FAMILIES UNDER FIRE

ROUTLEDGE PSYCHOSOCIAL STRESS SERIES
Charles R. Figley, Ph.D., Series Editor

1. *Stress Disorders Among Vietnam Veterans*, Edited by Charles R. Figley, Ph.D.
2. *Stress and the Family Vol. 1: Coping with Normative Transitions*, Edited by Hamilton I. McCubbin, Ph.D., and Charles R. Figley, Ph.D.
3. *Stress and the Family Vol. 2: Coping with Catastrophe*, Edited by Charles R. Figley, Ph.D., and Hamilton I. McCubbin, Ph.D.
4. *Trauma and Its Wake: The Study and Treatment of Post-Traumatic Stress Disorder*, Edited by Charles R. Figley, Ph.D.
5. *Post-Traumatic Stress Disorder and the War Veteran Patient*, Edited by William E. Kelly, M.D.
6. *The Crime Victim's Book, Second Edition*, By Morton Bard, Ph.D., and Dawn Sangrey.
7. *Stress and Coping in Time of War: Generalizations from the Israeli Experience*, Edited by Norman A. Milgram, Ph.D.
8. *Trauma and Its Wake Vol. 2: Traumatic Stress Theory, Research, and Intervention*, Edited by Charles R. Figley, Ph.D.
9. *Stress and Addiction*, Edited by Edward Gottheil, M.D., Ph.D., Keith A. Druley, Ph.D., Steven Pashko, Ph.D., and Stephen P. Weinsteinn, Ph.D.
10. *Vietnam: A Casebook*, By Jacob D. Lindy, M.D., in collaboration with Bonnie L. Green, Ph.D., Mary C. Grace, M.Ed., M.S., John A. MacLeod, M.D., and Louis Spitz, M.D.
11. *Post-Traumatic Therapy and Victims of Violence*, Edited by Frank M. Ochberg, M.D.
12. *Mental Health Response to Mass Emergencies: Theory and Practice*, Edited by Mary Lystad, Ph.D.
13. *Treating Stress in Families*, Edited by Charles R. Figley, Ph.D.
14. *Trauma, Transformation, and Healing: An Integrative Approach to Theory, Research, and Post-Traumatic Therapy*, By John P. Wilson, Ph.D.
15. *Systemic Treatment of Incest: A Therapeutic Handbook*, By Terry Trepper, Ph.D., and Mary Jo Barrett, M.S.W.
16. *The Crisis of Competence: Transitional Stress and the Displaced Worker*, Edited by Carl A. Maida, Ph.D., Norma S. Gordon, M.A., and Norman L. Farberow, Ph.D.
17. *Stress Management: An Integrated Approach to Therapy*, By Dorothy H. G. Cotton, Ph.D.
18. *Trauma and the Vietnam War Generation: Report of the Findings from the National Vietnam Veterans Readjustment Study*, By Richard A. Kulka, Ph.D., William E. Schlenger, Ph.D., John A. Fairbank, Ph.D., Richard L. Hough, Ph.D., Kathleen Jordan, Ph.D., Charles R. Marmar, M.D., Daniel S. Weiss, Ph.D., and David A. Grady, Psy.D.
19. *Strangers at Home: Vietnam Veterans Since the War*, Edited by Charles R. Figley, Ph.D., and Seymour Leventman, Ph.D.
20. *The National Vietnam Veterans Readjustment Study: Tables of Findings and Technical Appendices*, By Richard A. Kulka, Ph.D., Kathleen Jordan, Ph.D., Charles R. Marmar, M.D., and Daniel S. Weiss, Ph.D.
21. *Psychological Trauma and the Adult Survivor: Theory, Therapy, and Transformation*, By I. Lisa McCann, Ph.D., and Laurie Anne Pearlman, Ph.D.
22. *Coping with Infant or Fetal Loss: The Couple's Healing Process*, By Kathleen R. Gilbert, Ph.D., and Laura S. Smart, Ph.D.
23. *Compassion Fatigue: Coping with Secondary Traumatic Stress Disorder in Those Who Treat the Traumatized*, Edited by Charles R. Figley, Ph.D.
24. *Treating Compassion Fatigue*, Edited by Charles R. Figley, Ph.D.
25. *Handbook of Stress, Trauma and the Family*, Edited by Don R. Catherall, Ph.D.
26. *The Pain of Helping: Psychological Injury of Helping Professionals*, by Patrick J. Morrissette, Ph.D., RMFT, NCC, CCC.
27. *Disaster Mental Health Services: A Primer for Practitioners*, By Diane Myers, R.N., M.S.N., and David Wee, M.S.S.W.
28. *Empathy in the Treatment of Trauma and PTSD*, By John P. Wilson, Ph.D. and Rhiannon B. Thomas, Ph.D.
29. *Family Stressors: Interventions for Stress and Trauma*, Edited by Don. R. Catherall, Ph.D.

30. *Handbook of Women, Stress and Trauma,* Edited by Kathleen Kendall-Tackett, Ph.D.
31. *Mapping Trauma and Its Wake,* Edited by Charles R. Figley, Ph.D.
32. *The Posttraumatic Self: Restoring Meaning and Wholeness to Personality,* Edited by John P. Wilson, Ph.D.
33. *Violent Death: Resilience and Intervention Beyond the Crisis,* Edited by Edward K. Rynearson, M.D.
34. *Combat Stress Injury: Theory, Research, and Management,* Edited by Charles R. Figley, Ph.D. and William P. Nash, M.D.
35. *MindBody Medicine: Foundations and Practical Applications,* By Leo W. Rotan, Ph.D. and Veronika Ospina-Kammerer, Ph.D.
36. *Understanding and Assessing Trauma in Children and Adolescents: Measures, Methods, and Youth in Context,* By Kathleen Nader, D.S.W.
37. *When the Past Is Always Present: Emotional Traumatization, Causes, and Cures,* By Ronald A. Ruden, M.D., Ph.D.
38. *Families Under Fire: Systemic Therapy with Military Families,* Edited by R. Blaine Everson, Ph.D. and Charles R. Figley, Ph.D.

FAMILIES UNDER FIRE

Systemic Therapy With Military Families

Edited by

R. Blaine Everson and Charles R. Figley

This book is part of the Psychosocial Stress Series, edited by Charles R. Figley.

Routledge
Taylor & Francis Group
270 Madison Avenue
New York, NY 10016

Routledge
Taylor & Francis Group
27 Church Road
Hove, East Sussex BN3 2FA

Routledge is an imprint of Taylor & Francis Group, an Informa business

Printed in the United States of America on acid-free paper
10 9 8 7 6 5 4 3 2 1

International Standard Book Number: 978-0-415-99847-5 (Hardback)

Library of Congress Cataloging-in-Publication Data

Families under fire : systemic therapy with military families / edited by R. Blaine Everson and Charles Figley. -- 1st ed.
p. cm. -- (Psychosocial stress series)
Includes bibliographical references and index.
ISBN 978-0-415-99847-5 (hardcover : alk. paper)
1. Families of military personnel--Services for--United States. 2. Military dependents--Mental health services--United States. 3. Soldiers--United States--Mental health services. 4. Family psychotherapy--United States. I. Everson, R. Blaine. II. Figley, Charles R., 1944-

UB403.F353 2010
362.196'89156--dc22 2010007845

Visit the Taylor & Francis Web site at
http://www.taylorandfrancis.com

and the Routledge Web site at
http://www.routledgementalhealth.com

Dedicated to the memory and service of
Cmdr Charles "Keith" Springle, USN

Contents

Series Editor's Foreword

The Psychosocial Stress Book Series is happy to welcome our latest book, the 39th in the series. This latest book, *Families Under Fire*, as all others in the series before it, must address the three elements of all books in the series: adaptation to stressful environments (e.g., military, post-disaster area, public high school, child protection case work), contributions in understanding the psychosocial stress of particular units of intervention (family, group, individual, child, couple), and trend-setting impact on the field. Let us see how this book fits the series.

First, this book is about military service and adapting well to its rigor. The series started with *Stress Disorders Among Vietnam Veterans*, which some argue was written during the earliest days of the modern history of trauma. There have been at least 22 books in the series that either exclusively focus or partially focus on war-related stress. Second, the book is about families. There are 18 books in the series that exclusively or partially focus on families and family stress. Third, this book is a trendsetter, ushering a new era of utilizing the more powerful systemic therapies in many important domains including military families.

R. Blaine Everson and I wanted *Families Under Fire* to provide guidelines for systems-based practice for the broad spectrum of civilian mental health practitioners who provide professional services to military personnel, their spouses, and their family members. Civilian practitioners may not be as familiar with the military system and do not receive the same military mental healthcare training as providers on military installations, yet they are increasingly likely to provide services to these families as the provider networks on military bases are overwhelmed by the volume of new cases.

Working therapeutically with military couples requires an understanding of the dynamic nature of the lives they lead. It also requires the understanding that some therapeutic models developed for couples and families in one branch of the armed services may have only limited applicability to other branches. The editors provide a nuts-and-bolts approach to military families utilizing a systems-based practice that is effective with families in the military, regardless of branch of service or the practitioner's therapeutic preference.

This book helps to complete the vastly expanded collection of books designed for those working with military members who survived one or more deployments, including family therapists. More and more, behavioral health experts responsible for military readiness recognize the critical role of family and especially spouses in maintaining the morale and mental focus of military family members.

An example of a group of soldiers who are both warrior and savior who need the care and support of family members more than most are the combat medics. More than 90 percent of those I interviewed draw strength and guidance from their families and feel that what they are doing as soldiers is, in part, contributing to keeping their families safe.

The dozen practitioner authors, knowledgeable about systemic thinking and research, offer wisdom about working systemically with particular military families (e.g., Marine families are very different from Air Force families). Everson and the other contributors provide the blueprint and many examples for working with military family systems and relationships. This book should be useful to most practitioners who work with military families. Far from being limited to military families, this book is applicable to corporate families, families in the process of retirement, and others on which there is little research.

The Routledge Psychosocial Stress Book Series is happy to welcome this book to its long list of celebrated books. War consequences can be more effectively managed with this new book as a useful resource for family therapists working systemically with the families of heroes.

Charles Figley, Ph.D.
Series Editor
Tulane University Disaster Resilience Leadership Academy
New Orleans, Louisiana

About the Editors

Charles R. Figley is the Henry Paul Kurtzweg, MD chair in disaster mental health at Tulane University where he holds several faculty and scientist appointments. He is a former U. S. Marine sergeant who served early in the Vietnam War who went on to help invent the modern field of trauma through his more than 200 scholarly articles, chapters, and a number of books starting with his two classic textbooks, *Stress Disorders among Vietnam Veterans* (1978) and *Strangers at Home: Vietnam Veterans since the War* (1980). *Combat Stress Injuries* (2007), his 20th book, ushered in a paradigm shift toward understanding and promoting resilience in combat veteran and away from psychopathology. Dr. Figley was voted family psychologist of the year (1996) and head of the Interdivisional PhD Program in Marriage and Family at Florida State University in Tallahassee, and was founding editor of the influential *Journal of Family Psychotherapy*. Dr. Figley has two new books slated for publication. In 2011, his next book, *First Do No SELF Harm: Promoting Physician Stress Resilience*, will be published followed in 2012 by the *Encyclopedia of Trauma.*

R. Blaine Everson is a marriage and family therapist in private practice with the Samaritan Counseling Center in Athens, Georgia. He earned a Ph.D in Family and Child Science from Florida State University in Tallahassee. He is clinical member of the American Association for Marriage and Family Therapy. His practice includes extensive work with military families and readjustment issues associated with military service, along with a special interest in family level recovery from emotional trauma. He is a part-time member of the teaching faculty in the Department of Child and Family Development at the University of Georgia. Dr. Everson is currently working on his next book, *War, Society and Families.*

Contributors

Alan N. Baroody is the executive director of the Mary Lou Fraser Foundation for Families, Inc. (The Fraser Counseling Center) in Hinesville, Georgia, home of Ft. Stewart and the U.S. Army's Third Infantry Division. He received his BA from Wofford College, his MDiv from Princeton Theological Seminary, his ThM from Union Seminary, and his Doctor of Ministry from Lutheran Theological Southern Seminary. He is a licensed marriage and family therapist in Colorado and Georgia, an approved supervisor for AAMFT, a fellow in the American Association of Pastoral Counselors, and a certified EMDR practitioner. As a minister in the Presbyterian Church (USA) for more than 32 years, he has held pastorates as well as directed counseling centers.

Craig Boydston has worked as a senior therapist at Bridgeway Center Incorporated for over 20 years. He is a licensed clinical social worker and has held licensure in Florida since 1987. His specialty is in family therapy. He worked for 2 years as a family advocacy outreach worker (FAOW) at Eglin Air Force Base, Florida (1987-1989). He has retired from the Army National Guard and just prior to retirement spent a 1-year tour in Iraq as a brigade safety officer (Aviation). He is married and has four grown children and six grandchildren.

Thomas G. Camp is a clinical member and approved supervisor of the American Association for Marriage and Family Therapy, holds a certificate in advanced clinical pastoral education, and earned an MDiv from Emory University and an MS in family studies from the University of Georgia. He has been director of Samaritan Counseling Center of Northeast Georgia for 24 years and holds adjunct faculty status at the University of Georgia. He is married to Lacy Middlebrooks Camp and they have two adult sons.

Don Catherall obtained his PhD in clinical psychology from Northwestern University in 1984. He is an adjunct associate professor in clinical psychiatry at the Feinberg School of Medicine, Northwestern University, and teaches at the graduate level at Northwestern and at the University of Chicago. He maintains a clinical practice in downtown Chicago, specializing in couple therapy and the treatment of trauma disorders. His interest in trauma and the impact of trauma on relationships stems in part from his experience as a child of a Marine infantryman who served in the South Pacific during World War II, as well as his own experience as a Marine infantryman in Vietnam. He is married and has two children.

Natasha Elkovitch is a doctoral student in the Clinical Psychology Training Program at the University of Nebraska Lincoln. She received a BS in human development from Cornell University and an MA in clinical psychology from the University of Nebraska at Lincoln. She is currently completing a predoctoral clinical internship at the University of Mississippi Medical Center. Her research interests include child maltreatment and family violence, youth violence, and juvenile justice.

Leigh Ann Haigler is a social worker in private practice in Savannah, Georgia. She has worked extensively more than 20 years in variety of clinical social work settings. In 2005, she trained in marriage and family therapy with an emphasis on military family systems at the Whit Fraser Family Institute.

Lynn K. Hall recently retired as a professor of counseling from Western New Mexico University. Lynn received both her master's degree and doctorate from the University of Arizona; she worked in Tucson as a school counselor and in private practice specializing in marriage and family counseling. Prior to her 7 years at WNMU, she spent almost 10 years as a school counselor in both middle and high schools for the Department of Defense Schools in Germany. From this experience, as well as her work as a counselor educator, came her interest in working with military families that led to the 2008 publication of the book titled *Counseling Military Families: What Mental Health Professionals Need to Know.* Dr. Hall is currently living in Tucson, Arizona.

Joseph R. Herzog is an assistant professor in the School of Justice Studies and Social Work at the University of West Florida. He graduated with a master's in social work from the Florida State University and a PhD from the University of South Carolina. Joseph's social work career began in 1992. He has worked in both public and private nonprofit agencies providing clinical supervision for staff and direct services for clients. His dissertation research was on secondary trauma in military families and he continues to be involved military family research. Joseph is currently an external clinical consultant to the Veterans Center in Pensacola.

Judith A. Lyons is a clinical psychologist at the Veterans Administration Medical Center in Jackson, Mississippi, and associate professor of psychiatry and human behavior at the University of Mississippi Medical Center. She studied in Montreal at McGill and Concordia universities, then interned in Jackson, Mississippi. After serving as the founding clinical director of the National Center for PTSD at the Boston VA Medical Center (1985–1987), she returned to Jackson, Mississippi, to establish the Trauma Recovery Program at the G.V. "Sonny" Montgomery VA Medical Center. She assesses and treats traumatic stress through her work with the VA, consults on personal injury and criminal cases, and disaster response work with the American Red Cross. Post-trauma resilience, moral conflict, cognitive appraisal, and family strain are her major clinical and research interests. She has published more than 40 papers on traumatic stress. Enjoying nature, fostering shelter dogs, and engagement in Rotary and faith-based activities balance her trauma interests.

Lt. Col. Judith Mathewson is a member of the Air National Guard and has served as a teacher, counselor, and mental health professional in the armed forces and public education for the past 23 years. She created the Tragedy Assistance Program for Survivors Good Grief Camp for the children of military members who died in the line of duty. She assists spouses of veterans experiencing PTSD symptoms and volunteers as a mediator for both the Florida Supreme Court and school mediation programs. Her focus on current veteran issues drew her to grant writing for Welcome Home Vets, Inc., a not-for-profit organization in Brevard County, Florida. She is completing her PhD in marriage, couple, and family therapy from Barry University.

Kathryn D. Rheem, MS, is a licensed clinical marriage and family therapist, certified EFT therapist, supervisor, and trainer and has worked extensively with combat-related trauma and the impacts of high stress on couple relationships. She has worked with military service members and their families at Fort Belvoir, Virginia and is currently the director of the Couple and Family Therapy Center, LLC, located in Bethesda, Maryland, which serves military and civilian couples. Kathryn presents EFT internationally and, along with Dr. Sue Johnson, is the founder and director of Strong Bonds, Strong Couples, LLC, which provides EFT-based weekend retreats for soldiers coming home from Iraq and Afghanistan and their spouses. Kathryn may be contacted at krheem@hotmail.com.

Gwendolyn W. Smith is a licensed clinical social worker and registered play therapist in Augusta, Georgia. She earned her master's degree from the University of Pittsburgh. In addition, she completed a postgraduate program in child abuse and neglect through the University of Pittsburgh as well as a 2-year program in attachment and bonding sponsored through Georgia's Office of Adoptions in Atlanta. She has worked with families and their children in various capacities through domestic violence and rape crisis programs, hospital settings, and private practice. Her approach to clients is to guide them to find and utilize their core strengths, while maintaining a keen interest in mentoring parents to better meet the needs of their children during times of crisis.

Chaplain (Lieutenant Colonel) Lance Sneath, MS, MDiv, is the director of the U.S. Army Chief of Chaplain's Family Life Chaplain Training Center at Fort Hood, Texas where he trains and supervises Army and Air Force chaplains in marriage and family therapy in an internship program associated with Texas A&M and Central Texas University. The Family Life Chaplain Training Center provides thousands of treatment hours annually to the soldiers and families of the Fort Hood community. Chaplain Sneath was a presenter at the AAMFT Winter Institute for Advanced Clinical Studies in Asheville, North Carolina in 2009. He is an approved supervisor and clinical member of AAMFT, an LMFT with the state of Texas, and a diplomate of both the American Association of Pastoral Counselors (AAPC) and the College of Pastoral Supervision and Psychotherapy (CPSP). Chaplain Sneath is also an EMDR certified therapist with EMDRIA. He completed an externship in EFT under Dr. Sue Johnson at the Ackerman Institute in New York. He has presented twice at the AAPC annual conference on treating combat veteran families with EFT. Chaplain Sneath is a combat veteran who deployed to Saudi Arabia and Iraq in 1990 and 1991 in support of Operation Desert Shield, Operation Desert Storm, and Operation Provide Hope.

Commander Charles "Keith" Springle, a licensed clinical social worker, served 21 years in the U.S. Navy. He was a known leader in the field of Navy social work and a passionate advocate for deploying Navy social workers into coalition battlefields in Iraq and Afghanistan in an effort to positively impact the well-being and mental health of deployed service members. He earned a PhD from the University of Alabama in 2003 and served as director of the Counseling Services Branch, Marine Corps Base, Camp Lejeune, North Carolina. He received three Navy Achievement Awards, three Navy Commendation Awards, the Army Commendation Medal, and the Bronze Star. Commander Springle was one of five active duty personnel killed May 11, 2009 inside a combat stress clinic at Camp Liberty, Iraq.

James D. Whitworth, PhD, LCSW, is the director of behavioral medicine and research at the Eglin Air Force Base Family Medicine Residency Program, Florida. In this capacity, he coordinates all behavioral and scholarly training for 31 family medicine residents and 11 faculty physicians. Dr. Whitworth is the former chief of Air Force Family Research at the Pentagon. He also served as the director of operations and research for the Air Force Family Advocacy Program. He is an active clinical social worker who treats military members and their families. He has deployed to Iraq where he treated military members with post-traumatic stress disorder and mild traumatic brain injury.

Charlotte M. Wilmer is a licensed clinical social worker at the Marine Corps Base, Camp Lejeune, North Carolina. She is a co-author of "Painting a Moving Train: Working with Veterans of Iraq and Afghanistan," a curriculum to educate and train civilian health and mental health professionals to work effectively in the military culture. She is a member of the faculty for "Treating the Invisible Wounds of War," the on-line course adapted from that curriculum. Before her work in mental health, she had a political and government relations career in Washington, DC.

Introduction

On a plane from Norfolk, Virginia to Atlanta, Georgia, the captain of the Delta Airlines flight asked that the full cabin of passengers remain seated so that a Chief Petty Officer Simmons* could deplane first. He was escorting a young U.S. Marine medic home for the last time. Not only did the passengers comply with the request, they applauded as CPO Simmons walked smartly down the aisle. The young sailor being escorted home will be greeted for the last time by friends and family whose lives will be touched forever. This scenario has been repeated many times in the past few years. Except for these close encounters, Americans often forget the hundreds of thousands of lives that have been or will be affected, and who are the focus of this book.

There has been a great deal of media attention surrounding the lives of members of the U.S. armed services during the past several years, as a result of U.S. military involvement in Iraq and Afghanistan. Perhaps at no other time in modern history has so much attention been paid to what family members of military personnel experience as a result of their lives in the military. Family supports have been implemented by the various branches of the military and by organizations within many local communities near military installations. Research into the experience of warfare, both at home and abroad, has begun to proliferate as these conflicts continue as part of the global war on terror. Of course, some scholars have suggested that these conflicts represent the beginning of a worldwide war where globalized market forces clash with fundamental regionalist ideologies and that the United States will remain involved due to our further expanding economic interests (Ferguson, 2006). New threats to U.S. interests at home and abroad seem to emerge around the world on an almost weekly basis. Ferguson (2006) further asserts that the new century has already been colored by increased ethnic strife, heightened economic volatility in developing nations, and challenges to the global hegemony of long-standing super-states. At the heart of these current and potential conflicts are U.S. service members and their loved ones.

Some may wonder about the reasons for writing a handbook for helping military families when the number of services provided through the military, community, and veterans organizations seems to be increasing as the impact of the conflicts in Iraq and Afghanistan permeates American society. The answer is simple. By the middle of the next decade, these large-scale conflicts will likely be over, the military may once again be downsized, and most of these service members will have returned to their lives as civilians. Whether these conflicts end or future conflicts begin, the constant cycle of personnel into and out of the military system will continue unabated (Morgan, 2006), as will the need for well-trained providers of mental healthcare services. By that time, many service members will be privately insured or receive assistance through the U.S. Veteran's Administration, while

* Pseudonym.

many other veterans and their families will require assistance beyond the capacity of existing services and resources (Camacho, 2007). Our society will bear the responsibility and intangible costs of helping veterans of these conflicts, and their families, for many years to come (Tiegen, 2007). Civilian mental healthcare practitioners will be called upon to assist many of these veterans and their family members as they cope with their combat-related experiences. We hope to provide basic guidelines for systemic practice with this population, whether the provider works in a veteran's clinic, a community agency, or in private practice.

FOCUS OF THIS BOOK

The focus of this book is on the systemic treatment of military families based on what we have learned so far in treating them and building on what we already knew about military families. Make no mistake: the current wars are very different and any practitioner wishing to work with military family members must understand these fundamental differences and act accordingly. Unlike previous conflicts where soldiers were deployed for the duration of the war (e.g., WWII) or where they were conscripted for an assigned 1-year tour of duty (e.g., Vietnam), the conflicts in Iraq and Afghanistan have been characterized for many by year-long combat tours. These tours are interspersed with periodic returns to their families for approximately a year and an eventual return to combat duty (Booth et al., 2007).

Many U.S. service members who are part of the ground forces in Iraq or Afghanistan have served for more than one combat tour depending on their military occupational specialty (MOS). Consequently, families have experienced multiple, long-term separations from their loved ones who have served in the military during the past 5 years. Service members are often unable to fully reintegrate into the family system before they are required to prepare for deployment and separation again (Everson, 2005). Many of these families have been emotionally overburdened as a result of the increased impact of their affiliation with the military system.

Multiple Challenges upon Return

In addition to the strain imposed upon marriages and parent–child relationships, many service members have returned with multiple problems as a result of their exposure to an urban style of warfare. Many service members associated with the U.S. ground forces in Iraq have experienced some form of post-traumatic stress disorder (PTSD; Hoge et al., 2004), while others have experienced other symptoms associated with the general stressors and strains stemming from extended exposure to combat (e.g., depression, anxiety, and substance use). In response, Figley and Nash (2007) outlined the criteria for combat stress injury and treatment associated with this condition. The secondary stressors on families with a service member suffering from PTSD or physical wounds have been documented as a significant strain and a potential predictor of familial dissolution (Dekel, Goldblatt, Keidar, Solomon & Polliack, 2005).

Challenges of Reintegration

The reintegration of service members back into the family system has become a constant facet of the military way of life and the specter of redeployment has created a constant strain for families of U.S. ground troops in particular (Doyle & Peterson, 2005). The impact has permeated American society in terms of increased marital failures, a growing number of family dissolutions, and heightened reliance on healthcare services for families of service members. These trends are commonly observed within large societies during wartime and have been associated with extended conflicts in America's past (Ruger, Wilson, & Waldrop, 2002).

A report in *The Washington Post* from April 22, 2005, citing increases in claims to ValueOptions/Tricare indicated that military-related healthcare expenditures alone have nearly doubled annually since 2001 to exceed $36 billion, suggesting that the stress associated with a military lifestyle likely contributed to increased utilization of the military healthcare system and will continue to do so for the foreseeable future. In a related finding, Fulton, Lasdon & McDaniel (2007) reported that a further $120 million was needed annually to improve U.S. Army hospital performance due to increased demand for services.

Acute Need for Military Family Therapy Services

With the recent acceleration of combat-related deployments among the U.S. armed forces, the return of service members to their families from war-torn countries, the family burden of reintegrating these members into the household, and increased utilization of behavioral healthcare services by families in the military system, several facts become clear. These factors have converged, creating a need for a major volume in the field of family therapy that outlines the issues confronting practitioners who conduct clinical work with these families and providing detailed guidelines of systemic techniques to better assist those they see in daily practice.

Outline of Major Topics

The purpose of this book is to provide a set of guidelines for providing clinical mental health services to service members and their families from a wide variety of systems-based frameworks, including cognitive–behavioral family therapy, structural–strategic approaches, family-of-origin therapy, emotionally focused couple therapy, and family systems-based psychiatric practice.

Therapeutic Approaches

Our approach is similar to the International Society for Traumatic Stress Studies publication that provides guidelines for the 12 most frequently used treatment approaches (Foa, Keane & Friedman, 2000). In addition, the primary therapeutic foci of couple counseling are addressed, as well as family therapy with children and adolescents and individually focused family therapy. In part, we hope to stimulate new and improved methods of assessing and helping military families.

Branches of Service

The four major branches of the American military (U.S. Air Force, U.S. Army, U.S. Marine Corps, and U.S. Navy) are distinct and distinctive systems with a very defined culture. Providers of military family systems therapy will benefit from first becoming familiar with these cultures before meeting with families. We have included chapters by practitioners affiliated with these branches in an attempt to address the need for specific interventions designed for each branch of service and to move beyond the notion that "military families" are an all-encompassing generic entity (i.e., are all one and the same)—a recently popular term that ignores the uniqueness of family lifestyles and the daily realities associated with life in each branch of military service. Thus, the major themes of this book are as follows:

- An introductory discourse of family systems theory and practice
- Family-systems-based therapy approaches to military family issues
- Family therapy as applied to problems associated with each branch of service
- Systems-based therapy approaches with unique issues and special populations (PTSD, secondary trauma, etc.)
- Summary and conclusions, with suggestions for further practice and theory development

OVERVIEW OF CHAPTERS

Chapter 1, *Seeing Systems: An Introduction to Systemic Approaches with Military Families*, written by R. Blaine Everson and Thomas G. Camp, provides the conceptual overview for the book. First, there is an outline of each of the major schools of thought in family systems theory as applied to psychotherapy practice. At the same time, Everson and Camp provide ideas for shifting the practitioner's thinking from an individual approach to a systems perspective. The authors provide discussion of the basic concepts and techniques utilized by systems-oriented practitioners. An overview of recent literature in evidence-based systemic practice and empirical research as applied to family therapy comprises the next section of the first chapter. The chapter concludes with a specific case example of individually oriented therapists undergoing supervision training in a systems-based approach and the transitions that take place in their thinking as applied to family dynamics. A large portion of the discussion details how systems-based practitioners conceptualize problems arising within the family system as a result of the daily interaction with other military organizations or the failure of members to adapt to a military way of life. The authors discuss the stress transmission model and the subsequent risk of "burnout" among families under excessive amounts of stress for extended periods of time. Some thoughts are offered for establishing treatment goals that are realistic for these families, given their unique situation, and planning for outcomes that are compatible with life in the military organization. The chapter ends by focusing on the practice of systemic therapy with families within the context of the larger military system.

The second chapter, written by Lynn Hall, provides an overview of the various aspects of military culture and the lifestyle issues that develop from living within the military system. The topics discussed in *The Military Culture, Language, and Lifestyle* also include the acculturation process that takes place among military family members within each branch of service as they learn a new language, adjust to new locales after relocation, and the adaptations experienced as they contend with a constant cycle of departures and returns. In this chapter, Lynn Hall incorporates into her discussion a variety of viewpoints including the work of Segal (1986) and others outlining the incompatibility between the family as a social institution and the organization of the military, as well as the problems arising from this conflict since the advent of an all-volunteer military force in the late 1970s.

The next section, Section II: Systemic Therapy Interventions for Various Military Contexts, includes five chapters that focus on one of the major treatment approaches appropriate for military families.

Chapter 3, *Structural Strategic Approaches with Army Couples*, by R. Blaine Everson and Joseph R. Herzog, is the first chapter in this section. The authors suggest that structural strategic approaches appear to be well suited for families struggling with the challenges of parenting in the context of military service. They discuss the therapeutic issues and techniques associated with the treatment of relational problems based upon their experiences with couples from the U.S. Army and the U.S. Navy. This chapter compares couples' experiences associated with the various cycles of deployment and reunification and contrasts some of the different ways these couples deal with the associated interpersonal issues, while offering a thought-provoking discussion of several different treatment modalities. Several examples of their respective work are offered in the case material and commentary presented at the end of this chapter.

The next chapter, Chapter 4, *Systemic Therapy with Adolescents in Army Families*, by R. Blaine Everson, Joseph R. Herzog, and Leigh Ann Haigler, deals with what we see as an overlooked area of family therapy and child development. As a society, we have experienced the extension of adolescence for some into their early 20s. While debate continues over the causes of this phenomenon, there are specific factors creating this problem for military adolescents. Everson, Herzog, and Haigler discuss the extra-familial factors (e.g., lengthy deployments) in the military system and the intra-familial adaptations (e.g., lack of reintegration) that create difficulties in the successful launching of late adolescents from some families in the military. They provide specific case examples of parents and late adolescents in therapy who are experiencing this phenomenon and the strategies they've devised for assisting families in dealing with the crucial step into adulthood. These practitioners offer their unique perspectives on working with adolescents within U.S. Army families as co-authors of this chapter.

In Chapter 5, *Systemic Therapy with Families of U.S. Marines*, Don Catherall discusses family systems therapy with members of the U.S. Marine Corps. This chapter provides further understanding of this often misunderstood branch of service and its families, incorporating recent information about the USMC's successful attempts to improve family assistance programming and reduce the length of time marines spend away from their families on combat tours. Systems-based case examples are provided, debunking some of the myths that have developed about these families in therapy.

Chapter 6, *Systems Approaches with Air Force Members and Their Families*, by Joseph R. Herzog, Craig Boydston, and James Whitworth, provides a discussion of family therapy with families and service members within the USAF. This chapter addresses the issues of couples in therapy, seeing children within a family context, and clinical work with USAF families before, during, and after deployments. The authors, who have a background in clinical social work, have included cases where families are seen as a result of a service member with PTSD and their orientation to these problems within families. Case examples provide information pertaining to the unique aspects of the family services provided by this branch of service and how private practitioners can serve as a valuable resource for these families.

In Chapter 7, *Emotionally Focused Therapy with Army Couples Coping with PTSD,* Lance Sneath and Kathryn Rheem offer a unique perspective on couple and family work in the military setting using emotionally focused therapy (EFT). They begin with an overview of this approach and then move on to the application of EFT with families dealing with combat stress and post-traumatic stress disorder in the U.S. Army. Extensive case examples illustrating the work done at the various stages provide the reader with an easily applicable guide for working with families in the military using this approach.

Chapter 8, *Attachment as a Consideration in Family Play Therapy with Military Families*, by Gwendolyn Smith, begins with a look at how play therapy may be used with younger children in military families. The author discusses a variety of techniques, including sibling inclusion, play therapy, and creative drawing, that may be included in systemic therapy with these children and their families. Her approach is based upon rebuilding attachments through the use of a variety of techniques within a family systems context. Case illustrations are given from U.S. Army families, but the primary focus is the approach to children under age 10 and how families may be incorporated into ongoing interventions.

In Chapter 9, *Spirituality and Trauma in a Time of War: A Systemic Approach to Pastoral Care and Counseling*, Alan Baroody approaches the problems facing military families from the unique perspectives of pastoral care and family therapy. Using a systemic approach to the spiritual problems associated with military life, he outlines the importance of understanding religious life in military families within the context of fostering coping and resiliency among family members before, during, and after deployments when a reconnection to the spiritual aspects of life may be crucial to service member reintegration. Baroody also offers a cursory discussion of the benefits of providing community support for military chaplains and training local clergy to assist military families during times of crisis.

Chapter 10, *Secondary Traumatic Stress, Deployment Phase, and Military Families: Systemic Approaches to Treatment*, by Joseph R. Herzog and R. Blaine Everson, is based on recent clinical practice with an emotional condition that has a truly systemic basis in its origin—secondary traumatic stress. The authors of this chapter provide an overview of the causes of secondary traumatic stress, the development of symptoms in family members, a course of treatment, and observed (desired) outcomes. There is also a discussion of the development of secondary traumatic stress in children based on the lead author's own research with national guardsmen. The authors provide a model of recovery based on recent research and their experience with families traumatized by the experience of a service member with post-traumatic stress disorder (PTSD). Case material includes excerpts from couple sessions and family sessions with children.

In Chapter 11, *In Support of Military Women and Families: Challenges Facing Community Therapists*, Judith Mathewson takes up the discussion of a truly unique aspect of modern military service. The author, from her own background as an officer in the U.S. Air Force, discusses the unique position of women in military service and the dual impact of deployment on these service members and their families. She uses her unique perspective working as a therapist who has designed programs to address women's issues, such as deployment stress, gender inequality, and sexual assault in the U.S. Air Force.

In Chapter 12, *Painting a Moving Train: Preparing Community Providers to Serve Returning Warriors and Their Families*, Charles K. Springle and Charlotte Wilmer present the reader with a systemic overview of the experiences facing members of the armed forces and their families as a result of their attempts to readjust to between deployments. It is a privilege for the editors of this volume to present this chapter and dedicate this book to Commander Charles "Keith" Springle who was killed in the line of duty while serving with the U.S. Marine Corps in Iraq. The authors outline a number of strategies for fostering readjustment and offer some basic approaches to helping heal from post-traumatic stress, combat stress injuries, and other combat-related injuries within a family-oriented setting. These problems are often observed as a result of the face-to-face combat experienced by U.S. ground forces in both Afghanistan and Iraq. The authors discuss the various ways of incorporating family members into the ongoing process of healing from these injuries. Case material outlining the unique challenges of incorporating these injured service members into family-oriented therapy sessions and helping them recover within a family context is included in this chapter.

The next chapter, Chapter 13, *Post Deployment: Practical Guidelines for Warriors' Loved Ones*, by Judith Lyons and Natasha Elkovitch, deals with the issue of long-term, combat-related deployments from the perspective of those family members who remain behind—particularly military wives. Many experience a variety of daily strains associated with financial and budgetary matters, household management, maintaining contact with the deployed family member, and dealing with various aspects of their children's lives. The authors seek to provide the reader with more in-depth discussion of these day-to-day aspects of military life during deployments. In this context, they discuss the development of psychiatric symptoms in both spouses and children during long-term deployments, while offering guidelines for healthier functioning throughout the deployment and as service members leave the armed forces after military service. Lyons and Elkovitch provide rich case material to demonstrate ways in which family systems-oriented practitioners can appropriately diagnose deployment-related conditions within an array of military family stressors, help build coping skills, and improve the well-being of their clients.

The final chapter (Chapter 14), *The Long Way Home: The Aftermath of War for Service Members and Their Families*, by R. Blaine Everson and Charles Figley, provides a summary of the content of this book while exploring new areas for systems-based practice and family therapy research. More information is provided for the civilian practitioner regarding family assistance services within each branch of military service and terminology to assist the therapist with making appropriate contact. The authors also provide thoughts on where they see the future of practice within a family systems-based model and how practitioners can improve their visibility in military communities. They conclude with final thoughts that reflect on their current experience and those experiences of colleagues who work with service members and their families during this very stressful time in our nation's history.

CLOSING THOUGHTS

This handbook is designed to further extend the application of family systems therapy into the realm of military families. Although many practitioners from a variety of training backgrounds work with military families, we have purposefully sought to incorporate material from experts we deem to be systemic in their focus. While most mental health practitioners may ascribe to some form of family systems, many are unaware of the extent to which these methods can be applied in daily practice. The lead author of this introduction is reminded of a conversation with another therapist who suggested that the family system is nothing more than a composition of interactions between its members. Any systems thinker will know that nothing could be further from the truth, since one of the core principles in the systems orientation is nonsummativity (i.e., the whole is more than the sum of its parts). No text is comprehensive to the extent that it encompasses all of the issues, techniques, and applications to each branch of service associated with a systems-based approach to working therapeutically with military families. We apologize for that shortcoming in advance. What we have attempted to do is bring together information provided by a wide variety of practitioners from a broad range of backgrounds who work with military families on a daily basis. The one commonality of the contributors is their family systems approach to psychotherapy practice. We hope that the readers will find the necessary tools to improve their own work with military families within this text.

REFERENCES

Booth, B., Segal, M. W., Bell, D. B., Martin, J. A., Ender, M. G., Rohall, D. E. & Nelson, J. (2007). *What we know about Army families: A 2007 update.* Fairfax, VA: Caliber.

Burrell, L. M, Adams, G. A., Durand, D. B. & Castro, C. A. (2006). The impact of military lifestyle demands on well-being, Army, and family outcomes. *Armed Forces and Society, 33*, 43-58.

Camacho, P. R. (2007). Veterans and veteran's issues. *Armed Forces and Society, 33*, 313-315.

Dekel, R., Goldblatt, H., Keidar, M., Solomon, Z. & Polliack, M. (2005). Being the wife of a veteran with posttraumatic stress disorder. *Family Relations, 54,* 24-36.

Doyle, M. E. & Peterson, K. A. (2005). Re-entry and reintegration: Returning home after combat. *Psychiatric Quarterly, 76,* 361-370.

Everson, R. B. (2005). *Quality of life among Army spouses: Parenting and family stress during deployment to Operation Iraqi Freedom.* Florida State University, Tallahassee, p. 2737.

Ferguson, N. (2006). *The war of the world: 20th century conflict and the descent of the West.* New York, NY: Penguin.

Figley, C. R. & Nash, W. P. (2007). *Combat stress injury: Theory, research, and management.* New York: Routledge.

Fulton, L., Lasdon, L. S. & McDaniel, R. R. (2007). Cost drivers and resource allocation in the military healthcare systems. *Military Medicine, 172,* 244-249.

Hoge, C., Castro, C., Messer, S., McGurk, D., Cotting, D. & Koffman, R. (2004). Combat duty in Iraq and Afghanistan, mental health problems, and barriers to care. *The New England Journal of Medicine, 351,* 13-22.

Morgan, M. J. (2006). American empire and the American military. *Armed Forces and Society, 32*, 202-218.

Ruger, W., Wilson, S. E. & Waldrop, S. L. (2002). Warfare and welfare: Military service, combat, and marital dissolution. *Armed Forces and Society, 29,* 85-107.

Segal, M. W. (1986). The military and the family as greedy institutions. *Armed Forces and Society, 13,* 9-38.

Teigen, J. L. (2007). Debt of a nation: Understanding the treatment of military veterans in the United States. *Armed Forces and Society, 33,* 438-444.

Section I

An Overview of Family Systems in the Military

1 Seeing Systems

An Introduction to Systemic Approaches with Military Families

R. Blaine Everson and Thomas G. Camp

CONTENTS

Without the foundation of the family, it's very hard to be a good person.

—Mikhail Gorbachev

The application of family systems theory and practice to families within the military system has been discussed periodically in the past, but has been identified as crucial to improving our understanding of military family functioning in the social and behavioral sciences literature (Hogencamp & Figley, 1983). This chapter seeks to provide the reader with a basic understanding of how family systems models may be applied to better explain the phenomena associated with military lifestyles and improve our understanding of many of the family situations that develop as a result. This chapter covers the general approaches and concepts found within the practice of family therapy, along with newer developments in empirically supported methods of practice commonly used today. The authors also provide an in-depth discussion of the systems-based approach to conceptualizing problems within military families and diagnosing within a systemic context.

It seems some therapists believe that they are practicing a systemic approach because they happen to be in a consulting room with two or more people who may be related. This is usually not the case, since this approach requires an in-depth understanding of family systems theory and the rigorous application of systems-based concepts. While it is possible to see families without a thorough grounding in systemic thought, we feel that the orientation to this particular set of assumptions is the key difference between "treating families" and merely seeing them for therapy as a collective of individuals. From its inception, family therapy has sought to distinguish itself in a variety of ways from other helping professionals in the mental health field. Like many systemic practitioners, we believe we have largely succeeded in our goal of distinction given the international recognition of our craft. In conversations with other family therapists, several common themes often emerge: (a) how we are trained is different from the training of other practitioners; (b) our methods and approach to problems require different ways of conceptualizing complaints; and (c) to a large extent systemic methods can be taught to others from different therapeutic backgrounds. Systems theory is especially applicable to military families because the family system and the military system are intertwined. They form a larger system in which the military system and the family systems are mutually influential across contextual boundaries For those readers less familiar with systemic approaches or new to the field of family therapy, we have provided a more extensive overview of systems theory and therapy in the appendix to this volume.

SOME SYSTEMS-BASED CONCEPTS

There is no way, within the context of a book chapter, to describe in detail the major concepts associated with understanding systems thinking as applied to helping families. Indeed, there are entire texts referenced at the end of this chapter devoted to the understanding of systems-related concepts. What we have attempted to do is to provide an overview of the major systemic concepts as they apply in daily practice with couples, children, and families in the military. These concepts will be discussed in three major categories related to a systemic understanding of family functioning and/or dysfunction: family structure, family processes, and the family developmental life span, where both structure and process tend to intermingle. It is difficult to separate structure from process in a family systems approach, and this should only be viewed as an attempt to do so in order to provide an easier way of explaining these concepts.

Family Structure

Boundaries

Boundaries are often defined as the personal and emotional space, or distance, that exists between individuals, groups, and larger systems maintained by communication patterns that fluctuate between cut-offs and fusion. Some boundaries are most often open, closed, or ambiguous. Boundaries are dependent on rule systems established within families and the assignment and/or acceptance of roles as expressed by family need. Boundaries tend to fluctuate through an ongoing symbolic and interactive process between members and run along a continuum of closeness or separation (diffuse versus rigid), except in cases where they are rigidly maintained by some pre-existing rule structure (Minuchin & Fishman, 1981).

Some examples of the wide range of boundaries are personal space around one's body, personal space in the house (my drawer, my closet), and personal possessions. There are also boundaries relative to chores (she does the laundry and I do the cooking, I am a stay-at-home father whose main responsibility is parenting and household maintenance, and she is the breadwinner). Boundaries are subsequently very important to the adherence to family roles and to rulemaking within family systems. Boundaries provide personal space and a sense of personal safety. Boundaries can also limit interaction and access to resources. These may be closed or ambiguous boundaries in which a husband manages the finances and does not allow his wife access to reserves or to financial information, or a wife who restricts the father's access to information about the children's health or schooling.

Boundaries are a significant aspect of personality structure. Each child develops unique ways of trying to get perceived needs met, and these particular ways of getting needs met are conditioned by the evolving family structure, emotional processes in the family, and genetics. Some children develop boundaries that keep intruders out while others develop open boundaries that invite others in. In object relations family therapy (Scharff, 1989, p. 208), the dynamics of the parent–child relationship are internalized by the child and become aspects of personality structure. The dynamics of this child's interpersonal relationships are determined by ways the child has learned to defend himself or herself against uncertainty about the integrity of her or his boundaries. Mastery of this key concept forms an important basis for the practice of systemic therapy.

Family Roles and Rules

Within the context of small group experiences, each member is expected to behave in ways that conform to the requirements of the other members. Roles and the rules that govern the execution of roles between members in families are intricately related to the boundary system within the family. In one sense, systemic problems can be seen as related to the *strain* associated with performing certain multiple tasks associated with a role, or *conflict* between competing roles (parent/spouse/employee) or with others who are performing adjoining roles. A common strain associated with roles is that between parenting children and the role of spouse or partner. Adult partners have roles such as breadwinner, homemaker, confidant, lover, companion, and friend. These roles often conflict with the parenting role of caregiver, nurturer, and disciplinarian. In addition to role strain, any two people will have at least slightly different approaches to performing the roles (i.e., rules), such as how to discipline children at various ages, how love is expressed, and standards of housekeeping. Another common strain associated with roles arises from inter-family interaction and social contact with the larger community. This strain is most commonly seen as an extension of the demands experienced as a result of work-related tasks for adults and the challenges adolescents face in balancing family relationships with the demands of peer interactions.

Triangles

Triangles serve as a way to conceive the emotional interactions within a human system. They illustrate the flow of emotional energy within the system and explain what stimulates actions that otherwise may seem irrational and even insane (Papero, 1990). An example of a triangle may be wife, husband, and child; or wife with a military career, child, and wife's parents. In families with a member who struggles with an addiction, the often unspoken addiction is a point in several interlocking triangles between the members who are interested, abstinence from addictive substances, and the person who's providing the individual with the substances, for example.

Triangles are both configurations and emotional entities (Friedman, 1991). According to systems theorists, the human dyad is an unstable unit susceptible to a variety of vulnerabilities, unless interaction takes place (with some regularity) with a third member. A relational triangle can serve as a stabilizing mechanism within families, or any other small group (for that matter), but the emotional states associated with triangulation can be fraught with tension and anxiety. The "double bind" is often associated as a negative byproduct of an emotional triangle. An example might be a husband/father returning from combat duty to experience his wife initially rejoicing in his safe return and then expressing anger at the heavy burden she has struggled with in his absence. The parentified daughter may bond with the father while the husband–wife relationship distances. The father is then triangled with the daughter and the wife is triangled out, thereby creating emotional tension between the child and the mother.

The double bind is often associated as a negative byproduct of an emotional triangle. The double bind is a dynamic in which the anxiety is chronic and stuck because there seems to be no way out of the bind without significant pain. In the example above of A trying to control the relationship between B and C, B may experience the double bind when she does not want to risk the relationship with A, but also does not want to be controlled. The effect of the double bind is extreme anxiety and physiological tension that can lead one to act in irrational ways and to feel confusion that may appear to be mental illness. The physiological stress and tension often also lead to illnesses and physiological dysfunction. As a systemic concept, emotional triangles form the basis of at least three major approaches in the practice of systems therapy, since Bowen, Minuchin, members of the Palo Alto group, and later the Mental Research Institute all saw these emotional structures as a primary basis for family problems.

Birth Order

Sibling position is an important aspect of familial structure and is strongly dictated by the order in which children are born. It is complicated by the time span between births, the gender of the children, remarried family and step-parent dynamics, and historical events. Next to heredity, birth order may be the most influential aspect of human and family life, and is thought to exert long-term influence on various aspects of our lives (Sulloway, 1996). Partner choice is a major aspect of our lives thought to be influenced by birth order and sibling relationships, while gender and sexual socialization will be discussed later in the chapter as important aspects of family structure as well. Generally, oldest children tend toward leadership roles, accept responsibility, and assume responsibility for the emotional needs of other family members, including the adults in the system, and are more often the recipients of the emotional dynamic leading to their *parentification* than other siblings simply because of their position in the birth order (Berg-Cross, 2000). This phenomenon is sometimes seen in military families as a result of long-term, repeated separations due to deployments, where an older sibling may attempt to offset the structural imbalance created by the absent service member by performing duties reserved for a parent, or may be thrust into that position by an incapacitated adult member.

Oldest children by virtue of their age tend toward family leadership roles, accept responsibility, and are often more conscientious (Carter & McGoldrick, 1998). They often experience responsibility for younger children and learn to act with authority and may be perceived as unyielding and judgmental. Oldest daughters may have the same experiences as oldest sons except that they often do not receive the same privileges. As an example of this unique sibling position, oldest daughters often feel more obligated for the arrangement of parental care than other siblings, which is an influence both of gender and birth order. Middle children often learn to collaborate and work out differences between themselves and the other children. They may also experience a sense of being unnoticed by parents while the parents appreciate the oldest and care for the younger child. Youngest children can have a sense of being unique and special. This may lead to creativity or to a sense of entitlement. Some younger children also experience abandonment by the older siblings if there is a significant age difference or if the younger child exhibits entitlement. Only children may have characteristics that combine those of oldest and youngest children. Some theorists argue that oldest children are more likely to obey rules and follow the examples of parents, while both middle and youngest children are more likely to risk new adventures or to be rebels (Sulloway, 1996), yet these personality tendencies should be viewed as generalizations when considering birth order and the position of siblings within the context of any given family system.

Sibling position in a family of two or three children is quite a different experience, as one can imagine, than that in a family of six or eight children. Each child has unique experiences of the family processes because of the absence or presence of other children and their personalities and needs, the ages of various family members, and the evolution of family structure and process. Considering the birth order of a person often clarifies the source of primitive experiences that affect personality structure and current emotional experience and perception (Nichols, 1996). It is important to remember that other influences affect personality characteristics, emotional experience, and perceptions. These influences may include the time span between births, the gender of the children, parental expectations, remarried family and step-parent dynamics, temperament, and historical events. These dynamics are not only shaped by family systems, but influence subsequent systems as children of various sibling positions age and establish their own families.

Ecosystems

Families exist in close proximity to a number of other systemic entities, such as extended kinship networks, and within larger social contexts, whereby they interact within the communities they inhabit and come into contact with other agents of socialization like churches and schools (Rothery & Enns, 2002). Ecosystems are comprised of intricately linked social networks that form the basis for interactions outside of family boundaries. These networks are not only influential on families in both positive and negative ways, but are influenced by the families that comprise them (Berg-Cross, 2000). For example, peer networks within an ecosystem may exert what some family members consider to be a negative impact and create conflict among members as a result of their influence on adolescents at this stage of development. Incongruence between families, social networks, and larger ecosystems may be stressful for members and result in a crisis at some point, and, of course, members may be particularly vulnerable after a separation or relocation (Walsh, 2003). The family's affiliation with the military constitutes such an ecosystem, in that it is made up of multiple social networks, is all encompassing of families and their individual members, is a social institution, and creates its own evolving culture requiring adherence to its norms and value systems. A particular difficulty families experience within military ecosystems stems from the prefabrication of networks (e.g., unit affiliation) and the expectation of compliance to systemic conventions by members of military families (i.e., adherence to standards of conduct by all members residing on a military installation).

Family Processes

Emotional Regression

In times of high stress and anxiety, systems tend toward reactivity rather than objectivity, as do the individuals within them. Due to the chronic anxiety experienced within most family systems, members may experience regression in a way that brings them closer together during times of stress (a centripetal, or other directed, function) or causes them to withdraw from others (a centrifugal, or self-centered, function) depending on the nature of the stressor(s), pre-existing relationship states, and previous personal experiences with anxiety within the context of family support (Beavers & Hampson, 2003). This process is often referred to as *reactance* in a particular time and place setting (e.g., a daughter may become exceedingly angry at her mother for not watching grandkids in the evening because of the grandmother's drinking problem). Because of reactance and regressive tendencies, members in families, and families themselves, often behave in very predictable ways and, at other times, very unpredictable ways. The nature of regressive tendencies also may stem from a multigenerational family process (Papero, 1990) as expressions of poor differentiation, and may wreak havoc, to some extent, on the family's attempts at re-establishing equilibrium, further perpetuating a crisis situation. Individuals during these times of duress may visibly act more immature toward each other as an aspect of their regressive natures. Therapists must make attempts to effectively deal with regressive states and the emotional reactance that accompanies these states in clients, as they are frequent, but little understood, sources of conflict in families under stress.

Differentiation and Separation

Differentiation is a Bowenian concept whereby individual members of families seek to establish autonomy from the family emotional system (Papero, 1990). It is related to the idea of separation, from attachment theory, in that they both require a mutual process on the part of family members. Bowen saw differentiation as an emotional necessity to be strived for, but never fully achieved, whereas attachment theorists (i.e., Ainsworth, Bowlby, etc.) discuss attachment and separation as organic evolutionary processes necessary for the survival of mammalian species. Needless to say, adherents to Bowenian theory hold a somewhat different view (from attachment theorists) of the emotion and psychological repercussions of failing to properly separate from one's family of origin. Failing to achieve the adequate differentiation influences marital choice, parenting styles, development of self, and reactions to a variety situations that families may encounter over the course of their lifespan. The issue of differentiation is crucial at the outset of the family life cycle because of the couple dynamic created when two similarly differentiated individuals form a marital partnership (Friedman, 1991) and influence the family interaction patterns from that point forward in history (i.e., becoming a new family of origin for their own children).

The difficulty associated with differentiating from one's family of origin is directly related to the presence of chronic anxiety experienced by members within a particular family system. For Bowen, the presence of chronic anxiety within families is a constant and only varies from system to system and in relation to family experiences at various points along the developmental continuum (Papero, 1990). The extent to which one is able to differentiate from the family of origin may serve to dampen the negative impact of the multigenerational influences discussed in the next section of this chapter, but in terms of family lifespan development, for example, adequate differentiation may be quickly replaced by enmeshment for middle-aged children as their elderly parents grow more reliant upon them for assistance toward the end of their lives. On a more positive note, as such a crisis passes or is managed properly, individuals and families tend to move back to their previous levels of differentiation.

Multigenerational Influences

The tendency to behave in predictable ways and experience similar emotional reactions across the span of time is perhaps the most relevant of all concepts to the application of systems thinking to family life and what sets apart the family systems approach from others. Family systems theorists and practitioners believe that patterns of interaction between family members are relatively stable due to the tendency toward homeostasis (balance) and resistance to change within all self-correcting systems. These patterns were proposed by Bowen (Papero, 1990) as transcendent from one generation into subsequent generations, along with their resultant pathologies. The emotional dynamics in family systems carry over from one generation to the next. Anxiety in particular is thought to be transmitted in this manner, since many relationships within families tend to be fraught with anxiety. The strengths and the problems that family members experience are influenced by these processes, which may be operating over several generations. In considering the unique effects of any external system on the family, such as military service experience of one or more family members, it is important to also consider the emotional processes that are already firmly entrenched within the family. The tendency toward resilience, as opposed to resignation, in the face of difficulties may be influenced by the recreation of these intergeneration dynamics within the current family system (Boss, 2002). Consequently, one goal of systems-oriented therapy is to disrupt the interactional pattern that exists as a part of the overall family dynamic and reduce the emotional reactance of the identified patient(s). Another primary goal is to improve the awareness of these influences altering the system dynamics as part of the therapeutic process, which allows for improved functioning as a family (Roberto, 1992).

Paradoxical Situations

Families and their members are beset by a number of incongruous and incompatible situations that cause stress for individuals and strains to the relational system (Haley, 1976). It is what *shouldn't be* but *is* that often denotes a paradoxical situation in family settings. For example, family members often complain about experiencing less interaction with each other and fewer hours for accomplishing important tasks in their daily lives, yet individuals have more free time on their hands now than at any other point in history according to recent U.S. Census data. Perhaps a more widely experienced example is the distance that many couples report among themselves within their marriages, in light of their expectations of closeness and security within what is thought to be the most intimate of all interpersonal relationships. Paradoxes are steeped in a family communication process, which contain what Bateson described as *negative injunctions* (Jones, 1993) where the two levels of communication (e.g., verbal and non-verbal) are contradictory. At a most basic level, paradoxical situations form the crux of the learned helplessness conundrum (i.e., "the hell which awaits me is worse than the hell in which I find myself") creating ongoing anxiety and stress among members, but the lack of will to change anything that would rectify the situation for fear of making matters worse (i.e., "damned if I do and damned if I don't" is a common expression in sessions where paradoxes are discussed). Ongoing and repeated confrontations lead to emotional cut-offs between family members, which create a sense of what therapists often refer to as "being stuck." Under the assumptions of the Milan school of family therapy (i.e., Selvini-Palazzoli, Cecchin, Boscolo, Prata, and others), paradoxes may originate as a result of multigenerational influences, family secrets, or other structural factors (Jones, 1993). A common paradox within military families results from the conflict associated with the joy of having a service member back home, but not being able to allow that member to easily re-integrate into the household again while being angry because the service member is unable to do so. Paradoxical situations give members the sense that something is wrong, but they are unable to resolve it, and that is often the point at which members seek consultation with a therapist.

Family Secrets

Secrets are universal and are thought to be reinforcing of boundaries between family members within the systems, and may also provide protection from the outside world. Secrets are also, in terms of anxiety, the most binding force within family systems, in that their divulgence may lead to emotional cut-offs, bitter conflict, and extensive mistrust (Nichols, 1996). There are several types of family secrets that have varying effects on family emotional processes: supportive, protective, manipulative, and avoidant (Berg-Cross, 2000). Secrets may fall into any of these categories at varying times, as in the case of extramarital affairs, which may be construed as *protective*, or *manipulative*, while the affair is occurring, but may become primarily *avoidant* after it is discovered by a loved one (i.e., certain aspects of the affair often remain secret, thwarting attempts at emotional recovery). Supportive and protective secrets are thought to have positive merits and be of therapeutic value at some level, but manipulative and avoidant secrets are a source of anxiety to the family systems, form the basis of emotional cut-offs, and are almost never helpful in the therapeutic sense (Imber-Black, 1993). Unfortunately, secrets within the context of military families tend to fall into the latter two categories, more often than not. Imber-Black (1993) asserts that a secret may be difficult to place into positive or negative categories because it may have varied meanings for family members and thus may be viewed differently by each family member. A teenager's delinquency during a service member's deployment may be a protective, avoidant, and manipulative secret, depending on perceived reactions of the service member, the wish to avoid excess problems in his or her absence, and the attempt to use the threat of divulgence as a means of controlling the adolescent's behavior in the future. As a process, family secrets are often evidence of an emotional triangle and its inherent cut-offs, and are in need of resolution by the therapist in order to improve the family members' lives.

Family Rituals

Families are embedded within a variety of contexts that require the performance of public and private rituals in order to signify the movement of individuals and families from one developmental stage to another successive stage (Carter & McGoldrick, 1998). Sociologically, rituals serve five unique functions for families: *protection*, *cohesion*, *communication*, *intergenerational learning*, and *identity development*, or maintenance (Berg-Cross, 2000). Many aspects of human and family life are steeped in rituals. These range from once (or twice) in a lifetime events, such as weddings, baby showers, graduations, and retirement parties, to annual celebrations of which a sense of tradition becomes an integral part, like birthdays and seasonal holidays. Rituals are crucial to the process of creating memories about events, provide a meaningful context for our existence, and help define who we are as individuals and families (Imber-Black, Roberts & Whiting, 2003). Within the military, for example, promotion ceremonies as formal rituals are indications of both personal achievement and family involvement in the service member's career, and serve to strengthen the connection between service members, their family, their unit, and their branch of service. Private rituals also develop within military families and commonly include a service member's spending personal time with each family member prior to or after a deployment. Rituals may evolve or develop anew in a variety of contexts and occasions (Imber-Black et al., 2003). This phenomenon may provide evidence of family health and well-being, if it evolves in a way that is inclusive and functional to all members. On the other hand, the inability of family rituals to evolve may represent inflexibility or unresolved issues associated with grief or loss for certain families.

Sibling Relationships

Parents and peers often take center stage when family therapists and researchers discuss influences on individuals within families. Birth order has long been thought to exert influence on emotional development as children age, but in recent years there has been a stronger focus on the positive and negative aspects of relationships between siblings across the entire lifespan (Sulloway, 1996). These relationships tend to be the longest lasting in which individuals are involved, and are often the most egalitarian (Berg-Cross, 2000). Sibling relationships may be influenced by birth order, but should be seen as different from this aspect of family life in that the discussion of sibling relationship denotes a family process rather than structure. Sibling relationships are as likely to be dictated by inherent characteristics as they are the position of siblings in the family or the stage within the family life cycle (Harris, 1998). As a testament to the power of the heredity influence, both authors agree that we are about as likely to hear "you're just like dad" when mediating disputes between siblings in adulthood as we are "you've always treated me like that (badly, etc.) because you're older (or younger) than I am," or "Mom liked you best because ...".

These relationships form the basis for a variety of interpersonal socialization patterns. *Loyalty*, *cooperation*, *obligation*, and *supportiveness*, or the lack thereof, are core values upon which sibling relations are based, and absence of these may produce intense rivalries lasting into adulthood and may form the basis of negative interactional patterns in variety of settings (Berg- Cross, 2000). Cohesion between siblings may be adversely influenced by maladaptive familial patterns, such as parental incapacitation, family stress, or divorce and remarriage (Nichols, 1996). Separation between siblings is often a source of anxiety in adulthood, and is reflective of associated lifespan changes and the maturation process, whatever the reason may be. Extensive separations may be a source of disruption to the extent of family dissolution in the military setting, and almost always negatively impact siblings as parents go their separate ways, loyalties are inevitably divided, and disagreements between siblings ensue. Systemic therapists should be keenly aware of the importance of sibling relationships as an influence within the context of their client's lives, and in their own, as these issues may be a primary source of counter transference in the therapeutic setting.

Family Development

Stages of Development in the Lifespan

Families move through various stages and phases of change driven by the ontogenetic processes associated with child development. As they move through these stages, a variety of larger social forces act upon families, thwarting their efforts, in some cases, at healthy transitions and creating crises for family members. Such is the case with military families, as they relocate from one installation to another, members deploy to duty, and families reunite after extended separations (Hall, 2008). While the number of agreed-upon stages and trajectory may vary depending on the source, the general consensus is that change within family systems is more or less constant across the span of time. This concept was first introduced within the study of marriages and families by Ruben Hill and Evelyn

Duvall (Duvall, 1957) in the 1930s, and was later elaborated on within the field of family therapy in the 1970s (Carter & McGoldrick, 1980). Family lifespan development is now considered one of the core paradigms for understanding family change within the fields of social work, professional counseling, gerontology, and medicine, to name a few. Three core suppositions exist, regardless of the various uses of this approach, pursuant to life cycle stages and the changes in families associated with each stage: (1) movement through stages is determined by the addition or subtraction of members (e.g., launching begins when the first child departs from the household); (2) changes are brought on by the movement of children to developmental maturity (i.e., bringing the family into contact with other facets of social life); and (3) family connections with other social institutions (i.e., work, school, healthcare, etc.) are altered as members age (Carter & McGoldrick, 1980, 1998).

The process of family lifespan development is generally thought to begin with the coupling (or pair bonding) of two individuals through marriage or a long-term commitment, although the circumstances may vary due to ethnic background, socioeconomic practices, or other demographic factors (Carter & McGoldrick, 1998). This initial phase ends with the birth of the couple's first child, and the couple must adapt to the changes brought on by the arrival of the newborn as they move into the families-with-young-children life cycle phase. Many systems-based practitioners see the movement into this stage as the beginning of a triangulation that de-intensifies the emotional strength of the adult pair bond that began the lifespan developmental process. The next stage begins with the aging of the child into the preschool years and subsequent birth of other children (in many cases), as well as the involvement of the family with the education system as a social institution. This stage may be broken down into other substages, including elementary school years and middle childhood, but nevertheless the family must adapt to ever-growing influences from outside of the family, including challenges to the norms and rules that govern family life, and the process continues to intensify into the next stage of lifespan development (families with adolescents).

The next stage after adolescence is commonly referred to as the launching stage as children begin to leave and move into their own adult life courses. As with all previous stages, the entrance into this stage is driven by the ontogenetic development of the oldest child in the sibling set and ends as the last child leaves home. Families must respond to the set changes accompanying this transition by realigning themselves accordingly in terms of creating new rules, accepting new roles, adjusting to new-found statuses, and understanding how each member functions in accordance with the expectations of other family members. Figure 1.1 provides an example of a military family life cycle typical of members of the U.S. ground forces in Iraq and Afghanistan in the early 21st century, where crises may erupt at any of the major transition points in the life cycle trajectory and remarriages may produce complex step-family systems. One notable exception between military families and other families, with regard to developmental lifespan theory, concerns the ontogenetic force behind the developmental life course. With families in general, it is acknowledged that the age and stage of the oldest child acts

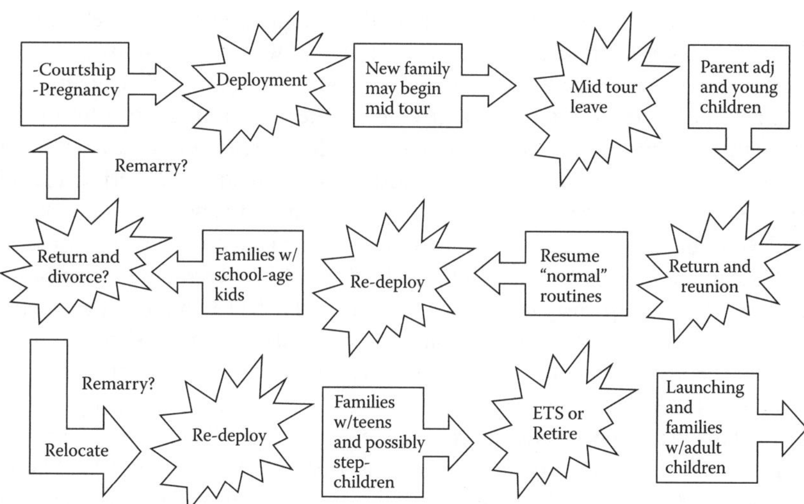

FIGURE 1.1 Developmental life cycle for career military families.

upon the family system in ways that forces transition into subsequent phases of the life cycle (Carter & McGoldrick, 1980, 1998). In military families, however, the service member's departure and return may act upon the system with equal or greater influence than the development of the oldest child.

Resilience and Vulnerability

Families are often perceived in terms of strengths and weaknesses. The notions of resilience and vulnerability stem from the attributions made in accordance with internal (intra-familial) perspectives on how much stress family members are experiencing, along with how well they are coping, and perceptions of members external to the family system (e.g., therapist). Boss (2002) defines resilience as the ability to meet challenges and cope with changes that threaten the integrity of the system while remaining intact and creating a positive environment for fostering member well-being. Some families are more resilient than others simply because of their member make-up, temperamental factors, and the way they are structured. Families also may be vulnerable as result of both internal factors (e.g., chaotic structure and inadequate rulemaking) and external factors, including excessive periods of time apart, economic downturns, or unforeseen catastrophic events. McCubbin, Thompson & McCubbin (2001), Olsen (2003), and Boss (2006) all denote myriad factors present along the resiliency continuum. Resilience is fostered by the ability of families to meet demands, such as stressors, strains, and transitions, adequately; their life cycle stage; their effectiveness at problem solving; their ability to marshal needed resources; their appraisal of the situation; and the capability to provide mutual support of members, in order to emerge from difficult situations and prevent negative outcomes that may render them vulnerable in the future.

Resilient families are also less prone to the development of crisis responses to catastrophic events; but of course there are limits to which any family system can be taxed emotionally, and any given family's ability to adjust to change and adapt to its circumstances is crucial to the idea of resilience. Families seen for therapy have failed at some level to adapt adequately to their circumstances and are therefore made more vulnerable as a result. Inadequate adaptations rendering a family more helpless in the face of adversity and the presence of new stressor events may also lead to increased vulnerability as result of a phenomenon known as "pile-up" (McCubbin, Thompson & McCubbin, 2001). The continued presence of unresolved demands (i.e., pile-up) eventually leads to emotional exhaustion under the tenets of the family resiliency model, which may lead to the development of mental health disorders or psychosomatic physical maladies in some family members. Further exploration is needed to fully understand the extent to which the inadequate resolution of demands in one generation leads to the expression of these influences in subsequent generations, but most systemic practitioners, from the beginnings of family therapy practice, commonly associate dysfunctional patterns within the family of origin (e.g., alcoholic, divorced, or anxiety-ridden family systems) as creating problems for current clients and their families.

Crisis in Families

The 2009 edition of the Merriam-Webster dictionary defines a *crisis* as "an unstable or crucial time or state of affairs in which a decisive change is impending, especially one with a distinct possibility of an unfavorable outcome." Systemic therapists define a crisis as an event, or a culmination of events, that exceeds a family's coping abilities and alters its perception of the event(s), resulting in a malfunctioning of emotions, cognitions, and behaviors (Webb, 2007). We mentioned in the previous section that the degree of a family's resiliency (versus vulnerability) renders it either susceptible to the experience or able to avoid a crisis. Within the context of family therapy and family science, there are several basic components associated with the development of a crisis in families. These are the severity of the stressor event, the family's ability to cope effectively with the event(s), its perception of its situation based on previous experiences with stressful situations, and its inherent ability to adapt based upon a culmination of the aforementioned factors, as well as the individual reactions and family style (McCubbin et al., 2001).

Olson (2003) proposed that the range of balance versus imbalance in families, along three continua of adaptability, cohesion, and communication, determine the extent to which they fail to properly respond to crises. Families who are considered more extreme toward the imbalanced end of Olsen's spectrum deal more poorly with stressors and strains, thereby placing them at greater risk for experiencing a crisis. Finally, we must mention the nature of the event itself. In some cases the event, or a series of occurrences, can so rapidly overwhelm families' problem-solving skills and their ability to utilize resources that they experience the event as *traumatic* and are subsequently helpless in the face of new demands for the immediate future. Trauma translates from Greek as "wound" (Webb,

2007), and the emotional nature of trauma has long been recognized as a part of the subsequent impact of calamitous experiences on individuals and families. Most of us are familiar with the traumatic nature of catastrophic events, whether man-made or natural in their origins, but some will experience the sudden death of a loved one or permanent injury on a more personal level as "traumatic" at some point in their lives. Within the military, death and incapacitation due to combat are constant sources of worry and strain, especially for family members during long separations as a part of hazardous deployments.

Illness or Incapacitation

Illness is perhaps the most common crisis within families and influences the onset of family crises due the nature of disease within the context of family structure. Illness may or may not cause incapacitation, but when it does, the loss of functioning related to incapacitation varies greatly by family style and type. Boss (2006) stresses the importance of loss as a key component added to the familial perception of illness or incapacitation as a crisis event, and the issue of the ill or incapacitated member's ability to return to a previous level of functioning is important as well. More recently, we have become familiar with the increased incidence of traumatic brain injury associated with the use of improvised explosive devices in Iraq and Afghanistan, and the long-term impact placed on the affected families and the healthcare system (Nash, 2007).

Separations

Separations within families occur for a variety of reasons and range in significance with regard to their impact upon the family system and its individual members. Separations in families occur for a variety of reasons, including divorce, relocation, occupational demands, military duties, and unfortunately, in some cases, incarceration. The ambiguity experienced by family members when loved ones are separated from them seems to create the greatest risk for the development of crises in family systems during their absence (Black, 1993). The absence of a family member alters the family's boundaries and emotional structure but the member is present in the memories of those who remain in the system, and they may be in frequent communication depending on the circumstances of their separation. Herein lies the ambiguous nature of the strain associated with separation, according to Boss (2002). Military deployments place extreme demands on family members and may serve to precipitate a crisis. Lengthy absences are not, however, without homecomings, which may be crisis provoking as well, depending upon the nature of the separation (Blount, Curry & Lubin, 1992).

Deaths

The death of someone close to an individual is often considered the most stressful life event one can experience and impacts families in a variety of ways. Death involves the experience of loss, the grief associated with that loss, and requires adjustment to the loss for those who remain (James & Cherry, 1988). The most typical emotional experience associated with the death of a family member is sadness, but it may be impacted by the events leading up the death of the individual (e.g., death after a long-term illness may result in a sense of relief for family members who experienced the suffering of the deceased family member). The stages of grieving may be complicated by the presence of emotional cut-offs between members of a family manifested by extreme guilt or regret as a result of the poor quality of the relationship between members of the system prior to death (Nichols & Schwartz, 1997). The death of a family member may result in a crisis as a mere result of the event itself or when the family is unable to fulfill the role requirements previously carried out by the deceased. The abruptness of death associated with military service most often causes extreme shock for family members and presents the system with a sudden void that they are unable to fill. Support from outside the family system is often necessary for stability and to forestall the precipitation of a crisis.

Beliefs and Spirituality

Social science research indicates that just as people are born with psychological, social, and physical potentials, they also have spiritual potential and seek out the sacred (Pargament, 2007, p. 61). Spirituality is recognized as one of the systems within which people live and spiritual coping methods have been found to contribute both positively and negatively to overall health (Pargament, 2007, p. 94; Walsh, 1998, p. 68). Belief systems often provide the basis for both overt and covert rules, family rituals, and the family's value systems. Clinicians and caregivers approach spirituality from their own religious perspective, from an open, curious perspective, or in ambiguity and unease. Those who approach spirituality from their own perspective are not always able to be open to someone who has a different religious perspective, and this can raise both clinical and ethical issues. Clinicians who approach spirituality in ambiguity and unease often ignore or deny it as a factor in the clinical situation. It is possible and helpful to invite a person or family to discuss their spiritual perspective and resources, and to assess whether the perspective and resources are helpful and integrating or hurtful and disintegrating.

A clinical interview should include questions about the person's spiritual perspective. "What beliefs and values give your life meaning?" is an open question that does not suppose a particular belief system or religion. There are great varieties of ways that people perceive the spiritual or religious dimensions of their lives. Some are traditional religious, involved in specific religious communities, have a particular way of conceiving of God, and try to adhere to the beliefs and commandments of their religion. Some people are less traditional and more oriented to rational, scientific explanations of life experiences. Others find spiritual connection in mystical experiences and practices such as meditation or in service to others and to the earth (ecology). Some people are disengaged from the spiritual dimension within their lives and are consequently searching for deeper meaning throughout the lifespan.

Tools for Understanding Families

Genogramming

A genogram is a drawing or graph of family structure and relationships. The use of genograms for assessing family problems has long been standard practice in the field of family therapy. Family practice medicine, social work, anthropologists, and geneticists have used some form of this technique for seeing family structure, tracing lineage, and mapping relationships (McGoldrick & Gerson, 1985). Genograms enable the family member to construct a representation of her or his family and the relationships in that family. It is a useful tool for family of origin self study, described below, in that it allows family members to develop a sense of the influence of interpersonal forces beyond themselves across space and time (i.e., intergenerational aspects). Genograms allow the clinician to learn about and remember the family structure, relationships, and primary triangles. In fact, more seasoned systems-oriented clinicians often report "thinking in terms of genograms," referring to the extent to which this diagnostic process becomes second nature to them.

There are several levels of representation in genograms. One level is the *structure* of the family over several generations—who married who, and the order and gender of their children. A second level of representation is *events and timing*—deaths, military service, accidents, illnesses, graduations, marriages, etc. An important third level is *indication of emotional process* through identifying the significant triangles in the genogram and the nature of the emotional energy in each relationship (negative, positive, open, closed, charged, etc.)

McGoldrick and Gerson (1985) describe many different ways to construct genograms with specific symbols that indicate marriage, divorce, affairs, death, unborn child, pre-natal deaths, addictions, triangles, sexual orientation, and other significant factors in a family's life experience. Berg-Cross (2000) also provides a basic set of notations useful in the construction of family genograms. Figure 1.2 gives an example of a military family genogram where the creation of a complex step-family has erupted into a process of conflict between the stepmother and stepdaughter due to the discovery of the stepdaughter's cannabis use. In this case, the therapist was able to rapidly assess multiple systemic problems and quickly help the family understand these processes through the use of a genogram. Several key points to consider when genogramming military families: the structural complexity of these depictions, the difficulty illustrating the emotional processes within these complex systems, and taking the amount of time needed to ensure the accurate portrayal of the family system. In this case, we have indicated the divorce slightly out of the recommended sequence in order to better portray the 16-year-old's inclusion in the reconstituted household.

Family Structural Analysis (Ecomapping)

A family structural analysis may be best described as a quick tool for using paradigmatic explanations for family problems. In some fields of practice, similar tools for gathering information about communication structures, interactional patterns,

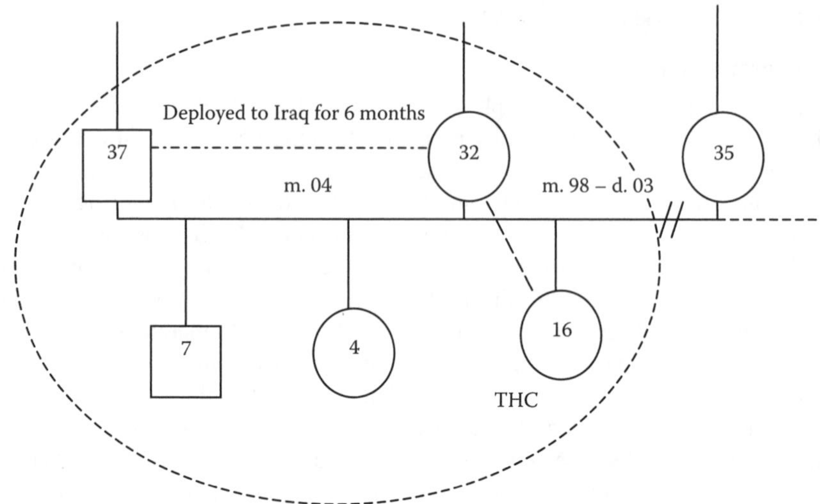

FIGURE 1.2 Sample military family genogram.

and linkages outside the family are referred to as ecomaps (in social work), or sociograms (in sociology). These ecomaps are useful because they include extrafamilial connections and their influence on family process, in addition to structure. Families find themselves coexisting within a larger social network that includes churches, communities, and civic organizations. These ecosystems and networks provide stabilization for families or may destabilize families as a result of their influence. An example of the ecosystems in which families find themselves are based upon *zones of intimacy* and range in affiliation from close friends and relatives to nominal personal affiliations (Berg-Cross, 2000). Given the embedded nature of military families within the larger system and that these families must recreate these networks as they relocate, for example, the clinician may more quickly develop an understanding of the stressors associated with this lifestyle and clarify problematic features of these issues very early in the course of therapy. We refer the reader to the work of Rothery and Enns (2001) for a more in-depth discussion of this diagnostic tool.

Family-of-Origin Self Study

This assessment of family-of-origin issues involves the client(s) as gatherers of information about multigenerational patterns currently causing distress within the family system. This technique has been used for a number of years in various family therapy training programs to assist young therapists in better understanding the influence of their families in their own lives. In training and supervision, we often recommended that students experiencing strong emotional reactance to a therapeutic issue or intense counter transference toward a client, couple, or family reassess their own family-of-origin issues. The utility of the family-of-origin self study with clients or couples is in the gathering of information as a way of processing current problems. Rather than taking a "hodgepodge" approach and gathering this information as these issues arise in sessions, focusing the clients on the process of family history gathering and personal reflections early in the therapy process provides insightful gains and often produces rapid results in family therapy. As a result of this process, clients are often able to gain a significant understanding of their emotional lives and the impact these sometimes intense emotions have on their interpersonal interactions in a variety of contexts.

SYSTEMS THINKING APPLIED TO MILITARY FAMILIES

The Bigger Picture

Marital and family relations seem to have been stretched beyond their capacities to accommodate individual needs for satisfaction and security within the context of postmodern life. The increased speed at which change occurs (vis-à-vis technology access and information management) and the constant adaptational requirements have led some family scholars to speculate as to the "proper" definition of family normality (Walsh, 2003). Suffice it to say that many families experience the travails of modern life in a way that renders them susceptible to a variety of difficulties that stem from these subsequent vulnerabilities, but the military institution is much slower to change than the groups of individuals that populate this structure, and it wields a tremendous pressure on families to conform to its prevailing social norms. Military families, with historically lengthy separations, frequent relocations, and constant strain associated with heightened occupational risk, may have provided us a glimpse through the window of how other families will appear in the very near future as a result of the ongoing process of globalization. Military families expect to move frequently, relocate to different parts of the world, spend excessive amounts of time apart, and live with the threat of the permanent loss of a loved one.

Regardless of their expectations, members of military families are just as likely to be rendered helpless by impinging stressors and vulnerabilities within the family as they are to be able to cope successfully with these factors. Figure 1.3 provides a simple look at the multiple contexts and structures in which military family members must exist on a daily basis. From this standpoint, the onset of problems associated with a military style of life is inevitable.

Commonly Observed Problems in Military Families

Perhaps the most common complaints among military families stem from the strain associated with balancing role requirements imposed by military service and the daily needs of family members. Many adult members of military families may be poorly differentiated from their families of origin, or originate from failed (or abusive) family backgrounds, placing them at higher risk for developing complex problems in the face of their already stressful lifestyles.

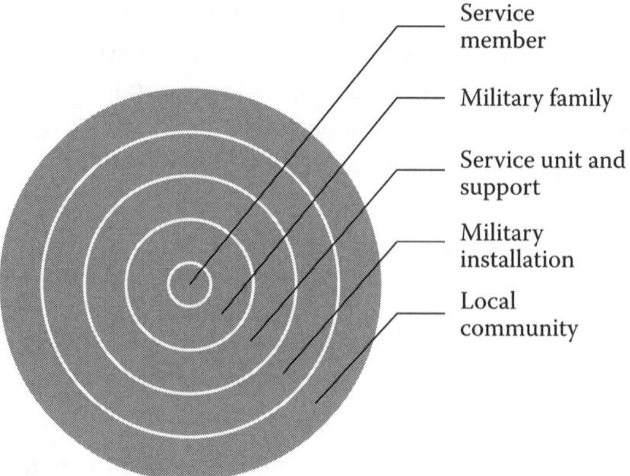

FIGURE 1.3 Military multi-systems.

The information presented in Table 1.1 provides a brief listing of factors associated with military service that render military families vulnerable to a variety of problems (Everson, 2005). The constancy of demands inherent to the cycle of deployment is depicted in Figure 1.4.

These vulnerability factors are common within the civilian population as well, but these factors may not, in and of themselves, cause dysfunction or dissolution of those family systems. Yet in the case of military families, again the strain associated with ongoing aspects of the military developmental life cycle may prove particularly troublesome. Developed out of a general systems framework and with returning WWII veterans and their families as its original focus (Hill, 1949), the family stress and resiliency model has become widely recognized and utilized by many family researchers and systemic practitioners as an integral part of making sense of the stressors and strains associated with a military lifestyle. This model, with its theoretical emphasis on the impact of stressors upon coping abilities, the perception of stressor intensity, and the availability of coping resources ultimately

TABLE 1.1
Current Military At-Risk Factors

Frequent relocations
Previous long-term deployments
Longer separations during combat-related deployments
More frequent combat-related deployments
Larger families and more dependents
Female spouses younger than females in the general population
Higher percentage of blended families due to remarriages
Lower median educational level
Lower median income
Spouses working outside home

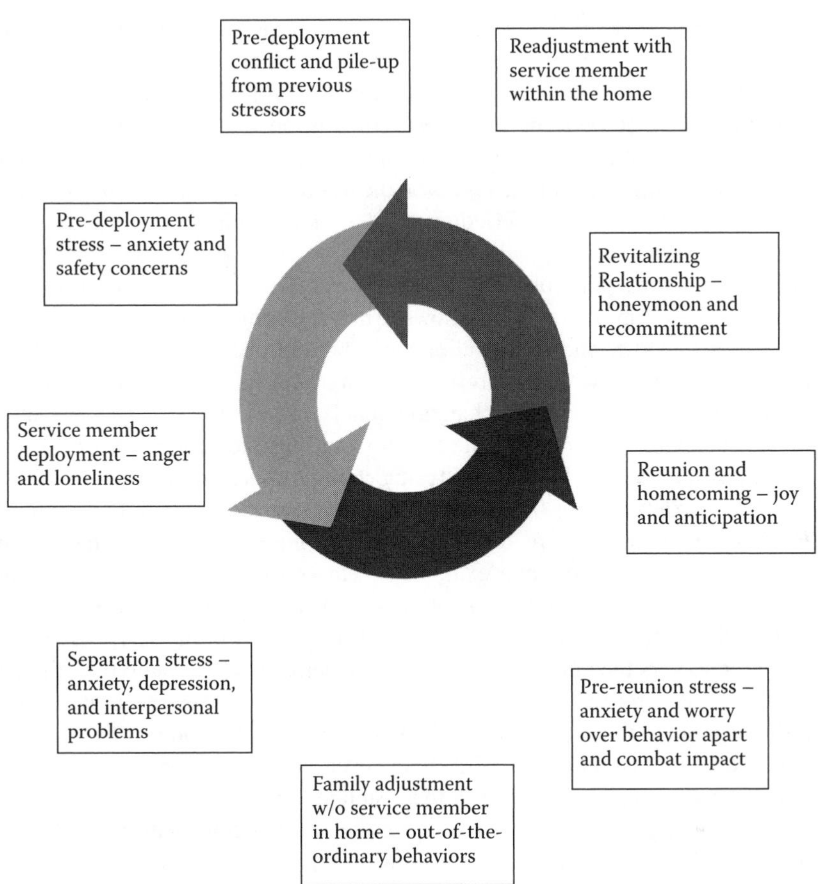

FIGURE 1.4 Stressors and strains associated with a typical deployment cycle.

allows for the explanation of the adaptive or maladaptive outcomes for families under stress (McCubbin et al., 2001). Many systemic problems within military families can be traced directly to the separation experienced during deployments. Disruption is experienced, in the words of one Army wife, "from the moment they cut his orders (for deployment)."

Conceptualizing Structural Problems in Military Families Systemically

One of the most basic elements of understanding problems within military families centers around the existence of an emotional triangle between the service member, his/her family, and the military as a systemic force that impacts the entire family system. As their name implies, emotional triangles in their simplest form only require the interaction of three individuals or a non-human entity. This point is particularly relevant to the military situation. The emotional triangles within the military context are particularly troublesome in that they are ultimately obligatory for the service member primarily, and the military family as a secondary function. In essence, service members are required to constantly balance their roles and status with their family and fulfill their obligatory duty to the military often at the same time. "Not going when your unit deploys," as one service member put it, "is simply not an option." This situation creates a classic double bind situation at multiple points on the triangle and at various times during the developmental life cycle (Friedman, 2007). The result is often the development of emotional pathology within the family system.

From Freidman's point of view, emotional triangles possess five basic *modus operandi*, which can be stated as follows: triangles form out of people's discomfort with one another and the situations in which they are involved; individuals within them function with self-preservation as a priority opposing any effort to change; they create difficulty in changing beliefs or behavior; triangles are interlocking and reciprocally reinforcing; and the resulting interactions transmit stress to the focal member of the system. Triangles often represent an attempt at first to mediate anxiety within the family system by drawing others into mediating roles, but often produce more anxiety within individuals as a result of the double binds that develop. A common example of emotional triangulating within the military system stems from the separations caused by deployment cycle that military families experience with a great deal of frequency. As the service member exits and re-enters the household as part of an ongoing obligation to the military (i.e., non-human entity), role shifts must occur, requiring systemic reorganization within the family of the service member. In this situation the spouse of the service member (and the parent of the military children, most often) becomes the focal point of the system and the bearer of the resultant anxiety in both cases.

Understanding the emotional triangle as the basic component of the family structure and process is, in our opinion, what separates our point of view from those of others in the helping professions. The interpersonal dynamics associated with triangulations are the source of much of the anxiety and tension found within family systems, and result in the impasses that are so common in therapeutic situations. In an attempt to reduce the tension so often associated with the emotional binds common to triangles, one or more members may engage in distancing behaviors in order to effect an emotional *cut-off* from the source of the tension (i.e., the impasse that created the double bind situation). Emotional cut-offs clarify boundaries in a negative way that most often results in the interpersonal *impasse* for which families initially seek treatment (Madanes, 1981).

Cut-offs often represent boundary shifts toward rigidity that can originate from the triangulated interaction pattern or surface as a result of the triangulation. The separation imposed by a deployment can be considered the source of a cut-off as a result of the ambiguous nature of the communication between spouses during these times. Information is often withheld by both members of the marital dyad in order to facilitate what is perceived to be a smoother separation for all members of the family, but, as is often the case, the result of withholding information forms the basis of deception that must be maintained as a *secret* between two or more family members (e.g., adolescent acting out in school while service

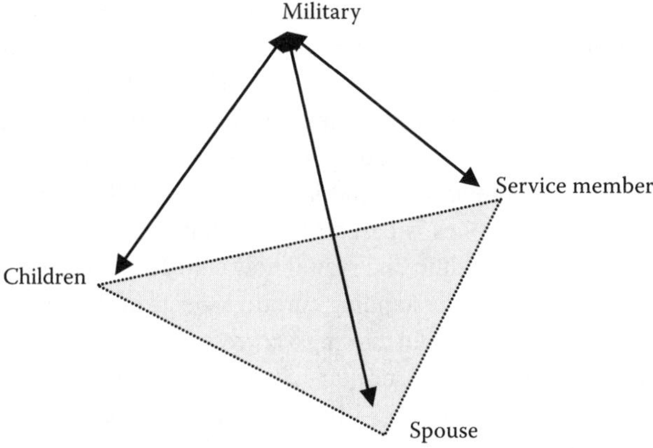

FIGURE 1.5 Basic emotional triangle between military families and the military system.

member is away). Of course, secrets may be intrapersonal and create a great deal of regret, remorse, dread, emotional distance, and reduced intimacy between the two members of the marital subsystem (e.g., extramarital affairs, the results of combat, etc.). Figure 1.5 provides a basic pyramidal depiction of the triangulation between the military defense system, the service member, and the members of a military family.

The Systemic Therapist as an Agent for Change in Military Settings

There has been a growing concern among mental health practitioners that military families may be stressed beyond their abilities to cope in the face of multiple deployments, repeated combat exposure, and constant life disruptions from a variety of sources (e.g., relocation). How can the systems-oriented therapist act as a force for positive improvement within these families who are often structurally and emotional entrenched. Simply put, the systems-oriented practitioner doesn't have to be hampered by the framework of an individually oriented practitioner. We begin with systems in mind, while other therapists do not. Quite a few conversations with individually oriented counselors have ended with their frustration over the military client's inability to make positive gains against what is perceived to be an unalterable bureaucratic, rule-laden, and inhumane entity. Indeed, while training and supervising individually oriented practitioners at an institute-based family therapy program, our primary focus was to deal with the initial frustration trainees felt as a result of feeling out of control in therapy due to their over-reliance on a one-to one perspective and the multiplicity of events occurring simultaneously in the lives of their military clients. One trainee compared therapeutic work with families in the military system to "being a ringmaster in a three-ring circus." This frustration may also be amplified by the disconnection created by the service member's adherence to the military's institutional norms and goals and those of their families. This disconnection becomes less of a barrier to improvement in family functioning when viewed as an aspect of the intense re-socialization process the service member undergoes beginning with basic training.

Sociologists tell us that language is the centrally organizing feature of any cultural system and the military is no exception. Theirs is a language heavily reliant on unique acronyms, abbreviations, and jargon (Hall, 2008). A crucial aspect of working with military families is based on understanding their unique language as a central feature of their culture, no matter how colorful or laced with expletives this language may be. Misunderstanding certain aspects of their language can, in some cases, mean the difference in making a correct referral for installation-based service and being informed by a military spouse that the Social Work Service doesn't handle a particular problem—"Installation Community Services does." A therapist new to work within military systems may have to become accustomed to coarse language from service members, their spouses, and even their children in the heat of a confrontation within a therapy session. Paradoxically, an Army wife, for example, may profess a devout belief in the divine in one sentence and curse worse than a proverbial sailor in the very next breath. It may take some time to desensitized oneself to the daily travails of working in this context.

As with other social systems, norms, values, and beliefs form the basis for acculturation and standards for conduct within the military system. Military dependents are expected to adhere to these standards as well, since disruptions in family life can negatively impact the service member in terms of potential assignments that enhance opportunities for promotion or the family being asked to leave the installation because of misdeeds by family members. Therapists working from a systemic perspective should understand the value of prudence when challenging some of the preconceived notions held by service members and their family members. Bravery and valor are very important, not only to service members, but to their families as well, and may conflict with the therapist's own deeply held convictions and preconceived notions about warfare. Many family members see what they do as an extension of the service member's commitment to the military and keeping their family lives running smoothly regardless of the situation (e.g., 6 months into a year-long deployment) is of the utmost importance. Our advice is to treat the military families and not the uniforms, or do not attempt to work with these families. Along these lines, a final caveat is appropriate for doing this work. In recent years, there has been a proliferation of seminars seeking to educate therapists on how to work with military families, as if they are a ubiquitous entity and are served by a "one size fits all" approach. We have found that these families are often as unique as the branch of the military in which they serve, the rank the service members hold, the installation to which they are assigned, and the length of time they have served in a specific branch of service. With these issues in mind, we hope that we've provided a useful integration of ideas and a wide variety of topics for this introduction to systemic practice with families within military settings.

CONCLUSIONS

This chapter was designed to provide practitioners with an overview of systemic principles that we feel are basic to working effectively with military families. Since no single chapter of this length could approach the complexity and delicacy with which systemic approaches may be applied, we have carefully chosen references that serve as standards of general family therapy practice and have provided them in the reference list. The reader will find this list to be varied in both focus and scope, but we consider these references to be basic to the understanding of a systems-based approach to working with families in general. We also refer the reader to the appendix at the end of this volume for information on the history and development of family therapy practice. We began by offering an overview of the historical development of systemically oriented family therapy before moving on to a more general discussion of the establishment of the field of family therapy. We then attempted to include some of the more basic concepts associated with the practice of systemic therapy and some of the tools used by systems therapists to provide clinical assessments for clients. We have concluded by providing an integration of these family systems concepts into a framework that relates specifically to problems associated with military family life, and how systemic practitioners can provide an impetus for positive change within these families. The remainder of this volume will include many of these concepts and will provide integration into the ongoing practice of systemic therapy with families within the military establishment.

REFERENCES

Berg-Cross, L. (Ed.) (2000). *Basic concepts in family therapy: An introductory text* (2nd ed.). New York, NY: Hawthorn.

Beavers, R. W. & Hampson, R. B. (2003). Measuring family competence: The Beavers Systems Model in *Normal family processes: Growing diversity and complexity*, Walsh, F., 3rd ed. New York: Guilford Press.

Black, W. G., Jr. (1993). Military-induced family separation: A stress reduction intervention. *Social Work, 38*(3), 273–280.

Blount, W., Curry, A. & Lubin, G. I. (1992). Family separation in the military. *Military Medicine, 157,* 76–80.

Boss, P. (2002). *Family stress management: A contextual approach* (2nd ed.). Thousand Oaks, CA: Sage.

Boss, P. (2006). Normalizing ambivalence in *Loss, trauma, and resilience: Therapeutic work with ambiguous loss*, 143–161. New York: Norton.

Cade, B. & O'Hanlon, W. H. (1993). *A brief guide to brief therapy.* New York, NY: Norton.

Carter, E. A. & McGoldrick, M. M. (Eds.) (1980). *Family life cycle.* New York, NY: John Wiley & Sons.

Carter, E. A. & McGoldrick, M. M. (Eds.) (1998). *The expanded family life cycle: Individual, family, and social perspectives* (3rd ed.). New York, NY: Allyn and Bacon.

Colapinto, J. (1991). Structural family therapy. In A. S. Gurman & D. P. Kniskern (Eds.), *Handbook of family therapy: Volume II* (pp. 417–443). New York, NY: Brunner-Mazel.

Duvall, E. M. (1957). *Family development.* Philadelphia, PA: Lippincott.

Everson, R. B. (2005). *Quality of life among Army spouses: Parenting and family stress during deployment to Operation Iraqi Freedom.* Florida State University, Tallahassee, p. 2737.

Freedman, J. & Combs, G. (1996). *Narrative therapy: The social construction of preferred realities.* New York, NY: Norton.

Friedman, E. H. (1991). Bowen theory and therapy. In A. S. Gurman & D. P. Kniskern (Eds.), *Handbook of family therapy: Volume II* (pp. 134–170). New York, NY: Brunner-Mazel.

Friedman, E. H. (2007). *A failure of nerve: Leadership in the age of the quick fix.* New York, NY: Seabury.

Gottman, J. M. (1999). *The marriage clinic.* New York, NY: Norton.

Gottman, J. M., Driver, J. & Tabares, A. (2002). Building the sound marital house: An empirically derived couple therapy. In A. Gurman & N. Jacobson (Eds.). *Clinical Handbook of Couple Therapy* (3rd ed.). New York, NY: Guilford.

Guttman, H. A. (1991). Systems theory, cybernetics, and epistemology. In A. S. Gurman & D. P. Kniskern (Eds.). *Handbook of Family Therapy: Volume II* (pp. 41–62). New York, NY: Brunner-Mazel.

Haley, J. (1976). *Problem solving therapy: New strategies for effective family therapy.* San Francisco, CA: Jossey-Bass.

Hall, L. K. (2008). *Counseling military families: What mental health professionals need to know.* New York, NY: Routledge—Taylor & Francis Group.

Harris, J. R. (1998). *The nurture assumption: Why children turn out the way they do.* New York, NY: Free Press.

Hill, R. (1949). *Families under stress: Adjustments to the crises of war, separation,and reunion.* New York: Harper.

Hogancamp, V. E. & Figley, C.R. (1983). War: Bringing the battle home. In C. Figley & H. McCubbin (Eds.). *Stress and the family: Vol. 2. Coping with catastrophe* (pp. 148–165). New York, NY: Brunner-Mazel.

Imber-Black, E. (1993). *Secrets in families and family therapy.* New York, NY: Norton.

Imber-Black, E., Roberts, J. & Whiting, R. (2003). *Rituals in families and family therapy, Revised.* New York, NY: Norton.

James, J. W. & Cherry. F. (1988). *The grief recovery handbook: A step-by-step program for moving beyond loss.* New York, NY: Harper and Row.

Johnson, S. M. & Denton, W. (2002). Emotionally-focused couple therapy: Creating secure connections. In A. Gurman & N. Jacobson (Eds.). *Clinical handbook of couple therapy* (3rd ed.). New York, NY: Guilford.

Jones, E. (1993). *Family systems therapy: Developments in the Milan-systemic therapies.* New York, NY: John Wiley & Sons.

Madanes, C. (1981). *Strategic family therapy.* San Francisco, CA: Jossey-Bass.

McCubbin, H. I., Thompson, A. I. & McCubbin, M. A. (2001). *Family measures: Stress, coping, and resiliency: Inventories for research and practice.* Honolulu, HI: Kamehameha.

McColdrick, M. & Gerson, R. (1985). *Genograms in family assessment.* New York: Norton.

McGoldrick, M. M., Anderson, C. A. & Walsh, F. (Eds.) (1989). *Women in families: A framework for family therapy.* New York, NY: Norton.

Minuchin, S. & Fishman, H. C. (1981). *Family therapy techniques.* Cambridge, MA: Harvard University Press.

Nash, W.P. (2007). The stressors of war. In C.R. Figley & W.P. Nash (Eds.). *Combat stress injury: Theory, research and management* (pp. 11–32). New York, NY: Routledge.

Nichols, M. P. & Schwartz, R. C. (1997). *Family therapy: Concepts and methods.* New York, NY: Allyn and Bacon.

Nichols, W. C. (1996). *Treating people in families: An integrative framework.* New York, NY: Guilford.

Olson, D. H. (2003). The circumplex model of marital and family functioning. In F. Walsh (Ed.). *Normal family processes* (3rd ed.) (pp. 514–548). New York, NY: Guilford.

Papernow, P. L. (1998). *Becoming a stepfamily: Patterns of development in remarried families.* Hillsdale, NJ: Analytic Press.

Papero, D. V. (1990). *Bowen family systems theory.* New York, NY: Allyn and Bacon.

Pargament, K. L. (2007). *Spiritually integrated psychotherapy: Understanding and addressing the sacred.* New York, NY: Guilford Press.

Remer, R. (2005). Family disruption—Chaos versus havoc: A chaos theory (dynamical systems) view of family structure and change. In V. L. Bengston, A. C. Acock, K. R. Allen, P. Dilworth-Anderson & D. M. Klein. (Eds.). *Sourcebook of family theory and research.* Thousand Oaks, CA: Sage.

Roberto, L. G. (1992). *Transgenerational family therapies.* New York, NY: Guilford.

Sulloway, F. J. (1996). *Born to rebel: Birth order, family dynamics, and creative lives.* New York, NY: Pantheon.

Walsh, F. (1998). *Strengthening family resilience*. New York: Guilford Press.

Walsh, F. (2003). Changing families in a changing world: Reconstructing family normality. In F. Walsh (Ed.). *Normal family processes* (3rd ed.). New York, NY: Guilford.

Webb, N. B. (2007). The family and community context of children facing crisis or trauma. In N. Webb (Ed.). *Play therapy with children in crisis: Individual, group, and family treatment* (3rd ed.) (pp. 3–20). New York, NY: Guilford.

2 The Military Culture, Language, and Lifestyle

Lynn K. Hall

CONTENTS

INTRODUCTION

In our attempt to work from a systemic perspective with military families, we first need to pay attention to the military culture. Civilian mental health professionals can make a major contribution to the needed services for military service members and families, but first it is essential that we understand the worldview, the mindset, and the historical perspective of life in the military (Hall, 2008).

Regardless of the framework that professionals work within, awareness of cultural diversity is a key component to their success. The unique culture of the military is one of those diverse groups in American society that some may indeed consider "foreign." As we know, "all experiences originate from a particular cultural context; the counselor must be attentive to this context and the role that cultural identity plays in a client's life" (Dass-Brailsford, 2007, p. 78). Certainly then, as Reger, Etherage, Reger & Gahm (2008) state, "to the extent that a culture includes a language, a code of manners, norms of behavior, belief systems, dress, and rituals, it is clear that the Army represents a unique cultural group" (p. 22). While the article written by Reger et al. focused on the Army, as they state, each of the military services has components that are both unique and common.

David Fenell (2008) points out that "by viewing the military as a distinct culture and developing interventions based on the recommendations contained in the American Counseling Association multicultural standards, counselors can increase their ability to help their military clients" (p. 8). Despite "cultural, religious and ethnic diversity within the military, the military is a culture in its own right" (p. 8). It is therefore our responsibility as ethical practitioners to be well versed in the three recognized areas of multicultural competencies (Sue, Arredondo & McDavis, 1992) of (a) becoming aware of our own behavior, values, biases, preconceived notions, and personal limitations; (b) understanding the worldview of our culturally different clients without negative judgment; and (c) actively developing and practicing appropriate, relevant, and sensitive strategies in working with our culturally diverse clients (Hall, 2008).

While it is not in the purview of this chapter to focus on all three multicultural competencies, it is my goal to consider the second competency of understanding the unique worldview and culture of the military in order for marriage and family therapists to withhold judgment and work to the best of their ability with this culturally diverse population. Understanding the worldview of the populations we work with in this case means the importance of obtaining the necessary knowledge to feel competent in working with military families (Hall, 2008). Some of the challenges for civilian mental health workers in working with military members and families include an understanding of the acronyms, including the rank and grade system; the beliefs and assumptions—both spoken and unspoken—held by most who chose this lifestyle; the fears, goals, and complications of living with long and frequent absences of one parent (or two in some cases); as well as the required frequent moves, and the more subtle lifestyle changes that families must endure and, in most cases, survive with amazing resiliency and success. Practitioners may sometimes also need to be aware of what is not being said, and understand the restricted nature of the military with its many boundaries, rules, regulations, and habits. It may also be necessary to acknowledge that some members of the military may actually feel trapped, particularly those who are from multi-generational military career families (Hall, 2008). This world has aptly been described as the Warrior Society.

REASONS TO JOIN THE WARRIOR SOCIETY

One way to understand the military is to consider why people join the military in the first place. Wertsch (1991) identified four key reasons why young people in our society choose to join the military. These are (a) family tradition, (b) benefits, (c) identification with the warrior mentality, and (d) an escape. While there are certainly many other reasons for people to join, there are usually aspects of these four that exist. We can also understand the motivation of those who remain in and make the military a career by understanding these key reasons for joining.

Family Tradition

When asked why a young woman chose to join and then make the military a career, she said she came from a military family so she understood the culture and didn't want to get out, as she was quite anxious about living in the civilian world. Having spent most of her life living on military installations, going to schools near or on the installation, she realized as an adult that she knew nothing about living "on the economy." As she experienced the civilian world through friends and a year or two of college, she found it was an uncomfortable, insecure world, with too many choices and too much freedom. Young people who grew up in the military later join the military because it is more comfortable than civilian life. That is not to say, however, that the majority of young people who grow up in the military eventually join (Hall, 2008). An Air Force veteran stated, "I think it is important to note that many families have numerous members who have served our country proudly and have provided them the emotional support to complete their tasks" (Wakefield, 2007, p. 23).

As noted above, women also share stories of wanting to follow in their fathers' footsteps. Kate Blaise (2006) says her interest in the military started with information about her ancestors during the Civil War. She shares that, more than likely, even though she heard of her father's military stories all her life, he probably never imagined he would eventually have not one, but two daughters leading troops in the middle east.

Benefits

Henderson (2006) suggested that money may be the main reason people join the military. She pointed out that those who join the military for the amount of money they will receive "tend to come from places that lack other economic opportunities" (p. 22). The military is often also seen as an option for young people who don't have clear future plans, and see this both as a transition as well as a place of service until they decide what they want to do with their lives. These young people tend to not see themselves as ready for college, but they do know that working for minimum wage is not what they want out of life.

In addition to the benefits of a steady income and a transition period, the military has been called the "great equalizer" for many in our society. A high percentage of lower income youth have correctly seen the military as a road to upward mobility, education, respect, and prestige that may have been impossible if they remained in the civilian world (Hall, 2008). The military has indeed set a standard for the integration of ethnic groups and gender, as it remains a relatively safe world for lower income service members and their families (Schouten, 2004). Wertsch (1991) shared that many of the African-American military "brats" she interviewed told of experiencing racism for the first time as adults in civilian communities and often "grew up acutely conscious of the contrast between their safe, secure life in the military and the tenuous existence of their civilian relatives in small rural towns or big city ghettos" (p. 338).

Identity of the Warrior

On a deeper, perhaps more psychological level, many who join the military feel a need to "merge their identity with that of the warrior" (Wertsch, 1991, p. 17). The structure, the expectations, the rules, even the penalties and overriding identity as a "warrior" are reassuring while, at the same time, the society provides service members with security, identity, and a sense of purpose. Those whose personality and needs fit with the military culture stay in. A San Diego therapist (Hall, 2008) noted that the profile of the service member who made the military a career during the time of the draft is often similar to those who now volunteer, as the military offers a reinforcement of a belief system and a personal identity.

Previous work on the topic of war (Nash, 2007) has explored the "psychology of war as a test of manhood and a rite of initiation among males in many cultures" (p. 17), so it is not uncommon for young men to merge their identity with that of a warrior by being a part of something meaningful, which is a motivation to join the military. Gegax and Thomas (2005) suggest that while military sons tend to talk about duty, when asked why they followed their fathers to war, their more personal motivations may be more difficult to understand. They suggest that combat may have been a test, and certainly in some cultures *the* test, of manhood throughout the history of warfare. "There is no better way to win a father's respect than to defy death just the way he did. Indeed, the effort to surpass one's father or brother's bravery has gotten more than a few men killed" (p. 26).

An Escape

The military also satisfies a need for some young people to get away from whatever they have experienced growing up, "a need for dependence … [drawing them] to the predictable, sheltered life … that they did not have growing up" (Wertsch, 1991, p. 17). Ridenour (1984) believes that military service can be that extended family system that was not experienced growing up, and that sometimes young married couples come into the military "as an escape from their respective families [only to] unconsciously run toward becoming part of a third extended family system" (p. 4). However, as Wertsch (1991) points out, "joining the military in order to put one's self in the care of a good surrogate parent is hardly the sort of thing one is likely to advertise; in fact, it is a secret so deep-seated that those who act upon it rarely admit it, and guard the secret carefully" (p. 17). This attempt to flee from problems at home, for the most part, however, does not end the problems; as in other segments of American society, sometimes the violence, gang mentality, or addiction issues are simply brought with them into the military (Hall, 2008).

CHARACTERISTICS OF WARRIOR SOCIETY

Most of the unique facets of military life, both positive and negative, that were described almost three decades ago remain true for military families today, including (a) frequent separations and reunions; (b) regular geographic household relocations; (c) living life under the "mission must come first" dictum; (d) a need for the family to adapt its natural growth and development to rigidity, regimentation, and conformity; (e) early retirement from a career in comparison to civilian counterparts; (f) omnipresent rumors and background threat of loss during a mission; (g) feelings of detachment from the mainstream of nonmilitary life; (h) the security of a vast system that exists to meet the families' needs; (i) work that more than likely involves travel and adventure; (j) the social effects of rank on the family; and (k) the lack of personal control over pay, promotion, and other benefits (Hall, 2008). These are, in summary, the plusses and minuses for the families living in the military. While "it is evident … that large segments of our society deal with one or more of these aforementioned concerns and stresses … there may be no other major group that confronts so many or all of them" (Ridenour, 1984, p. 3) at any given time.

Mary Wertsch (1991) defined this warrior society as a "fortress" to differentiate it from the democratic society of most U.S. citizens. "The great paradox of the military is that its members, the self-appointed front-line guardians of our cherished American democratic values, do not live in democracy themselves" (Wertsch, 1991, p. 15). I will share here a number of characteristics of this fortress that Wertsch discovered in her many interviews with adults who had grown up as military-dependent children. I can attest to the validity of these characteristics, having spent almost a decade working as a school counselor with military-dependent children and youth.

Authoritarian Structure

The first characteristic of the warrior society is that it is maintained by a rigid authoritarian structure. As previously noted, the family usually must adapt its natural growth and development to the rigidity, regimentation, and conformity required within the military system, as these characteristics often extend from the world of the service member into the structure of the home. It is important to point out, however, that while 80 percent of the military brats Wertsch (1991) interviewed described their families as authoritarian, "there are warriors who thrive in the authoritarian work environment without becoming authoritarian at home" (p. 25) so it is important to understand that authoritarianism is not the only model of military family life. However, within the authoritarian families, many of the characteristics discussed later in the chapter of what I have called parent-focused families (Hall, 2008) are present. Generally, in these families, there are clear rules for behavior and speech; there is little tolerance for questioning of authority or disagreements; there are often frequent violations of privacy; and often children are forbidden to engage in any activity that hints at individuation.

The military history and tradition of expecting that the service member "run a tight ship at home" has been an advantage to the career for many military men. Keith and Whitaker, back in 1984, shared the insight that "the military family lives in a community in which no one dies from old age, only violently ... lead[ing] to an illusion of eternal youth and vigor" (p. 156) and that the father (who is military) outranks his wife because he has a closer affiliation with the base commander. These authors contend that this imbalance in authority and permeability of the family boundaries causes problems as the families are often organized like miniature armies (Hall, 2008).

While this authoritarian parenting structure can work, at least while the children are in elementary school or if they are in schools on military installations, when families live "on the economy" (in a civilian community), the children, particularly once they reach adolescence, often rebel against this authoritarian parenting style because they see kids in other families with very different family structures (Hall, 2008). Within the military community this can be both comforting and suffocating at the same time. It is, in some ways, much like a "company town" mentality, where everyone knows everyone else's business. It is, in essence, a culture that is very inward focused, with consistent structure and hierarchy. The children often end up blaming the military for all their problems, as they see no way out and realize that even their extended family cannot step in to help. "They have a sense of betrayal by the military because they do not have the right to make the choices they see other young people making, but they realize their parents are not in a position to make many personal choices either" (Hall, 2008, p. 47).

Isolation and Alienation

The warrior society is also characterized by isolation and alienation from both the civilian world and the extended family as a result of the necessity for extreme mobility. As with so many professions, part of this isolation is magnified by the language, often spoken in acronyms and other idiosyncratic terms. "A therapist who does not understand ... a word or phrase is faced with a dilemma. She must balance the risk of missing important clinical information with the cost of asking for clarification " (Reger et al., 2008). This vocabulary is a significant part of the military culture and could have "important implications for psychological assessment and treatment" (Reger et al., 2008, p. 25). One of the obvious implications is that the military family may simply not be available for long-term treatment; "therefore, pragmatic reasons often force therapists to conceptualize treatment in brief terms" (Reger et al., 2008, p. 28) as well as the possibility that treatment could be interrupted for numerous reasons, suggesting that a mental health professional will need to pay attention to issues of continuity of care.

Another obvious example of isolation is that the average tour of duty is 3 years, but in many cases moves are much more frequent, for some as often as every year. I had many students in both the Department of Defense middle and high schools in Germany where I worked who had never visited their extended families' homes in the states or lived anywhere near their "home of record." The irony is that every time the family moves, it is called a PCS, or permanent change of station; permanent, that is, until the next move (Hall, 2008).

This isolation is often experienced as if life is temporary, so the focus is inward to the military world, rather than outward to the local community. For those families who spend time living abroad, the isolation may seem overwhelming as most housing areas in foreign countries are walled off from the outside culture, so the world of the Warrior Society becomes "an oddly isolated life, one in which it is possible to delude oneself that one is still on American soil" (Wertsch, 1991, p. 330). While there are those families who value the experience of living in a foreign country by learning the language and taking part in the culture, there are also those who are more anxious about this experience and may spend their entire tour of duty within the walls of the military installation. Frequently, students who lived in military housing talked about never leaving the base, as their parents were either too anxious or not interested in traveling in a foreign country (Hall, 2008). These families and students were often those who found fault with anything non-American and viewed all new experiences with distrust.

Even when military-dependent children attend public schools in the United States, they almost always have a sense of being different from the other students. Wertsch states that it is "next to impossible to grow up in the warrior society without absorbing the notion that civilians are very different and sometimes incomprehensible" (Wertsch, 1991, p. 315). Gegax and Thomas (2005) share that this isolation of the military from the rest of society can be readily understood because the United States is, in fact, divided between the vast majority who do not have military service experience and the tiny minority who do. Even those military members who don't feel isolated from the civilian world often share that they are unimpressed by aspects of the civilian work world, such as the civilian work ethic (Gegax and Thomas, 2005).

Class System

Nowhere in America is the dichotomy so omnipresent as on a military base; nowhere do the classes live and work in such close proximity; nowhere is every social interaction so freighted with class significance. … The thousands of people on a military base live together, have the same employer, dedicate their lives to the same purpose—yet they cannot, must not, socialize outside their class (Wertsch, 1991, p. 285).

The Warrior Society has two distinct subcultures, that of the officer and that of the enlisted ranks, each with very different lifestyles. The non-commissioned officers (non-coms), who are usually the top five enlisted ranks, seem sometimes caught in the middle, as one person Wertsch interviewed said, "They don't have enough power, but they have enough so that they have the appearance of having it" (1991, p. 299). But if you ask non-commissioned officers where they live and with whom they socialize, they will say with the enlisted, absolutely not the officers (Hall, 2008).

So while members of the military and their families experience a sense of isolation from their civilian counterparts, this rank structure creates a distance within the military itself. This impacts the families as well, as the spouses and the children are also expected to maintain their distance from each other. Wertsch points out that the military has its reasons for making these distinctions, and more than likely it could not exist without them, but it seems that "the only equality among officers and enlisted is in dying on the battlefield" (1991, p. 288).

The United States has made great strides in the past five decades to affirm and equalize the differences in society, but the assumption of all military systems in the world is that it is essential for the functioning of the organization to maintain a rigid hierarchical system based on dominance and subordination. It is also an essential ingredient in a clinical setting. Reger et al. (2008) point out that during the initial intake interview, rank can give the mental health professional important information, such as stressors, military history of the client and family, length of service, and possibly certain duties and experiences that will impact assessment and treatment. Another consideration pointed out by Reger et al. (2008) is that mental health professionals will more than likely be viewed by those in the military as "civilian/officer-equivalent/authority" figures. Practitioners may need to be aware that enlisted service members may respond differently from officers, based on this common belief, possibly leading to initial difficulties in establishing a therapist–client alliance.

While the children of the enlisted and officers go to the same school, they almost always are uncomfortable associating outside of school with children of the other rank. Housing is separated, with single military in one area, enlisted family housing in another, and officers' quarters in another, with clear distinctions in appearance, quality, and size (Hall, 2008). In speaking with numerous adult military brats, when the subject of rank comes up, virtually all will share that, as kids, they could almost instantaneously recognize an officer's kid or an enlisted kid. It is not a distinction to be taken lightly by civilian mental health professionals.

Parent Absence

This is a society with a great deal of parent absence and, with the changes in the military of the last two decades, sometimes both parents are absent at the same time. In 2003, graduation ceremonies from the high school where I previously worked were transmitted between the ceremonies in Germany and a location in Baghdad, Iraq, where nearly 40 percent of the graduating seniors had a parent deployed. This has continued during the current global conflicts and even expanded to connect a large number of high school graduations in Europe with Iraq, Afghanistan, Africa, and other locations around the world (DoDEA News

Release, 2007). "Despite very emotional examples like these, parent absence during important events can be crushing for young people, but for these families, it is nothing new. A parent is often absent for the prom, the big football game, the drama production, or graduation" (Hall, 2008, p. 51). But, more importantly, parents are absent for the routines of daily life, the first step, the first day of school, losing the first tooth, the first date, starting middle school, or starting high school. These are the times that cement relationships and often are missed by at least one parent. For single military parents, it is even more difficult.

Martin and McClure (2000) state that the conditions of military family life, "including long and often unpredictable duty hours, relatively low pay and limited benefits, frequent separations, and periodic relocations … remain the major stressors of military family life" (p. 3). Military parents are continually leaving, returning, leaving again, or working such long hours that their children cannot count on their presence; this is a condition of military life. Research from as far back as World War II documents that school work suffers, visits to the health clinics for both the spouse and children increase, and reports of depression and behavior problems go up when a parent is deployed. "Part of the training every military child receives is that one is expected to handle this disturbing fact of life in true stoic warrior style" (Wertsch, 1991, p. 66).

In understanding the military family system, it is also important that while the absence of parents is stressful, "sometimes this constant coming and going results in either the military parents protecting themselves from the pain of separation or the family forming a kind of cohesive unit that keeps the military parent out" (Hall, 2008, p. 52). The military parent may distance from the family, either physically by working long hours or spending time away from home, or emotionally through alcohol or other ways of soothing the self. Families, on the other hand, may become so comfortable in their roles without the military parents that when the service members return, they simply put up with the intrusion knowing that it won't be long before it ends. The military parent may also expect or demand major changes upon returning home, often adjustments that are resented by the other parent or children. "Counselors should be aware of the dynamics of military life that can introduce dissension into the relationship. Readjusting to family life, only to be pulled away yet again … places enormous stress on all those involved" (Dahn, 2008, p. 56). Frequently students in my school become more nervous and anxious prior to their military parent's return than before the parent deployed; the students and their non-military parent often became resentful that the family patterns would have to change again upon the military parent's return (Hall, 2008).

Importance of Mission

Martin and McClure (2000) point out that the conditions and demands of "a total commitment to the military—typically a commitment to one's unit, the unit's mission and its members" (p. 15) constitute the very essence of military unit cohesion. This felt sense of mission is, after all, the purpose of the military; for each service member, the commitment is not just about having a better education or training for a job, but is, in fact, a felt sense of mission to make the world a better and safer place (Hall, 2008). Houppert explains that basic training is not designed to bring an adolescent into independence, but rather to shift the recruit from dependence on his or her family to dependence on the team: "the soldier must learn that he can trust no one but his buddies" (2005, p. 84). Gegax and Thomas (2005) point out that as "incongruous as it may seem for the millions whose closest brush with battle is on cable [TV], soldiers and marines on the front line are proud to be there and willing to serve again. The overall effect is to heighten the sense that the military is becoming a proud cult that fewer and fewer outsiders want to join" (p. 26). Fenell (2008) points out that mental health professionals need to "recognize several common values shared by military personnel, including (a) always maintain physical fitness; (b) train hard before deployment to reduce casualties; (c) never abandon your fellow warriors in combat; (d) the mission and the unit always come before the individual; and (e) never show weakness to fellow warriors or to the enemy" (p. 9). While the last two items point directly to this issue of the importance of the mission, the first two also indirectly relate to the imperative to always be ready.

This dedication to the country and fellow soldiers (Fenell & Weinhold, 2003) can create difficult times for the family. Service members often see themselves as part of what might be described as a second family. Conflict can emerge when this second "military family" is perceived to be more important than the family left at home. While it has been shown that military service members who have solid families perform better on the job, it is always a difficult balancing act to be a part of two families who are so integral to the success of the mission, and to their personal career (Fenell & Weinhold, 2003). A therapist I interviewed while doing research for the book *Counseling Military Families* had been a career military officer's spouse and was, at that time, the mother of a career officer. She believes that this stance of the military that demands loyalty, dedication, dependency, and a sense of mission was virtually a form of brainwashing.

Gegax and Thomas (2005) reported that of the 100 or so generals who have children currently serving in the military, one is a mother. Her advice to her son as he went to Iraq was, "no matter what, you are there for your buddies" (Gegax & Thomas, 2005, p. 29). Mary Wertsch (1991) wrote that the real determining factor in most military families was that all-powerful presence that was often unacknowledged by the family called the Military Mission; she went on to explain that this presence went with them everywhere and gave their lives meaning. "From the viewpoint of the military's extended family style and demands, the mission takes precedence, and therefore, often the service member's relationship with his peers is found to take precedence over [the relationship] between himself and his spouse, children, or parents" (Ridenour, 1984, p. 7).

Preparation for Disaster

Civilians often seem to blithely overlook a central truth military people can never afford to forget, that at any moment they may be called upon to give their lives—or lose a loved one—to serve the ends of government. Even if it never comes to that, [they] sacrifice a great deal in the course of doing a job that most civilians on some level understand is necessary to the country as a whole" (Wertsch, 1991, p. 316).

If we look back at Fenell's list of shared values of military personnel, the first two regarding maintaining physical fitness and training hard before deployment speaks to this characteristic of preparation for disaster. Unlike most civilian occupations, with certainly a few exceptions like the police and firefighters, the Warrior Society is a world set apart from the civilian world because of its constant preparation for disaster. Unlike the first two decades after the inception of the all-volunteer military, which began in the early 1970s, this has definitely become a reality. Many who were deployed out of Europe in the early 1990s said, "But I didn't join the military to shoot people." This change has brought the military mentality back to the decades prior to the all-volunteer service (Hall, 2008). This constant preparation for disaster also places a great deal of pressure and stress on the military family. As Henderson shared, "Military readiness is like a three-legged stool. The first leg is training, the second equipment. The third leg is the family. If any of these three legs snaps, the stool tips over and America is unprepared to defend herself" (2006, p. 5). While the military cannot exist without this constant preparation, it means the family is also living under the constant threat of disaster, i.e., the potential for death or injury to the military parent.

PSYCHOLOGICAL CHARACTERISTICS OF THE FORTRESS

The above general characteristics of the military culture often lead to the three psychological traits that Mary Wertsch (1991) identified when interviewing a large number of adult military brats. These traits include

1. Secrecy, the importance of keeping what goes on at work separate from home, as well as making sure that what goes on at home stays home. The dictate about not talking about what goes on at work is also a part of many military job categories, so there is often a certain psychological shutting off even between spouses, let alone children.
2. Stoicism, or the importance of keeping up the appearance of stability and the ability to handle whatever stress the family is experiencing. Having to live under this constant preparation for change, whether it be disaster or just another deployment or PCS, means that if these fears and other feelings were expressed, families would have to acknowledge constant emotional turmoil.
3. Denial, or the need to keep all the feelings, fears, or even other "normal" developmental stresses of the family under wraps. While in a relatively few number of families this includes domestic violence, marital problems, child abuse, or other "reportable" offenses, what it does mean for most families is that feelings are not expressed, fears are not shared, and the need to ask for help or request assistance goes unnoticed.

Secrecy, stoicism, and denial are, in fact, crucial for success of the warrior, success of the mission, and ultimately success of the military (Hall, 2008). At the same time, these traits often determine whether military members seek treatment. "To the extent that seeking psychological treatment is defined as "weakness," soldiers may be slow to pursue services" (Reger et al., 2008, p. 27). Often this reluctance to seek help delays treatment, which ends up pushing many beyond tolerable stress levels. Addressing these beliefs during intake may lower the chance of military members minimizing symptoms, and thereby benefiting from a professional's ability to normalize their beliefs about fears, stigma, and future treatment (Reger et al., 2008).

These three traits of secrecy, stoicism, and denial also suggest that many military families may, on a regular basis, be experiencing Type II (*Grief and Trauma*, n.d.) trauma as a result of the constant fear, the constant planning for disaster, and the constant readiness for change. These restrictions from grieving may mean that military families are not allowed the growth that can come from the expression and "work" done in grieving the experience of loss. "When the culture encourages secrecy, stoicism and denial and discourages or even punishes the expression of fears and grief, families and service members are often faced with the same kind of consequences we see in clients who suffer from constant levels of Type II trauma" (Hall, 2008, p. 58).

HONOR AND SACRIFICE AND THE MALE MILITARY PSYCHE

These dynamics of secrecy, stoicism, and denial help us understand the concepts of honor and sacrifice in the military. It also might be difficult to understand the importance of the concepts of military honor and sacrifice without relating it to the male psyche and the traditional stereotypes of the military as a male domain. While we know that more and more women are entering the military, the culture of the military has historically been a very "male" culture. From the perspective of a therapist in San Diego who has worked with military service members for three decades (Butler, 2006), this issue could easily be overlooked or at least not understood, particularly by female therapists working with male service members. Because the military is still predominantly male, and most mental health fields are predominantly female, Dr. Butler's insights are invaluable. These concepts of honor and sacrifice help us understand the inherent stigma that is so predominant in the military. "Military personnel are expected to 'soldier up' and get through the rough times on their own" (Dahn, 2008, p. 56) because they have been warned that "seeking professional counseling could be detrimental to career advancement or seen as a sign of weakness by their chain of command" (Dahn, 2008, p. 56).

To work with men in the military, a therapist must give due attention to the concept of "honor" that is so central to the psychology of the military, and so central to male psychology. John Gilligan (1996), who wrote an amazing book on the topic of violence in society as a whole, points out that there is a marked difference between men and women in studying the culture of honor. The reality is that the military probably couldn't do its job without the strongly held beliefs of service members regarding the importance of honor.

Nash (2007) compares athletics and the military by stating that the genius of great athletes "lies in the ability to perform as if there is no distance or weight or danger" to overcome, and the genius of the warrior is to "fight as if there is no terror, horror, or hardship" (p. 14). Nash points out that "helping professionals … must always consider the possibility that they may do more harm than good by asking warriors in an operational theater to become more aware of their own stressors and stress reaction" (p. 15). One of the major tenets of war is generating combat stress in the enemy and thereby mitigating operational stress in their own troops. The concept of honor comes into the picture because, in order to inflict suffering on an adversary, the warrior must not identify with that adversary or feel remorse for the suffering of the enemy. That type of callousness cannot be turned on and off easily, so it "may be asking too much … to acknowledge their own or their comrades' vulnerability … at the same time they are exploiting their adversary's vulnerability to almost the same stressors" (Nash, 2007, p. 14). Through leadership, training, and unit cohesion, stress reactions are managed and honor is maintained; "searching for ways to become more comfortable or safe in war can be not only a distraction from the real business at hand, but also a serious hazard to success and even survival" (Nash, 2007, p. 15).

Sam Keen (1991) explains that throughout history men have been assigned the dirty work of killing and

> Have therefore had their bodies and spirits forged into the shape of a weapon. … It is all well and good to point out the folly of war and to lament the use of violence. But short of a utopian world from which greed, scarcity, madness, and ill will have vanished, someone must be prepared to take up arms and do battle with evil. We miss the mark if we do not see that manhood has traditionally required selfless generosity even to the point of sacrifice. (p. 47)

This isn't new to the 20th century. Gary Paulsen, the author of a small book called, *A Soldier's Heart* (1998), poignantly shares the story of one young soldier from Minnesota during the Civil War and his ability to be consumed by that sense of honor, even after watching and experiencing horrendous deaths and dismemberment of his fellow soldiers (Hall, 2008). "But he could not run away. None of the others had and he couldn't. … The training must work, he thought. I'm doing all this without meaning to do it. He felt like a stranger to himself, like another person watching his hands move over the rifle" (Paulsen, 1998, p. 33). As noted by Nash (2007), the soldier can be compared to the professional athlete—the need to go the distance, to work through pain, to be there for the team—but the athlete doesn't have to face the possibility of death. The concept of honor is so central to the teaching, training, and the mission of the military that it is inevitable that therapists working with military families will encounter this in their work (Hall, 2008).

Relationships at Home

Dahn (2008) points out the double bind that military personnel are left with. While they are restricted from seeking counseling, they are then also "admonished by their chain of command for any domestic matter in which the police are called" (p. 56), leading to more frustration on the home front and often domestic violence, which goes underground (read "denied") and allowed to persist. One of the obstacles that the concept of honor presents in therapy is that sometimes military men, because of the military commitments, believe they should be "given a pass when it comes to relationship issues with family and children" (Hall, 2008, p. 63), leading to a form of neglect at home. This neglect or inattention may endure for the 20 or more years of the military career, which is just the span of time it takes for children to grow to adulthood, often with an absent and emotionally self-contained father (Hall, 2008). In a metaphorical way, the career military male marries his military service and the male–female marriage becomes an extramarital affair (Keith & Whitaker, 1984).

A female therapist, who was also a wife of a former military officer, talked about family get-togethers when the officer husbands returned from deployment. She shared that invariably the military members wanted to spend the time together instead of with the families. While these were difficult times for her and the children, she began to understand that the time her husband spent with the other officers was the only time he believed that those around him would understand the left-over memories that were constant in this mind. She realized this was the only way the military husbands could cope with the tremendous shame for what they believed they had done and for what they had witnessed (Hall, 2008). One way of reframing this for families, especially spouses, is to point out, as Lyons (2007) suggests, that a reluctance to divulge horrible details may very likely be due to the importance of the home relationships, rather than an indication of the contrary.

The Power of Shame

Mejia (2005) writes about how the socialization of men requires an adherence to many masculine behaviors and attitudes, and one of the ways boys learn these behaviors and attitudes is through shaming.

The use of shame is one of a number of societal factors that contribute to the toughening-up process by which it is assumed that boys need to be raised. Little boys are made to feel ashamed of their feelings, guilty especially about feelings of weakness, vulnerability, fear, and despair. The use of shame to control boys is pervasive; boys are made to feel shame over and over in the course of growing up (p. 32).

Mejia points out that it is not surprising that boys who were socialized from a shame-based perspective find themselves a natural fit with the military culture because there are few healthy coping strategies for dealing with shame and trauma in the raising of boys. The military may be a natural extension to the socialization that taught them to "avoid shame at all costs, to wear a mask of coolness, to act as though everything is going all right, as though everything is under control, even if it is not" (Mejia, 2005, p. 33). Mahalik, Good, and Englar-Carlson (2003) suggest that, at the extreme end of a continuum, "violence and aggression may also be avenues through which some boys and men compensate for uncomfortable feelings such as shame and hurt" (p. 125), creating the ideal military warrior, who can act on his learned tendencies under the code of honor and sacrifice for the greater good. James Gilligan (1996), shares that

> Behind the mask of cool or self-assurance that many violent men clamp on to their faces—with a desperation born of the certain knowledge that they would "lose face" if they ever let it slip—is a person who feels vulnerable not just to the "loss of face" but to the total loss of honor, prestige, respect, and status—the disintegration of identity, especially their adult, masculine, heterosexual identity; their selfhood, personhood, rationality and sanity. (p. 112)

Gilligan writes that the "most dangerous men on earth are those who are afraid that they are wimps. Wars have been started for less" (1996, p. 66). Sam Keen (1991) says the true warrior psyche includes (a) a heroic stance; (b) willpower, danger, action, and a heightened awareness from the constant possibility of death; (c) identification of action with force; (d) a paranoid worldview; (e) black and white thinking; (f) repression of fear, compassion, and guilt; (g) an obsession with rank and hierarchy because obedience is required if there is a denying of one's freedom; and (i) the degrading of the feminine. This is not a condemnation of the military male, and certainly not all military male personnel fit this description, but in order to work with military families, therapists must understand that there is a history, a tradition in the military that would maintain this is the true description of a warrior, at least by degree (Hall, 2008).

This need for conformity to tradition may initially create many barriers to therapy, which requires an openness and critical examination of a client's assumptions about life. Families have traditionally been seen by the military as support services for the military mission. The demands of the wives and children are sometimes seen as interfering with the military man's duty. As the old Marine saying goes, "if the Marines wanted you to have a wife, they would have issued you one." While this is evolving since the beginning of the all-volunteer military in order to encourage more people into the military, the historical significance cannot be overlooked.

Ryan McKelley (2007) states that the general conclusion for men's aversion to seeking professional help points to the lack of fit between the culture of masculinity and the therapeutic process. The socialization of men continues to promote the avoidance of emotional expression, the absence of admitting weaknesses or vulnerabilities, and the need to solve problems without the help of others; this is the reality of the warrior society where stoicism, secrecy, and denial are key components. Research "indicates that traditional men are less attracted to feeling-oriented therapy and instead favor strategic problem-solving therapies" (Mahalik et al., 2003, p. 52). It becomes our challenge, then, to acknowledge and value the stereotypical roles of the military men that work for them in their commitment to the military, but then assist them in modifying these rigid roles and beliefs to assist in their goals of creating well-functioning families.

PARENT-FOCUSED FAMILIES

Another way of looking at the family within this fortress is to think of the military family as what I define (Hall, 2008) as parent-focused families. The characteristics are similar to those defined by Donaldson-Pressman and Pressman (1994), who began to track the families in their practice who had traits or dynamics of alcoholic or abusive families, but had no history of alcohol abuse, incest, physical abuse, emotional neglect, or physical absence. Wertsch (1991) found many of the same similarities in her interviews with adult military brats.

The consistent dynamic of the families Donaldson-Pressman and Pressman (1994) worked with was that "the needs of the parent system took precedence over the needs of the children" (p. 4), which is why I have chosen to use the term "parent-focused families." Developmentally, parent-focused families, and certainly many military families who are struggling, have difficulty meeting the fundamental needs of trust and safety for their children because the family has to be consumed with the needs of the parents—both the military service parent and the non-military parent. Military families have, as one of their major challenges, the need to learn how to operate within the larger external system of the military itself without complaint or unreasonable expectations (stoicism). This includes the importance of not allowing what happens in the family (secrecy) to impact the military parent's career. In many of these parent-focused military families, particularly when there is a child who is acting out or in other ways exhibiting behavior problems, there are certain characteristics we might look for, such as:

1. The belief that the child does not have a problem, instead he or she is the problem.
2. The child does not have a need, such as anxiety, a developmental delay, depression, or academic issues, but rather is given a label, such as lazy, stupid, or a class clown.
3. Children learn that their feelings are of little or negative value, and even may make things worse if expressed in the family, so they soon realize that detaching from their feelings becomes very functional.
4. When children discover early that their feelings are a source of discomfort in the family and may not be validated if they are expressed, they have difficulty developing a sense of trust in their own judgments. In so doing, they become either rebellious and/or reflective of others, which is often interpreted as inadequacy or failure.
5. Responsibility for meeting the emotional needs of the parents become skewed when the parents expect the child to become inappropriately responsible for meeting the parents' emotional, and sometimes physical, needs.

6. With the emotional unavailability of the parent, children may have difficulty letting down the barriers required for intimacy later in life (Hall, 2008; Donaldson-Pressman & Pressman, 1994).

These characteristics, when played out in military families, are a reflection of the secrecy, stoicism, and denial required of these families. Instead of providing a supportive, nurturing, reality-based mirror, the parents may present a mirror that only reflects their needs, resulting in children who grow up feeling defective. "When one is raised unable to trust in the stability, safety, and equity of one's world, one is raised to distrust one's own feelings, perceptions, and worth" (Donaldson-Pressman & Pressman, 1994, p. 18).

By examining the demographics of military families, we know that most military-dependent children are born to very young, immature couples who have been removed from their extended support system or other supportive older adults on whom they can rely. It should be pointed out, however, that the physical needs of military children are indeed met. And, while they are well nurtured and, in most cases, have both the physical and psychological needs met during childhood, when children begin to assert themselves and/or make emotional demands, which often begins in early to middle adolescence, the parental system may be unable to tend to the children's needs. Instead, parents who are under a great deal of stress may find themselves resentful or threatened by the needs of the children (Hall, 2008). The ability to understand how some families in the military are organized, not just because of who the parents are but, more importantly, who the parents are in the midst of the demands of the warrior fortress in which they live, is essential in working with these families.

PARENTING IN A DEMOCRATIC SOCIETY

A therapist (Hall, 2008) explained that, in his work with military couples, he found that they are often not faced with the typical life decisions or choices of civilian couples, like when to buy a house or whether to relocate to enhance the career of one of the spouses. At the same time, military couples and families are required to relate to and often live in our mostly democratic American world. This therapist works with adolescents and he often finds it necessary to point out to the parents that, while they might be comfortable living in the authoritarian, military structure, their kids, particularly those who are rebelling, often see the world in a different way. A typical parental response to a non-conforming teen is simply to tighten the rules, becoming more rigid, often out of the fear of losing control or his or her place as the head of the household. "Children of the military, whether they live on base or not, live, at least part of their life, in a democratic society; they go to democratic schools and their parents are serving the mission of defending a democratic nation. It is understandable, then, how those who face strictly authoritarian parenting or home life might be confused and perhaps become rebellious" (Hall, 2008, p. 119).

McKay and Maybell (2004) write about what they call the "Democratic Revolution," which they define as an "upheaval in all of our social institutions: government, education, the workplace, race relationships, gender relationships and families" (p. 64). During the last few decades, most social institutions and relationships in the United States have operated from an equality identity that includes attitudes of equal values and respect. These societal changes require new attitudes toward oneself and others, as well as a new set of knowledge and skills (McKay & Maybell, 2004; Hall, 2008). The military, on the other hand, has not changed to an egalitarian institution; it never will. But, regardless of how the military organizes itself and its members, the military family still lives, at least to some degree, in a democratic society and often struggles in its movement back and forth from the authoritarian world of the military to the democratic world in which it both comes from and continually has to step back into.

While McKay and Maybell outline the conflict in the greater society over the last few decades, the "tension, conflict, anger, and even violence ... as we move from the old autocratic tradition to a new democratic one" (McKay & Maybell, 2004, p. 65) are an ongoing challenge and struggle for the military family. These are valuable insights when understanding the children and the families of the military, many of whom may view the world outside of the military as quite appealing and then begin to rebel against the rigid structure they are forced to live within. This theoretical framework can be a useful tool for helping families move from the kind of rigid superior/inferior structure that often is brought from the military structure into the home to a more egalitarian structure that encourages and respects each individual in the family, but still maintains the hierarchical structure of parental control that is necessary for all functioning families (Hall, 2008).

One way to help families is to help parents understand their current parenting style, and then learn how to make modifications from those parenting styles that are discouraging for their children to those that are empowering and encouraging. McKay and Maybell (2004) describe three of the most common parenting styles: the Coercive Parenting Style, the Pampering or Permissive Parenting Style, and the Respectful Leadership Style. The first two are often discouraging to the healthy development of children; the third can be a respectful and encouraging style.

Coercive Parenting

The Coercive Parenting Style is often the style used to control children "for their own good" and is often the style of parenting used in parent-focused families. The parents maintain control by giving orders, setting rules, making demands, rewarding obedient behavior, and punishing bad deeds. The model is "limits without freedom." These parents, in most cases, have the good intentions of wanting to make sure their children avoid many of life's mistakes, and they want to teach their children "the right way" before they get hurt. This need for children to accommodate to a subordinate identity may work for a while, at least when the children are young. However, when children want to be acknowledged for their individuality or want to be respected as individuals, this style results in conflict and power struggles. "Kids tend to become experts at not doing what their parents want them to do and on doing exactly what their parents don't want" (McKay & Maybell, 2004, p. 71). The results of coercive parenting can be kids who need to get even, resulting in a constant war of revenge, or kids who submit to the coercion and learn to rely only on those in power to make their decisions (Hall, 2008), either of which can be destructive to the healthy development of children.

Pampering or Permissive Parenting

This parenting style is used by parents who want to make sure their children are comfortable and happy by either letting them do whatever they please, or by doing everything for them; this style is "freedom without limits." The result may be children who see themselves as the prince or princess and their parents as their servants. They can develop a "strong sense of ego-esteem with little true self- or people-esteem" (McKay & Maybell, 2004, p. 72). These children tend to have under-developed social skills and often become too dependent on others. Eventually parents start resenting how much they are doing for their children, leading to conflict and power struggles. With few limits, children believe they can do anything they want, leading to a sense of entitlement along with a lack of internal self-discipline or self-responsibility.

These first two parenting styles can actually exist in the same family, where one parent is the authoritarian (in a military family, usually the military parent) and the other is the permissive parent who tries to make up for the harshness of the authoritarian parent by lessening the rules when the military parent is absent (Hall, 2008). There were many examples of school behavior worsening upon return of the military parent from deployment; when asked, the young people talk about how things ran fine when the service member was gone, but now the parents are back to "cracking the whip," which usually instills rebellion, especially in the older teens.

Respectful Leadership

The third parenting style is the only encouraging style for children; it is the style of Respectful Leadership, or "freedom within limits." The parents value the child and value themselves as leaders of the family through the guiding principle of mutual respect in all parent–child interactions. Giving choices is the main discipline approach with the goal of building on strengths, accentuating the positive, promoting responsibility, and instilling confidence in their children. This parenting style, in both the civilian and military worlds, raises respectful, responsible children (Hall, 2008).

Helping parents understand how their parenting style impacts child development can often be our most valuable teaching tool. Parents all want the best for their children, and helping them promote responsibility and confidence by making adjustments to their parenting style can help them reach these goals. As early as 1984, Rodriguez wrote that in a rank-privileged and -oriented social system like the military, this mix of "caste formation" and egalitarianism may create a difficult dichotomy, particularly for children and adolescents struggling for their identity. This dichotomy can be exacerbated by parental concerns about how child misbehavior might affect the military parent's status in the military, and with whom children can associate within the rank hierarchy (Hall, 2008). Children become sensitive to this parental anxiety and the anger that follows when they break community rules or military social norms. In some military communities, particularly those that are isolated and where rules are strongly enforced, children have little room to make mistakes or test the limits of authority in a normal, developmental manner, without imperiling the family status or the military parent's career. This often leaves the child or adolescent with few choices but to internalize the identity and role conflicts or act them out behaviorally (Hall, 2008).

On the other hand, a caring relationship and low family stress are associated with resiliency and, if children have an emotionally supportive relationship with their parents, they are more likely to demonstrate high levels of self-esteem and healthy psychological development (Jeffreys & Leitzel, 2000). The study by Jeffreys and Leitzel (2000) of military families shows us that family climate promotes participation in family decision making and is positive for adolescent identity development. Effective communication patterns facilitate family interaction and are associated with social competence. This finding seems consistent with McKay and Maybell's (2004) Respectful Leadership style of parenting.

SUMMARY

These different aspects of the military family are all part of understanding the worldview of the military. Unless we understand the impact of the common characteristics of the military culture that lead to the need for stoicism, secrecy, and denial, we cannot work effectively with these families. In addition, understanding the commitment to the mission, and the role of honor and sacrifice, particularly for the military male service members, we cannot find our place when building a therapeutic alliance with the family. Last, we have to help families understand that changes in their parenting styles as they mature as parents can alleviate many current as well as future issues and behavior problems with their children. The majority of military families will seek mental health services because of issues with their children, so having a perspective of what life is like for those children and in those families is foundational for interventions and change. This change, however, must come from within the military framework and be consistent with the worldview of their culture, rather than attempting to move military families to believe or exist in what would be the norm for civilian families.

REFERENCES

Blaise, K. (2006). *The heart of a soldier: A true story of love, war, and sacrifice.* New York, NY: Gotham Books.

Butler, H. (2006, October 6). Love, honor and obey: Musings on working with military men and their families (personal communication).

Dahn, V.L. (October, 2008). Silent service in the soldier's shadow. *Counseling Today, 51*(4), 55–57.

Dass-Brailsford, P. (2007). *A practical approach to trauma: Empowering interventions.* Thousand Oaks, CA: Sage Publications.

DoDEA News Release. (2007, May 3). *Military parents in Iraq and Afghanistan to view graduations live via webcasts.* Retrieved June 15, 2007 from www.dodea.edu/pressroom/releasesDisplay.cfm

Donaldson-Pressman, S. & Pressman, R. M. (1994). *The narcissistic family: Diagnosis and treatment.* San Francisco, CA: Jossey-Bass.

Fenell, D. (June, 2008). A distinct culture: Applying multicultural counseling competencies to work with military personnel. *Counseling Today, 50*(12), 8–9, 35.

Fenell, D. L. & Weinhold, B. K. (2003). *Counseling families: An introduction to marriage and family therapy* (3rd ed.). Denver, CO: Love Publishing Company.

Gegax, T. T. & Thomas, E. (2005, June 20). The family business. *Newsweek, 145*(25), 24–31.

Gilligan, J. (1996). *Violence: Reflections on a national epidemic.* New York, NY: Random House.

Grief and Trauma. (n.d.) National Institute for Trauma and Loss in Children. Retrieved May 13, 2007 from www.tlcinst.org/griefandtrauma.html

Hall, L. K. (2008) *Counseling military families: What mental health professionals need to know.* New York, NY: Routledge: Taylor & Francis Group.

Henderson, K. (2006). *While they're at war: The true story of American families on the homefront.* New York, NY: Houghton-Mifflin.

Houppert, K. (2005). *Home fires burning: Married to the military—for better or worse.* New York, NY: Ballantine Books.

Jeffreys, D. J. & Leitzel, J. D. (2000). The strengths and vulnerabilities of adolescents in military families. In J. A. Martin, L. N. Rosen & L. R. Sparacino (Eds.). *The military family: A practice guide for human service providers* (pp. 225–240). Westport, CT: Praeger Publishers.

Keen, S. (1991). *Fire in the belly: On being a man.* New York, NY: Bantam Books.

Keith, D. V. & Whitaker, C. A. (1984). C'est la Guerre: Military families and family therapy. In F. W. Kaslow & R. I. Ridenour (Eds.). *The military family: Dynamics and treatment* (pp. 147–166). New York, NY: Guilford Press.

Lyons, J. A. (2007). The returning warrior: Advice for families and friends. In C. R. Figley & W. P. Nash (Eds.). *Combats stress injury: Theory, research and management* (pp. 311–324). New York, NY: Routledge: Taylor & Francis Group.

Mahalik, J. R., Good, G. E. & Englar-Carlson, M. (2003). Masculinity scripts, presenting concerns, and help seeking: Implications for practice and training. *Professional Psychology: Research and Practice, 34*(2), 123–131.

Martin, J. A. & McClure, P. (2000). Today's active duty military family: The evolving challenges of military family life. In J. A. Martin, L. N. Rosen & L. R. Sparacino (Eds.). *The military family: A practice guide for human service providers* (pp. 3–24). Westport, CT: Praeger.

McKay, G. D. & Maybell, S. A. (2004). *Calming the family story: Anger management for moms, dads, and all the kids.* Atascadero, CA: Impact Publishers.

McKelley, R. A. (2007). Men's resistance to seeking help: Using individual psychology to understand counseling-reluctant men. *Journal of Individual Psychology, 63*(1), 48–58.

Mejia, Z. E. (2005). Gender matters: Working with adult male survivors of trauma. *Journal of Counseling and Development, 83*(2), 29–40.

Nash, W. P. (2007). The stressors of war. In C. R. Figley & W. P. Nash (Eds.). *Combat stress injury: Theory, research and management* (pp. 11–32). New York, NY: Routledge.

Paulsen, G. (1998). *A soldier's heart.* New York, NY: Random House.

Reger, M. A., Etherage, J. R., Reger, G. M. & Gahm, G. A. (2008). Civilian psychologists in an Army culture: The ethical challenge of cultural competence. *Military Psychology, 20*, 21–35.

Ridenour, R. I. (1984). The military, service families, and the therapist. In F. W. Kaslow & R. I. Ridenour (Eds.). *The military family: Dynamics and treatment* (pp. 1–17). New York, NY: Guilford Press.

Schouten, F. (2004, April 1). No soldier's child left behind: Defense Department school system gets results. *USA Today,* p. D7.

Sue, D. W., Arredondo, P. & McDavis, R. J. (March/April, 1992). Multicultural counseling competencies and standards: A call to the profession. *Journal of Counseling and Development, 70*, 477–486.

Wakefield, M. (February, 2007). Guarding the military home front. *Counseling Today, 49*(8), 5, 23.

Wertsch, M. E. (1991). *Military brats: Legacies of childhood inside the fortress.* New York, NY: Harmony Books; Brightwell Publishing, St. Louis, MO at www.brightwellpublishing.net

Section II

Systemic Therapy Interventions for Various Military Contexts

3 Structural Strategic Approaches with Army Couples

R. Blaine Everson and Joseph R. Herzog

CONTENTS

Working therapeutically with military couples requires an understanding of the dynamic nature of the lives they lead. It also requires the understanding that some therapeutic models developed for couples and families in one branch of the armed services may have only limited applicability to other branches. For example, it is difficult to compare the deployment of an enlisted member of the U.S. Army as part of ground forces in Iraq or Afghanistan to the deployment of an enlisted member of the U.S. Navy serving on an aircraft carrier in the Mediterranean Sea. While both may be separated from their families for extended periods of time, the extra strain of being in daily combat makes service a very different experience for Army versus Navy families. We seek to provide a "nuts and bolts" approach to military families utilizing a systems-based practice that is effective with families in the military regardless of branch of service or the practitioner's therapeutic preference. Much of what is described in this chapter represents an attempt by private practitioners to provide services primarily to military family members. Although the service member may not be the identified client due to third-party payer constraints, he or she is as an integral part of the therapeutic approach.

This chapter is designed as a primer on a family systems-based approach to military couples seeking treatment for a variety of interpersonal and emotional problems. Physicians, social workers, counselors, community clergy, chaplains, and marriage and family therapists should benefit from exposure to this approach. We begin with an overview of the lifestyle of military couples, the problems that they experience, and the stress responses that often result. We move next into assessing, goal setting, and treating couples as they present in therapy. We will then focus on designing interventions with these couples. Finally, we end with specific case material associated with some of the more pertinent problems with military couples. We do not offer a preference for one school of thought in family systems therapy over another. Both authors use different approaches. One prefers a multi-generational family systems approach, whereas the other prefers a more emotionally focused approach to working with military couples. We both agree, however, that systemic approaches bring about the most rapid and long-lasting changes within these families.

A number of issues are unique to any discussion of therapy with military couples. These cases will be exceedingly challenging to therapists new to the profession and experienced clinicians alike. This population is very difficult to work with due to constantly changing set demands required by their lifestyle, so clinicians should be prepared to be frustrated at times in their effort to provide effective treatment as a result of trainings, relocation, and deployments. This chapter is timely given the fact that therapists will be seeing military families who have been impacted in some way by the conflicts in Afghanistan and Iraq for decades to come, even after these couples are no longer affiliated with the military. It is likely that the Veterans Administration will be unable to adequately serve former military personnel or their family members should current funding levels continue (see the Introduction).

SYSTEMIC FACTORS ASSOCIATED WITH MILITARY LIFESTYLES

The therapeutic approach to the dynamic lifestyles of military couples is systemic, and it is evolving to fit the needs of the couple in a specific situation. Segal (1986) pointed out that military families contend with four basic issues within the military system: geographic relocation, deployments, hazardous duty, and overseas assignments. To better understand the dynamic aspects of their lives from a therapeutic standpoint, we focus on these and several other key factors:

Relocation—These families experience a great deal of strain associated with moving every 3 to 4 years, or the strain may come from the inability to move because of a service member's particular job in the military (military occupational specialty [MOS]). Families often experience different levels of service from one duty station to another and varied responses when attempting to connect with resources on-post (or base). For example, the family may have lived in base housing at a previous duty station, but they may move to a military post with fewer family housing units, requiring them to reside in the community. When families move, they also must find new jobs for spouses, new schools for children, and new community activities for the entire family. Relocation can be particularly stressful for the non-military member of the couple and cause the couple to seek therapy, especially if the spouse is female and was in the military previously.

Separation—Service members typically deploy for 6 to 12 months depending on branch of service and the assignment. It is not uncommon for U.S. Army families to experience soldier deployments of more than 12 months with unit extensions during the Iraq conflict over the past several years. Many laypeople assume that when service members return from deployments, they are home for the duration of the redeployment. Many service members must participate in field exercises or complete schooling as part of their promotions (or changes of jobs) that require them to be away from their families for as little as a week or up to 3 months. The absence of a family member assails the structural integrity of the family like no other military stressor. Lengthy separation often causes poor communication between the spouses and creates emotional distance that is often difficult for them to surmount, creating the need for therapeutic interventions.

Peripheralization—Lack of re-integration of the service member into the family system after multiple separations and lengthy absences may create difficulty as the couple experiences devitalization of their marital quality. Conflicts tend to occur around the lack of affection, poor communication, disclosure (discovery) of extramarital relationships, poor participation in daily household affairs, and lack of involvement with children. Family members who remain behind may actually be more adept at living life without the service member, which runs counter to what most in the helping professions believe about the impact of long-term separations, and not allow re-integration to occur. Family members may exhibit distancing behaviors and social withdrawal while the service member is home, and behave normally when the service member leaves, as if they are happy to see him or her go.

Integration—Many military families find themselves in the midst of remarriage situations with children from previous relationships and are unable integrate all of the members into to new family setting. These problems are made worse by the constant adaptation required by frequent absences, relocation, and poor previous relationships between family members. Another issue plaguing these remarried military families centers around the problems within blended families of establishing sibling position as children settle into familial relationships, which may strain the parental marriage in the light of divided loyalties.

Hazardous Duty—Service member well-being while in a theater of operations is of utmost concern for each military couple. The risk of being wounded or killed in action has been a source of constant emotional strain for spouses of service members deployed to Iraq or Afghanistan in recent years. The worry and fear associated with such uncertainty are especially problematic for wives, regardless of the planning that goes into financially and emotionally "preparing for the worst." As practitioners, we have experienced the grief of widows of fallen service members and sat with families as they awaited word of their loved one's fate after a convoy ambush. We can attest to the fact that this fear has always been close at hand for these families during the past few years. The experience is life altering regardless of whether their service member is killed or wounded.

PRESENTING PROBLEMS OF MILITARY COUPLES

A number of problems stem from the dynamics associated with the military lifestyle. Three of the most difficult problems for the clinician working with a military couple are the presence of excessive conflict, emotional distance, and a lack of problem-solving skills as a couple. The conflict and emotional distance in the couple relationship may stem from a variety of sources. Most often the conflict is associated with interpersonal communication issues, but other areas of frequent conflict include disagreements over household finances, the children having problems, remarriage and blended families, the discovery of extramarital affairs, emotional distance in the relationship, excessive alcohol use by the service member (or spouse), domestic violence in the home, and trauma due to combat exposure. Segal (1986) suggested that the military system and families are both "greedy" institutions, and are at odds over the limited resources of service members. More often than not, many military couples will consist of a male service member and female spouse, but both may serve in the military in a number of cases, and the strains associated with military life are compounded by dual military service (Daley, 1999). The female members of dual-service military couples have the unique challenge of maintaining a household, continuing to function in their military occupation, and serving as a waiting spouse during the deployment. What follows is a more in-depth discussion of the primary issues facing clinicians working with families in a variety of settings within the military system.

Financial Problems

Problems due to finances (or a lack thereof) are frequently seen as part of couple treatment with military families. Many families of lower-ranking personnel, despite the variety of services provided by the military, live at (or below) poverty level. Even spouses of higher-ranking non-commissioned officers (NCOs) report that it's necessary for them to work outside of the home to make ends meet. While the horror stories of young military spouses liquidating a service member's assets during extended absences are occasionally true, a more common conflict stems from the mismanagement of financial assets by a spouse while the service member is away, or spending money on items not agreed upon prior to the service member's return. Another commonly observed problem, but less often reported, in therapy sessions is related to service members' misuse of monetary funds while away for training or deployment to the detriment of their families back home. In some cases, the service member may expect some type of self-reward (e.g., motorcycle, large-screen televisions, surround-sound systems, auto rims, etc.) for being away in a combat zone, and the "reward" may be in excess of family financial constraints, even with the accrual of hazardous duty pay, or may not be in line with the family long-term financial goals.

Mistrust is the underlying emotional issue associated with such cases, and power issues must be dealt with accordingly within the context of couple sessions. In many cases the emotional undercurrents of mistrust run deep and involve a deception that began with the latent financial benefits of being married in the military, including healthcare for the non-member spouse and an increase in the service member's basic allotment for housing (BAH). This increases the service member's overall monetary benefits and household income. There is also the issue of a proportional increase in the service member's hazardous duty pay associated with deployments in areas of conflict based on their base pay. In many older military couples, the situation has been resolved by allowing the non-military spouse the responsibility of maintaining the family budget and dealing with all other household matters before, during, and after deployments. Therapists will often experience a great deal of in-session conflict between military couples as result of unsettled financial issues.

Problems with Children

Children are affected by the military lifestyle in a variety of ways and may respond as a result (Kelley, 1994). They may be informed of the decision to relocate or of the service member's departure, but they have very little say in how such transitions take place. Severed attachments to a parental figure also prove detrimental to the child as the constant adaptation to required changes takes place against the contextual backdrop of the family life cycle. Many children in military families suffer myriad emotional and behavioral symptoms requiring enrollment into installation-based services, such as exceptional family member programs (EFMs). Many children also suffer from chronic anxiety or depressive disorder, all of which may be attributed to or exacerbated by the constant cycle of arrivals and departures of family members (Rosen, Westhuis & Teitelbaum, 1993). Older children may begin to suffer from academic problems, get into trouble in the community, or act out sexually as the strain associated with military transitions becomes too great to bear. Military spouses who remain behind must often handle these situations to the best of their ability on their own. These issues negatively impact the military couple as the service member often returns home to a very different setting from the home he or she left for deployment.

Remarriages

Given that the divorce rate is generally thought to be higher among military couples, it stands to reason that strains associated with remarriage should be a concern for clinicians engaged in practice with these couples. Although one member of the couple may be previously unmarried, often both members of military couples have been married previously, creating the basis for a *complex* stepfamily (Papernow, 1998). Within these stepfamilies, the system is comprised of children from previous relationships, as well as children from the union of the couple. Many military couples contend with the strain of dealing with the demands of ex-spouses and the constant financial constraints created by the dissolution of the previous relationship, while lengthy visitations during school breaks by non-residing children may create an added stressor for the remarried couple. Custodial arrangements are especially worth noting at this point due to the links between the current reconstituted family system and previous family systems in which one or both spouses may have been involved. Many times in our experience, as the service member is deployed, the current and former spouse(s) are often left to sort out the visitation arrangements and frequently do so with little or no conflict between the two families (if there is no negative relationship history between them).

Extramarital Relationships

Extramarital relationships among military couples are often characterized by a variety of situations. Extramarital affairs most commonly occur during the lengthy separations imposed by deployments. It is almost as common for a couple to request therapy after the wife's disclosure of an affair during deployment as it is for the service member to have been caught in an extramarital relationship. The secrecy that surrounds this phenomenon in the military is somewhat different from that observed in the civilian population and casts affairs as less detrimental to the military marriage. This may be partly due to the fact that extramarital sex is considered *bad conduct* on the part of the service member and is subject to court martial under the Uniform Code of Military Justice, yet there is a high incidence of extramarital sex reported for service members. It is also embarrassing to service members when spouses have affairs because it reflects poorly on the service member's ability to maintain a harmonious household environment and is considered detrimental to morale, especially if the affair takes place with another service member (often referred informally to as "friendly fire"). Many female spouses report succumbing to loneliness, fear of the unknown, emotional stress, and sexual deprivation, along with the attention of unscrupulous males, as a part of their reason for having extramarital relationships (Matsakis, 2005).

The taboos associated with spouses of service members having extramarital relationships are often overshadowed by the sexual permissiveness of service members. The service member who discloses an affair has the benefit of numerous factors that tend to reduce the likelihood of separation or divorce (i.e., health benefits for dependents, military housing, etc.). Regardless of whether the offending spouse is the service member or the spouse, the resulting emotions are similar to those observed with couples of the general population after an affair: emotional distress characterized by hurt feelings and intense anger, extreme jealousy and mistrust, and attempts by the offended spouse to regulate the behavior of the offending spouse. Extramarital activity is the most often cited reason for ended marriages within the civilian population; however, divorce is less often the result of an affair for military couples because of the lengthy separations. If these couples remain together, it is very common to see a great deal of passive aggression, occasional conflict, and extreme emotional distance (i.e., cut-offs) between them.

Emotional Distance

It is not uncommon for couples in the military to experience emotional distance due to extended periods of separation. This emotional distance is often accompanied by excessive efforts on the part of one to bridge the emotional distance while the other spouse seeks to maintain the emotional separation in the relationship. These separations are attempts to remain emotionally *cut off* in some way and are often the result of long-standing resentments between spouses (Berg-Cross, 2000). Some of the distance experienced may stem from the autonomy gained by the non-military member of the couple as she (generally) has learned to manage the household, children, and finances across the span of several deployments. These couples are generally in their 30s and may be nearing the end of the service member's career.

A frequent complaint heard very early in therapy sessions is the lack of sexual intimacy, which is expressed by a heightened desire to engage in sex by one partner and a hypoactive desire on the part of the other spouse. Very typically, the male (service member) of the couple will complain about a lack of sexual intimacy while the female spouse cross-complains about not feeling enough emotional intimacy to engage in sexual activity. This pattern is not uncommon in couples within the general population, but unique to military couples are the extended periods of separation and limited involvement within the household by the service member. In other cases, the lack of intimacy is accepted by both members of the couple and only comes to light after some exploration by the therapist.

Substance Use

Alcohol use by service members is fairly common. On occasion, the use exceeds the normal acceptable standards and becomes a problem for the spouse as the service member becomes more withdrawn or abusive to others as a result of excessive substance use. The excessive use of alcohol and other substances by the service member may be exacerbated by the prolonged experience of combat (e.g., 1 year in Iraq), cumulative injuries acquired as a result of military service (e.g., chronic lumbar pain), or an existing predisposition to substance abuse (i.e., a family history). Mood-altering substances, especially alcohol, may be the only acceptable form of self-medicating for the service member for any of the above reasons. What begins as a sporadic pattern of alcohol abuse may become a full-blown addiction for service members by mid-career and often becomes a difficult issue for the entire family. Referral for addiction-related services is often warranted in these cases.

Another often-overlooked problem for military spouses is the overuse of prescription medications. This particular substance use problem is often discovered by service members upon their return from deployment or as the result of a family-related emergency that requires their early return from duty. Perhaps the most frequent set of abused medications are anxiolytic benzodiazapines, such diazepam (Valium), alprazolam (Xanax), clonazepam (Klonopin), and lorazepam (Ativan), but more recently we have increasingly confronted dependence on any number of the oxycodone class of painkillers (Oxycontin, in particular). The difficulty associated with referral and treatment of prescription dependence is compounded by the need for the medication to combat any number of ongoing symptoms for which the medications were originally prescribed.

Combat Stress

Combat stress injuries, along with the presence of post-traumatic stress disorder (PTSD), can create a unique set of problems for couples and families, as the re-entry of a traumatized service member influences the entire family emotional system producing a variety of family-level responses that have been characterized as *secondary traumatic stress* transmission (Figley, 1998). This one issue separates therapy with family members of U.S. ground troops from therapy with other families of members of the armed services. Most often it is the spouse (mother) who serves as the "buffer" between the ailing service member and the rest of the family (Dekel, Goldblatt, Keidar, Solomon & Polliack, 2005). The resulting *triangulation* (Papero, 1990) frequently proves to be exceedingly stressful and may lead to the development of emotional problems for the non-military spouse. It is not uncommon for a clinician to see a depressed spouse of a service member with undiagnosed PTSD. This scenario presents a complex therapeutic situation for even the most experienced practitioner, and will be dealt with by the same authors in a later chapter.

Domestic Violence

A frequent manifestation of the stressors and strains associated with the rigors of military life is the development of domestic violence in the military couple relationship. The most common form of domestic violence is chronic verbal and emotional abuse between members of a couple (or one member abusing the other more often). It most often involves an escalation to physical violence after a couple has been arguing for an extended period of time. The couple may also be seen because the domestic violence may have been directed at a child in the household and the spouse's attempts to intercede resulted in a physical incident. According to a reputable source at one U.S. Army installation, it is one of the most significant family problems currently facing the military command structure and policymakers. Some episodes may also be related to the current strain of service in Iraq or Afghanistan for the service member. The clinician must be able sort out a possible combat-related incident from those maliciously perpetrated (e.g., a soldier holding his wife down or hitting her due to a nightmare while sleeping may not be considered domestic abuse, but a symptom of PTSD). Regardless of the cause, serious intervention is absolutely necessary.

These factors, when taken together or separately, may contribute to the higher rate of marital dissolution for military couples. A recent report issued by the National Healthy Marriage Resource Center (2006) suggested that military couples are at much higher risk of marital dissolution than couples in the general population because of lengthy separations, remarriages, relocations, and increased incidences of combat stress.

THERAPEUTIC INTERVENTIONS FOR MILITARY COUPLES

There are several unique features associated with working with military families. The first step any therapist must take is to understand that there is a socially constructed *cultural system* specific to military service and families associated with the military system (Daley, 1999). A primary part of this cultural system includes the language associated with various aspects of military life. Therapists must be able to understand and utilize this language to some extent when attempting to assist these families. For practitioners with no previous military service, simply asking service members or spouses to explain the meaning of terms like PCS, NTC, or MOS helps establish a basis for conversation within the therapeutic context. Also, the clinician should be prepared to hear some abrasive language (i.e., excessive use of profanity) by both members of the couple in some cases.

We have found it best for the clinician to approach military couples in a very direct, no-nonsense manner. Members of the military have been trained to respect authority and generally have no problem accepting direction from an authority figure like a relational expert. It has been pleasantly surprising to learn that male service members are generally very active participants in couple and family therapy and that it isn't difficult to secure a recurring schedule of regular appointments if the service members request permission from their superiors to do so. The clinician may facilitate this process by offering to write a letter to the service member's chain of command, after obtaining written permission from both members of the couple. Many times a unit commander may already be aware of the problems a military couple is experiencing and may have suggested counseling to the service member to remedy the situation as an expression of support.

Generally, couples seeking therapy are probably at a higher risk for marital failure than those in the community at large. Some of the couples we see are often at the point of break-up and considerable effort must be expended to find positive attributes for improving their marital situation. Practitioners should not be surprised to find themselves preparing couples for divorce, with an emphasis on co-parenting in the aftermath. Regardless of the situation, it is very important the establish rapport quickly with both members of the couple, along with reducing feelings of helplessness and hopelessness, as a way of beginning the therapy process. This "quick" start is often necessary as the number of sessions with a couple may be shortened by training exercises, upcoming deployments, or an impending relocation of the family to another military installation.

Assessment

This phase of treatment generally lasts from one to three sessions and involves a clinical interview of the identified patient based on DSM-IV-TR guidelines, plus the development of a genogram (Carter & McGoldrick, 1998; McGoldrick & Gerson, 1985) for each member of the couple. In addition to the standard problems, symptoms, and history-based initial session, the clinical interview of military couples should include questions about (a) previous duty stations and assignments, (b) rank of soldier and military occupation, (c) spouse's military history, (d) special needs children, (e) recent deployment history, and (f) standard family-of-origin and personal life history for both members. Systemic practitioners generally understand the importance of genogramming, but for military families who may be remarried or have children from previous non-marital relationships, this assessment tool can provide the quickest overview of problems within the couple (family) system. In one instance, using a genogram with a particularly distressed Hispanic couple brought to light their guilt over the (previously undisclosed) death of their first child from sudden infant death syndrome (SIDS) (the child had been born out of wedlock), how their family's reactions toward the death had caused deep animosity between the two of them (her family was more supportive of them), and helped us understand how their strict religious beliefs about marriage influenced their thinking about their prospect of a successful relationship and successful parenting of their two subsequent children (they didn't marry until after the death of their first child).

It is also useful to further explore the couple relationship using a variety of scales or instruments to assess various areas of personal and couple life. While we do not endorse any particular assessment instrument, the following list reflects some of the scales and instruments that we have found useful and is intended merely to provide a starting point for the clinician. To assess the extent of couple relational problems and marital satisfaction, we recommend the Index of Marital Satisfaction (Hudson, 1982), the Dyadic Adjustment Scale (Spanier, 1976), or the Locke-Wallace Marital Adjustment Test (Locke & Wallace, 1959). The clinician may find other instruments more useful for understanding the extent of distress within the couple relationship, his or her expectations for the relationship, or assessment of marital instability via the Marital Distress Scale, Relationship Beliefs Index, or Marital Alternatives Scale. It is useful to ask about domestic violence or substance abuse within the couple relationship, or one may assess these factors simply by using a variety of scales. Individual-level problems may complicate the clinical picture early on in the therapy, so the use of the Beck Depression Inventory (Beck, 1978), Zung Anxiety Scale, or the Generalized Contentment Scale (Hudson, 1982) to assess the extent of depression or anxiety is also beneficial. Given the diverse backgrounds and experiences of the military population, it is advisable to assess for previous traumatic experiences of each member of the couple using PTSD checklists or other trauma-based questionnaires (Corcoran & Fisher, 1987).

By the end of the third session the therapist should be well into *joining* with the couple. In the process, the therapist should have established an acceptable level of rapport and trust to allow for further goal setting and candid conversations about the couple's (and therapist's) ideas for change. Every attempt should be made at realism because military couples are capable of dealing with a matter-of-fact approach to their situation. Systemic-oriented practitioners understand that everything is important within the therapeutic context and that their involvement is part of an ongoing attempt to provide *corrective feedback* (i.e., reduce the influence of negative feedback loops that are contributing to the current distress) into the couple (family) system (see Klein & White, 1995).

This is also the point in therapy where another of the couple's secrets, previously undisclosed because of a lack of trust in the process (or the therapist), may be disclosed and change the way the therapist has framed their problems thus far. It has been our experience with military couples that the traditional feminization of interaction and language used in couple therapy is ineffectual and tends to alienate the service member in the military couple whether male or female. This is particularly true for the male service member who will often become actively engaged in therapy, as long as he does not continually feel that he is *scapegoated* for couple's problems.

Early Phases of Treatment

The next phase of couple treatment generally last four to eight sessions and involves the further exploration of the couple's problems, helping the couple understand the problems, and testing their ability to resolve those problems. Testing the couple's commitment to the process of therapy and beginning to initiate first-order change in the relationship is important at the beginning of this stage, such as reducing the level of conflict and tension, improving effectiveness of communication (of needs), and increasing the positive regard expressed by each member of the couple toward the other. Dealing with presenting problems and tertiary issues is very important within the first few sessions (e.g., an affair and the anguish associated with the affair). This may create a great deal of emotional tension for the couple and the therapist characterized by the frequent descent into conflict and arguing.

In some cases, the couple is actually allowed to argue for a few moments, before the therapist intercedes, in order to observe conflict tactics, the dynamics of the argument, who proposes that they stop arguing (softening from emotionally focused couple therapy [EFCT]), and who initiates repair attempts in the couple. Frequently these arguments will reveal, very early on, where the majority of the tension is within the relationship. In clinical supervision of younger therapists who may be newer to systems thinking, we have found that it is difficult to prevent therapists from stepping in too soon to stop the argument because of their own reactance and inability to manage their anxiety stemming from their own experiences. Knowing when to stop the process is an acquired skill and takes practice to develop the necessary instinct. Many therapists will observe the classic pursuer–distancer dichotomy taking place within the couple's communication process, where the male service member will act defensively and become agitated under constant criticism and contempt from the female spouse. On a number of occasions, the discussion of Gottman's "Four Horsemen" (criticism, contempt, defensiveness, and stonewalling) has served to educate the couple to their communication patterns and help them see that conflict is a normal interactive process in long-term relationships (Gottman, 1994).

The exploration of family-of-origin issues for each member of the couple is also important at this phase of treatment in order to understand their previous relational experiences, possible historical antecedents for current problems, and how their relationship expectations came into being. Parental divorce, any form of abuse, or abandonment, parental substance use, and addictions all influence the way adult partners behave in couple relationships because of the maladaptive attachments experienced during childhood. Such problems make it difficult to properly *differentiate* oneself from his or her family of origin, creating a perpetual cycle of anxious–regressive interactions during times of emotional strain within the couple (Papero, 1990). Family-of-origin work should take as long as the couple requires and may warrant referral to other therapists for individual therapy, if the situation dictates, or if the problem threatens to change the focus of the couple sessions.

Sometimes couples enter therapy because they need a "quick fix" and the service member is preparing to leave soon for training or deployment without wanting to make a long-term commitment to therapy. Flexibility should be a central component to working with military couples because of this tendency to enter therapy for a few sessions of short-term treatment. In such cases, reducing the level of conflict and tension, improving effectiveness of communication (of needs), helping them become more aware of the patterns that are problematic, and increasing the positive regard expressed are the primary goals of therapy. The therapist must keep in mind that the military system competes with the family system at every level for the service member's time and that the spouse (family) often loses out in the competition, creating resentment that the couple may find difficult to frame. It is important to understand that, like other couples, these families will need therapeutic intervention at various points in time as they experience their life cycle transitions. We have found it best to maintain an "open door" policy, so that couples and families may return as long as they'd like and as often as feasible.

Another important aspect of counseling military couples requires acknowledging the "time-out" of the marriage due to deployment. This acknowledgment is very important, especially with younger couples who have been married less than 2 years and may have been separated for half of that time due to deployment. It is not uncommon for a dating couple to marry a few months prior to deployment. Then the service member leaves for a year-long tour of duty a few months into their marriage. They are unable to achieve the balance afforded most couples during the role assignments, rule negotiations, and conflict management crucial to establishing *couplehood* during the first year of marriage. In some cases, the female spouse may have been pregnant and had a baby during the service member's deployment, creating further strain on the couple relationship when the service member returns. As a result, they may be at risk for break-up because they lack these essential relational skills. In essence, they are still experiencing the first year of their marriage and the therapist should be prepared to help the couple negotiate the return as such (i.e., a portion of the first year of marriage) very early in the process of therapy.

It should also be noted that military couples in general experience higher rates of marital dissolution whether they receive therapy or not, so ending therapy prematurely at this stage may be more common for therapists who work with military couples. It has been our experience that sometimes we begin with marital therapy and very quickly come to the realization that the couple may want to dissolve the relationship, but are unsure of how to proceed. At this point, the therapist may begin to focus on helping the couple part amicably, divide their assets, and help plan for the care of any children in the relationship if dissolution is imminent. Otherwise, as part of the initial phases of therapy, the therapeutic triad must work through a variety of presenting issues in order to immediately improve the quality of the relationship. Often some direction is required for how to regulate conflict, and rules for basic resolution tactics must be clearly established. Examples of directions for home interaction include avoiding negative start-up (Gottman, 1999), taking "five" (minutes or more) for reducing hostility in the midst of an argument and for allowing the physical stress response to abate, and establishing a pattern for returning to deal with the problem later (improving trust between members). As mentioned previously, these directives are derived from allowing the couple to argue without interference in some earlier sessions so that the therapist can observe the topics that cause conflict, the tactics they use to fight, and the ways they resolve their conflict (or not).

Later Phases of Treatment

The earlier phases of treatment should be characterized by decreases in conflict and decreased negativity, along with increases in commitment, cooperation, and emotionality as the relationship has improved. These first-order changes are important and should be acknowledged as progress by the therapist. The next phase of therapy should involve strengthening couplehood and continuing to reduce their reactance to change (or a reversion to previous levels of functioning). This phase of treatment may last anywhere from 8 to 12 sessions. This is often the point at which many couples will want to stop therapy because of the improvements seen during the earlier treatment phases, or an interruption will occur due to the service member's training schedule. This is a crucial transition point in couple therapy in general, but it is especially important for the military couple to remain engaged in the process because of the further changes needed to reduce the potential for relapse as they experience future life cycle changes.

This stage of treatment is important for solidifying second-order changes to the couple system, regardless of the particular approach. The therapy should focus primarily on helping set realistic expectations for their relationship, communicating their needs to one another in a respectful way, and continuing to help each partner meet the other's expectations within limits. As the couple continues along toward improvement, the therapist should help insulate them from failure in therapy by allowing for disagreement and conflict while controlling for inflammatory responses that may dishearten the couple. The therapist may introduce various topics to help build skills into their communication structure and bring them closer together. Discussing topics through to the point of compromise is a way to ensure continued improvement in the quality of the marriage.

This is often the point at which the therapist and couple will begin to work on other problems that were discussed at the beginning of treatment, but not introduced for work until a sufficient amount of rapport, trust, and confidence has been established. An example of a problem to be dealt with at this phase may be an issue of sexual incompatibility. It is not uncommon to see a military couple consisting of a sexually hyperactive male service member and sexually hypoactive female spouse. This relational state may have led to a great deal of tension between the couple or an affair on the part of the hyper-aroused member of the couple. (Many times a non-sexual "quasi-affair" with a co-worker or online affair may serve to call attention to the incompatibility problems in the relationship.) The standard protocols for treating such cases should be followed based on the therapist's preference of treatment at this point.

It is also important to include children within the therapy, when it is appropriate, at this point. We do this for two reasons: it keeps the couple honest in the process because the children hopefully have a vested interest in parental well-being, and the children may be the source of tension, especially if the couple is attempting to form a blended family system. The inclusion of children can also help parents understand the impact of poor marital relations and constant conflict on other members of the household. If a mental or emotional disorder warranting a medical referral was detected earlier in therapy, the positive (or negative) effects of the treatment should be discussed as part of the therapy. In some cases the spouse who was not suffering from an emotional disorder may be inclined to dismiss further therapy as unnecessary due to the improvement, but the therapist should interpret this as resistance and incorporate these improvements into the ongoing therapeutic process.

Toward the end of this phase of therapy, the couple should be comfortable with "ownership" of their therapy, and the therapist should have adopted a much less directive, more supportive approach as a result. Encouraging the couple to continue improvement while watching for relapse is the primary goal as this phase ends. The therapist should never work as hard in therapy as the clients, especially at this stage of the process. This phase of treatment may last a little longer if a personal issue, such as trauma, depression, or a medical condition, becomes a part of the treatment focus. The therapist may find that referral resources are limited due to the difficult nature of this work or lack of approved providers in the Tricare network within the referral area. This phase ends when the couple can manage their relationship interactions with little assistance from the therapist.

Ending Phases of Therapy

Ending therapy should take between one and three sessions optimally, and it should be understood that termination may be pre-empted by relocation to another duty station, the deployment of the service member, or the dissolution of the relationship. However, ending therapy should involve several basic components: resolution of the initial problem(s), assessing the couple's satisfaction with the therapeutic results, checking to see that desired changes have been implemented, and securing their commitment to return for therapy should previous issues re-emerge or if they are unable to make the desired changes permanent. Our approach is not short term in nature, and solution-focused or cognitive behavioral approaches are not discouraged from use. We prefer to take as long as we need for each situation.

THERAPEUTIC MODELS AND TECHNIQUES TO USE

Many reading this chapter may wonder about our preferred approach since we've mentioned numerous styles and models of couple therapy. Structural–strategic approaches to couple therapy lend themselves well to the short term of therapy many military couples experience because of their lifestyle. We have no particular aversion to brief or solution-focused models, and we both know a number of practitioners who are very skilled at those approaches with military couples. Cognitive behavioral therapy has translated very well into the realm of couple and family therapy, since behavior serves as a conduit for system-maintaining interactional patterns. As mentioned previously, each author prefers a slightly different approach to couples. The first author prefers more of a multigenerational family–systems approach, while the second author has become a recent adherent to emotionally focused techniques. As long as the techniques are systems based, then the reader should find them applicable to a wide variety of situations involving couples in family therapy. For more of this discussion (i.e., family systems concepts), the reader is referred back to the first chapter in this text.

CASE ILLUSTRATIONS

Finding Our Places

The following case illustrations are presented to help the reader further understand the application of systemic therapy techniques with military couples. The reader should note the use of multiple styles of therapy, as the authors' approach to family therapy practice differs slightly depending on the situation and personal preferences. This couple was seen due to adjustment problems after the service member's return from a second tour of duty in Iraq. He had suffered a non-combat-related injury during his deployment and was awaiting discharge for medical reasons. Many of their relational problems stemmed from his inability to connect with her preschool-aged daughter from a previous marriage, along with the emotional distance and sexual incompatibility experienced since his return from deployment. They had been referred by another therapist for couple work because of an argument that occurred during a family session in the presence of their daughter when an incident of domestic violence was disclosed. This session occurred well into their therapy and would be characterized as a middle-phase session, as the reader will note the discussion of previously disclosed problems.

Husband: We've had a pretty good week, I think—don't you (to wife)?

Wife: I thought it was crazy that you said we should be nicer to each other—I mean we're paying $100 an hour for that? We've been at it now for several weeks and it seems to be working.

Therapist: I think I intended to convey that the two of you should work harder at reducing the amount of negativity you express toward each other, but being nicer would be helpful.

Wife: You didn't really clarify what you meant.

Wife teases therapist using head gesture for emphasis—non-verbal message (contempt).

Therapist: Don't be a smart-ass (laughing)—you knew what I meant. Sometimes the simplest gestures or acts of kindness can initiate positive change within a relationship.

Husband: Well, we also got some good news from the medical board that has my case right now—that helped a little. We'll ETS (get out) later this spring and hopefully they'll give me more than 40 percent disability because of my injuries.

Wife: He's right. I know that it's not his fault or that he has no control over what they do, but it's hard for me not to get in "one of my moods," as you so famously put it [*Teasing, once again, indicating recognition of issues.*] when I don't see him following up on things the way I think he should. It has been better.

Therapist: There you go again making fun of me and something I said or pointed out to you (to wife), but you both are right in this case—the ambiguity associated with open-ended ETS dates and boards that don't act according to our time tables creates a lot of stress for people who are holding off making major decisions like moving.

Therapist acknowledges her point and reinforces her recognition of problem.

Wife: Speaking of that, I'm going to fly back home for a couple of job interviews next week.

A good sign that she's more committed to the process of staying married and relational improvement.

Therapist: And you're going be here with the little one (to husband)?

Husband: Yeah, she's left me in charge of a preschooler for two whole days.

Wife: Well, he's been following your suggestions about fathering and I've been giving him more time with her, so she's really started bonding with him a lot better and doesn't cry when I go to work anymore.

Husband: We've also been working in family therapy to get her more used to me.

Acknowledging that their efforts have paid off.

Therapist: That sounds like an improvement because I suggested to you both that these issues were linked and causing strain in your marriage and your relationship with your step-daughter.

Wife: I realize that it (his parenting or lack thereof) was really raising my anxiety about a lot of things, as far as our marriage was concerned. I mean—I saw it as if he wasn't trying to make an improvement (with her), so why would he try to do anything different in our relationship. That's less of a problem now—I feel more confident.

Wife alludes to an issue raised earlier in therapy regarding her experiences with her distant father who suffered PTSD from service in Vietnam.

Husband (to therapist): But you pointed out that I wasn't used to that situation (of parenting) having never been married—I thought I would be, but the reality was overwhelming.

Wife: I'm just glad things are getting back to normal and we'll be leaving soon, hopefully. I've been checking his medical records to make sure he doesn't get screwed-over by the military.

Again, concern over what happened with father and use of her background as a healthcare professional—family-of-origin issues we'd previously explored.

Therapist: Well, that's something that you'll have keep on top of as time goes on, if previous treatment of veterans is any indication of what's coming—let's hope for the best and prep for the worst.

Session ended later with digression into his ETS date and medical discharge status.

In this case the therapist dealt with two primary issues: blending the husband into a step-family situation and the strain on their marriage as a result of their frustration with the military establishment. The two issues were inextricable and created a bind for all members, especially the couple in question, given the mother's concern about her daughter's well-being. It should be of interest to the reader that while the first author was working with the couple in marital therapy, the second author was working with the daughter in play therapy aimed at incorporating the step-father into the family and improving their relationship. The couple eventually moved back to the Midwest after he left the military and continued therapy. Through several e-mail correspondences, they seemed to have been successful in transitioning from the military to civilian life. They were also able to "catch up" on some of their first year of marriage, which was missed because of his deployment soon after they married. The daughter did well with the move, since they were relocating near her biological father with whom she had a strong relationship.

The Surreal (Cyber) Life

This case illustrates several aspects of military life that are not often discussed within therapeutic texts. The reader will see that couple systems are not only embedded within family and institutional systems like the military, but are part of overarching worldwide systems accessible through new media technologies and are susceptible to systemic transitions for which a couple may not be fully prepared. The following depiction and session dialogue demonstrates how these seemingly unrelated macro-systemic issues culminate in day-to-day work with couples and families.

A recently retired service member was compelled by his estranged wife to seek services as a result of a recent liaison with another woman in another state. He had left his wife to be with the other woman after an online relationship (over the Internet) turned physical. He was in his late 40s and had retired from the military a few years earlier, after a year-long tour of duty in the early phases of the Iraq conflict. He had been deployed to the most major area of operation since the mid-1980s and had served during the Persian Gulf War in 1991. After his retirement, he and his wife had settled into the community to be near the military installation where he was employed as a civilian. He acknowledged that they had been apart for over half of their marriage and had little interaction when he was home since their children were now adults with families of their own. He complained that his wife was very distant when he'd returned from the two previous deployments before retirement (i.e., the Balkans and then Iraq). He felt guilty about leaving her after over 25 years of marriage, but confessed that he'd only returned home because of her attempted overdose on antidepressants a few weeks earlier, which made him feel more guilty and disingenuous. His wife had been in therapy with another therapist and had improved since her suicide attempt. He initially planned to divorce his wife and move "out West" with his girlfriend.

As it turned out there was more to the online affair than was initially disclosed in the early phases of therapy. In addition to numerous extramarital affairs during many of his deployments, he had been involved in several affairs in recent years that began as online encounters. (He related that the military's prohibition against sexual encounters in many Muslim countries where U.S. troops are now deployed, coupled with the increase in Internet access, had contributed to a rise in this type of behavior among service members in recent years.) However, this particular incident was different in that it involved his living in the alternate cyberworld of *Second Life*® with this woman for over a year. More surprising was the fact that he was living in this alternate online universe as a woman (i.e., having a same-sexed, or lesbian, relationship), prompting his wife to become overly concerned about his heterosexuality at one point later in therapy. (He confided individually that women were less inclined to talk to men online, so he'd initially pretended to be female and simply kept the ruse going for longer than he intended.) The other woman had also continued to seek his companionship physically, even after he'd returned home to his wife and "moved out" of their online relationship. At one point, he actually returned to the other woman's home for three days before the divorce was finalized, but realized that he didn't like her as much in person and asked his wife for another chance to make their marriage work (to which she agreed).

The three main issues are as follows: life cycle transition (mid-life crisis and retirement); a devitalized marriage that had stemmed from a seemingly congenial arrangement earlier, based on Cuber and Harroff's typologies; violation of implicit rulemaking in the relationship; and his own personal feelings of inadequacy. He was diagnosed with an adjustment disorder with mixed emotional features and a narcissistic personality disorder was a rule-out Axis II diagnosis using DSM-IV-TR criteria. Since he had initially sought individual services, we had initiated some ground rules for working with them as a couple. We discussed what he should disclose prior to each session in order to not violate his confidentiality from his private sessions (e.g., the number of affairs during deployments, etc.). As it turned out, the wife had engaged in several extramarital relationships during his numerous deployments, and the therapist in this case suspected that she may have sought to leave him at one point as a result of intense feelings associated with the most recent of these relationships. The case material presented is a portion of one of approximately six sessions during which they were seen together as a couple.

Husband: We discussed what you and I talked about last time this week and she admitted that she had developed strong feelings in that relationship.

Referring to discussion of her affair.

Wife: It was the first time I'd been able to admit that to myself, much less anyone else. We had a moment, but he was overall very supportive.

Therapist: Why didn't you leave and go away with the other person?

Therapist is looking for clarification of the implicit rules within their relationship.

Wife: Because they ended the relationship before I had a chance to make a decision. It was very difficult for me, but it was also a violation of our rules.

Therapist: You mean "don't ask-don't tell," or "what happens in Korea stays in Korea?"

Wife: Something like that—I guess.

Husband (jumps into the conversation very quickly): In all of this, though, I understand now how what I did was a rule violation also. I mean I'm not trying to make it out as something less than what it was, but I didn't know what was going on at the time. It didn't really matter. All I could think about was the distance between us—she didn't want me around and the fact that we couldn't talk about it at all without arguing, that is.

Husband picks up a theme from previous session.

Wife: That doesn't justify having a whole other life with somebody though. I mean, come on!

Wife challenges notion that it's all about her infidelity.

Therapist: I would propose that the two of you had been doing that very thing for quite some time anyway and that this alternate life was perhaps an extension of all that. Let me ask you a question though (to wife)—what bothered you more: the online live-in relationship or the fact that he decided he'd rather be somewhere else with someone else?

Therapist clarifies the symbolic nature of the online affair in relation to their double life as a couple and pushes wife for more clarity.

Wife (angrily): Both! Isn't that the craziest thing you've ever heard of?!?! As another woman—come on (to husband).

Therapist: It certainly makes my Top 10 list of most shocking things I've heard in session—that's for sure, but we've already processed that to a large extent. I get the feeling that you're still struggling with this issue though.

Using humor to defuse anger and maintain positive direction of conversation.

Husband: I've already explained why I did that!

Alluding to the purported lack of conversation in chat groups between men and women.

Wife: I can only imagine what she thought when she finally found out that she was living a lie, too!

Therapist: She apparently didn't think too much about it—she took him in when he went out there—not once, but twice. But as you've said (to husband) given the reality of the situation, it would have been better if the relationship had been kept online.

A little reality check for both.

Husband: Let's not go there again. She was nuts. When I called her (looking at wife), and told her that I wanted to come back, if she'd have me, and she said there'd be a ticket waiting at the American Airlines terminal when I got to the airport (begins to cry)—man, you just don't know—I can't describe how I felt at that time. There was such a wash over me of emotions.

A pivotal moment in the session as the realization of what happened cannot be denied.

Wife (holds his hand as he sobs): He doesn't cry a whole lot, but he has cried more since all this—we've both shed a lot of tears. That's how I know he's sincere—we're both sincere about this now.

Softening.

Therapist: Not necessarily a story you'd want to share every detail of with the grandkids, I guess, but nevertheless your repair attempts seem to have worked well in light of your situation.

Therapist keeps them "in the moment" for a chance at a deeper corrective emotional experience.

Wife: You just don't know—we were less than 48 hours from the divorce being final and the second thing I did, after getting his ticket home, was to call the lawyer.

Husband: I know we still have a long way to go, but I feel like we have come a long way in the past couple of months.

Therapist: You think? I'd say so (joking).

Therapist and wife have been at odds over letting him decide on his own to leave—she felt that the therapist should have taken more preventive action.

Wife (glares at therapist, but then smiles): I don't know how with ALL your "help" (referring to therapist not doing more to keep husband from leaving). I guess that's what you guys call using "reverse psychology."

Therapist: Something like that (smiling). Unfortunately, we tend to learn best in therapy from experience.

Therapist disagrees, but refrains from discussing paradox.

Husband: That was a hard lesson, but many years coming I think.

The session continued with discussion of their recent attempts to improve their relationship and ended later with another appointment, along with a commitment to continue processing information from at-home conversations and repair attempts.

This case illustrated the intricate nature of working with military couples where spatial proximity and the span of time are relative to the therapeutic interactions. At one point, the lead therapist considered the option of creating avatars for the wife and himself in *Second Life* in order to confront the issue of deception and help the former partner move on emotionally, but refrained from doing so due to ethical concerns associated with the use of such a new technology and the uncertainty of involving a former partner from an online relationship in therapy. The AAMFT Code of Ethics has yet to advance into the realm of cybertherapy. We did, however, role-play this scenario in couple therapy using a variation of the "empty chair" technique (i.e., talked through the end of the affair as if the former partner was present). Individually, we worked on insecurity and self-esteem issues that stemmed from a number of instances of childhood verbal and physical abuse from the husband's father. The wife continued her own therapy and both reportedly experienced an improvement in their marital relationship. Needless to say, this is one of the most unusual and interesting cases the authors have ever been involved with or consulted on as supervisors.

Note: A final clarification is needed in this case regarding psychodynamic processes in relational systems. The therapist (first author) later connected the same-sexed nature of the online cyber relationship to deeper unconscious factors related to the husband's recent blood pressure problems and difficulties with maintaining an erection after the prescription of a beta-blocker and the intractable prospect of failing at another relationship because of sexual issues (i.e., being a woman helped ensure that this issue never arose in the online relationship).

SUMMARY AND CONCLUSIONS

Many clinicians are adept at working with couples, and many texts have been published attesting to this fact, but the challenging nature of couple therapy within a military setting would stretch any therapist's skills to their limits. At times, we have been left overwhelmed and feeling inept as the multiplicitous nature of the problems that these families experience presents itself session after session. The challenges to normalcy in military marriages are many. Long-term separations, reunifications, personal loneliness, extramarital temptations, and the ever-present strain of possible harm constitute a few of the more prominent challenges associated with being married in the military. It is our hope that the recent recognition of these issues by the Department of Defense and the implementation of new marital enrichment programs will improve the odds of success for these couples. Regardless, mental health practitioners working with military couples in all branches of service should remain aware of the value of systemic techniques as applied to presenting problems discussed within this chapter.

Although these methods were derived from clinical work with Army couples, there are several key points from this chapter that the reader should consider when doing systemic work with couples in any branch of service. First, be aware that there may be multiple issues operating at multiple levels of the various systems in which the therapist is working. Second, make sure that all of the information needed for effective treatment is at your disposal. Also, be patient with the process and do not work any harder in therapy than the clients are working. Although it may seem that the stressors are overwhelming, even to the clinician, these families are competent at dealing with a great deal of turmoil and strain. It's only when their coping resources are taxed beyond their limits that the couple often seeks professional assistance. Understand also that the therapy may be time limited and disrupted by training, deployments, and relocation. Finally, keep in mind that self-care is important given the strenuous nature of the work with this population. Stay in supervision or remain involved with a consulting group with others who are familiar with these populations. Working with these couples can be very stressful, but the rewards of improved clinical skills and enhanced therapeutic competence are worth the effort on the part of the clinician.

REFERENCES

Beavers, W. R. (1985). *Successful marriage: A family systems approach to couples therapy.* New York, NY: Norton.

Beck, A. T. (1978). *The depression inventory*. Philadelphia: Center for Cognitive Therapy.

Berg-Cross, L. (Ed.) (2000). *Basic concepts in family therapy: An introductory text* (2nd ed.). New York, NY: Hawthorne.

Carter, E. A. & McGoldrick, M. M. (Eds.) (1998). *The expanded family life cycle: Individual, family, and social perspectives* (3rd ed.). New York, NY: Allyn and Bacon.

Corcoran, K. & Fisher, J. (Eds.) (1987). *Measures for clinical practice: A sourcebook.* New York, NY: Free Press.

Daley, J. G. (1999). Understanding the military as an ethnic identity. In J. Daley (Ed.), *Social work practice in the military* (pp. 291–303). New York, NY: Hawthorne.

Dekel, R., Goldblatt, H., Keidar, M., Solomon, Z. & Polliack, M. (2005). Being the wife of a veteran with posttraumatic stress disorder. *Family Relations, 54,* 24–36.

Dirkzwager, A., Bramsen, I., Ader, H. & van der Ploeg, H. (2005). Secondary traumatization in partners and parents of Dutch peacekeeping soldiers. *Journal of Family Psychology, 19(2)*, 217–226.

Figley, C. R. (1998). *The transition from registered to certified traumatologist.* Invited address to the Green Cross Projects Annual Conference, Tampa, Florida.

Gottman, J. M. (1994). *Why marriages succeed or fail ... and how you can make yours work.* New York, NY: Simon and Schuster.

Gottman, J. M. (1999). *The sound marital house: A theory of marriage in The Marriage Clinic.* New York: Norton.

Gurman, A. S. & Jacobson, N. S. (Eds.) (2002). *Clinical handbook of couple therapy* (3rd ed.). New York, NY: Guilford.

Hudson, W. W. (1982). *The clinical measurement package: A field manual.* Homewood, IL: Dorsey.

Kelley, M. (1994). The effects of military-induced separation on family factors and child behavior. *American Journal of Orthopsychiatry, 64*(1), 103–111.

Klein, D. M. & White, J. M. (1996). *Family theories: An introduction.* Thousand Oaks, CA: Sage.

Leiblum, S. & Rosen, R. (Eds.) (2000). *Principles and practice in sex therapy* (3rd ed). New York, NY: Guilford.

Locke, H. J. & Wallace, M. (1959). Short marital adjustment and prediction test; Reliability and validity. *Marriage and Family Living, 21*, 251–255.

Marchant, K. & Medway, F. (1987). Adjustment and achievement associated with mobility in military families. *Psychological Schools 24*, 289–294.

Matsakis, A. (2005). *In harm's way: Help for the wives of military men, police, EMTs, and firefighters.* Oakland, CA: New Harbinger.

McGoldrick, M. & Gerson, R. (1985). *Genograms in family assessment.* New York, NY: Norton.

National Healthy Marriage Resource Center (2006). *Retrieved February 13, 2007.*

Newby, J. H., Ursano, R. J., McCarroll, Xian, L., Fullerton, C. S. & Norwood, A. E. (2005). Post-deployment domestic violence by U.S. Army soldiers. *Military Medicine, 170(8)*, 643–647.

Papernow, P. L. (1998). *Becoming a stepfamily: Patterns of development in remarried families.* Hillsdale, NJ: Analytic Press.

Papero, D. V. (1990). *Bowen family systems theory.* New York, NY: Allyn and Bacon.

Rosen, L., Westhuis, D. & Teitelbaum, J. (1993). Children's reactions to the Desert Storm deployment: Initial findings from a survey of Army families. *Military Medicine, 158*, 465-469.

Rotter, J. C. & Boveja, M. E. (1999). Counseling military families. *Family Journal—Counseling and Therapy for Couples and Families, 7,* 379–382.

Ruger, W., Wilson, S. E. & Waldrop, S. L. (2002). Warfare and welfare: Military service, combat, and marital dissolution. *Armed Forces and Society, 29,* 85–107.

Segal, D. R., Segal, M. W. & Eyre, D. P. (1992). The social construction of peacekeeping in America. *Sociological Forum, 7,* 121–136.

Segal, M. W. (1986). The military and the family as greedy institutions. *Armed Forces and Society, 13,* 9-38.

Segal, M. W. & Harris, J. J. (1993). *What we know about Army families (ARI Special Report 21).* Alexandria, VA: Army Research Institute for the Behavioral and Social Sciences, U.S. Department of Defense.

Spanier, G. (1976). Measuring Dyadic Adjustment. *Journal of Marriage and the Family, 38*(1), 15–28.

Walsh, F. (Ed.) (2003). *Normal family processes* (3rd ed.). New York, NY: Guilford.

4 Systemic Therapy with Adolescents in Army Families

R. Blaine Everson, Joseph R. Herzog, and Leigh Ann Haigler

CONTENTS

This chapter is an attempt to provide a better systemic understanding of the processes of late adolescence and its associated problems within U.S. Army families. During the past half-decade, many military family members have experienced multiple deployments of a service member to Iraq and Afghanistan. These deployments are both long term and hazardous, creating added stressors for those family members who remain behind as the service members deploy for long periods of time (Cozza, Chun & Polo, 2005). These families, along with the military parent, present clinicians with a unique set of challenges as they experience a variety of issues and problems associated with the military lifestyle. Given the recent focus of media attention on military families and the level of support provided both on-post and in local communities, many may be led to think that these families have limited problems. Nothing could be further from the truth (Daley, 1999).

First, we outline a set of problems unique to adolescents within the military culture, such as frequent long-term separations from one (or both parents) due to deployments, geographic *hypermobility* resulting from frequent relocation, dealing with a parent after his or her return from a combat tour, and failing to achieve the appropriate milestones for launching into early adulthood. We also seek to identify common treatment issues associated with adolescents and their families in the U.S. Army, such as parent–child conflict stemming from losses associated with relocations and deployments, academic problems experienced by the adolescent, coping with a family situation where a member may be experiencing combat trauma, and substance abuse issues often associated with late adolescence. Another of our goals in this chapter is to provide some clinical examples of adolescents, from 16 to 19 years of age, within these families and our attempts to deal with them therapeutically. While a fair amount of work exists regarding adolescents in psychotherapy, much of it tends to over-focus on the problems of the adolescent without fully regarding the systemic nature of the problems, and the remainder focuses on adolescents in their earlier teens. Finally, we offer suggestions for those working within military communities in general for programming, counseling services, and policymaking.

We realize that many military children are able to achieve the appropriate family support and the developmental trajectory allowing a successful transition through the launching phase of the developmental life cycle (Carter & McGoldrick, 1998), yet this phase is fraught with ambiguity as the adolescent and family seek to strike a balance between maintaining familial ties and asserting independence (Boss, 2002). From a child development standpoint, the adolescent is dealing with a number of transitional issues, including choosing a career path, selecting a potential mate, adopting a value system to guide behavior, and achieving socially acceptable behavior, all made more difficult by interactional failures in any of the significant social systems that serve as contexts for the adolescent's development (i.e., family, school, community). Ideally, adolescents should be able to maintain closeness with their families, be emotionally mature, and act with some autonomy. Very often, this is not the case. Figure 4.1 illustrates our trisecting view of the adaptation of adolescents within military family systems.

Following are some detailed analyses and examples of those teenagers who do not successfully navigate such transitions. Military children seem to fall into three broad categories of adaptation when it comes to the rigors associated with military life. Some seem to adjust fairly well to frequent relocations, lengthy deployments, and new social environs without exceptional difficulty. On the other end of this spectrum, some adolescents are unable to adjust, suffer emotionally, and/or act out behaviorally. They may get into trouble both academically (poor

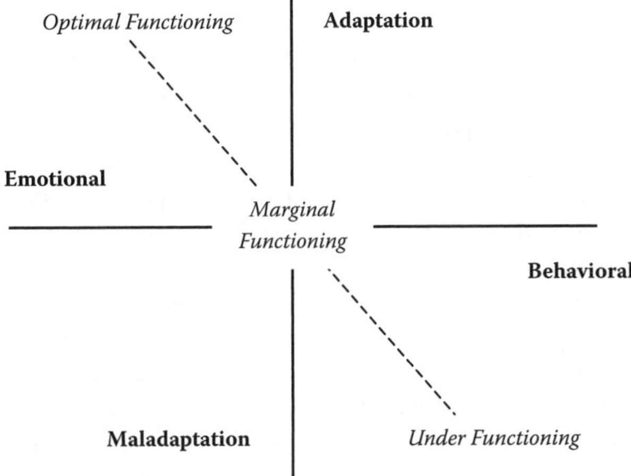

FIGURE 4.1 Three-dimensional continuum for adolescent adaptation in military families.

grades, truancy, suspensions, etc.) and within the community (curfew violations, shoplifting, vandalism, fighting, etc.). These adolescents may be referred for therapy at some point, but the referrals are usually sought through the juvenile justice system or installation-based agencies and less frequently are self-motivated. The middle ground within this categorization system involves adolescents who remain withdrawn in a new setting, marginally complete their schoolwork, and suffer from emotional problems, which makes them and their families good candidates for family therapy. These situations most often are overlooked, given their failure to capture the attention of those in the best position to potentially make a referral if needed.

MILITARY LIFESTYLE

Military family issues have been at the forefront of the debate on America's involvement in various troubled spots around the world, especially for the past half-decade. In the 1990s, Segal and Harris (1993) identified a number of lifestyle issues associated with the military and suggested ways to assist Army families in particular. Various military support organizations (e.g., National Military Family Association) assist families before, during, and after deployments, and provide varying types of information on financial management, childrearing, and self-care on their Web sites (e.g., www.nmfa.org). All branches of the armed services have recognized the problems that develop due to strains associated with the military lifestyle and the need for family support as a result (Pincus, House, Christensen & Adler, 2004). We discuss several of the more pertinent lifestyle issues that may lead military families to seek the assistance of a helping professional.

Deployments

Much has been written about the difficulties associated with the long-term separations imposed by military deployments (Black, 1993; Kelly, 1994). There is no other facet of the military that stresses military family members more and assails their coping abilities (Blount, Curry & Lubin, 1992). Since the beginning of the conflicts in Afghanistan and Iraq, the average length of deployments has nearly doubled from 6 months to around a year (since the Balkans peacekeeping missions of the late 1990s). Many service members have been deployed multiple times to Iraq, which means that the average service members involved with U.S. ground forces in Iraq or Afghanistan spend less time per year with their families and more time away from home. Deployments usually follow a cycle of pre-deployment preparation, deployment of the service member, sustainment during the deployment, and redeployment or post-deployment adjustment (Pincus et al., 2004). All of these stages place different demands upon the family system and require unique coping skills from each member.

Adolescents may be particularly susceptible to the negative effects associated with frequent and long-term separation due to deployments. As the adolescent moves toward adulthood, more rituals and milestones associated with the end of a secondary academic career (i.e., homecoming, prom, graduation, college visitation, etc.) are occurring (Carter & McGoldrick, 1998). Deployed service members may miss these important aspects of late adolescence and crucial planning necessary for successful movement into young adulthood. Family systems-based practitioners may facilitate these interactions by helping families become more aware of better ways to keep a deployed family member informed during the separation and assist families in smoothly re-integrating service members when they return home.

Relocation

Military families move every 3 to 4 years on average. These moves require that all family members adjust to unfamiliar communities, new schools, and different social expectations within each setting (Finkel, Kelley & Ashby, 2003). Service members make this transition more smoothly because of the work-related connection to the military system. Other than deployment, there is no situation within the military lifestyle that children feel less control over than relocation, and relocation is perhaps worse, due to the adjustment required by a complete change of social contexts (Weber & Weber, 2005). Relocation is particularly stressful for adolescents because of the intense relationships that they have generally formed with peers by this age. The U.S. Army generally discourages moving families with children in high school for this particular reason, although it occasionally happens.

Relocation requires that the adolescent adjust to new social, emotional, and relational situations after a move. How the children or adolescents cope with moving is often related to how the non-military spouse manages the relocation (Finkel et al., 2003). In many cases, relocation is more stressful for adolescents than younger children due to the disruption of normative events during the adolescent phase of the life cycle, such as peer group formation, romantic attachments, and academic success. Relocation requires that the adolescent begin anew the social processes required in forming new relationships, and for many teens, starting over in a new place may be too much for them emotionally and psychologically (Pittman & Bowen, 1994).

Blended Families

The higher divorce rate associated with military marriages tends to produce a higher incidence of remarried couples and, as a result, blended families with children from previous relationships occupying the same household. A very common type of blended family in the military is the *complex* stepfamily, where the remarried parents have children from previous relationships, plus children of their own as a couple (Papernow, 1998). In a number of cases, these families are not only blended, but face the unique challenge of both parents serving in the military (i.e., dual military couples) or one on active duty and the other in the military reserves. Therapists may see these families in crisis when both spouses are ordered to deploy, as has been the case with more frequent deployments in recent years, and be required to assist with the design of a family care plan (i.e., designating a guardian of their children while they serve overseas).

A frequent problem associated with military families stems from the deployment of the biological parent, while the step-parent remains behind to contend with the conflict often associated with caring for a child who is *not* biologically related. For many couples, this situation causes a great deal of strain between the remaining spouse and the deployed service member, as well as children who are already in the home, and frequently ends with the step-child being returned to the previous custodial parent. Often, children from a previous marriage or relationship may have felt neglected and act upon their anger because of the presence of younger kids with the new spouse, or simply feel as if they have no place within the new household. Be mindful that the child from the previous relationship may not have a great of relational experience with the new biological parent because of the military lifestyle (e.g., hypermobility). In addition, these children often come into these families at the adolescent stage of development, making the transition even more difficult. Systems-oriented therapists realize the importance of establishing a "new face" for the new family quickly through church and other community involvement, the value of allowing everyone time to adjust to the new family environment and values system, and reducing emotional reactions to each other and the children. It may take some time to adapt to new situations and experiences in the new family life, and family therapists can facilitate this process.

Transient Family Members

In some ways, the arrival of an adolescent for visitation into a blended household is similar to the problems discussed in the previous section. For that period of time, each member of the family system is presented with a unique set of challenges. The father may be unfamiliar with the child due to a lack of consistent contact since divorcing the mother. Step-parents are faced with trying to incorporate a new member into the family, while balancing the needs of their own children and maintaining a healthy marital relationship, which may be threatened by the arrival of an adolescent from a previous relationship. The reactions frequently differ based on the sex of the step-parent. In some cases, step-mothers may find themselves handling the visitation of a child who is biologically unrelated to them or their children, in the absence of a deployed husband.

Often these visitations will result in a change of custody as the adolescent decides to become a part of the biological parent's new household. While some of these transitions go smoothly, others strain the family's ability to cope with the new situation. Most often these problems begin with conflict between the newcomer and the other children in the household. The biological parent is caught in a *double bind*, given the relationship expectations of the new(er) spouse and the loyalties to the biological child (Berg-Cross, 2000). The financial benefits associated with the military are incentives that make this an all-too-frequent phenomenon that therapists who work with military families will experience in their practice.

Soldier Retirement

An often-overlooked phenomenon associated with the late adolescent within the military is the retirement of the service member from active duty. This often requires a restructuring of the family system with the service member remaining at home rather than leaving for deployments, training, and specialty schools. This process may create a situation of conflict between the child in late adolescence and the retired parent because of a lack relationship history between parent and child due to frequent separations. Often the parent is unfamiliar with the expectations of distance from the children based on previously limited contact vis-à-vis lengthy separations. This presents the family with a set of dual normative stressors at this phase in the life cycle not typically experienced by other families, due to the relatively young age at which service members retire from the military. Launching of an adolescent and retirement of the service member may complicate family situations until adjustments have been made (Walsh, 2003).

Often, the non-military spouse and the family experience conflict with the retired service member as they must adjust to the service member being at home for longer periods of time. They may view the increased presence of the military retiree as an intrusion on an already established way of life, family structure, and the household regulation. The retiree must also adjust to a new job situation, re-entry into the post-secondary educational system, and the loss of status along with military identity. Systems-oriented practitioners will be asked to help families through this transitional period in their lives. We must see the needs of the individuals within the family system, but understand that successfully navigating this transition requires striking a balance between competing individual and family-level needs.

COMMON THERAPEUTIC ISSUES

There are a number of therapeutic issues arising from the interaction between older adolescents and relational structures associated with families in the military system. We will attempt to discuss the most prevalent issues that we confront in daily therapy practice with adolescents and military families, including launching, peripheral family involvement of a service member parent, a troubled parent suffering from combat exposure, alcohol and drug abuse, domestic disputes with parents, and problematic sibling interactions.

Failing to Launch

This term has become a cliché in American popular culture and has been trivialized to the extent that it sometimes diminishes the seriousness of the problem for many adolescents and their families. However, many adolescents in military families find it difficult to transition to adulthood for a variety of reasons, including school failure, developmental delays due to separation loss, and current deployments disrupting the life cycle rituals associated with this stage (i.e., parent missing graduation). Many adolescents in military families may find that they have little or no chance of going to college because of poor academic performance or the lack of preparation on the part of parents to help them through this transition.

Systemically, the failure to launch centers around an inability to properly *differentiate* from a child's family-of-origin (Papero, 1990) and should be looked at by the clinician as a triangulation or an emotional double bind. The double bind may stem from the emotional over-reliance on the adolescent, or *parentification* (Berg-Cross, 2000), by one or both adults within the household. This systemic phenomenon is not unusual in military families given the frequent long-term absences of the service member, the presence of younger children within the household, and the addition of more daily responsibility.

Marginalization of Service Member

Over the course of many deployment cycles, military families will adapt to having the service member absent by acting as if the member isn't there when he or she returns. The service member may be part of the physical structure of family, but not participate in the emotional processes, instead leaving that arena for their spouses. This peripheral connection to the system by the service member is often an attempt to make the transitions between deployments and reunifications easier. This situation is problematic for the family because the mother bears the burden of being overly involved in parenting and household affairs without the benefit of assistance from the service member who remains detached from the system.

A similar issue results from service members trying to re-connect with an uninterested adolescent late in his or her career. This experience can be disruptive to the family balance because it upsets the homeostatic balance the family system has established without the service member. Also, the clinician must consider the presence of family *secrets* resulting from occurrences in the household when the service member was away that require loyalty to the established status quo and continue the marginalization of the service member (Karpel & Strauss, 1983). At a behavioral level, the adolescent may simply be mimicking the allied parent's attitude toward the returning spouse.

Secondary Traumatic Stress

Secondary traumatic stress has recently become a topic of interest for systemic practitioners and researchers, primarily due to the fact that the process through which stress permeates families is both a communicative and a structural aspect of an evolving family system. In order for this process to begin, a member of the family must be exposed to a potentially traumatic situation or event. This situation or event may or may not cause a psychiatric condition and, most commonly, post-traumatic stress disorder (PTSD). Simply having a family member in harm's way is enough to activate secondary traumatic stress symptoms in family members (Dirkzwager, Bramensen, Ader & van der Ploeg, 2005). The stress of having a family member in danger and/or coping with the ailing member's condition becomes a strain for all family members involved, leading to emotional fatigue and burn-out in those family members (Figley, 1998). As many as one in three service members returning from Iraq may suffer from PTSD or some form of combat stress injury.

This process is more easily defined within adults in close emotional proximity to the traumatized individual, as in the case of spouses of service members, but secondary traumatic stress may manifest differently in children and adolescents. While adolescents may have the requisite cognitive and emotional skills to negotiate secondary traumatic stress, they may also have a greater depth of awareness of the traumatic event(s) and the effect of such event(s) on their parent. This phenomenon is transmitted much like any other anxiety-based symptom within the context of the *family emotional process* (Berg-Cross, 2000).

Substance Abuse

Many teenagers actively use alcohol or drugs on a regular basis. The use of illegal substances can be treated as both a symptom of the underlying emotional and behavioral problems or as the primary focus of treatment, depending on the nature of the referral. Screening for types of substance and the extent of use can be difficult, but is critical for determining whether outpatient or inpatient treatment is the appropriate level of care (Vik, Brown & Myers, 1997). Adolescents are often reticent to disclose the amount or type of substance use due to possibly worsening already poor familial relationships. This lack of disclosure can mean the difference between a correct diagnosis and a misdiagnosis of a substance use problems (i.e., substance abuse versus a more serious dependence). Along with the use of illegal substances (we include alcohol as illegal for this age group, because of the drinking age limit of 21 years in most states), conduct problems associated with peer interactions may act as a barrier to eliciting accurate information from children at this age. Substance-related symptoms may co-exist with an emotional disorder such as anxiety, bipolar disorder, or major depression, creating the need for a dual diagnosis of the adolescent and a decision as to which symptoms take precedence in terms of their immediate well-being (Corcoran & Fisher, 1987).

Anxiety and Mood Disorders

Mental disorders, such as generalized anxiety, major depression, and bipolar disorder (DSM-IV-TR), are often the result of a variety of systemic factors akin to those previously discussed. Regardless of their origin, the symptoms comprising these conditions often bring the family into therapy. More often than not, the adolescent will begin to experience emotional problems as a result of the strains associated with a military family experience over which they have little or no control. The anxiety of the military adolescent may stem from early childhood when he or she first experienced a long-term separation from the military member of the family. The adolescent often manifests behavioral symptoms (e.g., oppositional defiance) at a younger age, due to an inability to articulate feelings associated with frustration experienced. As they get older, their anxiety may become more generalized with the development of constant worry or phobias, or situational anxiety, as they experience sudden onsets of panic symptoms (Barrios & Hartmann, 1997). Each evaluation must include an assessment of anxiety- and mood-related symptoms, as the potential risk for self-harm is generally greater with late adolescents than with any other age group.

Emotional and Behavioral Disorders

The previous emotional conditions may also co-exist with any number of behavioral diagnoses, such as attention-deficit hyperactive disorder (ADHD), conduct disorder, impulse control disorder, or intermittent explosive disorder (APA, 2000). Other commonly observed emotional and behavioral problems include eating disorders, personality disorders, sexually acting out, and self-mutilation. The decision as to which symptom set warrants clinical attention or psychiatric referral rests with the clinician, but a systemic practitioner should very quickly seek to address familial sources of stress that may exacerbate these symptoms (i.e., see the adolescent's symptoms as part of a larger systemic context) and work with families to reduce these intra-familial tensions. Sometimes adolescents with conduct problems and the associated sociopathy may become involved in gang activity and drug dealing associated with gang membership. The difficulty associated with the social reinforcement provided by such affiliations and the potential legal problems may thwart any efforts to foster a positive change in familial relationships. Gang membership may also provide continuity between one setting and another as these youths relocate frequently in the military system.

A BRIEF OVERVIEW OF THERAPY WITH LATE ADOLESCENTS IN MILITARY FAMILIES

Therapy with late adolescents often begins with the family seeking treatment for the teen as the focus (i.e., source of family's problems or the identified patient). The family typically enters therapy as a result of the adolescent's conduct problems, substance use issues, or a mood disturbance. These avenues into therapy are often opened by a recent deployment, move, new family situation, or a crisis created by the adolescents themselves. Part of the initial assessment process is the clinical interview, which should include as many family members as possible in order to provide the most information about the family system in a short time period. The individual and family level of problems, as well as their creation and maintenance should be considered as part of the initial evaluation (Karpel & Strauss, 1983). Referral for psychological testing may be warranted if the clinical picture is unclear, or for medication management if the therapist deems that rapid stabilization of symptoms is a necessary part of treatment.

The early phases of treatment should begin with the therapist and the adolescent trying to build a trusting relationship where a free exchange of information and therapeutic disclosure can take place. Family members should be encouraged to look for ways that they can begin to mimic this process in their own relations with the adolescent when not in therapy, through the use of positive communication and reflective feedback. Within this systems-based approach to late adolescents, we very quickly begin to look for ways to reduce the admitting complaints to a level that is acceptable to both the individual and family members. This approach does not differ drastically from other brief therapy models where therapists seek to test commitments and look for exceptions in previously stated ways of interacting as they join with the family in the early phases of treatment (O'Hanlon & Bertolini, 1998). Our approach also centers on the improvement of communications, enhanced decision making, and behavioral demonstration of the ongoing improvements. For example, compliance with a family therapy regimen for a dysthymic, substance-using adolescent and his or her family would include support group attendance, sessions with a substance abuse professional, and submitting to regular substance abuse testing. Sometimes families leave treatment after the alleviation of the presented problems and the amelioration of their admitting complaints, but often families will need further assistance as the adolescent transitions through the emotional strains associated with this life stage and family context.

As therapy proceeds, adolescents may be seen alone from time to time without other family members. As long as these sessions do not become a mechanism for co-opting the therapist into secret-keeping as a way of letting the family "off the hook," or triangulated position, the therapist may continue with tandem sessions. Adolescents often rely heavily on the relationship with the therapist, especially if they come to see the benefits of the process. If there are siblings in the household, it is sometimes helpful to include in them in the adolescent's sessions separate from the parents. The family sessions should provide the family with a "secure" space for solving ongoing problems and addressing new concerns, as well as helping the adolescent express his or her feelings about the situations the family may be experiencing. The journaling of thoughts, feelings, and ideas at this developmental stage is a very effective way of helping adolescents cope with frustration and externalize their negative feelings about problems. We utilize this with some effectiveness with improving mood disturbances and reducing self-mutilating behavior. More in-depth interaction with the adolescent and his or her family is possible as the relationship between the participants deepens. It is not uncommon for the teens and their families to exchange e-mails with therapists as a way of relating information about daily life and topics for upcoming sessions.

CASE ILLUSTRATIONS

The cases presented in this section are designed to illustrate the previously discussed problems with military children in late adolescence and represents the authors' attempts to deal with these complex issues from a systemic standpoint. The interventions in the first case are generally of a structural–strategic nature, and these approaches have been applied to bring about rapid and dynamic changes within family systems since their introduction in the 1970s. All of the cases used for illustration are also multi-focused in that the reader may pick out two or more therapeutic issues from these conversations. The format of the dialogue involves both content, where much of the conversation is depicted, and process, which consists of the therapist's commentary on the events of the session.

Let Me In (or Not)

The following dialogue is a case illustrating of the first author's attempt to realign the family structure where the father (a service member) has been marginalized through adaptation by other family members after numerous deployments and is unable (unwilling) to take an active part in the rule-making in the household regarding cell phone use. The mother and daughters had been in therapy for a number of months prior to his return from Iraq due to the girls' ongoing behavior problems and not following household rules. The older daughter was 17 and the younger daughter was 15 at the time of the depicted session. Their father attended three or four sessions after his return.

Mom: They (teenage daughters) go over their minutes every month! This is ALL we fight about now!

Therapist: Surely, there are other things to fight about (jokingly).

Therapist is attempting to tease out extent of problems using humor.

Dad: I can't believe this sh*t—for the second month in a row the bill's over $500.

Therapist: This isn't the first time we've discussed this problem. How much do you believe is an acceptable amount?

Mom: I'd like to see them not go over their minutes at all, but I don't know what to do anymore. They (phones) go off constantly and the girls are always talking or texting someone. They don't clean their rooms or do any other chores.

Therapist: What about you, sarge? What's an acceptable amount?

Engaging the father.

Dad: I don't know. I come back from Iraq and this [situation] is what I got to put up with. Their mom usually handles this kind of thing, but I know I'm not going to do this anymore. Things are going to change!

Therapist: So what are you going to do instead?

Therapist suspects daughters frequently use parental quarrels as a chance to exploit the rules.

Mom: Nothing! You heard him say that he lets me deal with this stuff, as if he's not there at all.

Dad: That's bullsh*t! (*begins arguing with mom*)

Girls: It's true—this is what always happens … so sick of this!! (Oldest daughter pauses and begins to text message someone on her cell phone.)

Therapist (to daughter): Give me your phone, please. (Takes phone, switches it off, and places it in his desk drawer.) Now when you come back in two sessions, you can have the phone back.

Corrective action modeled by therapist.

Dad: Hey, wait a minute!! I pay the damn bill on that cell phone—you don't!!

Therapist: You're right. This should save you some money. There shouldn't be any overage charges at all for the next month.

Therapist relieves tension between mom and dad by engaging in argument with dad.

Oldest Daughter: They'll just find something else to complain about (*as her younger sister giggles*).

Mom (angrily): They don't do anything, unless he yells at them and then they still don't do what he says half the time then.

Dad: I get sick of that [yelling] too. It's seems like that's all I do when I'm home.

Youngest Daughter: It is all you do. He tries too hard to control things and doesn't let us do anything. It's always a fight with him to do anything when he's home.

Mom: They generally just blow him off—and me too.

Dad: No respect at all.

Therapist: So, by that rationale, he may actually feel more like a part of things in your household when he can dictate the conflict to some extent.

Pointing out paradoxical nature of the interaction.

Dad: I don't know about all of that, but if you're saying that they shut me out otherwise—you're right.

Mom: You mostly choose to be out of the loop. When's the last time you actually did something with the girls?

Mom correcting his point of view.

Dad: It hasn't been all that long ago.

Younger Daughter: You can't count sending us to our rooms as an activity (laughs).

Youngest daughter always uses humor to defuse.

Therapist: She's got a good point it seems. What would you like to do with him? I mean are there any of your activities that he could be a part of?

Mom: Drama club, or the band concert? He will show up for her [youngest daughter's] soccer games when he can get off early.

Checking for openness of boundaries or cut-offs.

Therapist: Let me guess which one of you is into drama (*younger sister points to older sister*). I said let me guess (*jokingly*).

Attempting to engage the angry older daughter, but younger one again picks up the interaction.

Dad: I do things with them, but I can't relate to them without getting into an argument about something.

Younger Daughter: We're not arguing now.

Therapist: That's an excellent observation, but part of this [developmental stage] is that they are teenagers and are subject to their own points of view—this is normal and they may or may not grow out of it.

Dad (laughing): So there's not a cure for this.

Therapist: I'm afraid not, but it [adolescence] goes into remission sometime in the early 20s.

Mom: They just grew up too fast, I think.

Therapist (handing cell phone back to dad): Do you think that you three could begin to negotiate this [phone usage] now? You need to be part of this too (to older daughter).

Empowering dad by symbolic gesture and re-establishing hierarchy.

This is an example of a pivotal session interaction and an early-stage attempt at structural realignment with an Army family where the father was deployed to Iraq for a year prior to entering therapy. The therapist has joined the family and has attempted to help reassert parental hierarchy by re-engaging the father who returned from deployment to Iraq 6 months earlier. This family improved over the course of several months of treatment, but began to experience similar problems with misbehavior later as the father prepared for redeployment to Iraq. The family later dropped out of therapy.

Don't Fail (to Launch) Me Now

The next case illustrates difficulties that late adolescents sometimes experience with launching from military families. The 17-year-old daughter had been seen on a number of occasions, both individually and as part of her family. She was initially referred from another therapist because she had been sexually assaulted by an older male at age 13. She had sexually acted out and became very depressed afterward. Her mother left for Germany and our therapy continued as she remained in the United States with her grandmother and younger brother. Her behavior problems led to her eventual relocation to Germany with her mother, where she became pregnant and underwent an abortion. She also began drinking every day during that time. She returned to the United States and began acting out sexually, staying out late, and by dating a drug dealer who was much older. She returned to therapy as a stipulation of her probation due to absconding for a number of days with him. He was charged with kidnapping.

Her mother returned from Germany after completing a year-long tour in Iraq, and began attending therapy with her daughter again upon the discovery of her prolific sexual behavior after she was diagnosed with a sexually transmitted disease (STD). In many ways, Mother and daughter related more like sisters than mother and child. The daughter was about to turn 18 and had failed the first course of her senior year in high school (meaning that she would not graduate on time), although she had been a good student throughout many of her problems. The following excerpt takes place a few months into the last round of therapy, before the mother's prospective return to Iraq, and consists of a portion of a conversation about the problematic dynamic that has developed between the two of them. The daughter had become more anxious and depressed since mother had received her orders and had needed an additional inpatient stay to stabilize her condition. The daughter had turned 18 at the time of the session depicted here.

Mom: I just couldn't deal with those folks down at the hospital—they just wouldn't deal with me and I didn't think they were doing her any good.

Therapist: So you went and got her out AMA (against medical advice)?

Mom: Yes, I did.

Daughter: She didn't like the way they were doing my treatment between the A and D unit and the adolescent program. You know how she is.

Mom: We talked about it on the phone and you know how I felt (to therapist).

Therapist: I know how you felt and I disagreed with your decision given the urgency with which we admitted her before Christmas—I still do [disagree], but that's neither here nor there. How have you been since you got out (to daughter)?

Challenging mom's decision making as disruptive to ongoing assistance.

Daughter: I feel okay and I haven't drank anything—I'm going to that AA meeting over at the church on Thursdays and we go to Al-Anon on Sundays. I still feel a little depressed and have a little trouble sleeping, but less anxious.

Therapist: Good.

(Later in the session.)

Therapist: Let's switch gears and talk about how you guys are preparing for the deployment in a few weeks.

Mom: I just got to do what I got to do to get ready to fly out week after next. We've talked a good bit about it. She's still very upset when we get on the topic.

Therapist: That's because she doesn't want you to go.

Daughter: She doesn't really get that—I don't think!

Pointing out the double bind.

Therapist: What doesn't she get? You've told her repeatedly and you've basically shown her that things are going to remain on hold until she comes back next year—you're not going to finish high school, not going to college, not going to do anything remotely resembling moving on with your life.

Daughter: That test you gave me on how I feel about the war* should have summed up how I felt about whole thing.

Mom: But she doesn't understand that I don't see combat at all on my deployments—I never leave the FOB (forward operating base) when I'm there.

Daughter: It doesn't matter—something could still happen.

Mom: I know, but it's not likely.

Detailing the problems for both moher and daughter from a systemic perspective—a reframe.

Therapist: She's caught in the middle of those feelings either way you look at it. So are you. You've got to do one more rotation before you retire and there's nothing we can do to change that, but this represents a bigger set of issues that we've been dealing with on and off for the past five years—you've missed a lot and when you have been here it's nothing but conflict, for the most part, when you've tried to act like a mom. It's been this way since she was assaulted in the spring of 2002.

We have previously discussed their problems stemming from the sexual assault.

---

* War Attitudes Scale.

Mom: I wish I could go back and undo all of that and there's another case of letting the job get in the way; I should have come earlier that day like I was planning to and I could have prevented that from happening—something came up, though. (Becomes tearful and daughter's knee begins to tremble as a result of anxiety related to discussion of this topic.)

Therapist: You still feel guilty about that—not coming home early to prevent the boys from coming into the house.

Daughter is still anxious about the topic in spite of previous therapy.

Mom: I'm very sorry that I didn't. She knows that. It essentially changed everything and effectively ended my marriage—things were never the same between us again either (looking at daughter). Things seemed to speed up and haven't slowed down since.

A reference to early entry into sexual behavior, post-traumatic stress, and to trauma therapy three years earlier.

Therapist: Do you mean your coming and going, leaving them behind (daughter and younger brother) with relatives? It's difficult being mom when you're not here.

Mom: Yeah. I wish this was all over with now, but I gotta do one more [deployment].

Therapist: She and I have talked previously about how that incident set into motion a lot of things that she wasn't prepared to deal with.

Therapist (to daughter): What do you wish could happen?

Daughter: I wish it was 2008 already.

Therapist: She'd be back from Iraq then. What are you going to do between now and then to move forward and not put things on hold in your own life?

Daughter: I guess I need to keep working on my schoolwork and be more choosey about my relationships—like we've talked about. I'm kind of tired of all this drama with guys.

Therapist: And you've certainly had some drama with guys over the past year.

Reference to earlier contraction of STDs and older men talking to her all the time.

Mom: Uh-huh. (Daughter rolls her eyes and laughs at mom. Mom laughs too, but becomes serious again.)

Mom: That's all over now, I hope. It's not going to be easy, but we've talked about ways, in here and at home, that we can handle this deployment differently this time. I can be a part of the college selection process and keep up better with her school performance online.

Therapist: That sounds like a good plan and we've gotten a good start on it in here. Of course, you know you can always call or e-mail me any time.

Re-iterating their plan for handling the deployment.

Mom: I think it's going to be okay.
Daughter: I just want it to be over with.

The client was seen by the therapist for another few months after the mother deployed back to Iraq. The client was eventually referred to another therapist, after a lengthy period of closure, when the attending therapist moved away. This case was interesting in that the client actually seemed to function better (in some ways) when the mother was away, as opposed to when she was home. She improved after her mother deployed, returned to school, began following grandmother's rules better, and continued to volunteer at the local public health clinic. Later follow-up with her new therapist revealed that she was working and attending college part time.

Sgt. Dad

Tom, a 17-year-old African-American, started therapy with his mother, father, and brother when he was 16. Absent from the therapy session was Tom's older sister who was in college. The presenting problem offered by Tom's parents was that Tom was beginning to be involved with peers who had a history of substance use and other illegal behaviors. Tom also had conflicted relations with his father. Tom's father was a senior enlisted soldier who had gone on several deployments and been absent from Tom's life for extended periods of time. Tom saw his father as "Sgt. Dad" who demanded immediate obedience from him much like he did from his soldiers. While Tom's father was beginning to make decisions concerning his retirement, his mother was transitioning from her role of a stay-at-home military spouse to employment outside the home (as is often the case in military families nearing retirement). In fact, Tom's mother was in the process of completing her teaching degree and was to soon be employed with the local school system.

Tom was seen for a series of counseling sessions with his parents and his brother. The sessions focused on Tom's relationship with his father, as well as the parents' relationship with each other. Tom's brother was only marginally involved in the sessions. Tom and his father continued to be conflicted with incremental improvement. Tom and his father were able to pursue some activities together, but the tension between them failed to resolve. Tom's mother graduated from college and this was a major event for this family. Soon after the graduation Tom was involved in an incident at school, for which he was suspended and became involved with the juvenile court. The court's judgment was swift and Tom was sentenced to serve time in a youth detention center. This sentence was later changed after intervention by his family, this therapist, and community leaders, and Tom was ordered to complete a residential treatment program.

This case illustration deals with the circumstances surrounding the relationship between an authoritarian parent and a late adolescent involved in the juvenile justice system. Children often act out behaviorally when a parent is deployed and the non-military parent is left to manage the household as a single parent would. The mother was over-involved in her own career attainment, and the father expected compliance in his children upon his return from deployments, thereby exacerbating an already tense situation. Tom's substance abuse issues were of great concern to the therapist in charge of the case, and ongoing addiction treatment was a vital part of his residential program, along with family therapy sessions requiring the participation of all members.

SUMMARY

This chapter serves as a basic guide to working with families within the military using systemic applications in the assessment, treatment, and management of therapy with late adolescents. We sought to express a number of issues commonly seen in the practice of systems-based therapy with military families. This chapter began by pointing out some of the factors associated with the military lifestyle that lead families to seek assistance from mental healthcare providers and ended with case illustrations of military families with adolescents in therapy. The 16- to 19-year-old adolescent in a military family must be viewed within a unique situational context spanning two crucial life cycle phases. While many families have difficulty adjusting to structural changes within the family system during late adolescence, few in the civilian population are faced with the rigors of families with members associated with the U.S. ground forces in Afghanistan and Iraq during the past few years. In some cases, the adolescent has become a member of the military establishment through enlistment and has begun his or her own military family. Therapeutic intervention at this stage of development may be crucial to moving on into the early adult phase of the life cycle and the emotional well-being as a young adult, regardless of status (i.e., either as a part of a military household or as a head of household in the military).

Clinicians providing services to these families must be aware of a number of considerations in addition to ones that we have discussed. While the cases presented for illustration were U.S. Army families, the reader should see more similarities than differences among the various branches of service as far as deployments, frequency of relocation, overseas assignments, occurrence of remarriage, and adolescent problems are concerned. We have hopefully provided the practitioner with some helpful information and tips for providing systemic remedies for addressing problems within military families.

REFERENCES

American Psychiatric Association (2000). *Diagnostic and statistical manual of mental disorders (4th ed., Test Revision) (DSM-IV-TR).* Washington, DC: APA.

Barrios, B. A. & Hartmann, D. P. (1997). Fears and anxieties. In E. J. Mash & L. G. Terdal (Eds.), *Assessment of childhood disorders* (3rd ed.) (pp. 230–327). New York, NY: Guilford.

Berg-Cross, L. (Ed.) (2000). *Basic concepts in family therapy: An introductory text* (2nd ed.). New York, NY: Hawthorn.

Black, W. G., Jr. (1993). Military-induced family separation: A stress reduction intervention. *Social Work, 38*(3), 273–280.

Blount, W., Curry, A. & Lubin, G. I. (1992). Family separation in the military. *Military Medicine, 157,* 76–80.

Boss, P. (2002). *Family stress management: A contextual approach.* (2nd ed.). Thousand Oaks, CA: Sage.

Carter, B. & McGoldrick, M. (Eds.) (1998). *The expanded family life cycle: Individual, family, and social perspectives* (3rd ed.). New York, NY: Allyn and Bacon.

Compas, B. E. (1997). Depression in children and adolescents. In E. J. Mash & L. G. Terdal (Eds.), *Assessment of childhood disorders* (3rd ed.) (pp. 197–229). New York, NY: Guilford.

Corcoran, K. & Fisher, J. (Eds.) (1987). *Measures for clinical practice: A sourcebook.* New York, NY: Free Press.

Cozza, S. J., Chun, R. S. & Polo, J. A. (2005). Military families and children during Operation Iraqi Freedom. *Psychiatric Quarterly, 76,* 371–378.

Daley, J. G. (1999). Understanding the military as an ethnic identity. In J. Daley (Ed.), *Social work practice in the military* (pp. 291–303). New York, NY: Hawthorne.

Dirkzwager, A., Bramensen, I., Ader, H. & van der Ploeg, H., (2005). Secondary traumatization in partners and parents of Dutch peacekeeping soldiers. *Journal of Family Psychology, 19*(2), 217–226.

Figley, C. R. (1998). Burnout as systemic traumatic stress: A model for helping traumatized family members. In C. R. Figley (Ed.), *Burnout in families: The systemic costs of caring.* Boca Raton, FL: CRC Press.

Finkel, L. B., Kelley, M. L. & Ashby, J. (2003). Geographic mobility, family, and maternal variables as related to the psychosocial adjustment of military children. *Military Medicine, 168,* 1–6.

Karpel, M. A. & Strauss, E. S. (1983). *Family evaluation.* New York, NY: Allyn and Bacon.

Kelley, M. (1994). The effects of military-induced separation on family factors and child behavior. *American Journal of Orthopsychiatry, 64*(1), 103–111.

O'Hanlon, B. & Bertolini, B. (1998). *Even for a broken web: Brief, respectful solution-oriented treatment for sexual abuse and trauma.* New York, NY: Wiley.

Papernow, P. L. (1998). *Becoming a stepfamily: Patterns of development in remarried families.* Hillsdale, NJ: Analytic Press.

Papero, D. V. (1990). *Bowen family systems theory.* New York, NY: Allyn and Bacon.

Pincus, S. H., House, R., Christensen, J. & Adler, L. E. (2004). *The emotional cycle of deployment: A military family perspective.* Retrieved from *www.hooah4health.com* on February 13, 2007.

Pittman, J. & Bowen, G. (1994). Adolescents on the move: Adjustment to family relocation. *Youth and Society, 26*(1), 69–91.

Segal, M. W. & Harris, J. J. (1993). *What we know about Army families (ARI Special Report 21).* Alexandria, VA: Army Research Institute for the Behavioral and Social Sciences, U.S. Department of Defense.

Vik, P. W., Brown, S. A. & Myers, M. G. (1997). Adolescent substance use problems. In E. J. Mash & L. G. Terdal (Eds.), *Assessment of childhood disorders* (3rd ed.) (pp. 717–748). New York, NY: Guilford.

Walsh, F. (2003). Family resilience: a framework for clinical practice. *Family Process, 42*(1), 1–18.

Walsh, F. (Ed.). (2003). *Normal family processes* (Third ed.). New York, NY: The Guilford Press.

Weber, E. & Weber, D. (2005). Geographic relocation frequency, resilience, and military adolescent behavior. *Military Medicine, 170,* 638–642.

5 Systemic Therapy with Families of U.S. Marines

Don Catherall

CONTENTS

Systemic issues arise in work with all families, and interface issues arise with all military families. There are more commonalities than differences in the interface issues that appear across the different branches of service, but some of the differences are noteworthy. This chapter focuses on some of the characteristics that distinguish members of the U.S. Marine Corps. As the nation's oldest branch of service, the Marine Corps has a long history and a distinct culture. As with families, knowledge of that history and culture can facilitate our understanding of individual Marines and the issues that arise with their families. Marines are a particularly proud and loyal group, highly disciplined, competent, and prone to arrogantly boasting about the Corps and devaluing the other branches of service. We will begin by exploring the idea that it can be useful for family therapists to think of the Marine Corps as a family.

"THE CORPS, THE CORPS, THE CORPS"*

The Marine Corps needs to be regarded as more than just another institution in a client's life. It is an institution, but the degree of (a) loyalty to the Corps and (b) influence from the Corps is more similar to that seen in families than in more impersonal institutions.

Once a Marine, always a Marine. From a sociological perspective, the armed services are well-defined communities in which the members interact within a rigid system of mores, values, and boundaries that distinguish them from non-members of the community. Each service has its own distinct culture, traditions, and peculiarities. For example, the Marines utilize naval jargon for many everyday activities (e.g., stairways are "ladders"; the bathroom is the "head"; the commander is the "skipper"), even though the activities of Marines have expanded far beyond their original function aboard ships.† The use of jargon links current Marines with the long tradition of the Marine Corps family and, like all jargon, helps define the in-group status that distinguishes Marines from non-Marines. To be a Marine is to feel a strong personal identification with the Marine family. Like a nuclear family, an individual can move away yet still feel part of it.

"Don't forget that you're First Marines! Not all the Communists in hell can overrun you."‡ The intensity of the attachment between the Marine and the Marine Corps is similar to that found in families. The Marine Corps shares many dimensions with families; it can be examined through the same lenses that therapists use to understand families. We can describe the family of the Marine Corps in terms of the hierarchy, the family structure, the roles, the rules, the emotional climate, and even in terms of intergenerational effects. For example, if a Marine's unit took heavy losses or played a pivotal role in a battle, the Marine is likely to feel he or she has a legacy to live up to. The First Marine Division achieved the first offensive victory against the Japanese in WWII at Guadalcanal. The same division (but with different Marines constituting its membership) faced overwhelming odds at the Chosin Reservoir in Korea, which prompted the quote above.

Marine identity within *the family of the Corps.* You can make genograms of the Marine's family network within the Corps that include the history of the units in which the Marine has served. Each Marine has a unique history within the Corps that can be readily understood by another Marine. Simply by identifying previous units, battles, duty stations, occupational specialties, and the like,

---

* This quote is from Army General Douglas MacArthur's retirement speech at West Point, when he identified the three things that had been the most important to him. Clearly, MacArthur was a Marine wannabee.

† Of course, the use of naval jargon does not mean that Marines embrace the relationship with the Navy. Many Marines are disdainful of the Navy—a "bus ride into battle and free medical and dental"—but the Navy corpsmen who operate in the field with Marine units are highly respected.

‡ Chesty Puller, motivating his Marines at Chosin Reservoir, Korea, when the First Marine Division was surrounded by 22 enemy divisions (Davis, 1991). The quote captures the Marine attitude that they are the toughest troops in battle as well as the historical value of Marine units. Puller was the most highly decorated Marine (five Navy Crosses) and, more than any other individual, his attitudes epitomize the culture of the Marine Corps. He is frequently quoted by Marines.

a Marine can quickly develop significant insight into another Marine's unique experience. The ribbons and other insignias on the dress uniform can provide astonishingly large amounts of information about people in the service.

Consider the power of the dress uniform. Two unacquainted Marines can meet and, before the first word is spoken, each knows something about how long the other has been in the Corps, what rank he or she has achieved, and whether he or she has ever been wounded, decorated, served in certain theaters of war, achieved special training, or demonstrated skills with particular weapons. A Marine can often infer what special assignments the other may have participated in and even what kinds of experiences another is likely to have had. Members of the Marine family share a level of mutual understanding that far exceeds their formal relationship (the one defined by rank and duty assignment).

Every salute must be returned. The Marine Corps is a system par excellence, and circularity abounds. The military hierarchy is so clearly defined that units continue to function even when the leaders are removed because the hierarchy clearly prescribes who will assume leadership responsibilities. This is obviously adaptive for an organization that must constantly prepare for crisis, but it may contribute to a more authoritarian parenting style among many Marine parents.

He gave his life so that his comrades might live. The attachment between individual Marines can be as intense as those in nuclear families, especially in combat units, where the Marines depend upon each other to stay alive. Marines in combat typically form bonds as strong as any family relationship; they rely on each other and they take care of each other. Marines and corpsmen attend to wounded Marines with the same care as a loving mother with her infant.

No Marine will be left behind. Another characteristic of the Marine Corps is its undying commitment to its members. Every Marine knows that he or she will never be abandoned in combat. This is the essence of what comprises secure attachment in a family. Marines are secure in their relationship with the Corps, and at the same time they are the Corps—just as family members influence each other even as they are influenced by each other. Marines know their Marine family will be there when needed, and therefore they must be there for other Marines when needed. This is a large part of what is meant by duty—I must be there for you because you are there for me.

Every Marine is a rifleman. The Marine Corps differs from other services by requiring that all Marines become qualified combatants. Marine training treats every member of the Corps the same—before they learn any kind of specialization, they must first achieve competence as infantrymen. Every recruit, whether enlisted or officer candidate, must achieve competence as an infantryman before he or she will be called a Marine. The entire Marine Corps thus maintains a warrior culture and a sense of elitism that is usually limited to smaller units, such as the Navy SEALs or the Army Rangers. Elitist military units confer a sense of pride on their members, but the price is usually high. Life is dangerous for warriors.

A Marine is prepared and resourceful. The Marine Corps trains hard because its goal is to constantly be prepared. Two lessons of combat are that (a) it is essential to be prepared and (b) the plan goes awry in the first minute of combat. Hence, a fundamental aspect of preparedness is training Marines to be resourceful so that they will adaptively deal with situations for which they were not (initially) prepared.

One of the great ironies about the Marine Corps is that low-ranking members are treated as though they are totally unable to think for themselves, yet the real expectation is that every Marine will be able to function on his or her own. The "dumb treatment"—couched in accusations of inferior intelligence and applied mostly in training—is actually about discipline and obedience. The training and the culture of the Corps explicitly demand intelligent decisions and behavior. This is not the "getting loud in the tavern" side of Marine culture—this is the "knowing how to assemble a gas-operated weapon in the dark" side. Being a Marine means being very competent. In combat units, Marines regularly assume positions of responsibility and leadership beyond their rank. Corporals and lance corporals lead squads and non-commissioned officers (NCOs) frequently end up commanding platoons without any diminished functioning of these units (Rooks, 2009).

As an organization, the Marines demonstrated their capacity to anticipate and prepare for potential dangers during the years before World War II. Members of the Corps recognized the likelihood of Japanese encroachment in the Pacific and the Corps instituted training in amphibious landings, which proved invaluable for the war in the Pacific theater. During the Vietnam guerilla war when America's goal was to win the hearts and minds of the populace, the Corps argued the value of placing small units in the villages and fighting alongside the local forces. This strategy was never accepted by the Army, which ran the overall war, but the Marines employed such units in their geographic area of responsibility (I Corps). Their insistence that guerilla wars must be fought differently from conventional wars is an example of the Marine Corps' traditional emphasis on adapting to the situation at hand. The point here is that Marines are indeed expected to think for themselves, to anticipate dangers, and to adapt resourcefully when they encounter the unexpected.

A TRAUMATIZED FAMILY

The Marines are one of the world's premier fighting forces (Marines would say *the* premier force). When the Marines of the First Division were cut off from American forces and had to fight their way out of the Chosin Reservoir during the Korean War, they inflicted the highest casualty rate on an enemy in the history of modern warfare. Typically Marine, this was no retreat—it was advancing to the rear. The First Division, which numbered 12,500 men, destroyed seven enemy divisions, each of which numbered more than 16,500 men, as they fought their way to the American lines. Achieving and maintaining that kind of combat efficiency is the primary goal of the Marine Corps: the philosophy, the commitment, and the culture of the Corps are all in the service of that goal.

The Corps has endured tremendous trauma in the course of its history and come through it intact. But no system can experience so much trauma without being affected. The Marine Corps family is not dysfunctional, but it is a traumatized family that has adapted to living in a world in which continued trauma is expected. The lessons of past trauma are woven into the fabric of Marine culture.

Take all you want, but eat all you take. The Marine Corps takes care of the needs of its members, but they are expected to maintain a high level of self-discipline, and infractions are punished. Much of daily life is highly structured, and all Marines are expected to maintain a high level of performance. This produces a workmanlike approach to tasks that is uniquely Marine. For example, senior NCOs* often assume the role of teacher, describing tasks in terms of clear tactics and objectives. There is even a characteristic cadence and vocal quality to the way these non-commissioned officers talk when they provide instruction.

The more you sweat in peace, the less you bleed in war. Errors in combat are deadly, so the Marine Corps strives to keep Marines at their highest levels of performance. The individual Marine is encouraged to push himself or herself to the limit, and individuals who do not push themselves lose status. Sometimes the group is used to pressure individuals who do not seem to be pushing themselves enough. In boot camp, scapegoating is common and can be quite destructive for those recruits who end up on the receiving end of a platoon's ire. The overall message is that Marines must always push themselves to perform at the highest levels.

First to fight. The Marine Corps is organized as a rapid deployment force, allowing the United States to establish a ground presence in foreign locales before the occupation of a large army can be initiated. The Corps has fought in every American armed conflict. The Marine Corps also has special duties, including missions in direct support of the White House and the State Department, as well as providing security at American embassies, legations, and consulates. The ideal Marine is a delicate balance between (a) the exquisitely disciplined and controlled man or woman in dress blues standing at attention outside the door of the embassy, and (b) the fiercely aggressive combat Marine about to storm an enemy position.

Take me to the Brig. I want to see the real Marines.† The Corps recognizes the need for aggression in a fighting force. General Puller's quote reflects a popular belief in the Corps that a certain amount of aggression and acting out, such as drinking and fighting, must be tolerated (despite official sanctions against such behavior) because it is an unfortunate side effect of maintaining a proper level of aggression. The Corps' mission requires its members to be mentally, physically, and emotionally tough, and this leads to increased tolerance of some rough behavior.

What'd you say about my mama? Drill instructors purposefully find something personal to say about every recruit. The lesson is that insults are not to be taken personally. A Marine must demonstrate self-control and not allow an opponent to control him through taunts. The training process of boot camp seeks

---

* NCOs are non-commissioned officers, the enlisted men and women who achieve higher rank and have primary responsibility for supervision of the lower-ranking Marines.

† Another quote from Chesty Puller, then a lieutenant general (Davis, 1991).

to remake recruits emotionally. They learn to (a) control their feelings by enduring taunts and challenges, (b) channel their aggression into prescribed outlets, such as bayonet training, and (c) push themselves beyond their existing limits of tolerance for adversity (both physically and emotionally). The result is much more than physical strength; it is an emotional hardiness. The recruits who bust out of boot camp and fail to achieve the title of Marine more often fail because of the emotional demands than the physical ones.

A Marine can take orders and a Marine can give orders. In all military organizations, the taking and giving of orders is done through a highly ritualized procedure that makes the process impersonal. The two individuals refer to each other by rank rather than by name. They step away from any personal relationship and the giving and accepting of orders occurs through their formal roles. Personal feelings are not allowed to interfere. Some military organizations may be less rigorous about the formality of this process, but in the Marines it is a key component.

Death before dishonor. The Marines are a culture of honor, similar to the Japanese Samurai warrior culture. The emphasis on honor serves to strengthen individual courage. If dishonor is seen as worse than death, then fear of dishonor can help Marines to face death. Many of the young men and women who enter the Marine Corps are seeking this sense of honor because of previous difficulties with feeling competent or adequate during adolescence. The downside of honor cultures is that shame has enormous power in those cultures.* Shaming and scapegoating are often used to shape Marines' behavior during their training. Concern about not shaming oneself or one's unit is a significant motivating factor in the Corps.

Sounds like a problem for the chaplain. Emotional vulnerability is avoided in traumatized families. Most career Marines treat emotional problems as an inevitable difficulty that simply must be endured. Thus, the expression of vulnerable emotions is discouraged and self-control is rewarded. The difficulty many Marines have accessing their more tender feelings is similar to the post-traumatic stress symptom of a diminished capacity for positive feelings. After tours of combat, Marines are especially hardened and many find it difficult to regain access to their emotional center.

"You don't hurt 'em if you don't hit 'em."† The Marine emphasis on marksmanship is another lesson learned from combat. It teaches every Marine to be an independent threat to the enemy. To be a good marksman in combat, the individual must be able to relax, focus on the target, and ignore incoming fire. This leads to a greater internal locus of control and allows Marine riflemen to prevail against numerically superior forces. This internal locus of control extends beyond marksmanship; it is a central component of the Marine identity.

---

* In 1996, the ranking admiral of the Navy killed himself because it had been revealed that he was wearing an unauthorized decoration. This is the power of shame in honor cultures. See Catherall (2007) for an in-depth discussion of shame and its role in male fraternal organizations.

† Chesty Puller made this remark at the Army Infantry School in Fort Benning, Georgia, where he was arguing the Marine emphasis on accuracy of marksmanship over volume of firepower (Davis, 1991).

Lead by example. The Marine family is split between officers and enlisted, and between higher and lower ranks. The Marines maintain a very high level of family cohesion, despite the split, by (a) not misusing the privileges of the ruling class* and (b) leading by example (lieutenants and captains have a high casualty rate because they are on the front lines right alongside their men).

"Paperwork will ruin any military force."† The Marines emphasize pragmatics and individual competence. The leaders who are the most highly revered are those who can stand shoulder to shoulder with the lowest-ranking Marines. The Corps often eschews sophisticated designs and fancy machinery, choosing to rely instead on the competence of the common Marine. For example, the Corps has often been behind the other services in its acquisition of modern exercise equipment, preferring to make use of naturally occurring challenges, such as carrying logs and running in sand.

Semper Fidelis. The Marine Corps motto, which means always faithful, reflects the sense of family that sustains every Marine individually and the Corps as a whole. Perhaps the greatest lesson from the accumulated trauma of our country's many wars is that Marines must always stand together, regardless of the odds. The same love and loyalty that hold families together hold the Corps together.

A CODE OF UNDERLYING PRINCIPLES

> They were the old breed of American regular, regarding the service as home and war as an occupation; and they transmitted their temper and character and viewpoint to the high-hearted volunteer mass which filled the ranks of the Marine Brigade.
>
> **—"The Leathernecks," John W. Thomason, Jr. (1926)**

To really see how the Corps works, look at the role of the non-commissioned officers, the NCOs and senior NCOs (SNCOs). They embody the living knowledge of the Corps and they keep that knowledge active for all Marines. Here are the words of some instructors at the Second Marine Logistics Group's Battle Skills Training School from an interview conducted in 2008. These NCOs are not training infantrymen, they are preparing support personnel for their role in the combat zone.

> Every Marine is a rifleman. We fight on the frontlines of war, so everyone has to be prepared for the worst.
>
> **—Sgt. Johnathan D. Nash**

> It's knowledge that could one day save their lives. If they don't know how to operate a machine gun, they won't be able to protect the convoy they're on. If they don't understand the convoy order process, they won't understand the mission they're on.
>
> **—Sgt. Shane R. Burge**

---

* General Chesty Puller was known to refuse the traditional privilege of officers to cut to the front of the chow line.

† Another quote from General Chesty Puller (Davis, 1991).

> If one of those seven [support personnel] falls, the infantrymen have to stop and get into a defensive position because they will no longer be getting the support they need to continue.
>
> **—Staff Sgt. Stephen A. Farage**

These NCOs speak in terms of the basics of survival and accomplishing the mission. Their priorities are crystal clear, and the clarity is no accident. They are the embodiment of the Corps, doing its job of keeping its personnel prepared for combat. The trained Marine deals with challenges by relying on well-rehearsed principles. The training helps the Marine to respond quickly during times of crisis when untrained people are more likely to be overwhelmed and become ineffective. The principles underlying surviving and accomplishing the mission are the common denominator that defines the Marine Corps experience. Being a Marine means adhering to that code of principles.*

CORPS ISSUES

The depth and intensity of that code inevitably extends beyond combat. For the Marine, many choices reduce to (a) life and death and (b) accomplishing or not accomplishing the mission. Therapists dealing with Marines and Marine families need to understand (a) the culture of the Corps, (b) the strong attachment Marines make to the Corps, and (c) the ways in which trauma has shaped the culture of the Corps.

IMPACT ON THE NUCLEAR FAMILIES OF MARINES

The Marine can be considered to have multiple family influences and family loyalties. The Marine Corps family is similar to the family of origin in regard to its influence on the Marine's relationship with his or her nuclear family. The Marine will usually refer to "the Corps" when talking about his or her Marine Corps family.

PARENTING

The Corps emphasizes discipline and obedience, and this influences the way most Marines approach parenting. Obedience and acceptance of the hierarchy is expected in the Marine's family. Children growing up in such a world usually accept this as a given, but children exposed to a greater variety of parenting styles may resist the hierarchical structure. Spouses who come from a less regimented background may have difficulty adapting to family life with a Marine.

---

* Yep, that's what those non-coms are yelling at their Marines, a well-rehearsed code of principles that are designed to maximize survival and successful accomplishment of the mission. "No, your left foot, not your right! Do you not know your left from your right? Did your Mommy not teach you the difference between your left and your right? When you're shooting one of my machine guns, are you going to shoot it to the left when I tell you right? Are you going to shoot your fellow Marine?"

Partnering

The Marine is a responsible hard worker. Cooperation is paramount, but a partnering relationship is seldom emphasized in the Corps. Many Marines struggle with the interpersonal dynamics associated with the partnering demands of modern love relationships. Decision making is usually not a democratic process in the Corps. And loyalty conflicts can occur in which the Marine must choose between the wishes of a partner and what is deemed right according to the Corps. These loyalty conflicts are similar to those that can occur between a nuclear family and family of origin.

The Marine Spouse

Spouses of Marines do not fare well if they cannot operate on their own. With their Marines serving on long deployments and evening and weekend duty requirements, spouses must be able to manage without their Marine spouses. Younger spouses and those from sheltered backgrounds often struggle with marriage to a Marine. It is not a typical marriage, and the spouses must understand and accept this fact if they are to have a successful relationship. Spouses of career Marines in successful marriages tend to be independent people who have accepted the rigors of life in a Marine marriage.

The Interface

The Marine family is subject to all the problems of any other family, with the additional dimension that a family member is a Marine. Sometimes the needs of the Corps supersede those of the Marine's family—as when the Marine is deployed overseas. Sometimes the needs of family members—such as needing the Marine to be more emotionally accessible—conflict with the culture of the Corps. And sometimes the Marine's exposure to trauma interferes with the functioning of the nuclear family—as when a former combat Marine remains hyperaroused and cannot respond to the family's emotional needs.

Trauma and the Family System

Not only is the Corps a traumatized family, but many Marine nuclear families are themselves traumatized. When a Marine is psychologically injured by his or her exposure to combat and traumatic loss, the family is affected. The systemic impact of trauma on families is well accepted by most clinicians; it is primarily documented in the literature on secondary traumatization (Nelson Goff & Schwerdtfeger, 2004). Other family members are at increased risk for developing symptoms when one member has been traumatized.* The nuclear family can

* See Catherall (2004) for a discussion of the different avenues through which a trauma survivor can secondarily traumatize other family members.

encounter obstacles if the family's style of dealing with these stressors conflicts with the Corps' style of dealing with stressors. Management of these differences is best handled through implementing a therapeutic structure that categorizes and prioritizes the needs of the family and the needs of the Corps. The emotional safety model can be useful in accomplishing this goal.

Emotional Safety Model

The model posits that the needs of the Corps can be prioritized when necessary—as long as it is done in such a way as to not diminish the emotional safety of family members. Emotional safety refers to the safety of (a) the relationships and (b) the selves of family members. Emotional safety exists in a family when the members feel that (a) their attachment relationships are secure and (b) their personal self-esteem is not threatened (Catherall, 2007). It is quite possible to meet the needs of the Corps without sacrificing emotional safety in the nuclear family as long as the two realms of emotional safety are adequately addressed.

Attachment Realm

A parent's extended overseas deployment is a great stressor on a child, but it will not cause the child to lose emotional safety as long as the child knows that the attachment is secure. First, the parent must take steps to ensure that the child receives adequate care in his or her absence. Second, the deployed parent must communicate (through phone calls, email, instant messaging, letters, and gifts) that he or she is thinking about the child and will return to resume normal parenting.

The child still must cope with an enormously stressful situation, and developmental problems can occur as a result of the parent's absence. Additionally, if the parent is deployed in a combat zone, the child must also cope with his or her anxiety about the parent's well-being. So emphasizing the child's emotional safety does not preclude the development of problems spawned by the Marine's service. But the sources of these kinds of problems—a parent away for an extended period and the child's awareness that the parent is in danger—cannot be avoided. What the Marine family can ensure is that the relationship between parent and child is protected. As long as the child feels that the attachment relationship is secure, he or she will not be upset about the relationship itself. The other problems will not have disrupted the functioning of the relationship system.

When there is a breakdown in the attachment system, the children in the family are at increased risk for other problems, including inadequate social learning. If they are also exposed to inappropriate modeling from the parents, they have the triad of deprivation that is associated with chronic difficulties in personality functioning (Gold, 2004).

The need to know that the attachment is secure is not confined to the children. Both spouses must also feel that their relationship is secure. The Corps has a duty to do what it can to facilitate and support the family relationships of Marines. This is why it is important that mail get through to deployed Marines, even in the combat zone. In our modern electronic age, deployed Marines need access to email and other forms of contact with their families. Thoughtful NCOs and officers have always paid attention to whether their Marines were receiving mail and writing home.

It is also important to remind the reader of the value of the attachment relationships between individual Marines and between Marines and the Corps. Marines must be prepared to endure long separations from their families. A significant factor in making these separations successful is that many of their attachment needs continue to be met within the Corps. Especially during tours of combat, the attachment relationships between Marines may play a greater role in preserving their sense of security than their attachments to nuclear family. This is particularly salient when a deployed Marine receives the dreaded "Dear John" letter.

Esteem Realm

In addition to having secure attachments, family members must feel personally accepted and respected in order to feel emotionally safe. The regimentation that occurs in many Marine families is not destructive as long as the self esteem of the children is not damaged in the process. However, this dimension can run awry because of some of the undesirable elements of the Corps' approach to influencing Marines. As noted above, the Corps sometimes resorts to shaming and scapegoating as motivational techniques. This often produces casualties—many of those individuals who fail to live up to the Corps' standards leave with damaged self-esteem. The Marine parent needs to understand the difference between motivating Marines and raising healthy children. It is never appropriate to shame children, and many parents (Marine and civilian alike) unknowingly shame their children because the shaming things they say and do are so common as to be invisible to them.

Self-esteem grows as a consequence of successfully meeting personal challenges (Branden, 1971, 1983). Enduring the rigors of Marine training and the disciplinary demands of Marine life is a tremendous source of self-esteem, and has helped many thousands of young men and women to develop pride in themselves. The concept is no different with children, but the challenges are very different. Simply following the developmental path—learning to walk, talk, socialize, and regulate their emotional state—is a great challenge for young children. Older children meet daily challenges in school, relationships, and on the athletic field (to name just a few). Shame is a response to failure and setbacks, and it comes from within the child; it does not need to be imposed by anyone else (Nathanson, 1992). The best way to motivate children is to recognize their personal challenges—since what constitutes a challenge differs for each of us—by celebrating their achievements and supporting them through their setbacks.

Marines who have been heavily influenced by the Corps' approach to building esteem may be vulnerable to overdoing it with their nuclear families. The Corps builds the self-esteem of individual Marines by pushing them physically, mentally, and emotionally, as well as resorting to shaming and scapegoating. The primary error that Marines are likely to make with their families is to resort to too many of these same tactics. With children, a little pushing may help, but too much can have devastating consequences. In my opinion, shaming never helps and should be avoided altogether. Since Marines live in a culture of shame versus honor, they are at increased risk of bringing these values into their family lives.

Shame inducement (as opposed to shaming) can play a more appropriate role. It occurs regularly between spouses, though most of us don't stop to realize that is what we are doing. For example, when a spouse says, "You're not going to leave me to clean up this mess all by myself, are you?" he or she is motivating the partner by inducing some shame (or the prospect of some shame if the other spouse were to fail to do his or her share of the work). The line between inducing healthy shame to motivate versus shaming people and damaging their self-esteem is not always clear, and therapists may need to educate Marine families in this regard.

The Family System and the Corps System

I have tried to show how it can be useful to apply family concepts to the Marine Corps family. However, most of what I have described falls under the category of culture; it is primarily the depth of the attachment that makes the Corps more like family. Ultimately, the Corps is only "like family." The Corps and the family are both systems, but they operate somewhat differently. The family system operates in a tightly structured feedback network in which members are simultaneously influencing and reacting to each other (Watzlawick, Beavin & Jackson, 1967; Watzlawick, Weakland & Fisch, 1974). This circular causality occurs in all systems, but the Corps' formal structure places greater controls on the ways in which members influence each other. The formal roles are more far-reaching. For example, rank and role remain active factors whenever Marines interact, even during non-work hours—much more so than in many professional organizations. This is more similar to enduring institutions like the church (or the family), where the strength of formal roles serves to preserve the institution. It is no accident that members of the Corps celebrate the Corps' birthday every November.

This institutionalized independence of the Corps, combined with the strength of its formal roles, produces a situation in which influence between Corps and family is largely unidirectional. The Corps has more influence on the family than the family has on the Corps. This means that spouses and families of Marines must accommodate to the needs of the Corps much more than the Corps is likely to accommodate to their needs. In the words of a wife of a senior NCO, "The Marine Corps is a way of life and not a job. If you can't accept it on those terms, then your marriage is doomed to fail."

Therapists dealing with the interface between family and Corps also must accept many aspects of the Corps' influence as givens and not amenable to intervention. The interplay of influence most amenable to change still occurs between family members. If the family maintains emotional safety, then problems can be addressed as they occur. But if emotional safety is lacking, the family will not operate well as a group and may even be dysfunctional. Safety is typically lost in a circular fashion. One member says or does something that another member perceives as a threat in one of the two realms (attachment and esteem), and the second member's reaction creates a reciprocal threat for the first member (or for another member, who reacts in turn).

For example, a Marine father might criticize or shame his son, leading the boy to perceive this as a threat to his self-esteem. If the boy responds by attacking the father, that might threaten the father's self-esteem. Or the boy might respond by withdrawing, and that could threaten the father's feeling that the relationship is secure (it's not just the children who need to feel their attachments are secure). In the first scenario, the boy responds to an esteem threat in a manner that creates a reciprocal esteem threat for the father. In the second scenario, the boy's response creates an attachment threat for the father. Alternatively, the boy might act out in a manner that creates a threat for one of the other family members. The circularity of the pattern is controlled by these maladaptive responses to a perceived threat. If the boy's reaction creates a reciprocal threat for the father and the father reacts maladaptively, then the father's reaction again creates a threat for the boy, the boy reacts to that, and the pattern continues endlessly.

After a while, practically all of the behaviors that create the perception of a threat are themselves responses to perceived threats. The therapist's goal is to break the cycle by helping members to stop reacting in ways that create the perception of a threat for other members.

Example

Rather than use clinical material, I will describe issues that emerged in my own family life, which I consider to be directly related to my father's service in the Marine Corps during WWII. He was a drill instructor in the states and then served as an infantryman in the First Division in the assaults on Peleliu and Okinawa. Thus, he had large doses of two major components of Marine influence—discipline and combat. As a senior drill instructor, he was responsible for inculcating fledgling Marines with a constant awareness of the fundamental priorities of survival and accomplishing the mission. Combat reinforced those priorities, perhaps loosened his inhibition of aggression, and exposed him to much trauma and loss. His company suffered unprecedented losses on Peleliu, where he was in some of the worst fighting in the Pacific. The war ended for him when he was shot during the final month of fighting on Okinawa. He experienced a great deal of trauma and traumatic loss during his tour of combat in the Pacific.

Like so many men of that generation, my father successfully recovered from his wounds and returned home to raise a family. And like the Corps itself, he manifested some post-traumatic sequelae yet continued to function effectively. But the legacy of his experience definitely influenced our family life—he passed on the lessons learned from combat and from the Corps. He was intent that I grow up strong, able to face fear, and able to defend myself. He taught me to box and to shoot at an early age. He demanded that I demonstrate self-discipline, correcting my posture and inspecting my fingernails before meals just as he had with his recruits. He dressed and carried himself with the discipline of a drill instructor. A Marine drill instructor always looks impeccable: his uniform is freshly pressed;

his shoes are spit shined; he is clean-shaven and his hair is cut high and tight. He is in top physical condition and never looks tired, even as his troops are barely able to keep up with him. He never whines or complains, except to yell at his recruits to tell them what pitiful specimens of humanity they are. He is, in effect, a living model of what the recruits must aspire to become.

When my father gave orders, we were expected to follow them without protest—the Marine way. All discipline starts with self-discipline, and this was a lesson we were taught early on in my family. Sometimes this provided me with an advantage, and sometimes it led to other problems in the family. For example, my father insisted that I eat all I took at meals. Worse yet, he added foods to my plate that I had not chosen and didn't want to eat. We had many power battles at the dinner table where I was not permitted to leave until I had cleaned my plate. In the long run, the Marine lessons in discipline and self-control have served me admirably, but my father's efforts to impose discipline at an early age were sometimes unrealistic.

The impact of his combat experience was never far away. Sometimes he would talk about it with a look of pain and anger on his face. Several times, he walked out of the room expressing disgust at the unrealistic portrayals of combat on the television. Once, as he was driving down the street, a boy pointed a toy gun at our car and my father slammed on the brakes and yelled at the boy. On summer nights, he would sit in the dark for hours at a time, uncommunicative with the rest of the family.

Pretty early in my life, I came to understand the reasons for a lot of my father's behavior. I could see his pain and deep grief; he didn't cry but would talk and look off into the distance in a manner that conveyed his struggle with grief. When I could see the link between his behavior and his combat experience—such as when he reacted to the toy gun—it was easier to accept behavior that might otherwise seem unacceptable. When he was frustrated with me, he sometimes resorted to shaming. He also pushed me physically at times and treated me like a recalcitrant Marine. This was distinctly different from his approach to my sisters—boys were treated like young Marines but girls were to be protected and handled more gently.

At the same time, he was a powerful model. He maintained the bearing and self-discipline of the indestructible drill instructor, and his integrity was admired by the people who knew him. Despite the occasional shaming, he had a feeling for the difference between training troops and raising children, and he rarely mistreated us. Some of the benefits of his Marine experience were highlighted in crisis situations. For example, when we happened upon a terrible automobile accident in Mexico, my father instantly assumed command. He organized the people on the scene—who were just standing around and staring at the victims when we arrived—and he bandaged and provided first aid to several badly injured people. The local papers later referred to him as an American doctor who had saved the people's lives. But, of course, he was no doctor; he was a Marine, who is a particularly good person to have around in a crisis.

My family never developed problems of sufficient magnitude to bring us into contact with the mental health system, so I cannot say how that would have unfolded. Also, my father was discharged from the Marine Corps before I was born, so my family's experience does not represent that of families dealing with the ongoing demands of a Marine on active duty. What my personal experience does convey, to some extent, is the impact of combat and the Marine Corps culture. That impact is reflected in the emphasis on (a) discipline; (b) being mentally, physically, and emotionally tough; (c) doing what is necessary to survive; and (d) accomplishing the mission. The impact is also visible in the avoidance of feelings of grief and vulnerability—though within my family, and surely many Marine families, those kinds of feelings were tolerated among the female members. The increased involvement of women in the Corps may be affecting that gender gap in emotional expressivity, but probably not very much.

CONCLUDING THOUGHTS

I have contended that the Corps' influence is that of both a culture and a family. The values underlying survival and accomplishing the mission are central to understanding the Corps. Similarly, the impact of past trauma and the expectation of more trauma must be appreciated. For Marines who do not have significant bonds outside of the Corps, it is their only family. But for Marines who do have families, the needs of the Corps can collide with the needs of the family. That interface is best handled by accepting that (a) the Corps will not be doing the accommodating, (b) the spouse must be able to operate independently, and (c) emotional safety must be preserved in the family. Despite lengthy separations, the Marine and his or her family must maintain a secure attachment. And, despite living in a world in which shaming and scapegoating are not uncommon, Marines must treat their family members with complete respect. As long as both the Marine and his or her family members maintain a secure attachment and feel highly regarded by one another, the inevitable interface issues should not disrupt the emotional relationships in the family.

Family members must be able to accommodate the needs of the Corps, but their Marines must accommodate the dual worlds of Corps and family. At home, the Marine must be able to be a sensitive spouse and parent. This need to maintain a healthy division between Corps and family was expressed most clearly by the wife of a drill instructor at Parris Island, who told her husband, "When you leave to come home, hang your hat (the drill instructor campaign hat) on the gate. You can get it in the morning when you go back."

ACKNOWLEDGMENTS

Special thanks to William F. Dyer Jr., MSgt, USMC Retired, and his wife Susan, for their many insightful contributions to the manuscript. They are living evidence that a Marine family can thrive and raise healthy children.

REFERENCES

Branden, N. (1971). *The psychology of self-esteem*. New York, NY: Bantam.

Branden, N. (1983). *Honoring the self: Self-esteem and personal transformation*. New York, NY: Bantam.

Catherall, D. R. (2004). *Handbook of stress, trauma and the family*. New York, NY: Brunner-Routledge.

Catherall, D. R. (2007). *Emotional safety: Viewing couples through the lens of affect*. New York, NY: Routledge.

Davis, B. (1991). *Marine: The life of Chesty Puller*. New York, NY: Bantam.

Gold, S. N. (2004). The contextual treatment model. In D. R. Catherall (Ed.), *Handbook of stress, trauma and the family* (pp. 347–365). New York, NY: Brunner-Routledge.

Nathanson, D. L. (1992). *Shame and pride: Affect, sex and the birth of the self*. New York, NY: Norton.

Nelson Goff, B. S. & Schwerdtfeger, K. L. (2004). The systemic impact of traumatized children. In D. R. Catherall (Ed.), *Handbook of stress, trauma and the family* (pp. 179–202). New York, NY: Brunner-Routledge.

Rooks, Aaron, Cpl. (January 7, 2009). Infantrymen bring combat knowledge. In *Today in the Military, Marine Corps News*. Retrieved from Military.com

Thomason, J. W. (1926). *Fix bayonets!* New York, NY: Charles Scribner's Sons.

Watzlawick, P., Beavin, J. H. & Jackson, D. (1967). *Pragmatics of human communication*. New York, NY: Norton.

Watzlawick, P., Weakland, J. & Fisch, R. (1974). *Change: Principles of problem resolution*. New York, NY: Norton.

6 Systems Approaches with Air Force Members and Their Families

A Focus on Trauma

Joseph R. Herzog, Craig Boydston, and James D. Whitworth

CONTENTS

INTRODUCTION

Established in 1947, the U.S. Air Force is a unique entity among military departments. The mission of the Air Force is to "fly, fight, and win ... in air, space, and cyberspace" (United States Air Force [USAF], 2009). To accomplish this mission there are over 300,000 individuals on active duty in the Air Force with another 200,000 or more serving in the Air Force Reserve and Air National Guard. The Air Force retains and recruits a different type of military member than the other services employ. Given their primary focus on gaining and maintaining air and space superiority, along with ensuring cyberspace dominance, most Air Force members manage highly technical roles to accomplish this mission. Extensive initial and ongoing technical training is required for nearly all Air Force enlisted and officer positions. The vast majority of Air Force members are employed full time in computer, avionics, aerospace mechanics/weaponry, or medical functions. Although the Air Force has strategically sought to re-focus each member on a role as a military war fighter, Airmen generally think of their Air Force Specialty Code (AFSC) as their primary function. They pursue and obtain specialized training and higher education degrees more than members within the other services. These individuals are heavily involved with Operation Enduring Freedom (OEF), Operation Iraqi Freedom (OIF), as well as other missions around the world. Deployments for OEF and OIF have appreciably impacted Air Force members and their families. This chapter highlights the stress and strain of deployments, especially those to combat zones, for Air Force families, including those that occur after redeployment and reunion.

HISTORY OF AIR FORCE MENTAL HEALTH

The Air Force implemented social welfare programming as early as the 1950s (Daley, 1999). Mental health workers can be found in a variety of Air Force institutions such as hospitals and correctional facilities working with service members and their families. One of the earliest programs was Project Children Have a Potential addressing the needs of Air Force families whose members have special needs. This program later became part of the Department of Defense's Exceptional Family Member Program, which now encompasses the Air Force Special Needs Identification Assignment Coordination Program. In the mid-1970s the Air Force established the Child Advocacy Program to deal with child abuse. This advocacy program began to also address spouse maltreatment and became known as the Family Advocacy Program (FAP) in the 1980s. FAP focuses on the prevention and treatment of family maltreatment through outreach and prevention programs, new parent support and counseling, assessment, and treatment interventions.

The Air Force has also been active in treating substance misuse, abuse, and dependence among its members with the first inpatient treatment program opening in 1966 (Daley, 1999). A yearly average of 5300 alcohol-related incidents occur for Air Force individuals (Ogle, 2009). Alcohol misuse is involved in 33 percent of suicides, 57 percent of sexual assaults, and 28 percent of domestic violence cases (Ogle, 2009). Public intoxication and underage drinking are also notable alcohol-related incidents. Ogle (2009) described the 0-0-1-3 Alcohol Prevention program initiated at a USAF base at the 2009 Hidden Casualties of War Symposium. The 0-0-1-3 program was aimed at the individual, base, and community levels and met with impressive results, significantly reducing alcohol-related incidents and improving workplace productivity.

Air Force mental health providers have partnered with on- and off-base helping agencies, installation leaders, and informal support networks to build formal and informal community connections and resiliency (Huebner, Mancini, Bowen & Orthner, 2009). This partnership is fostered through the use of two specific committees (i.e., the Integrated Delivery System [IDS] committee and the Community

Action Information Board [CAIB]) on each installation, Major Command, and at Headquarters USAF. The IDS is the "working group" of helping agencies, while the CAIB formulates policy and interfaces with higher levels of leadership. The drive for promoting such collaboration is grounded in the belief that when agencies, leaders, and others work together they can build a community's capacity for managing stressful events such as deployments (Huebner et al., 2009).

Air Force deployments in support of OEF and OIF have led to increased mental health issues in Airmen. Mental Health Advisory Team (MHAT) V (2008) recently reported on the mental health status of military members serving in Iraq. Members deployed to Iraq and Afghanistan are at increased risk for acute stress disorder, depression, and anxiety. Air Force members, and their spouses, report that deployments negatively impact their family, personal, and professional lives (2008 Air Force Community Assessment). They also describe feeling less supported by leadership and are less satisfied with the Air Force after a deployment (Air Force Community Assessment, 2008).

Air Force members are increasingly employed in direct combat roles. They are also more frequently deployed to OIF and OEF areas where they are directly exposed to mortar or rocket blasts, improvised explosive devices (IEDs), or providing medical care to wounded military members and civilians. These members who are directly exposed to such threats, and those indirectly exposed (e.g., on a base that regularly has mortar and rocket attacks) report higher percentages of post-traumatic stress symptoms than members who have not deployed since September 11, 2001 (Air Force Community Assessment, 2008). Combat exposure has been a strong predictor of post-traumatic stress disorder (PTSD) in veterans (Foy & Card, 1987). PTSD rates were significantly higher for Marines and soldiers after combat duty in Iraq (Hoge et al., 2004). Soldiers who experience high levels of combat were three times more likely to have had mental problems when compared to those who have low levels of combat experience (MHAT IV, 2006). Hoge et al. (2005) indicated that 17 percent of troops deployed to Iraq experienced symptoms of PTSD. Individuals with PTSD have been more likely to have a substance abuse disorder than those without PTSD (Regier et al., 1990). Between 36 percent and 50 percent of individuals seeking treatment for substance abuse met criteria for PTSD (Brady, Back & Coffey, 2004; Brown, Recupero & Stout, 1995). Deployment length and frequency were risk factors for mental health and well-being in soldiers deployed longer than 6 months, and those who have deployed to Iraq more than once are at greater risk for problems (MHAT V, 2008). In addition to PTSD, traumatic brain injury (TBI) has been common to Iraq war veterans. Combat veterans have experienced irritability, memory problems, headache, and difficulty concentrating as a result of the blast explosions (Hoge et al., 2008). Air Force suicide rates, 9.9/100K (FY 97-07) and 9.7/100K (FY 08), even among deployed/redeployed members, are lower than the rates reported by the Army and Marines (Talking Paper on Air Force Suicide Prevention Program, 2008). Compounding these issues are a lack of access to and a continuing stigma from seeking mental health care.

AIR FORCE FAMILY LITERATURE REVIEW

The literature on Air Force families is scarce and much less is known about these families when compared to other military families. Some of the earliest work is found in the Families in Blue series (Orthner & Bowen, 1980; Orthner, Bowen, Brown, Orthner & Mancini, 1980; Orthner, Bowen, Mancini & Robinson, 1982). In *Families in Blue: Phase II*, Orthner and Bowen (1980) found families stationed in the Pacific Air Force (PACAF; i.e., Asia, Alaska, Guam, and Hawaii) to be much like those in the Continental United States (CONUS) and Europe. The authors found no differences in these families on issues of marital stress, parental adjustment, family support needs, or general support for the Air Force. Among the differences were the number of Asian-American marriages, lower levels of spousal employment, and higher dependency on Air Force base agencies and services.

Work and family stress has been examined for effects on Air Force personnel. Single parenting has been identified as a source of stress dating back to the early 1980s with family stability, childcare, and work performance as important concerns (Orthner et al., 1980). Single-parent, active-duty Airmen have been found to successfully adjust to the demands of an Air Force career and single parenting (Bowen & Orthner, 1986). These single parents reported satisfaction both with their careers and with their relationships with their children.

Efforts to build military installations' community capacity (i.e., interagency collaboration and leadership involvement) have been found to help Air Force members and their families adapt and cope with military stressors (Bowen, Martin & Ware, 2004). In a 2003 Air Force-wide survey, married members' positive views of their community capacity directly affected self-reported symptoms of depression (Bowen et al., 2004). Knox, Litts, Talcott, Feig & Caine (2003) reported lower suicide rates when Air Force communities implanted changes to foster community capacity as part of the Air Force Suicide Prevention Program.

FACTORS UNIQUE TO AIR FORCE FAMILIES

The average age of Air Force officers is 35, whereas the average age of enlisted Airmen is 29 (Air Force Personnel Center, 2009). Women compose almost 20 percent of the Air Force. Active duty Airmen support over 440,000 family members with 59 percent being married and just over 17,000 being dual military couples (Air Force Personnel Center, 2009). Twenty percent of the Air Force serves overseas.

The Air Force culture has been described as having several distinct classes (Daley, 1999). Among the most prestigious members of this class system are the aircrew, especially pilots, whose designation as mission-essential allows for special benefits. Officers compose another grouping within the class system with higher ranking officers afforded more privilege and responsibility. Enlisted personnel compose a third group. The enlisted corps is made up of non-commissioned officers and lower ranking enlisted personnel. A significant portion of

Air Force enlisted members are well educated, with many having bachelors or masters degrees. The last group consists of the family members. Daley (1999) describes family members as essential but peripheral in that "the family should be highly visible as a nurturing support system but as peripheral as possible with any life crises" (p. 251).

Air Force families face the stressors typical to military families in general. These stressors include periods of separation between service members and their families as well as frequent geographic relocation. Dual military families face the possibility of separate assignments. Spouses of military members may have difficulty gaining employment after a geographic move and find their career trajectories interrupted.

METHODS

The therapists in the following cases demonstrate multiple approaches based on the presenting issues. They operate from this eclectic point of view due to the vastly different problems they see. One of social work's core values is to start where the client is, and eclecticism lends itself well to this value. The following cases were chosen to exemplify the cases mental health providers might typically see when providing services to Air Force members and their families. These cases contain multiple issues and the therapists tailor interventions in light of these factors.

The first case, the Smiths, occurs as Ms. Smith is preparing for deployment. The Smiths have a troubled relationship complicated by an upcoming deployment. The therapist utilized guided imagery for the trauma symptoms Ms. Smith was experiencing. Guided imagery has been found to be helpful in reducing nightmares in trauma survivors (Germain et al., 2004). It is an experiential technique used for stress management and it promotes relaxation, self-awareness, and uses the power of the imagination for self-healing. A type of exposure therapy was also used with Ms. Smith to reduce trauma symptoms. Ms. Smith was experiencing a great amount of unresolved guilt in addition to fear and anxiety stemming from her previous deployments. The therapist utilized a writing exercise to both desensitize Ms. Smith as well as to help her work through unresolved grief and the associated guilt. After reducing the trauma symptoms the therapy then focused on relationship issues in Ms. Smith's life.

The next case, SSgt Rodriquez, portrays trauma Air Force members are exposed to and the type of treatment available to them during deployment. In addition to a referral to a primary care physician for medication evaluation, SSgt Rodriquez underwent a course of brief exposure therapy utilizing audio recordings of his trauma history and relaxation breathing. Exposure therapy has been found to be effective in the treatment of forward-deployed troops (Cigrang, Peterson & Schobitz, 2005) as well as veterans with chronic PTSD (Rauch et al., 2009). SSgt Rodriquez dealt with his irrational guilt through cognitive behavioral technique (CBT). CBT has also been proven to be an effective treatment for PTSD symptoms (Harvey, Bryant & Tarrier, 2003). SSgt Rodriquez also benefitted from a psychoeducational intervention on the effects of trauma symptoms both for himself and for his family, and has been given referral information should he need services upon redeployment and reunion with his family. Behavioral family therapy may be helpful for those with combat-related PTSD, especially in regard to problem solving (Glynn, Randolph, Randolph & Foy, 1999).

Lastly, the Palmers are dealing with trauma symptoms many years after the deployment in which the trauma occurred. Mr. Palmer, a disabled veteran, presented with chronic PTSD symptoms as well as other serious health concerns. His wife presented with generalized anxiety and appeared enmeshed with Mr. Palmer. Spouses of chronic PTSD combat veterans have been found to have enmeshed relationships with their husbands, especially concerning their emotional lives (Dekel, Goldblatt, Keidar, Solomon & Polliack, 2005). Mr. Palmer was unable to discuss his trauma history in individual therapy. The therapist then enlisted Mrs. Palmer in the therapeutic process. Mrs. Palmer was a catalyst in helping Mr. Palmer to begin to deal with his trauma. The Palmers began to work through Mr. Palmer's trauma history in conjoint therapy. Mr. Palmer then continued to work on his trauma history individually. The therapist used a dual approach in working with the Palmers, focusing on the trauma history while recognizing strengths both possessed. The strengths-based approach is a therapeutic technique designed to empower people by focusing on their inherent strengths (Saleebey, 1996). In the case of the Palmers, the strengths-based approach helped them cope with the overwhelming problems of disability, chronic PTSD, and terminal illness.

CASE EXAMPLES

The Smiths

The Smiths are a military family consisting of a 24-year-old active duty Air Force (ADAF) husband and his 28-year-old wife who are separated. Ms. Smith is a nurse in the Air Guard facing her third deployment to Iraq. This case exemplifies an Air Force member and her spouse dealing with post-trauma.

Ms. Smith sought therapy because she has been having intrusive memories of her work as an operating room (OR) nurse while in Iraq. These memories are interfering with her ability to work or rest. She had been coping "OK" with her stress from two previous tours in the war zone until recently when she began experiencing weight loss, irritability, and sleep disturbance. She recently attempted to view a movie in which a violent military scene was portrayed. She had to leave the theater. She then began having nightmares and daytime flashbacks to the emergency medical scenes while she was in Iraq. She also reports difficulty feeling comfortable around men, particularly men wearing Muslim robes and headwear. She is irritable while in training and fears being sent back to the war. She has bad memories of her childhood. Her father was a substance abuser. As the oldest child in her family she had to take care of her younger siblings. She coped by "cleaning constantly."

During the therapy sessions she talked about her difficult conversations with her estranged husband. She reported having difficulty setting boundaries with him. She felt guilty because she had submitted divorce papers. She was unable to sleep.

She continued to report intrusive thoughts about her service in Iraq with injured and dying soldiers who would often ask her if they were going to live or die.

Ms. Smith's treatment followed in two stages. First, I introduced her to the deep relaxation/guided imagery technique to help her manage her anxiety. Once she was relaxed (breathing properly, muscles relaxed, hands warm, etc.) I began the guided imagery with a request she imagine herself as an animal in the wild and create a scene including that animal. Animals such as wolves, horses, lionesses, etc., have some common characteristics in that they have been given mastery over their environments and due to size, senses, etc., can keep themselves safe and secure. The whole exercise takes about 15 to 20 minutes. Then we debrief. I ask her to imagine a scene in the near future when she might experience those same feelings of safety, control, and security that she experienced in the guided imagery exercise.

For example, "where would you be, what would you be doing, thinking, feeling?" If she can complete this exercise then I move to the second stage. Ms. Smith was able to do the exercise. As I recall her symbol was the lioness. If she were unable to imagine a scene in the near future that created the security, etc., needed I would go back and ask her to consider choosing another animal symbol that might work better for her. The next stage involved revisiting the traumatic event as a type of desensitization but also to look for unresolved guilt. She felt guilty about not being able to tell the wounded soldiers they would be OK or if she did and they did not recover she would be haunted by the memory. At this point I worked on the "forgiveness" process involving writing letters to the soldiers asking forgiveness, and writing letters from the soldiers giving forgiveness. These two interventions were designed to address the PTSD and by her report were useful. She reported a significant reduction in anxiety, intrusive thoughts, and nightmare activity. Once the PTSD symptoms were under control, Ms. Smith began to address relationships in her life. Specifically, boundary setting became an issue as she discussed her tendency to be drawn to abusive, self-centered, and controlling males.

The following is an excerpt from a session:

Client: What is it about me? … I always fall for the wrong sort of guy.

Therapist: What do you mean?

Client: Only that it seems like the guys I am attracted to become abusive later in the relationship.

Therapist: How so?

Client: You know that my husband was abusive … especially if he had been drinking … just like my Dad was. … Even after everything he (her husband) put me through I still feel terrible about serving him with divorce papers.

Therapist: You seem to have a strong desire to help others … where you seem to miss the mark is in setting boundaries.

Client: Yeah … I know.

Therapist: Let's talk about how you can set appropriate boundaries in relationships.

In this excerpt, the therapist reaches for clarification and specificity, then reframes the client's codependent behaviors as a strength (desire to help others) while offering a solution (setting boundaries). Once she got this piece in place she did much better.

SSgt Rodriquez

SSgt Rodriquez is an Air Force Reserve member from Alabama currently completing his third tour in Iraq. He came to the Combat Stress Clinic to seek help at the request of his supervisor who told him that he needed to learn "anger management skills" so that he can get along better with his co-workers. He reported having ongoing headaches, intrusive memories, hypervigilance, irritability, insomnia, and nightmares. His nightmares generally focused on an incident that occurred several months earlier during the middle of the night. A mortar hit a portable bathroom just outside his quarters. One of his fellow Airmen was in the bathroom when the mortar hit, causing him to lose his leg. SSgt Rodriquez was one of the first people to try to help the injured Airman. He remembers being very angry at the others who responded because "they just stood around looking shocked and didn't really help him."

SSgt Rodriquez works as a Security Forces member. His unit's mission is to escort truck convoys throughout the surrounding region. During one of their recent convoys his vehicle was partially destroyed by an IED. He was not hit by any debris from the blast, but the shock wave caused him to lose consciousness for about 15 seconds. This was the fourth IED blast that he had been exposed to during all his tours in Iraq. His headaches have been persistent ever since the blast. He had seen an Army medical provider within his unit who told him that he had a moderate concussion (mild traumatic brain injury or mTBI) from this most recent blast. SSgt Rodriquez is quite concerned about getting pain relief for his headaches and he would like help with his irritability. His father, whom he described as an alcoholic, was in the Army in Vietnam and had rather significant PTSD that he never sought treatment for. SSgt Rodriquez stated early on in his treatment that he wanted help so that he would not "turn out like Dad."

SSgt Rodriquez was initially referred to a primary care physician who treated his headache pain with Topamax (topiramate) and initiated the use of an antidepressant medication (Zoloft [sertraline]). He then was released from normal work activities for 1 week to obtain appropriate rest in order to recover from his concussion (mTBI). He was treated using brief exposure therapy. This included first helping him understand the purpose and benefits of exposure therapy followed by training on how to use relaxation breathing techniques to decrease his feelings of autonomic arousal. He then participated in imaginal exposure employing audio recordings of his most traumatic experiences, which centered primarily on the incident where his fellow Airman was harmed in the portable toilet. His first recordings were generally vague and addressed mostly minimal facts about the traumatic event. He continually (three to five times per day) listened to these recordings on his MP3 player. Over time he began to add significantly more details about the event including what the injured Airman's body looked like, the sounds (i.e., yelling and screaming) that he had heard, and how he felt (i.e., angry and scared) throughout the incident.

During the third week of treatment he agreed to participate in an in vivo exposure session during which he and his therapist revisited the bathroom area where his fellow Airman was harmed. During the imaginal and in vivo sessions SSgt Rodriquez described some initial hesitancy to go through the exposure treatment. However, as he started to experience reductions in his hypervigilance, nightmares, and anger about the incident he significantly increased his participation. Cognitive behavioral therapy techniques were used to address SSgt Rodriquez's irrational guilt (cognitive distortion) after another Airman was more seriously injured in the most recent IED blast. This included having him list and describe any facts he had to support his conclusion that he might have been able to help the Airman from being harmed along with the facts contrary to this conclusion. He was only able to list one or two facts to support his feelings of guilt, while he had a much longer list detailing his inability to stop the event from occurring or changing how others responded. SSgt Rodriquez was also asked to imagine he had been the Airman injured in the incident. Would he have been angry at others who lived near him? He denied that he would have been angry at them, but he persistently believed that he would have been mad at those who did not quickly respond to incident.

SSgt Rodriquez experienced a significant reduction in his headaches, which helped him to get more sleep. His mood slowly became less irritable over the 2 months that he participated in treatment. He was seen by his mental health provider three to four times per week. SSgt Rodriquez reviewed psychoeducational material on trauma, trauma symptoms, and its impact on both himself and his family members. SSgt Rodriquez noted that his wife was extremely concerned for his safety and well-being and that she was very anxious to the point of panic when they were unable to communicate. He was informed that family members can suffer secondary trauma symptoms and may benefit from behavioral family therapy and was advised to have his wife talk to a chaplain about her concerns. He was given referral information for individual and family counseling should he or his family need further services. At treatment closure, he reported having far fewer nightmares, limited hypervigilance, and significantly more hope that he would be able to successfully return to his family and police officer job back in Alabama.

Mr. Palmer

Mr. Palmer is a disabled veteran who decided to come for therapy about a year ago to deal with past trauma as well as a tendency to "fall emotionally after something good happens." He described his wartime trauma and an incident in the early

1990s when he was shot by sniper, which led to the eventual amputation of his right leg below the knee. He was in a coma for 3 months after being shot, spent the next 14 months in a hospital, and then the next 5 years in a wheelchair prior to getting a prosthesis that worked for him. Other symptoms included not being able to "get started" on a project or to finish a project he started. He reported restless sleep with frequent recurring nightmares and intrusive memories of wartime events.

He lives with his wife, whom he met and married after the events mentioned above. She is described and describes herself as his only emotional supporter. Mrs. Palmer was enmeshed with Mr. Palmer, especially concerning with trauma symptoms. She was impacted significantly by night terrors and deteriorating health. Her symptoms took the form of generalized anxiety and she endured many sleepless nights, social isolation, and his distrust of and lack of contact with extended family.

Mr. Palmer talked about one intrusive, recurring memory involving him and his unit when on patrol. An incoming rocket-propelled grenade (RPG) killed the man standing next to him. He expressed guilt that he couldn't have given better warning to protect the members of his squad. He stated he often feels like he is trapped in a sandpit in which he tries to pull himself out but keeps slipping back to the bottom. He worries that he might "turn out like my parents" who were both alcoholic. (He denies abusing substances.) He expressed extreme distrust of the government. He reported some past suicidal feelings. If it hadn't been for his wife he believes he would have committed suicide. He suffers from chronic pain, a chronic bacterial infection, and other health conditions that he knows will shorten his life. He often watches the military and history channels, and his wife wonders if some of his symptoms might be triggered by these shows. She stated he often refuses to talk about his past traumatic experiences.

Interventions with the Palmers took the form of a strengths-based approach. Mr. Palmer explored the many strengths he had. First and foremost of these was his ability to endure chronic pain and health-related issues. Mr. Palmer provided a positive example for those who knew him as a patriot and a loving husband. An additional strength Mr. Palmer identified was his ability to establish a sense of safety and security in and around his home. Mr. Palmer was able to draw on these strengths as he continued to endure chronic pain and acknowledged the reality of his terminal condition. Similarly, Mrs. Palmer explored strengths she possessed as a loving wife with a sophisticated knowledge of health-related issues as well as being a person capable of providing a great deal of emotional support. Mr. Palmer was challenged on several beliefs he held including the view that he could have done more to control the situations that led to the death or injury of his men. Mr. Palmer discussed these past incidents and believed that there will always be "remnants" of trauma to deal with. These interventions occurred over the course of a year and became apparent toward the end of treatment as the client experienced symptom relief.

CONCLUSION

This chapter provides mental health providers working with Air Force members and their families with a fuller understanding of the issues particular to the Air Force. While a distinct service, the Air Force has much in common with other military branches, including exposure to traumatic situations. Whether air crew, officers, or enlisted, Air Force members deployed in support of the global war on terror are at risk of exposure to traumatic situations. While the literature on Air Force members and their families is not broad, it is important for mental health personnel working with Airmen and their families to be well grounded in their culture and climate.

This chapter highlights Air Force mental systems, Air Force family literature, and provides case examples of the stresses and strains of Airmen deployed to OEF and OIF areas and their families. An eclectic group of interventions was designed by the therapists in this chapter to start where the client was impacted. The Smiths were an estranged couple facing an upcoming deployment; for SSgt Rodriquez, it was a traumatic incident that occurred during deployment; while the Palmers struggled to deal with long-standing combat-related trauma and health issues. Mental health workers play a critical role with Air Force members and their families experiencing the impact of deployment-related trauma, and this chapter provides a focus for that work.

REFERENCES

Air Force Community Assessment (2008).

Air Force Personnel Center (2009). *Air Force personnel demographics*. Retrieved on July 11, 2009 from http://www.afpc.randolph.af.mil/library/airforce personnelstatistics.asp

Bowen, G., Martin, J. & Ware, W. (2004). Community capacity and the health of married active duty members. In G. L. Bowen (Chair), *Community capacity and the health of military families*. Symposium conducted at the National Council on Family Relations 66th Annual Conference, Orlando, FL.

Bowen, G. & Orthner, D. (1986). Single parents in the U.S. Air Force. *Family Relations,*

Cigrang, J. A., Peterson, A. L. & Schobitz, R. P. (2005). Three American troops in Iraq: Evaluation of a brief exposure treatment for the secondary prevention of combat-related PTSD. *Pragmatic Case Studies in Psychotherapy, 1*, 1–25.

Daley, J. (1999). *Social work in the military*. New York, NY: Routledge.

Dekel, R., Goldblatt, H., Keidar, M., Solomon, Z. & Polliack, M. (2005). Being a wife of a veteran with posttraumatic stress disorder. *Family Relations, 54*, 24–36.

Germain, A., Krakow, B., Faucher, B., Zandra, A., Nielsen, T., Hollifield, M. & Koss. (2004) Increased mastery elements associated with imagery rehearsal treatment for nightmares in sexual assault survivors with PTSD. *Dreaming, 14*(4), 195–206.

Glynn, S., Randolph, S., Randolph, E. & Foy, D. (1999). A test of behavioral family therapy to augment exposure for combat-related posttraumatic stress disorder. *Journal of Counseling and Clinical Psychology, 67*(2), 243–251.

Harvey, A., Bryant, R. & Tarrier, N. (2003). Cognitive behavior therapy for posttraumatic stress disorder. *Clinical Psychology Review, 23*, 501–522.

Hoge, C. W., McGurk, D., Thomas, J. L., Cox, A. L., Engel, C. C. & Castro, C. A. (2008). Mild traumatic brain injury in U.S. soldiers returning from Iraq. *The New England Journal of Medicine*, *358*(5), 453–463.

Hoyt, G. B. (2006). Integrated mental health within operational units: Opportunities and challenges. *Military Psychology, 18,* 309–320.

Huebner, A., Mancini, J., Bowen, G. & Orthner, D. (2009). Shadowed by war: Building community capacity to support military families. *Family Relations, 58*, 216–228.

Knox, K., Litts, D. Talcott, W., Feig, J. & Caine, E. (2003). Risk of suicide and related adverse outcomes after exposure to a suicide prevention programme in the US Air Force: Cohort study. *British Medical Journal, 327*, 1376-1380.

Ogle, A. (2009). *Post-deployment(s) alcohol use and abuse: Renewed freedom vs. maladaptive coping*. Presented at the *2nd Deployment Mental Health Symposium Hidden Casualties of War: Moving to Solutions.*

Orthner, D. & Bowen, G. (1980). *Families in blue: Implications of a study of married and single parent families in the U.S. Air Force*. Greensboro, NC: Family Research and Analysis, Inc.

Orthner, D., Bowen, G., Brown, R., Orthner, B. & Mancini, J. (1980). *Families in blue: A study of married and single parent families in the U.S. Air Force.* Washington, DC: Office of the Chaplains, USAF.

Orthner, D., Bowen, G., Mancini, J. & Robinson, C. (1982). *Families in blue: Phase II insights from Air Force families in the Pacific*. Washington, DC: Office of Chief of Chaplains, USAF Bolling Air Force Base.

Rauch, S., Defever, E., Favorite, T., Duroe, A., Garrity, C., Martis, B. & Liberzon, I. (2009). Prolonged exposure for PTSD in a Veterans Health Administration PTSD clinic. *Journal of Traumatic Stress, 22*(1). 60–64.

Saleebey, D. (1996). The strengths perspective in social work practice: Extensions and cautions. *Social Work, 41*(3), 296–305.

Talking Paper on Air Force Suicide Prevention Program (2008). *United States Air Force Suicide Prevention Program.* Retrieved on July 11, 2009 from http://afspp.afms.mil/idc/groups/public/documents/afms/ctb_101896.pdf

United States Air Force (USAF) (2009). *United States Air Force mission.* Retrieved on March 4, 2009 from http://www.airforce.com/learn-about/our-mission/

7 The Use of Emotionally Focused Couples Therapy with Military Couples and Families

Lance Sneath and Kathryn D. Rheem

CONTENTS

INTRODUCTION

Combat-related trauma and the impacts of deployment have once again been pushed to the fore due to the current global war on terror. Like shell shock from the World Wars and combat fatigue from the Vietnam War, combat-related psychological symptoms have now impacted 31 percent to 38 percent of our post-combat deployed military service members (Munsey, 2007). Of those with psychological symptoms, 17 percent were diagnosed with post-traumatic stress disorder (PTSD), major depression, or generalized anxiety (Hoge et al., 2004). Typically, the military service member with PTSD or combat stress is treated individually (APA Presidential Task Force on Military Deployment Services for Youth, Families, and Service Members, 2007), despite the known negative relational impacts of deployment and combat stress on service members and their spouses and children (Sherman, Zanotti & Jones, 2005). Just as deployment and combat stress are associated with mental health disorders such as PTSD, depression, anxiety, suicidal tendencies, and substance abuse (Hoge, Terhakopian, Castro, Messer & Engel, 2007), additionally, marital distress often increases (Basham, 2008).

To date, focus on the impacts of deployment and combat trauma on the soldier's marital relationship and family has been sparse (Basham, 2008). If the echoes of battle are not contained, the result for military service members and their spouses is increased impact of trauma resulting from deployment and combat. In a securely attached relationship, spouses become protective factors against the echoes of battle and help the soldiers contain and ameliorate the stressors of deployment and combat. In an insecurely attached marriage, deployment and combat exacerbate the lack of relationship safety and connection, and typically increase distrust, vigilance, and fear (Basham, 2008). Most of the mental health services provided for soldiers and their families are based on cognitive-behavioral interventions (Armstrong, Best & Domenici, 2006; Riggs, 2000), which fail to address the soldiers' marital and familial relationships as an attachment bond. Not only does the soldier bring the battle home, but the battle lives on within the couple's relationship and threatens their bond.

Additionally, the need for systemic understanding of the impacts—how deployment to a war zone and combat exposure impact the primary relationship of those serving—is growing, and thus is the focus of this chapter. Clinicians need to understand the service member's marriage and its relationship dynamics, not just the service member individually, in order to provide effective clinical interventions.

EMOTIONALLY FOCUSED COUPLES THERAPY

Emotionally focused therapy (EFT; Greenberg & Johnson, 1985) is an approach based on John Bowlby's (1969) attachment theory. Attachment theory "addresses how relational partners deal with their emotions, process and organize information about the self and others, and communicate with loved ones" (Johnson, 2004, p. 36). Attachment theory—as a theory of relationships—integrates with systems theory (Bertalanffy, 1968). When viewing relationships from a systemic perspective, relationship dynamics can be seen within the relationship context while patterns of communication and interactions are the focus. From a systemic perspective, "emotions link self and system" (Johnson, 2004, p. 15). To a lesser degree, EFT also integrates experiential and humanistic theory (Rogers, 1951) and structural theory (Minuchin & Fishman, 1981). Since the focus of EFT is on emotions, which are viewed as the leading elements in couple dynamics, EFT could be particularly well suited for military couples facing the echoes of battle and distress resulting from post-traumatic stress.

THE EMOTIONAL CYCLE OF DEPLOYMENT AND ADULT ATTACHMENT THEORY

Researchers have observed an emotional cycle to the deployment process that coincides with the deployment cycle (Pincus, House, Christenson & Adler, 2006). This emotional cycle is correlated with the three military stages of pre-deployment, deployment, and post-deployment. The three stages are further understood in a seven-stage emotional model as anticipation of loss and detachment and withdrawal in the pre-deployment stage; emotional disorganization, recovery and reorganization, and anticipation of homecoming for the deployment stage; and reorganization of the marital bond, and reintegration and stabilization for the post-deployment stage.

The current body of research supports the correlation of a cycle of emotional turbulence that parallels the cycle of military deployment with families. The relationship between emotion and attachment is firmly established in attachment theory (Johnson, 2004), and this explains the turbulent effects upon the marriages and families of service members as they move through the deployment cycle. A recent study by Faber, Willerton, Clymer, MacDermid & Weiss (2008) showed ambiguity among family members of reservists regarding both the perceived presence and absence of their soldier family member during the various cycles of deployment. McLeland and Sutton (2005) also found in their study that men's marital satisfaction dropped significantly by simply receiving orders for deployment. The Walter Reed Army Institute for Research Land Combat Study (Hoge et al., 2007) found nearly 20 percent of the soldiers reporting problems in their marriages after a deployment to Iraq.

During the pre-deployment stage, service members and their family members begin to experience a deep sense of anticipation of loss and detachment due to the impending deployment. The marriage relationship is most often the first place this is felt, and one or both spouses may begin to shut down and withdraw—especially if they are still recovering from a previous and recent deployment. Due to some of the frequent deployments associated with the global war on terror, some military members and spouses acknowledge that they find it difficult to get close to each other between deployments because of the anticipated pain of being separated again. This often establishes a negative interactional cycle in marriages of one being the pursuer and the other a withdrawer, or both partners shut down and withdraw, accepting loneliness and isolation as safer options. Emotionally focused therapy, which is especially effective in helping couples identify and overcome negative interactional cycles to achieve secure attachment, is especially effective for this reason.

During the deployment stage, service members and their family members initially experience emotional disorganization for several weeks to several months. Eventually, the military family reorganizes to find a sense of emotional stability and reorganization. These periods of emotional reorganization are times of particular vulnerability for spouses to pursue in affairs, and for children to find peer friendships that could be a negative influence on them. Most often, military service members form secure bonds with fellow service members, and family members strengthen bonds with family and friends in order to experience the companionship and comfort of healthy attachment. As the end of the deployment nears, the service member and family members begin to anticipate the homecoming, and oscillate from excitement to anxiety as they sense things are not the same, and realize that adjustments will be required for them to reunite after the homecoming.

The post-deployment stage is a more challenging time of adjustment for attachment relationships than most people realize. Data gathered by the Walter Reed Institute for Research Land Combat Study (Hoge et al., 2007) showed soldiers experiencing an increase in marital relationship distress for the first 12 months after the deployment. The re-organization and renewal of the bond is a significant challenge due the nuance of emotional intimacy involved in couple attachment relationships. Much of marital communication is emotional and nonverbal in nature, and after 12 or more months apart, partners find they frequently misinterpret each other emotionally. The emotional repertoire required of service members deployed in combat is very adaptive for the lethal environment that calls for vigilance and a highly regulated emotional response in order to accomplish the required missions in this lethal and uncertain environment. Spouses who remain at home, on the other hand, adapt as necessary to their new demands as they change their emotional repertoire to primary caregivers to children, and learn to lean more on friends for emotional support. This "emotional re-wiring" of the couple system is not easily sorted out or even recognized when couples first re-unite after re-deployment, and frequently results in a great number of negative interpretations as to the nature of what is happening in the relationship.

The miscommunication of emotional and nonverbal cues for couples in the re-integration stage can escalate into a negative cycle that requires therapeutic intervention to help the couple re-connect and get back "in sync" with the very sophisticated emotional communication that intimate partners share with each other. Recent studies show that deployed service members who have PTSD-related symptoms experience a greatly restrictive range of emotion and tend to use a great deal of emotional energy trying to regulate and suppress emotions (Litz, Orsillo, Kaloupek & Weathers, 2000; Miller & Litz, 2004). This normally affects the relationship by the non-deployed spouse interpreting the seeming lack of emotion as lack of interest and the couple begins to go through a fear-driven cycle with the pursuing spouse believing the re-deployed spouse may have stopped caring for him or her and the relationship. Accusations or suspicions of unfaithfulness often accompany this negative interactional cycle due to the perceived emotional aloofness of the re-deployed service member. This often puts even greater emotional distance between couples, and it is very difficult for them to see the correlation between their negative interactional cycle and the impact the deployment had on their relationship bond through all the "emotional re-wiring." The EFT therapist helps couples sort out this negative cycle by serving as an "emotional linguist" as couples in session experience emotional clarity and understand the changes the emotional cycle of deployment brought to their relationship. This reframe of the emotional cycle of deployment as the culprit that emotionally re-wired the couple then helps facilitate taking steps toward each other in session where they experience the deep emotional connection they are longing for in their marriage.

The post-deployment stage is completed when the family is re-integrated, accommodating all the changes, stable in emotional expression and connection with each other, and having a sense of resilience from the entire experience. More will be said later in this chapter about the relationships with the children, but from a structural therapy point of view (Minuchin & Fishman, 1981), the children are most secure and responsive when the parental relationship is securely connected and emotionally responsive. The EFT therapist offers these couples struggling in the deployment cycle a road map to secure an emotionally responsive love. The skills of working with emotion, and the lens of attachment relationship to understand the emotional cycle of deployment, can be a real lifeline to hurting and confused military couples.

WHEN COMBAT STRESS COMES HOME

Movies like Sylvester Stallone's *Rambo* and Chuck Norris' *Missing in Action* series stereotype combat-related PTSD to the degree that anyone would recognize it—if it only looked like it does in the movies! When combat stress comes home, it often seems to have disappeared, at least initially. Many combat-stress-related mental health problems seem to have no immediate connection to a deployment that the service member returned home from months ago, when all appeared just great at homecoming. When the combat stress symptoms begin to re-appear, they often wear different clothes and have many faces.

Soldiers experiencing combat stress often find themselves experiencing intense emotional reactions to triggers that involve the marriage and the family. For some soldiers, the fear of losing their families while deployed and coming home to nothing is their worst fear in combat. This fear gets played out in imaginary scenarios, and happens over and over again to couples as they go through the emotional cycle of deployment. The re-integration stage of the emotional cycle of deployment is often the stage where the soldier and spouse realize something is wrong and come to a therapist for help. The EFT therapist can be of great help by recognizing the presence of combat-related fears driving the cycle as PTSD has put on the civilian clothes of the marriage relationship.

Combat-related PTSD often drives negative marital interaction cycles through nightmares imagining the worst from a mate, resulting in a hyper-vigilance that results in over-reaction at anything the spouse does that triggers fears related to a perceived vulnerability to affairs. This perception of vulnerability to affairs can provoke fears that are linked back to nights in the combat zone where the imagination ran rampant with fearful scenarios and nightmares of spouses "taken" by predatory males back at home station. This often presents as a hyper-vigilance in the male soldier that his wife could very easily be taken from him at any time or occasion when other males may be present like clubs, parties, swimming pools or any other settings where spouses are dressed in a less modest fashion. These normal social settings for young adults then become the triggers for anxious reactions that are related to combat PTSD. This PTSD-driven cycle often looks like irrational jealousy to the spouse of the soldier, and its relationship to combat-related PTSD is often missed. The EFT therapist can help the couple make the connection of this irrational fear with the soldier's combat experience, and highlight the secondary traumatization and "morphing" of PTSD as it puts on civilian "party clothes" when it comes home.

EFT AS A THERAPEUTIC MEANS OF HEALING WITH MILITARY COUPLES

Researchers are in agreement that the single greatest predictor of the ability to recover from human trauma is the ability to derive comfort from another human being (Figley, 1989; Johnson, 2002). The relationship with the spouse then offers promising potential for bringing about healing responses, as well as empathic interaction for the soldier returning home from combat. At the same time, the marriage relationship also has the negative potential through secondary traumatization to become a re-traumatizing relationship. The marriage relationship then has the potential to either become a relationship of cyclical and elongated re-traumatization, or it becomes a relationship for safe haven and healing. Our experience indicates that without help, most relationships experience cyclical and elongated re-traumatization unless they receive effective clinical intervention.

The EFT therapist works within this dynamic to assess and minimize the impact of secondary traumatization and optimizes the relationship for its healing potential. This kind of potential in the marriage often does not come naturally, but must be developed and heightened through therapeutic encounters with the EFT therapist. The EFT therapist trusts that within the marriage relationship, there exists the potential for recovery and healing once the marriage re-establishes secure attachment and the couple develops and puts into practice their own healing theory (Johnson, 2002). The EFT therapist reframes the negative interactional cycle as a normative response to very abnormal traumatic experiences, and facilitates the journey of the couple into a healing and transformational kind of relationship.

THE EFT MODEL AT WORK: STAGE ONE, STABILIZATION

The first stage of EFT is focused on helping the couple make sense of their negative cycle of interaction (Johnson, 2004). The EFT therapist, working on behalf of the couple's relationship, is a process consultant who is focused on how each partner's attachment needs, fears, and longings are met or not met. These attachment needs compel spouses to be close and to seek safety in the arms of a loved one. When the distress grows and the echoes of battle are hard to contain, the couple's negative cycle of interaction takes over their relationship and makes it hard for them to connect or to feel the love they have for each other. The goal of stage one is to de-escalate the couple's negative pattern (Johnson, 2004).

To achieve de-escalation, the EFT therapist provides a safe, genuine, and empathetically attuned environment. From this non-judgmental stance, the therapist starts to understand the nature of the couple's distress. How do they reach for each other? How do they soothe one another? When they argue, how do they repair? These types of questions help the therapist and the couple connect with the pattern underlying their relationship. Once the therapist understands the underlying pattern, the next step is to identify and access the primary emotional experience for each partner (Johnson, 2004). This internal experience, such as fear or anxiety, drives the partners to act in ways that either pull their loved ones close or, in distressed relationships, push their loved ones away. This pushing is the beginning of the couple's cycle.

The final part of stage one is helping the couple see that this cycle is a most potent enemy that keeps them from comforting one another, from sharing their fears and vulnerabilities, and from working together. At this point, the EFT therapist helps the couple unite against this enemy in order to limit the impacts of disconnection and emotional isolation (Johnson, 2004). When working with couples struggling with PTSD, the therapist puts the triggers and symptoms of PTSD into the couple's cycle. These triggers and symptoms complicate the cycle and are added to it so both the couple and the therapist can better understand and work with the PTSD. As the couple work together to make sense of their cycle, this is their first step in uniting against the cycle in order to interrupt and redirect it in stage two of EFT.

Slogging through the Bogs of Combat-Related PTSD

The soldier with combat-related PTSD often has the more complex version of PTSD, Type II (Schiraldi, 2000). Though soldiers with this more complex form of PTSD may point to one or more incidents of trauma during their tours of duty, they have actually acclimated to as much as a 15-month-long tour of traumatic duty. These soldiers have acclimated to a lifestyle of trauma, and it has become somewhat integrated into their personality for the sake of survival in the high-threat environment. This survival-oriented integration is primary in the formation of their emotional response repertoire, and it will not simply leave with the soldier's return home from the combat zone. The EFT therapist must watch for the "morphing" of PTSD and look for the presence of PTSD in the marriage wearing the disguise of marital clothes. This requires patience on the part of the therapist, and the EFT therapist must look for hyper-vigilance and anxiety at work in the marriage in ways that the couple would not consider as normal, especially before the experience of the soldier's deployment.

The metaphor chosen here, "slogging through the bogs of combat-related PTSD," reflects the sense of slow progress and constant search for secure footing that therapists and couples will seek in the recovery from combat-related PTSD in the marriage. The soldier has frequently faced an enemy that has ambushed him or her in very sneaky ways, and this enemy has sought to completely take away the soldier's sense of security. As a result of this prolonged exposure to an enemy committed to undermining security, the soldier will most likely be looking with anxious anticipation for any evidence of the undermining of security in the secure base at home—the marriage and attachment relationship. The EFT therapist must vigilantly tune into this dynamic of hyper-vigilance, and be ready to reframe irrational anxiety in the marital relationship in terms of the combat experience of the veteran. The following case study demonstrates this dynamic in therapy.

Case Study for EFT Stage One with Soldier Having PTSD*

The soldier recently returned from a 15-month deployment in Iraq as an infantryman. He has been diagnosed with PTSD due to frequent nightmares, flashbacks, intrusive thoughts, and a high degree of anxious thoughts and hyper-vigilance. He survived a very serious attempt at suicide with a gunshot wound approximately 7 months after returning home. He is a 24-year-old Caucasian male married to a 23-year-old Asian American female. Together they have a 1-year-old baby they conceived immediately before he deployed and just after they were married. He was married 3 months before deployment and their daughter is a 15-month-old baby when he presents for counseling. Their presenting problem is his PTSD and its many ramifications for their life and future. The wife reports, "He's just not the same as when he left." An Army psychiatrist diagnosed him officially with PTSD. The following excerpt comes from their sixth session after the suicide attempt.

Therapist: So how do you feel the PTSD currently continues to affect your relationship? Now that you have been home for about 7 months, and you have been out of the hospital for about 2 months, how do you think it is still affecting how you connect with your wife?

Therapist is reframing the negative interactional cycle around PTSD and is initiating a search for the "morphing" of PTSD.

Husband: She seems to be scared of me. I don't think she feels safe with me anymore. She seems to be running from me or hiding from me all the time. We just don't talk to each other any more.

Therapist (to Husband): You feel like she is trying to avoid you and that maybe she's actually frightened by you now? What's that like for you, when you feel like she may be frightened of you?

Therapist is empathically attuned, heightening, clarifying, and tracking emotion that is driving interactions.

Husband: Yeah. It's hard. I get really uncomfortable and irritable. It's just not the same. She can be really quiet, and I don't know what's going on with her now. It's killing me.

---

* All case studies were conducted by the first author at major U.S. military installations with active-duty soldiers.

Therapist (to Wife): When your husband shares how uncomfortable he gets, how different things are between you, how he says, "It's killing me," when he wonders if you're scared of him, what is this like for you to hear?

Wife: Well, I don't know if I am scared of him, but he is acting really weird, and I don't know what to do. He has these dreams in the middle of the night and he talks and says things that are strange. When he wakes up, he's quiet. I'm really worried that he might try suicide again.

Therapist (to Wife): So, you're not sure how scared you are, but you're really feeling a bit worried about what's going on with him right now, especially at night, and you're still feeling worried that he might try another suicide attempt. When you feel worried, either about his sleeping or trying suicide again, how do you share that with him?

Therapist once again shows empathic attunement, then expands, clarifies, and tracks emotion that is driving the interactional cycle.

Wife: Well, I don't. I can't. I don't want to burden him. So, I just get quiet, like he's saying. I guess I give him space.

Therapist: Right, yes, you give him space. You get quiet, feeling worried on the inside but don't know quite how to share your worry with him? Is that it?

Wife: Yes, I don't know what to say so I get quiet and distant.

Therapist: So, when you feel this worry, you get quiet and give him some space. Are these moments when you find yourself withdrawing? Distancing and pulling away from him?

Wife: Yea, withdrawing, not being sure what to say or how to connect with him.

Therapist: Right, right, that makes sense. Pulling away when you feel worried or maybe even scared? Does "scared" fit?

Wife: Yes, worried and scared. Like he's a different man and that scares me. I don't always feel like I know him.

Therapist (to Husband): What's it like to hear your wife describe how she gets worried and scared and pulls back, not being sure what to say to you? Not being sure how to connect with you after a rough night or in her moments of worry?

Husband (tight, edgy tone): Yes, my nights are miserable. I never know what I'm going to dream. I can't wait until the night is over. I didn't realize that she noticed. But I have no desire now to commit suicide. I hope she sees how hard I'm working on things.

Therapist: You don't want her to worry, you're saying you're safe now, you're working on things but that your nights are really hard. Miserable you said. It must be really hard to go to bed, trying to sleep, never knowing how the night is going to go.

Husband: Yes, many nights are miserable. But, I don't want her to worry. I didn't know she noticed. But, I do wake up quiet—I'm quiet on the outside but it's different on the inside.

Therapist: On the inside of you, it's not so quiet? It's different, kind of …

Husband: Noisy.

Therapist: Right, noisy, that makes sense. On the outside you're quiet but on the inside you're having such a different experience. It's noisy and maybe chaotic?

Husband: Yea, noisy and chaotic but I didn't think she noticed.

Wife: Oh, yeah, I notice! I couldn't help but to notice. But you smother me, and you get really weird, especially just after you get up in the morning.

Therapist invites more from the wife to expand the correlation between the emotional "smothering" and the interactional cycle of the couple.

Therapist (to Wife): You do notice, as you say, and you feel smothered?

Wife: Yes, I do feel smothered and, well, he just follows me around, and seems to just be stuck to me like glue. It's creepy, like he's afraid I am just going to leave him.

Therapist (to Wife): So, you guys help me understand … I think what I'm hearing you both say is when you (husband) have a rough night, you get quiet but on the inside it's noisy and chaotic. When you wake up with this feeling, you try to connect with her, follow her around, want to be with her, but she feels smothered. And, when you (wife) feel smothered, you get worried and scared and pull back from him. And, I wonder, when he feels you pull back, you (turning to husband) get worried that she's going to leave you, you need reassurance so you cling to her? Have I got this right? This is the cycle that keeps you both from feeling connected with each other, feeling safe and secure together especially when the rough nights happen?

Wife (nodding): Yeah, it's like he's guarding me or something. And, I do pull back. I'm just not sure what else to do?

Therapist (to Husband): Right and then you feel like she might leave you?

Therapist invites the husband to clarify this emotion the wife is picking up on as they together track the negative interactional cycle.

Husband: Yeah, I'm afraid she's going to realize how messed up I am and decide this is too hard and leave me. Every night I was in Iraq, I kept worrying that she would leave me like some of the other guys' wives left them. Then when we have a fight, and she slams the door on me and goes into the bedroom, I feel like I'm going to die. It's like there's no oxygen in the house!

Therapist (to Husband): So when the two of you are having a marital spat, your mind goes back to Iraq when others learned their wives left them?

Husband: Yeah, like it was just yesterday.

Therapist (to Husband): You said that when she closes the bedroom door, "that you might die. Like there's no oxygen in the house" and that's excruciating for you? The thought of losing her is terrible, she's so important to you, you care for her so much that when she closes the bedroom door, you feel that noisy chaotic feeling so intensely?

The therapist invites more expansion of the underlying emotion to access more positive attachment-related desires.

Husband: When she closes the door, it feels like that's the end of the marriage. When she does that, I feel like I'm going to die. The thing I was more afraid of than dying in Iraq was that I would come home to nothing. I still am afraid that it's just a matter of time.

Therapist: You feel like you are going to die, that there is nothing left, that you might come home to nothing? (Husband nodding.) So, then you cling, smother was her word, you seek connection so intensely because this fear is nearly unbearable? This fear is just so hard to tolerate?

Husband: Right … yea. All the air goes out of the room, like all the life and hope goes out of the marriage and I get scared and panicky. And (with sadness), she's right, I follow her around, like glue, because I don't know what else to do.

Therapist: You get so scared when she closes that door. Like she might be closing the door on the marriage? On you? You get scared and panicky, cling to her, seeking reassurance, and she feels smothered and pulls back.

Therapist (to Wife): Did you realize he felt that way when you close the door?

Wife: No, I just needed some space because I get so confused, and he seems so intense at those times. I just need some time and space for a break, that's all.

Therapist (to Wife): Can you share a little more of what it means to be confused and a bit scared when you feel he's "smothering you"?

The therapist validates her emotions and invites her to re-engage emotionally as she accesses deeper emotion and expresses it in session.

Wife: I just feel like I can never understand him or be enough for him. It's really overwhelming for me. I mean, I want to be there for him, but I don't know if I can ever be enough for him.

Therapist: Right, that makes so much sense, you want to be there for him but get scared and confused and then you pull back when you feel overwhelmed. He feels you pull back, and he gets worried and so he starts "smothering" you, seeking reassurance, not wanting you to leave him. This cycle, this process of him clinging and you pulling back keeps you both from feeling connected. You both end up feeling alone, loving the other so much but not knowing how to connect when this cycle kicks up and takes over your relationship. You both feel worried and scared but haven't known how to turn to the other and share the fears, share how much you miss each other, how much you long to feel close?

Husband and Wife (with sadness and softness on their faces) nod with affirmation of this encapsulation of their negative cycle of interaction.

This session concludes with the therapist summarizing by helping the couple see themselves in this negative interactional cycle. The cycle is driven by the husband's intense fears of his wife leaving that are rooted in his combat experience in Iraq, and by the wife's fears that she will be overwhelmed by everything going on in the relationship. The husband over-pursues out of his intense fear of losing his wife and child. The wife withdraws to put distance between herself and the husband out of her intense fear that she cannot handle everything going on with him psychologically. The therapist helps the couple to see how the fear driven by combat-related experience drives this cycle in a way that amplifies their fears way out of proportion. This reframes the problem around the aftermath of combat and highlights the authentic love and commitment the couple has for each other. This session's encounter helps set the conditions for eventual movement into stage two therapy for EFT.

STAGE TWO OF EFT

In stage two of EFT, the therapist works to create new interactional patterns that create a safer connection and pull the spouses closer (Johnson, 2004). So, at the end of stage one, the couple was aware that their relationship had been taken over by this enemy and they are now standing together against it. Stage two is a second-order change that actually changes how partners interact with each other and what they share and do when they feel distress. The goals of stage two are helping the withdrawer achieve emotional engagement and helping the demanding partner soften and share vulnerabilities. With these new positions and interactions, the couple's cycle changes.

Starting with the partner who withdraws, which is more often the male, the therapist helps him own his attachment needs that have been unmet in the relationship. As his needs have gone unmet, he generally will have coped by hanging out a lot with his buddies, perhaps drinking too much, trying to find practical solutions to non-practical problems, and staying in his head. Typical withdrawers report feeling like failures and they are afraid that they will never measure up (Johnson et al., 2005). Helping the withdrawer share his fears with his spouse is a key change event in EFT and the start of creating a new interactional pattern (Johnson, 2004).

As the withdrawer is engaged emotionally, the focus of the therapy shifts to the demander. In distressed relationships, the demander has been experienced as critical and blaming. Demanders typically feel that they are not important, their needs do not matter, and they usually report feeling very alone (Johnson et al., 2005). These internal experiences fuel their demands for attention and connection, although closeness rarely results until the demander can share his or her vulnerabilities.

Helping demanders identify and access their tender spots is vital in this stage of EFT. Rather than being critical and demanding attention, demanders share how lonely they have felt and how scared they are that their needs have gone unmet. When their needs have been unmet, generally demanders up the "ante" to make sure their needs register in the mind and heart of their partner. This softening of the blamer is the second key change event of stage two (Johnson, 2004).

As the withdrawer and the demander go through stage two, an important element for the therapist is to help each partner accept their partner's new position in their interactional pattern. For the first time in years, the demander may be hurt rather than threatening. The withdrawer may be scared rather than disinterested.

The therapist works on each partner's behalf to put their needs and distress in attachment context, and supports each partner in sharing more authentically with his or her loved one. These safe moments of sharing are the bonding events that are the hallmark of EFT (Johnson, 2004).

Case Study for EFT Stage Two with Soldier Having PTSD

The same couple has participated in 14 sessions of therapy to this point since the husband's suicide attempt, and they have de-escalated their negative interactional cycle. The soldier husband who is the anxious pursuer is recognizing the effects of PTSD in his daily life with more attunement. The couple presents with more connection and they are seated very close together for the first time in therapy.

Therapist: I notice that the two of you are sitting much closer and look much more relaxed with each other than you have in other sessions. You seem to me to be much closer and more connected emotionally, but I wonder what that means to you?

The therapist is expanding the emotional experience and heightening the couple's awareness of the restructuring of their emotional bond that is taking place.

Husband (smiling and making intimate eye contact with his wife): We have been a lot closer lately and we talk a lot more.

Wife: Yeah, it's been a lot better at home. I think we're doing a lot better.

Therapist (to Wife): Wow, that's awesome! What do you notice different about the relationship?

Wife: Well, I feel close and connected, but I don't feel like he's watching my every move. It feels more relaxed. It's more normal now.

Therapist (to Husband): Wow, that's awesome! She thinks you're chilling, dude! So, how has your PTSD been lately?

Husband: Well, I still have the "tramp dreams," but I don't worry about them as much and I realize that it's just the PTSD working on me at night.

Wife (looking at husband with surprise): You're still having the dreams? Why aren't you saying anything to me about them?

Husband (to Wife): Well, I know that it's not real and that you're not really going to cheat on me, so I try not to bother you with all that stuff.

Therapist (to Wife): You're surprised that he's still having the dreams? Can you tell us what that's like for you?

The therapist picks up on the emotion displayed in the nonverbal display of surprise and invites her to share with her husband with the potential for more "softening" and emotional re-engagement in the relationship.

Wife (to Husband): I'm glad you really are starting to trust me, but I really want you to know that I married you for life. I'm not going anywhere! I love you, and I want you to feel like you can talk with me about anything—including these weird dreams. I understand now why these dreams are happening, and I want to be able to be there for you when you wake up in the morning after a night like that. I know I'm not a tramp! (She laughs—and the husband and therapist also laugh with her.)

Therapist (to Wife): You want to be there for him? You want him to turn to you? You were surprised and maybe a bit scared when he just shared that he's still having those dreams?

Wife: Yea, yes, exactly.

Therapist: And, when you get surprised and scared, in the past you might have pulled back but now you're saying, "Tell me, turn to me, I want to be there for you … I'm not going anywhere but I need you to share with me. I get surprised and scared when you don't share with me." …

Therapist (to Wife): You get surprised and scared and don't want to pull back like before. You want to stay connected even when it's uncomfortable or hard for you.

Wife: Yes, I don't want to distance any more or pull back. But, I do still get scared.

Therapist: Right, getting scared … getting scared that you'll get overwhelmed, feel like you're not enough, feel scared that you're failing with him?

Wife: Yea, like the old days, that I can't be there for him in the ways that he needs.

Therapist: That's scary.

Wife (with sadness in her eyes): Yea, scary, like we're going to lose ourselves again.

Therapist: Can you turn to him? Can you turn to him and tell him how scared you get of losing this connection? How scared you get of not being there for him … but you really want to be there for him, especially after one of these dreams?

Wife (turning to Husband): I do get scared that I'll not know you've had one of those dreams or that I won't get a chance to be there for you. I get scared to lose you. I really want to be there for you.

Husband (pulls Wife closer, kisses her): I know you're here for me and you're not going anywhere. If I need to talk with you, I will. It helps waking up with you beside me, just knowing that's true.

Therapist (to Husband): Can you hear her? She is here, she's not going anywhere and she just took a big risk to share her fears with you. Can you hear her saying, "I want to be there for you, I want you to turn to me, share with me. I want you to trust me and tell me when you have one of those dreams. I don't want to lose you to one more of those dreams." … What's that like to hear her say?

Husband: It feels good. I guess it's like she's closer to me now; I don't have to worry that she's going to leave. It's reassuring.

Therapist (to Husband): And, when you have another one of those dreams, can you imagine turning to her and sharing it with her and pulling her close like you just did here?

The therapist seizes the moment to focus on genuine emotional connection and invites the couple to seize the moment of connection in a way that is a type of celebration together.

Husband/Wife (each pull together even closer, look at each other with affection, and speak in unison): Yeah, I think so.

Therapist: What's happening at home now between the two of you? You came in here looking like you have already been to therapy. Can I get the name of the therapist you're seeing between our sessions? (The couple and therapist laugh.)

Wife: We're just talking a lot more now, and we are able to just be ourselves with each other, and relax. It feels good.

Husband: I don't feel like I need to chase her anymore. She's there for me, and we're a lot more affectionate with each other. It feels like it did before I went to Iraq.

Therapist: It feels like it did before you went to Iraq. Can you say more about that?

Therapist invites the husband to expand more of self and heightens the potential of the relationship to overcome the combat-related PTSD.

Husband: When we first got married, we were a couple that was just in love, having fun and carefree with each other. After I got back from Iraq, it felt like we were both strangers and everything was so hard. We're starting to be the way we were with each other when we were first married again. It feels good.

Wife: Yeah, the relationship doesn't feel like so much work like it did when he came back. I don't feel like I have to watch everything I say or do. It's definitely more natural for us.

In this segment of case study, we can see key events occurring for stage two of EFT. In the first stage of EFT, we achieved de-escalation (the husband started slowing his pursuit and demonstrating more trust and patience with his wife and the wife was more accessible emotionally). He's not as anxious about attachment needs now. In stage two of EFT, we focus on the wife (as the withdrawer) sharing her emotions. As a result of her being more accessible and responsive, she has emotionally re-engaged in the relationship, and together they are experiencing a more secure connection in their relationship bond. She is more emotionally available and responsive, which helps him feel more secure in the relationship. This kind of withdrawer re-engagement event in session is key to restructuring the marital bond, and even more, is key to reframing the marriage relationship as the primary context for healing the wounds of war in the souls of this couple. After the withdrawer re-engagement, the EFT therapist works towards "blamer softening," the second change event in stage two of EFT. This event in session gives the couple hope that they will overcome the effects of PTSD in their marriage, which also offers hope they can overcome the effects of PTSD in their individual lives as well.

STAGE THREE OF EFT

The final stage of EFT, stage three, is focused on helping the same couple consolidate their relationship's new interactional patterns (Johnson, 2004). Each partner has achieved and maintained his or her new position in the relationship's dance, which compels connection and closeness. As a partnership, they have integrated the process of how they got stuck and how they have repaired their relationship. As each of them is in a new and different place emotionally, new solutions to old problems emerge (Johnson, 2004). Couples are now able to solve long-standing pragmatic problems that had previously threatened their bond.

Integration is the key to stage three of EFT. Each partner is now able to reach for the other and have the other be emotionally accessible and responsive (Johnson, 2008). When distressed, partners are able to turn to each other and ask for their needs to be met. The loved one knows how to respond and responds in ways that are reassuring and comforting. The couple nurtures their relationship and focuses on the quality of their connection.

CASE STUDY FOR EFT STAGE THREE WITH SOLDIER HAVING PTSD

In the case we have been following, the soldier with PTSD and his wife have made steady progress with some minor set-backs. Therapists working with the more complex combat-related PTSD should anticipate that there will be set-backs after going into stage two. The very nature of combat-related PTSD will result in unanticipated reactions to previously unknown triggers, and therapists should be careful to not join clients in a quick "flight into health." In this session, number 31, the couple comes in after recently recovering from set-backs.

Therapist: How are the two of you doing?

Husband: I believe we are doing much better, even though we had a couple of rough weeks.

Wife (looking surprised): Really?

Husband: Yeah, I had a dream last night that I wanted to talk about here in session.

Therapist: Okay, let's hear it. I'm interested!

Wife (looking at husband with curiosity): I am too!

Husband: I had a dream last night that was initially like the other "tramp dreams" where I found out that my wife cheated on me while I was deployed. (Wife gives a non-verbal facial grimace towards her husband.) But my response was different this time from before. Instead of being angry and either wanting to leave her or get even with her, I felt like that was a long time ago, and that we had worked really hard on the marriage. So, I decided in the dream that we had too much good going for us in our marriage and I just forgave her and decided to move on.

Wife (looking puzzled): And this is good, how?

Therapist: Yeah, help her understand what's at the core of this for you that makes this good.

The therapist shows faith in the couple to problem solve and trusts that they have the kind of relationship security to discuss this dream.

Husband: I think the dream says that I am feeling so good with the marriage, that I don't want to keep looking back at that part of my life and the way I felt that was so crazy.

Wife (looking deep in thought, and not saying anything).

Therapist (to Wife): Help him understand what you're feeling right now as you're taking all this in right now.

Therapist displays empathic attunement with wife and invites her to embark on a conversation that will take them deeper in a more integrated way than in past sessions.

Wife (turning to Husband): I guess I'm really glad that you believe our marriage is a lot better, and I think it is too. I'm feeling much better about us now. I guess I still have problems—I feel surprised—when I hear that your dreams still have me cheating on you. I never have cheated on you, and I never will. I really want you to believe that about me. I so want to be trusted.

Husband (to Wife): I believe you with all my heart and I know that you wouldn't cheat on me. I think what's so good for me to feel, is that in my dream, that didn't have the kind of power over me that it used to have. It was like my love for you was so much stronger! I do trust you! And, it feels really good to trust you, trust us, and realize this dream isn't the truth.

Wife: Okay, I get it now. That is good. I'll be glad when you don't have those dreams any more.

Therapist (to Wife): Can you reflect on what he just said, "It was like my love for you was so much stronger!" Can you let him know how that really feels deep down?

The therapist is sensing more resilience in the relationship that the husband's dream reveals, and invites the wife to explore that with the husband.

Wife (moved emotionally): It really feels good to know your love is stronger than those crazy dreams! (Sobbing.) I have been wondering if you would ever really trust me real deep down. It feels good to know that you really are starting to trust me in your sleep.

Therapist (to couple): I also am thinking this is about the idea that the two of you are beginning to move beyond the grasp of PTSD in your relationship. I wonder if this dream, and even this session, represents a watershed event taking place within both of you that will carry you beyond the grip of the war and PTSD in your lives?

The therapist describes the couple in a more resilient, and even a victorious sense in their war against PTSD.

Husband: I believe it is. I feel better about us than I ever have. What do you think (looking at his wife)?

Wife: Yeah, I do feel like we keep getting stronger, and it really helps me to hear you say that. Things feel more and more "normal" at home, like we're a "normal" young couple again, whatever that is (they both laugh).

This session demonstrates how the EFT process has become a corrective therapeutic experience in the couple who are now changing their intra-psychic experience and their sense of overall faith and hope in their relationship. Their journey together through the valley of the shadows of war is beginning to shed some light onto their path, and they are beginning to feel more secure about life. Together, they are starting to view the future as a life without the total domination of the husband's combat experience. The EFT therapist serves as a guide that helps shine a light into some of the areas of the heart when those shadows of war and PTSD make those areas a bit unclear. The EFT therapist in this third stage helps the couple see more clearly beyond the shadows of war. This kind of successful journey of experience through adversity results in a kind of resilience in the human spirit that brings deep meaning and connection as a couple in a very profound way.

EMOTIONALLY FOCUSED FAMILY THERAPY IN FAMILIES WITH CHILDREN

The authors of this chapter both find that the majority of military families initially present for therapy with marital problems that are attachment related. Hall (2008) in her book related to counseling military families describes a dynamic in military families that she refers to as "parent-focused families." Due to the mission focus and the warrior culture of the military, the needs of the children often take a backseat to the needs of the parents so that the military family can function when a service member deploys. This functional re-alignment of the family system often results in attachment needs going unmet in the family, or in the children finding those needs in other ways with peers. Children sometimes become parentified in order to take care of the family business to keep the home running while one or both of the adult members are away for extended periods of time. The family often gets re-structured in ways that orient around efficiency, while the attachment and developmental needs of the children suffer. Many problems that military families present with children should first be looked at through the lens of attachment needs, and the therapist should help the family maintain emotionally expressive and responsive ways that are developmentally appropriate for the children involved.

Emotionally focused family therapy (EFFT) in military families with children generally resembles an integration of structural family therapy, experiential family therapy, and emotionally focused therapy. EFFT addresses the structure of the family by paying attention to the marital dyad as the executive relationship for the family. As the marital dyad expresses and responds emotionally to provide attachment needs, so goes the rest of the family. EFFT therapy will first look to the marital relationship as an emotional barometer for what is going on in the family. EFFT integrates experiential family therapy modalities in session, counting on genuine encounters of emotional interaction that are corrective in nature to bring about real and lasting change in the family system.

Case Study of EFFT in Military Families with Children

A military family presents for therapy just 6 weeks after the husband returns from a 12-month tour of duty as an infantry non-commissioned officer (NCO) in Iraq. The spouse called for an appointment because their 14-year-old daughter slit her wrists at school, and was arrested over the weekend for shoplifting. The school required them to get family therapy before they would allow the daughter back into school. The family consists of a 32-year-old Caucasian male Army infantry NCO married 13 years to a 34-year-old Caucasian female. The husband adopted the 14-year-old daughter from the wife's previous marriage, as well as a 15-year-old daughter. The couple has a biological 4-year-old autistic son. The father, mother, and 14-year-old daughter present for therapy, and the parents ask to talk with the therapist first. The husband and wife come in and sit down some five to six feet apart from each other.

Husband: I don't understand what's going on with her. Ever since I've been home, she has been acting weird, and she started dressing Gothic and hanging around with a bunch of weird kids in the Gothic crowd.

Wife: Yeah, I don't understand what happened to her. We seemed to be close before the deployment, but I feel like she just slipped away this past year during the deployment. I feel like I don't really know her anymore, and we used to be close.

Therapist: How has the reunion and reintegration been going since you came back from Iraq?

(Husband and Wife look nervously at each other.)

Husband: Well, we've been pretty busy, and money's been really tight. We have been fighting about finances a lot, I guess.

Wife: Yeah, raising a family on E6 pay is hard, and with all three kids, and our youngest son having autism, we felt I really shouldn't work. We have been trying to get help for our son, and I guess I have been giving most of my attention to him lately.

Therapist: So would it be safe to say that maybe your daughter got sort of lost in all the stuff going on in your lives right now?

The therapist reframes the problem around the family simply trying to take care of its many needs in a very stressful time.

Wife (very thoughtfully): I guess so. I hadn't thought about it, but I guess I just took her for granted. She's never given us any trouble before.

Husband (just nods thoughtfully as though in agreement).

Therapist: Well, I have an idea, but I really want to bring her in to be part of our discussion. If it's all right with you, I'm going to ask her in now.

Therapist (stepping outside to daughter): Would you be willing to join us now, or would you like to have some time alone with me?

The therapist offers a time alone with the daughter in order to provide a sense of mutuality with the daughter.

Jane (fictitious name): No that's all right, I don't need any time with you. (Her non-verbals indicate she really does not want to be there, and she's dressed in solid black Gothic style.)

Therapist (to Jane): It sounds like you have had a very rough time recently. (Looking at her slit wrist) It looks like you have been in a lot of pain.

The therapist joins with the client and empathizes with her pain and position.

Jane (shifts a bit in her chair): Yeah, I guess so.

Therapist: Can you share what it's like for you with your family right now? You're really struggling and …

Jane: I just don't feel loved in this family. Especially by my dad. He's never told me if he loves me and so I don't think he does.

Therapist: This is really hard for you, Jane. Not to have heard these words from him. He's so important to you but you get scared that maybe he doesn't love you?

Jane: Yea.

Therapist: Can you tell him how scared you are that he doesn't love you because he doesn't say, "I love you?" It seems like you really need to hear it, hear the words, especially when you wonder if he does loves you …

Jane (looking sadly at her dad): I do wonder. I don't think you love me. You just stay so mad at me … like I'm the burden.

Therapist: Dad, what's it like to hear Jane's experience?

Father: I do love her, truly love her, but she's right, I don't say it. I don't really say it to anyone …

Therapist: It's unfamiliar for you, those words, sharing such strong feelings out loud is new or different for you?

Father: Yes, I don't know the last time I said it or it was said to me …

Therapist: Would it feel good to be able to say it? To let your family know you do love them? *Father*: Yes, yes it would. I do want my family to know that I love them.

Therapist: Could you turn to Jane and tell her, "I do love you. Even though I haven't said the words, I truly do."

Father: I do love you. I really do.

Jane (doubling over, and sobbing loudly): That's all I've wanted to hear! That's all I've wanted to hear!

Mom (sobbing loudly): I want to hear that too! I want to hear that too!

Father (sobbing loudly): I'm sorry. I didn't know. I just didn't know. (The family seems to simultaneously move toward the center together and have a long family hug, with all of them sobbing.)

When children and adolescents are present in session, the EFFT therapist should seek to rely much more heavily on experiential processes and techniques to help children and teens access emotion in session. The first author has found the use of experiential family sculpting to be effective during EFFT with families that have experienced deployment. While family sculpting is not a typical EFFT technique, its experiential nature works well when integrated with other emotionally focused skills and interventions. The EFFT therapist can use a sculpt to help the family experience and track their own emotional cycle of deployment, using emotionally focused skills to access and heighten the attachment-related emotional experience in session. The EFFT therapist working with the family choreographs movement through the sculpt in a way that the family can portray and experience the emotional distance in relationships at whatever point in the deployment cycle they are currently at in session. The EFFT therapist invites exploration of emotional closeness and distance with the family members throughout the process and works to heighten the expression of emotion. The therapist uses the EFT lens of attachment theory for assessment and as the road map for therapeutic change. Children are wired developmentally for the safe nurture and expression of emotion, and without it, all symptomatic behavior can be viewed as a cry for help.

An example of a family sculpt session with Jane and her parents:

Therapist: I've been thinking about what it must be like for you in your family right now with so much going on and your dad recently returning from Iraq, and I feel like trying something a little different. Would it be all right with you if I do something a little artsy? It's called sculpting. Sometimes I like to pretend I'm an artist and direct the family in a sculpting exercise—sort of like a play.

Jane (laughs sort of nervously as the parents squirm anxiously in their chairs): Yeah, that's okay with me.

Therapist: Dad and Mom, are you willing to try this with me?

Dad and Mom (looking at each other nervously): Yeah, sure.

Therapist: I want to use this room to help you picture the emotional distance in the family relationships through the deployment and after redeployment. Dad if you could stand over by the door to represent your being in Iraq, and Mom, if you could stand in the center of the room, we'll start there. Jane, you can stay where you are until they get positioned.

The therapist is choreographing the sculpt giving clear directions and intent on the experiential exercise. The father goes to the door and turns toward his wife who is standing in the center looking at him.

Therapist: Now, I want you all to move somewhere in this room that pictures where you felt you were in terms of emotional closeness or distance with each other during the deployment. So you would stand closest to the person you felt closest to during the deployment.

The father takes a couple of steps toward his wife as the daughter, Jane, moves over to stand quite close beside her mom. The father stops when he sees the two of them standing side by side, and he looks very surprised.

Therapist: Dad, you looked quite surprised and stopped. Would you be willing to share what is going on in you emotionally right now?

Dad: I am feeling just like I did while I was deployed, like I'm on the outside of my own family looking in. I feel like I'm an intruder.

Therapist: Feeling like an intruder in your own home must be lonely and somewhat confusing, yeah?

Dad: Yeah, it is very lonely sometimes, but in Iraq, I stayed very busy and had soldiers to take care of, so that helped me deal with it.

Therapist: Mom, what are you feeling when you hear him say he felt like an intruder?

Mom: I guess I'm a bit surprised. I didn't think he really missed us that much because he always seemed so busy. I know that I was close to Jane and the other kids while he was gone, and we seemed to be there for each other emotionally.

Therapist: Jane, you moved to be with Mom pretty quickly. What are you feeling right now as you stand close to her?

Jane (somewhat choked up and gently sobbing): It feels good. I liked it so much when Mom and the rest of us just hung out together, especially on the weekends when we went to the beach or went shopping. We don't do that now that Dad's home. (Mom reaches over to pull Jane in close and hugs her to provide her comfort.)

Therapist: It looks like you and your Mom got really close during the deployment, and standing beside her right now brings up the memory of the emotional connection you have had, and you really miss it.

Jane: Yeah, I do really miss being with her. (Her mother wipes off a tear from her eyes.)

Therapist (pauses for some moments): This is a great picture of the two of you to just kind of soak in together. I want you to just be there in this moment with each other. (They hug each other and there are some more tears.)

The therapist is letting the daughter, and her mother, acknowledge and focus on the experience of the attachment needs that are being met in this therapeutic moment.

Therapist: Now I want to ask you to change your positions of the sculpt here in the room in a way that pictures the emotional closeness or distance that is present in your relationships since Dad redeployed and returned home.

The therapist observes the daughter move toward the door, passing her father without even a glance. The husband then takes a few steps closer to the wife, while the wife just looks at him rather stoically. The family has a very disjointed/disconnected look to it with significant distance between all three persons in the room.

Therapist: Jane, I see that you very quickly moved to the door and moved away from Mom, while Dad seemed to move a little closer to Mom. What are you feeling right now as you have made this move? I'm wondering what it must be like for you standing there right now.

The therapist is now evocatively responding to Jane, inviting the expression of emotion from her that will call attention to the present condition that brought this family into therapy, which are the attachment needs of the child that appear to be unmet in this family at this crucial time of reunion.

Jane: I'm feeling very sad and alone. I feel like I'm on the outside looking in and I don't belong now.

Therapist (to Jane): Hmm ... You do look lonely standing there right now. It seems like I just heard your Dad say similar words when he was standing where you are—alone and on the outside.

The therapist is heightening and validating the emotion, while maintaining a sense of mutuality with Dad.

Therapist (to Dad): Dad, when you see Jane standing where you just were and feeling all alone, and on the outside looking in, what can you say to her right now?

Dad (pauses and looks at her with his eyes moistening): Jane, I want you to know that I really do love you.

Jane (doubling over, and sobbing loudly): That's all I've wanted to hear! That's all I've wanted to hear!

Mom (sobbing loudly): I want to hear that too! I want to hear that too!

Father (sobbing loudly): I'm sorry. I didn't know. I just didn't know. (The family seems to simultaneously move toward the center together and have a long family hug, with all of them sobbing.)

This case study demonstrates how the military family can get so focused around the function of the family that the deeper needs of attachment can get lost for members of the family. The EFFT therapist used an experiential intervention to facilitate emotional awareness regarding how the deployment cycle has impacted the family attachment relationships. The intervention also facilitated in-session emotional connection in the family's attachment system, and awakened the desire and awareness of the family for attachment needs. The EFFT therapist sensed that the father simply had difficulty expressing love and that the deployment had impaired his ability to express the soft attachment-related emotion his family so desperately wanted from him. The therapist used the family sculpt in an experiential way that helped them get in touch with their deeper attachment longings that words could not seem to reach.

The therapist never discussed the specific problems regarding the daughter's behavior outside of the session, since the therapy focus was on the attachment relationships within the family. The family concluded the session in a group hug, and said they were going to go home and bring the rest of the family into the group hug. The husband and wife followed up with seven sessions of EFT couples therapy where they both revealed they had traumatic experiences in life that made it difficult for them to express emotion and respond to each other emotionally.

CONCLUSION AND SUMMARY

Military families going though the emotional cycle of deployment and experiencing the demand of combat tours are stressed at the very deepest levels of the human experience. The human need for intimate emotional connection as described in attachment theory is at the core of the struggle our military families face. The EFT therapist brings unique skills and theoretical perspectives that can assist these courageous families to overcome unparalleled hardship and build amazing resilience. It is the hope of the authors that more EFT therapists will bring their skills to the home front into the fight to save military families serving in the global war on terror.

REFERENCES

American Psychiatric Association (2001). *Diagnostic and statistical manual of mental disorders* (5th ed.). Washington, DC.

APA Presidential Task Force on Military Deployment Services for Youth, Families, and Service Members (2007). *The psychological needs of U.S. military service members and their families: A preliminary report.* Washington, DC: American Psychological Association.

Armstrong, K., Best, S. & Domenici, P. (2006). *Courage after fire: Coping strategies for troops returning from Iraq and Afghanistan and their families.* Berkeley, CA: Ulysses Press.

Basham, K. (2008). Homecoming as safe haven or the new front: Attachment and detachment in military couples. *Clinical Social Work Journal, 36*, 83–96.

Bertalanffy, L. (1968). *General system theory.* New York, NY: George Braziller.

Bowlby, J. (1969). *Attachment and loss: Vol. 1.* New York, NY: Basic Books.

Faber, A., Willerton, E., Clymer, S., MacDermid, S. & Weiss H. (2008). Ambiguous absence, ambiguous presence: A qualitative study of military reserve families in wartime. *Journal of Family Psychology, 22,* 222–230.

Figley, C. (1989). *Healing traumatized families.* San Francisco, CA: Jossey-Bass.

Greenberg, L. S. & Johnson, S. M. (1985). Emotionally focused therapy: An affective systemic approach. In N. S. Jacobson & A. S. Gurman (Eds.), *Handbook of clinical and marital therapy.* New York, NY: Guilford Press.

Hall, L. (2008). *Counseling military families: What mental health professionals need to know.* New York, NY: Routledge.

Hoge, C. W., Castro, C. A., Messner, S. C., McGurk, D., Cotting, D. I. & Koffman, R. L. (2004). Combat duty in Iraq and Afghanistan, mental health problems, and barriers to care. *New England Journal of Medicine, 351*(1), 13–22.

Hoge, C. W., Terhakopian, A., Castro, C. A., Messer, S. C. & Engel, C. C. (2007). Association with posttraumatic stress disorder with somatic symptoms, health care visits, and absenteeism among Iraq War veterans. *American Journal of Psychiatry, 164*(1), 150–153.

Johnson, S. M. (2002). *Emotionally focused couple therapy with trauma survivors: Strengthening attachment bonds*. New York, NY: Guilford.

Johnson, S. M. (2004). *The practice of emotionally focused couple therapy: Creating Connection* (2nd ed.). New York, NY: Brunner-Routledge.

Johnson, S. M. (2008). *Hold me tight: Seven conversations for a lifetime of love*. New York, NY: Little, Brown and Company.

Johnson, S. M., Bradley, B., Furrow, J., Lee, A., Palmer, G., Tilley, D., et al. (2005). *Becoming an emotionally focused couple therapist: The workbook*. New York, NY: Routledge.

Litz, B. T., Orsillo, S. M., Kaloupek, D. & Weathers, F. (2000). Emotional processing in posttraumatic stress disorder. *Journal of Abnormal Psychology, 109*(1), 26–39.

McLeland, K. C. & Sutton, G. W. (2005). Military service, marital status, and men's relationship satisfaction. *Individual Differences Research, 3*(3), 177–182.

Miller, M. W. & Litz, B. T. (2004). Emotional-processing in posttraumatic stress disorder II: Startle reflex during picture processing. *Journal of Abnormal Psychology, 113*(3), 451–463.

Minuchin, S. & Fishman, H. C. (1981). *Family therapy techniques*. Cambridge, MA: Harvard University Press.

Munsey, C. (2007). Serving those who serve: Transforming military mental health. *APA Monitor on Psychology, 38*(8), 38–41.

Pincus, S., House, R., Christenson, J. & Adler, L. (2006). The emotional cycle of deployment: A military family perspective. Retrieved January 17, 2009, from http://www.hoah4health.com/deployment/familymatters/emotionalcycle.htm

Riggs, D. (2000). Marital and family therapy. In E. B. Foa, T. M. Keane & M. J. Friedman (Eds.), *Effective treatments for PTSD* (pp. 280-301). New York, NY: Guilford Press.

Rogers, C. (1951). *Client-centered therapy*. Boston, MA: Houghton-Mifflin.

Schiraldi, G. (2000). *The post-traumatic stress disorder sourcebook: A guide to healing, recovery, and growth.* Los Angeles, CA: Lowell House.

Sherman, M. D., Zanotti, D. K. & Jones, D. E. (2005). Key elements in couples therapy with veterans with combat-related posttraumatic stress disorder. *Professional Psychology: Research and Practice, 36*(6), 626–633.

8 Attachment as a Consideration in Family Play Therapy with Military Families

Gwendolyn W. Smith

CONTENTS

It is the aim of this chapter to introduce the clinician working with children of military parents to a variety of play therapy techniques arising from the history of family play therapy as a modality that has proven useful in assisting families to re-build relationships. In addition, it is proposed that blending several key concepts from family play therapy with techniques originating in the field of attachment, and keeping these at the forefront of the work with family members experiencing parental–child military separations, may guide the clinical work more effectively. Using research and techniques from the two fields of family play therapy and attachment therapy, clinicians can more succinctly impact the healing of relationships within military families in such a way as to restore family roles and reconstruct levels of intimacy after multiple short-term separations or even extended deployments. The stress of parental absences on children of military parents has been well documented, and it is not the intent of this chapter to examine the findings of studies. (Please see Herzog and Everson [2007] for a more thorough review of such research.)

BENEFITS OF PLAY THERAPY

First, a look at what the field of family play therapy has to offer. According to Eliana Gil (1994), family therapy (minus the play aspect) received a boost in acceptance as a legitimate treatment approach following the work of several groups of practitioners in the early 1950s. Prior to that time, traditional family therapy had been viewed as a lengthy intervention anchored in psychoanalytical theory based on Freudian influences. Inclusion of the patient's family was not a favored approach due to the underlying belief that the patient's dysfunction was originating from struggles of the id, ego, and superego. With the exploration into new approaches initiated by the likes of the groups of Gregory Bateson, Don Jackson, John Weakland, Jay Haley, and later accompanied by Virginia Satir, the work between therapist and family members took several novel turns. Such family clinicians began to propose that other dynamics were at work within the family such as sub-systems among the members that influenced the identified patient's, and actually the family's, functioning. Meanwhile, the work of Murray Bowen and Lyman Wynne with schizophrenic families at the National Institute of Mental Health, along with the growing realization of the importance of family roles in Nathan Ackerman's work at the Child Guidance Clinic at Menninger helped to guide the family therapy field further into unique interventions. These researchers helped lay the groundwork covering the various roles and coalitions within a family unit instead of focusing only on the person who was exhibiting the symptoms of difficulty in functioning. A primary example of a sub-system is the marital parental unit, as opposed to a mother–daughter or father–son subsystem. Focusing on the sub-systems and utilizing all the relationships between family members allowed the new genre of family therapists to coach changes more effectively into the family system as a whole, as well as alleviating the identified patient of all the responsibility for change.

In the case of military families, sub-systems exist as well, of course. However, these sub-systems are different from those of non-military families in that they cannot avoid being splintered due to the absence of a military parent responding to the call of duty. Most families do not experience or even anticipate the loss of a marital partner or parent (Herzog & Everson, 2007). However, in military families, one absence can be counted on to impact several roles and sub-systems. This can be seen when considering a three-member family of father, mother, and one child. Should the military parent receive orders requiring parental presence in the field for 2 months of training or for a year of deployment, the marital/parental sub-system as well as the father–child and mother–child sub-systems or dyads are all impacted. The marriage is now missing a partner, necessitating the remaining spouse to seek forms of support, (i.e., childcare) outside the immediate family, the parenting is now shifted to accommodate the remaining parent taking on both roles and the military parent–child dyad is left without one of the partners as well, leaving the child to struggle with all the tensions that absence or loss (even a temporary one) brings.

Historically, the clinical work of Virginia Satir and Carl Whitaker was among the first to include children in addressing clinical issues with families. They designed interventions that could be undertaken through the participation of all family members. During the 1960s and into the 1970s, techniques from the field of play therapy evolved into their family therapy sessions. Both clinicians wrote of their experiences and encouraged others in the field to consider the inclusion of all family members, young, old, nuclear, and extended as well, if need be in the same therapy session. In addition, with support from a grant from the National Institute of Mental Health in 1981, Whitaker, with his colleague David Keith, proposed to practitioners in both the play therapy and family therapy fields, that treating the "whole" family permitted a change that took into account the developmental needs of children within the structure of the family therapeutic experience. Including all family members allowed the therapist to address the many dyads and coalitions found within the family system, while strengthening the overall family functioning.

Still, it was not until the 1980s that family play therapy was accepted within the treatment field in its own right, with clinicians debating the benefits regarding the inclusion or exclusion of children and/or play in the therapy session. Today, family play therapy is widely recognized as a skilled and acceptable intervention for families. This treatment can be useful and effective in working with military families whose children are often exposed to interruptions in family relationships and changes in family roles. In addition, giving attention to the dynamic of attachment found inherently within all relationships is a strong ingredient in family play sessions with military parents and their children who have sought assistance from the author. So what is attachment exactly, and why is it a potentially significant aspect of family play therapy with military families?

Attachment is often defined as the presence of a mutually affective or emotional relationship between self and others. In the early life of infants, it is commonly referred to as the mother–infant bond and can be seen in the emotional quality of the connection between the infant and primary care-giver, again, usually the mother. Attachment is developed in the mundane everyday interactions that occur countless times as well as in the deliberate interactions of "play time or togetherness" between care-giver and baby. A care-giver's consistent response to the infant's needs regarding hunger, warmth, touch, socialization, and other primary elements of human life is the foundation of attachment. Nancy Thomas refers to the first year of attending to the comforts of the infant as enthroning the infant because the infant's needs are a priority for the parents to focus on. Crying is the language of babies calling for comfort and help. Responding primary care-givers (hereafter referred to as mothers for the sake of continuity) read or understand the cries and give relief with diaper changes, food, rocking, etc. Trust builds between the dyad of mother and infant and the infant eventually learns to be soothed by the mother's voice as the infant knows her attention to his or her needs will follow her voice shortly. A growing infant can be observed to cry, stop, and listen, before resuming a cry or whimper to solicit his or her mother. Such is the evidence of a growing mutual relationship built on trust and reciprocity.

By introducing the world to the infant in consistent, small interactions that answer the baby's needs for comfort and growth through experiences, the mother sets up a reciprocal relationship in which her efforts are rewarded implicitly and explicitly with smiles, efforts to please, and trust from her infant. The mother, in turn, then judges her infant's needs for further experiences, and again provides the opportunities for the infant to grow physically, socially, and emotionally. This interactional pattern assists attachment through the process that Ainsworth and Winnicott referred to as attunement. An attuned mother reads her infant's needs and attends to them in a way that validates the infant's emotions, drives, and experiences. She decodes the cries, sees the needs, and responds to them in such a way that the infant moves into toddlerhood with security and confidence. The relationship is well on its way to a healthy status; so much so, that in the second year of life when infants require dethroning (by way of limit setting), as Nancy Thomas has referred to it, infants have built up enough trust that they can tolerate the word "no" from the mother even as they feel frustrated in not obtaining what they want.

Unfortunately, several factors can disrupt the bonding or attachment process. Just as the timely, consistent response through attunement of the primary care-giver to the infant's needs facilitates attachment and bonding, the lack of a timely, consistent response; abusive/neglectful experiences; or several changes of care-givers within the critical first 3 years of age can impede attachment and/or delay its formation in the child. While abusive and neglectful experiences can occur in any family across all socio-economic, cultural groups, the military being no exception, this is not the dynamic that is of concern here. What is clearly known from research in the area of attachment, especially the field of foster care and adoption, is that repeated changes of the primary care-giver are likely to impact the ability of a child to form attachments or to remain securely attached to adults. Extended and/or multiple breaks in the relationship of the infant–parent dyad alter the affective reciprocity and the warm, loving relationship with a parent. Their relationship, specifically the trust and certainty elements, can be diminished through the physical and emotional absence of the primary parent or care-giver.

IMPACTS OF PARENTAL ABSENCE

The consequence of the parental absence, planned or unplanned inherent within military families, needs to be addressed when returning parents encounter difficulties navigating their way back into parental roles with their children and the warm, loving aspects of those family relationships as well. For regardless of how much thought, care, and angst go into the selection of a responsible adult/surrogate parent figure to care for the children while a military parent is gone, the primary attachment figure/parent is no longer present and the child must internally sort out the missing relationship. All the time the primary care-giver has invested in recognizing and addressing the needs of the infant/toddler now must be attempted by another adult. The trust, understanding, and communication between child and parent that was present and deepened through repeated experiences from birth is no longer available with one party absent. Even for the older child, parental expectations, rules of the home or relationship, and styles of demonstrating loving regard are all up for change as the child struggles to accommodate to the physical absence of the parent. In addition, the infant and child have extra, often unacknowledged and unspoken tasks to attend to just as the parent has the duties of the military calling to fulfill. He or she must wait out the loss of the beloved parent without the ability to understand the nature and duration of the time frame involved. The daily routine of the home is altered, possibly by having to go to a relative's home for care while a parent is away. This is especially true in single-parent households.

As if this isn't emotionally taxing enough, yet another factor interrupts the parent–child dyad. By requesting a grandparent, aunt, uncle, neighbor, or close friend to enter the role of primary care-giver to temporarily replace the parent, the chosen adult is placed into the middle of an already formed relationship. Now both giver (adult) and receiver (child) must work cautiously to align their lives together (all without the proximity and coaching of the parent). The adult has to make room in the home and heart for an additional child, while the child is mourning the loss of his or her parent and trying to adapt to a new lifestyle within the nuances of a new relationship and home environment offered by the adult. The trust, emotional intimacy, and certainty that existed between parent and infant/child cannot be easily replaced regardless of the well-meaning intentions or nurture offered by this new care-giver. Yet, the infant/child is expected to receive the care offered and continue to grow physically, socially, and emotionally without a prime relationship. Is it no wonder that military families often find the return of the parent into the home and family relationships stressful? Although their love and bond for their child is secure within themselves while they are gone in service, their infant/child has had to bond to another adult to endure the painful absence of the parent. Routines have been changed to acclimate to the surrogate or changed family system and the care, rules, or expectations cannot mirror exactly what was known in the birth home when two parents were present. Even with the present-day availability of Internet, Web-cam, and phone calls making daily contact possible in some deployment situations, the emotional, social, and physical components of the parent–child relationship are strained.

Yet, it isn't necessary to forecast all doom and gloom. For years military families have demonstrated resiliency in surviving the necessary absences that accompany military life. With efforts on everyone's part, experience has proven that babies and children can accept what is offered in the uniqueness of the new surrogate relationship or an altered home structure as a necessary dynamic of growing up in a military family, and learn to accommodate to the new caretaker. In the best of situations, the temporary care-giver provides needed support and hope for the child while the experience of "missing Mommy or Daddy" has to be endured. After years of studies in the fields of family play therapy and attachment, clinicians are in the best position possible to assist families to strengthen relationships among the various sub-systems when an absent parent returns.

It has been the experience of this author in working with military families that even in the most successful cases of a child adapting to the absence of a primary care-giver where the child has been more than adequately supported (with fears calmed and mourning addressed), the weeks and months following the homecoming are where problems are likely to emerge. With the celebration and relief that the return of the parent brings, the return also permits the reunited parent to step back in the role of care-giver. Assuming all the privileges of the roles within the original dyad of nurturer, disciplinarian, and mentor of their child since the child's birth is fairly automatic for the parent barring serious physical or emotional injury. However, in receiving the returning parent, the infants/children are now asked to disrupt the relationship they had to form with either the remaining parent or the surrogate care-giver and re-align once again, not only with daily routine, but emotional ties as well, to the original care-giver.

For many families, this expectation that things can return to normal with little or no upheaval is enough and the dyad picks up where parenting and childhood would normally intersect. For other families, however, the return of a deployed parent carries with it difficulties in re-establishing the connection within the parent–child relationship. It is difficult to predict which families can weather the changes, needing no outside assistance, and those who go on to experience more than minimal difficulties trying to transition back into life as it was before deployment. However, in the author's observations of clinical work with military families, paying attention to the dynamic of attachment is a necessary element in assisting military family members when difficulty reassuming family roles and/or relationships is experienced.

ASPECTS OF ATTACHMENT

In obtaining a social history at intake, it is helpful to inquire about the nature and the quality of attachment prior to deployment or multiple field trainings, to assess a possible breach in the relationship of the parent–child dyad. How emotionally close, how difficult was it to get their child to cooperate with daily tasks of brushing teeth, picking up toys, etc., and how easily was affection demonstrated between the dyad can be useful information as a baseline. Then asking how the child now responds to parental demonstrations of love and caring such as smiles, hugs, or eye contact in general and to parental requests of daily family life allows the clinician to listen for disruptions in the parent–child dyad. While emotional distancing from the parent and behavioral reluctance or non-compliance to parental or teacher requests can have many etiological explanations, an unresolved conflict surrounding the interrupted parent–child relationship can be a cue that something is amiss in the dyad. It can be expressed as anger, disrespect, oppositional behaviors, and/or mistrust (that the parent won't leave again).

Such families can present for therapy with behavioral or emotional difficulties of the child. At times, the misbehaviors can be happening in the school environment in moderate to more severe disruptions of the classroom. Perhaps the parent presents with complaints that the child has low motivation regarding the learning experience and isn't studying, doing homework, or keeping the parent informed. At other times, emotional upheavals are the presenting complaint. Angry outbursts, irritable defiance to adult requests, or subtle, repeated manipulations are described as interfering with the daily functioning of the family, and the parent complains of feeling angry or overwhelmed, if not puzzled, by the child's reactions to his or her homecoming. Other signs that a breach in the attachment may be underlying the child's difficulty in daily or relationship functioning are poor eye contact, avoidance of physical contact such as hugs, little joy expressed in reciprocity to the parent's overtures, few shared smiles, or general happiness is absent as in depression. Infants and toddlers may be difficult to soothe when distressed and may turn from the parent when intimate contact is offered. With teens, one also may find a higher than normal tendency to isolate themselves from home interactions, little effort to contribute to family conversations, and avoidance of social family interactions, especially with the returning parent. Again, there may be other factors involved in the emotional or behavioral state of the child that may need to be ruled out such as a mood disturbance, etc. However, consideration of an attachment-related etiology can be a factor in not only diagnostic impressions, but in choosing a treatment modality that could be useful in addressing the presenting complaints. Should attachment issues appear in the assessment phase, family play therapy offers a wealth of techniques as do treatment strategies from the attachment field itself. Such approaches offer a much different clinical approach from working solo with the child on anger management or other skill-building techniques.

Attachment clinicians often refer to several basic elements in their work with children experiencing difficulty with relationships and/or bonding. One is attunement. Deciphering a child's inner experience of self as well as outer expression toward others is necessary in all clinical work with children. Decoding this for both the child and parent, and then strengthening the attunement between the dyad reinforces the dynamic of their attachment. Daniel Hughes, Ph.D., has provided a clear description of the attunement process in his book, *Facilitating Development Attachment* (1997). A therapist demonstrating attunement during a session with a child would be monitoring and noticing the child's emotional state, his or her ability to engage in eye contact, and toleration of a parent's physical touch, as well as the child's ability to read and understand facial gestures and self-moderation of physical movements in response to the interactions at hand. Observing out loud to the parent what the therapist notices about the child is one way of highlighting attunement for the parent. Using childhood finger frolics is a fun way of attuning, making sure to incorporate age-appropriate frolics in the play. Most parents are familiar with several of the more common ones such as itsy bitsy spider, but a host of others may be found in *Finger Frolics* (1985). Another way of strengthening attunement between parent and child is to use techniques from Theraplay. Theraplay is a treatment approach that uses attunement in its engagement phase in which the therapist first interacts with the child in a brief, structured playful interaction that involves something specific about the child, followed by the therapist inviting the parent to join in the interaction with the child. The therapist then deliberately extracts him- or herself, leaving the dyad fully in the experience together.

Another element attachment therapists use that can be incorporated into family play therapy is touch. Viola Brody underscored the helpfulness of touch in healing relationship and attachment difficulties in her book, *The Dialogue of Touch* (1993). She described an interactional vignette in which the therapist sits on the floor with the parent and child. Taking a bottle of lotion, the therapist pours a little amount out in dots on the child's hand and engages the child in imaginary play with the lotion. The lotion becomes different colors of face paint in which circles, squares, hearts, etc., are "drawn" on the child's cheeks and forehead. The parent can be invited to join in and given the child's other hand with different pretend colors of lotion to draw shapes on the child's face also. Simply, tender touch is thus facilitated between parent and child and often eye contact and smiles are intermingled in such family play sessions. An attuned parent can often be observed to use soft strokes and linger in the play, pushing back the child's hair or demonstrating other affectionate gestures during such interactions. The family play permits the child to drop the anger and oppositional nature of home behaviors and enjoy the parent in the moment, thus re-establishing the relationship on a more positive level.

Still another simple but effective family play technique that encourages the attachment dynamic of touch is to have a play medical kit present in the family session. After some therapeutic discussion involving how much of the child's life was missed by the parent while away, the therapist can ask the child to point to all the different parts of his or her body that were hurt or sick. Children will often search their arms and legs first for evidence of scratches, scrapes, or scars and point eagerly. Some may touch their tummy or heart. The parent is then asked to look in the doctor's kit and find something that might soothe such hurts. A stethoscope to listen to the child's heart beats, a play thermometer under the armpit, multiple applications of actual band-aids, M&Ms or Skittles in a clear plastic baggie used for pretend medicine (if cleared with the parent beforehand) may start the interactional play that follows, with the parent making all the soothing sounds the parent would have made had he or she been there when the scrape occurred. Such techniques afford the parent the ability to offer verbal and emotional nurture within the physical touch component of the play.

Still another element found in attachment healing is competence—competence within the belief of the child's ability to grow respectful, responsible, and fun to be around, as Nancy Thomas described it. Because military parents miss months if not a year or more of their child's life, stages of development and the appropriate accomplishments by the child are missed as well. Incorporating fun challenges into family play sessions catches the parent up to the accomplishments while giving the child an appropriate stage by which to demonstrate competence. From the background to the foreground, a growing sense of competence and the validation of that competence by the parent assists the child in letting go of the need to act out behaviorally and begin to demonstrate self-control in an effort to please the parent. One finds a return to the reciprocity found in the original infant–parent dyad with mutual affection growing in place of the presenting symptoms of anger, isolation, or uncooperativeness.

With a younger child a therapist may introduce pairs of shapes such as purple circles, red squares, yellow hearts, blue triangles, orange hexagons. Having prepped the parent beforehand, the therapist can introduce the activity by acknowledging how hard it must have been for the military parent to have been gone when the child learned so much. Parents can be invited to add their own comments and stories about how they spent time wondering what wonderful things their child was doing while they were away. The therapist can then ask the child to show the parent how smart he or she has become by listening to directions and sticking the various shapes on the specific body parts named by the therapist. The therapist then asks the child if she knows colors and/or shapes. With a yes response, the therapist then asks the child to select the yellow shapes. If the correct color shape is chosen, the parent beams and verbally praises the child (having been prepped for this previously). Next, the therapist asks the child to name the shape. If unable to, the parent is to teach the shape by naming it and outlining it with his or her finger and having the child copy it also. Using double-sided tape, the therapist directs the child to stick the yellow hearts on her shoulders. Of course, the parent is to smile and cheer the child on. Then the parent can ask the child to find the blue triangles, teach color or shape as needed, and ask the child to place them on her knees, for instance. Again, validation of cooperativeness in listening to adult instructions and making the correct choices as to placement follows. Play continues until all the shapes are placed somewhere on the child's body. Time is allowed to let the parent marvel over the smartness of the child and how much was learned while that parent was away. Play is then reversed in that the child is asked to close his or her eyes and guess one at a time where each pair of shapes was stuck to the child. For a correct guess (the blue triangles are on my knees), the child is allowed to open her or his eyes and take the blue triangles and stick them on the parent's knees! Once the child has successfully guessed, and hence stuck all pairs on the parent's body, the child is allowed to ask the parent, who has been instructed to close his or her eyes, where each colored pair of shapes is. As the parent guesses and removes the shapes, they are placed in a plastic baggie so they can be sent home with the parent and child for family interaction time as "homework."

Further examples of competence can be found in the Theraplay literature under the challenge activities. School-aged children can be invited to thumb wrestle or stack hands upwards and downwards in increasingly rapid succession (incorporating touch with competence). The therapist can introduce a bottle of bubbles and ask the child to pop bubbles using a specific finger, such as the pointer finger on the left hand. When turning over the play to the parent, the parent can expand the activity by asking the child to show competence in counting bubbles by popping only three, or five, or every other one, again, using a specific finger. Furthering the activity, the parent can ask the child to show how clever the child is by popping bubbles with the right elbow or left knee, or even the child's nose! An indirect advantage of competence activities within family play therapy is that the child has actively listened to the adults, both therapist and parent, and followed directions without opposition or complaints because of the inherent nature of enjoying play. This furthers a rebuilding of respect between parent and child and also permits the parent to quietly regain the role with parental authority in a fun way that can be easily transferred to the home or school environment.

All such family play activities are done in a lighthearted manner, encouraging the child when tasks are not met exactly and weaving in the delight of the parent to be catching up on all the activity missed. Of course, it is very important to prep the parents beforehand to allow the child to demonstrate successfully, and explain that it is the process of interaction between the dyad that is important, not the winning or gaining advantage over the child in any of the competitive-style play interactions.

An additional element from the attachment field of nurture is also a helpful addition to family play sessions with military families. Often it is difficult for children to articulate emotional needs to parents, or anyone for that matter, hence their acting out behaviors. Children become their feelings through behavioral outbursts or maneuverings such as slowing up the family morning routine by refusing to get dressed in a timely fashion, thus making parents late for work. Structuring nurture opportunities within family play sessions allows time for rebuilding verbal and emotional closeness and gives the parents time to share how much they missed all that their child experienced while they were away. It helps to repair the emotional bond in the dyad and reinforces the reality that the parent was absent, not by choice, but by design of the career path and/or job responsibilities.

Nurture can be incorporated in sessions through a variety of ways. Have the parent bring a favorite snack of the child and a blanket to create a picnic atmosphere. Only have the parent sit on the blanket and hold the child in his or her lap while the parent feeds the M&Ms, Goldfish crackers, gummy bears, blueberries, etc., into the child's mouth. With an older child, have the dyad sit across from each other and feed each other, taking turns, of course. With Skittles or M&Ms, have the child or parent close their eyes and guess what color was plopped into their mouth! With both the younger and older child, make sure the parent is prepped with the goal of the activity of re-creating emotional closeness, security, and trust, and is willing to incorporate verbal musings into the interaction. An example would be for the parent to ask whether their child still loved the red M&Ms the best or if the sour gummy bears were still too sour for the child as they feed each other back and forth.

Still other ways of adding the nurture element can be found in storytelling or narratives. The therapist can assign a category for storytelling for the session, such as how names are chosen in families. If possible, the therapist gets out a book of names and their meanings. The therapist then tells a story about how a friend's child was named, or a sibling's name was chosen, etc., and looks up the name in the book and reads the background to that name. The turn passes to the child, who is encouraged to tell about naming a pet, doll, or stuffed animal. The child is helped by the parent to look up the name in the book and the parent reads the description to the child. Next, of course, it is the parent's turn to tell a story. Having been prepped previously by the therapist the parent relates how they got their name, who chose it, what other names were considered, whom the child was named after, and so forth. The parent hands the book to the child and assists the child in finding the parent's name and reads the description to the child.

Often what follows next is the natural course of events. The child asks how he or she was named. Should the child have asked this question prior to everyone taking a turn as assigned by the therapist, the child is asked to wait until everyone has had their turn. This quite naturally builds suspense in the child, similar to mild anxiety or a bit of agitation at having to wait. Once everyone has had a turn or the child asks at the end of the turns, the parent invites the child into his or her lap and semi-reclines the child. This facilitates eye contact, touch, smiles, anticipation, snuggling, and a whole host of other positive bonding elements that immediately soothe the child from any suspense-like emotions. It also provides a reparative experience for the parents who weren't there when their children felt distressed by their absence, but they can soothe now within the play experience. The parent then takes his or her time and tells the whole birth story of the child, adding in whatever details the parent feels would delight the child, whether it was the wiggling in the womb, or the many discussions at the kitchen table as to what names were considered prior to the chosen one. The therapist may interject questions to facilitate the interaction and/or be an appropriate audience with ohs and ahs as needed.

Other themes for narratives in following sessions are to have the parent hold the child and talk about what he or she likes, loves, and hopes for the child, giving five examples of each before moving to the next. Should time permit, the child is encouraged to share back with the parent what he or she likes, loves, and hopes for the parent. The therapist may need to assist in reframing wishes or hopes of the child, such as hoping the parent never goes away again. A reframe could be that, should the parent have to train in the field or deploy, the child would understand it as a temporary trip, just longer, such as how the child leaves every morning for school and returns every afternoon. Military parents have to leave for trips for school or duty, but always intend on coming back at the end of the time/assignment.

Using four different colors of pick-up sticks as props, this same theme can be addressed by assigning likes, loves, hopes, and dislikes to the various colors of the sticks. In a follow-up session or for an older child, the four colors could be labeled favorite childhood stories or heroes, memories most thought of while a parent was away, words describing happy experiences (enjoyment, satisfaction, bliss, elation, cheerful, glad) and a story that happened within the family that matches the word, words describing sad experiences (upset, distressed, crying) and, again, stories to match. With each stick successfully picked up without moving another stick, the participant tells a real life story about that color stick. For example, if the green sticks are hopes the parent/child/therapist tells a hope for that family. Again, the therapist is to facilitate a fuller discussion of the theme through questions and clarifying points, creating opportunities for the dyad to share more deeply. The turn passes to the next participant when another stick is moved while attempting to pick one up, just as in the regular rules of pick-up sticks. It is helpful to prep the parent beforehand to allow the turn to pass on to the child after getting a stick or two themselves. The inherent competitive nature of adults sometimes takes over without a gentle reminder, and the parent can inadvertently capture most of the sticks!

SUMMARY

Overall, family play therapy that addresses attachment elements can be a process that provides opportunities for reciprocal enjoyment of the parent and child even while they are experiencing difficulty in the reunification of the homecoming. Using elements of attunement, competence, and nurture, both parent and child can be guided and supported to repair the emotional connection that was broken by the physical absence of the parent. By combining family play activities with attachment dynamics, the therapy experience of each member of the dyad can be enriched with smiles, laughter, touch, and eye contact. This approach allows the child to settle the residual emotions of the temporary loss of the parent in a non-threatening and non-punitive manner in which the parent is invited to become an integral part of the healing process. The child is given the opportunity to re-align with the original care-giver and a sense of balance is returned to the roles of each family member as the relationship is re-established. In addition, military parents are presented with the experience of witnessing the growth and development of their child, something they certainly missed while being deployed.

REFERENCES

Boynton, R., Kobe C. & Peters, L. (1985). *Finger frolics* (Revised ed.), as compiled by L. Cromwell, D. Hibner & J. R. Faitel. Pleasant Hill, CA: Discovery Toys

Brody, V. A. (1993). *The dialogue of touch: Developmental play therapy.* Treasure Island, FL: Developmental Play Training Associates.

Gil, E. (1994). *Play in family therapy.* New York, NY: Guilford Press.

Gitlin-Weiner, K., Sandgrund, A. & Schafer, C. (2000). A scale for assessing development of children's play. In *Play diagnosis and assessment* (pp. 15–57). New York, NY: John Wiley & Sons.

Guerney, L. F. (1995). *Parenting: A skills training manual.* Silver Springs, MD: Relationship Press.

Harvey, S. (2008). An initial look at the outcomes for dynamic play therapy. *International Journal of Play Therapy, 17*(2): 86–101.

Herzog, J. R. & Everson, R. B. (2007). The crisis of military deployment in military service: Implications for play therapy. In N. B. Webb (Ed.), *Play therapy with children in crisis* (3rd ed.). New York, NY: Guilford Press.

Hughes, D. A. (1997). Therapeutic interventions. In *Facilitating developmental attachment: The road to emotional recovery and behavioral change in foster and adopted children* (pp. 93–136). Northvale, NJ: Jason Aronson Inc.

Jernberg, A. M. & Booth, P. B. (1999). *Theraplay: Helping parents and children build better relationships through attachment-based play* (2nd ed.) San Francisco, CA: Jossey-Bass.

Sher, B. (2002). *Spirit games: 300 fun activities that bring children comfort and joy.* New York, NY: John Wiley & Sons, Inc.

Thomas, N. L. (1997). *When love is not enough* (pp. 7–10). Glenwood Springs, CO: Families By Design.

9 Spirituality and Trauma during a Time of War

A Systemic Approach to Pastoral Care and Counseling

Alan N. Baroody

CONTENTS

This chapter* seeks to redefine the nature of the religious experiences of combat veterans, and thus heighten the awareness of clinicians and chaplains to the religious nature of the personality changes within the soldiers. It also seeks to provide alternative interventions that may assist them in recovering a renewed sense of self, reintegrating back into the family system, and normalizing life within the culture from which they came. When one recognizes the spiritual nature or basis of the presenting symptoms, then interventions that infuse hope into the therapeutic process can lead to resilience and a greater sense of *well-being*. The term used for *well-being* in this article is a word taken from the Hebrew language—*shalom*.

What happens to spirituality during times of war? What part does faith have in trauma recovery? What is the function of religion in the enabling of resiliency among military dependents, veterans, and the chaplains who serve them?

* In order to protect client confidentiality, all names used in case illustrations are pseudonyms.

When asked to address these issues for this chapter, I queried our staff of therapists at the Fraser Center to find out how often the overt issue of spirituality or religion surfaced in their work with returning Iraq war veterans and their families. Out of 10 therapists, none could recall where the subject of religion became a therapeutic issue or where clients talked about their faith in relationship to either primary or secondary trauma experienced as a result of deployments.* Similarly, my work with military chaplains returning from deployments to Bosnia, Afghanistan, and Iraq has been centered primarily around the effects of traumatic stress on their lives and the lives of their families. There has been very little talk of or about religion in these sessions. Thus, the void with regard to overt religious experiences, practices, or language becomes a subject for exploration.

* * *

While serving as pastor of a Presbyterian congregation on Jekyll Island, Georgia, where there were numerous retired veterans (WWII, Viet Nam, the Korean War), I listened to many so-called "foxhole" conversion stories where faith was strengthened and provided extraordinary solace in the midst of terrifying conditions. Many were quite moving and resulted in lifelong change, which strengthened these retired veterans' perceptions of God's presence in their lives.

In contrast, there was also the funeral of WWII veteran Robert Jacobs. Robert, too, had a life-long changed relationship with the Almighty on the field of battle. He began as the commander of a tank on D-Day. From Normandy, he crossed the continent experiencing numerous life-threatening engagements with the enemy including a stint in a German POW camp. The most powerful religious experience, as Robert told it, was his entrance into the Buchenwald concentration camp. His platoon was one of the first to enter. He said that their first thoughts were, "My, they must have eaten well, look at all of those ovens!" The reality of sights, senses, and smells quickly set in, reshaping his concept of God and religion. A man from a faith-based family, who prior to WWII was known for his beneficent character, Robert returned from war with a heart hardened to religion. He preferred solitude to groups, had few close friends, and remained emotionally distanced from (if not abusive to) his wife and children. His life, post-WWII, was focused on becoming a successful businessman—there was no room for religion. His personal relationships suffered and his use of alcohol was excessive. Rarely did he speak of the trauma experienced or the medals of honor received. He died a multi-millionaire war hero of the "Greatest Generation." His funeral eulogy was titled, "A Scarred Soul."

As soldiers continue to return from multiple lengthy deployments to Afghanistan and Iraq, we are still trying to discern the place of spirituality and religion, and

* The Fraser Counseling Center is a non-profit, faith-based, ecumenical counseling center located in Hinesville, Georgia, the home of the U.S. Army's 3rd Infantry Division out of Ft. Stewart and Hunter Army Airfield. My colleagues and I work with soldiers and their dependents from both Ft. Stewart and Hunter Army Air Force Base in Savannah. Our statistics from the year 2006 show that we have worked with more than 260 military families and more than 100 soldiers apart from their dependents.

differentiate between that which makes for a "resilient spirit" and that which makes for a "scarred soul." This chapter does not contain answers to deep questions based on analytical research; rather, they are anecdotal assumptions based on the author's life experiences as a pastor and a clinician working to facilitate the healing process of the souls scarred by such deployments and warfare.

* * *

There was a time during my training as a marriage and family therapist, and pastoral counselor when pastoral counseling, or pastoral psychotherapy, was the only legitimate field in which one could mention anything about spirituality or religion. Most practitioners who strolled down the pathways leading from psychology were warned to keep personal values as well as religion out of the 50-minute session (unless, of course, it involved symptoms arising from psychosis). We have now reached an age where not only do we use a client's religious beliefs and faith community as strengths in the therapeutic process, we also delve into those once verboten realms in order to actively incorporate the dynamics of a person's spirituality into the healing process. To see how far we have come, one need only review an article such as D. R. Hodge's "Spiritual Assessment in Marital and Family Therapy: A Methodological Framework for Selecting from Among Six Qualitative Assessment Tools",* or a book such as Griffith and Griffith's *Encountering the Sacred in Psychotherapy: How to Talk with People About Their Spiritual Lives.*†

How do we utilize therapeutic permission, given the apparent lack of overt religious language from veterans and their dependents in these recent deployments as compared with veterans from past military engagements? Could it be that the subject is ever present, but the nature of trauma and length of deployments have changed the language?

DEFINING SPIRITUALITY AND RELIGION

Often, *religion* and *spirituality* are used interchangeably. For the purpose of this treatment, spirituality will refer to the subjective way in which one experiences one's ultimate concern within the context of one's religion or culture. This definition is similar to one presented by Felicity Kelcourse in "Spirituality or Religion, Reintegrating Our Faith." She understands spirituality as the intuitive counterpart of faith, which "points to those dimensions of human experience that do not easily lend themselves to cognitive categories or descriptions but are nevertheless profoundly moving."‡ Spirituality is therefore a sub-context of religion and culture. As such it is totally dependent on personal experiences and the ability to

* Hodge, D. R. (2005). Spiritual assessment in marital and family therapy: A methodological framework for selecting from among six qualitative assessment tools. *Journal of Marital and Family Therapy*, 31, 341–356.

† Griffith, James L., and Griffith, Melissa Elliott (2003). *Encountering the sacred in psychotherapy: How to talk with people about their spiritual lives.* New York, NY: Guilford Press.

‡ Kelcourse, Felicity (2006). Spirituality or Religion? Reintegrating our faith. *Insights*, 122, 24.

perceive a relational connection with that which is greater than oneself—Higher Power, Ultimate Concern, or God.

One of the first problems encountered when addressing the issue of the effects of warfare-induced trauma on spirituality, and the relationship between spirituality and resiliency, is definitional. Definitions of what is meant by spirituality or religion abound in such numbers as to boggle the mind of anyone attempting to do an exhaustive review of current literature. Yvonne Farley in her article, "Making the Connection: Spirituality, Trauma, and Resiliency,"* gleans from the literature to derive a definition of spirituality based on Canada and Furman's use of spirituality as "[a]n aspect of a person or group dealing with a search for meaning, moral frameworks, and relationships with others, including ultimate reality."† Her work relating Canada and Furman's operational model of spirituality to a developmental model of resiliency is to be commended.

Eric Erikson in his book, *Young Man Luther: A Study in Psychoanalysis and History*, defines religion in existential terms:

> Religion … elaborates on what feels profoundly true even though it is not demonstrable; it translates into significant words, images, and codes the exceeding darkness which surrounds man's existence and the light which pervades it beyond all desert or comprehension.‡

This author prefers the more classic and general definition as proposed by Paul Tillich. Religion is "[t]he state of being grasped by an ultimate concern." In his work, "Aspects of a Religious Analysis of Culture," he is quick to point out that this state (religion) cannot be restricted to a special realm. He explains:

> This unconditional character of this concern implies that it refers to every moment of life, to every space and every realm. The universe is God's sanctuary. Every work day is a day of the Lord, every supper a Lord's supper, every work the fulfillment of a divine task, every joy a joy in God. In all preliminary concerns, ultimate concern is present, consecrating them. Essentially the religious and the secular are not separated realms. Rather they are within each other.§

Thus, for Tillich there is no dichotomy or separation between culture and religion. *Religion is the meaning-giving substance* of culture, and culture is the totality of forms in which the basic concern of religion expresses itself. While not precluding Farley's definition, which emphasizes relationships and developmental theory, or Ericson's definition, which in summary defines the importance and relevance of hope to religion, Tillich's understanding of the relationship between culture,

---

* Farley, Yvonne R. (2007). Making the connection: Spirituality, trauma, and resiliency. *Journal of Religion and Spirituality in Social Work*, 26(1).

† Farley, p. 3.

‡ Naylor, Thomas, Willimon, William & Naylor, Magdalena (1994). *The search for meaning* (p. 203). Abingdon Press, Nashville, TN.

§ Tillich, Paul (1968). Aspects of a religious analysis of culture. In *The theology of culture* (p. 41). New York, NY: Oxford.

religion, and ultimate concern may shed light on the absence of religious language to describe the life-changing effects of battlefield trauma on soldiers and their families. Trauma, whether primary or secondary, changes one's relationships both with both culture and religion. A person's reason for being, or connection to his or her Ultimate Concern, is called into question. Culture shock and religion shock go hand-in-hand during lengthy deployments such as the Iraq engagements. The trauma of warfare can blur the lines between cultures, and thus bring about a dramatic shift in long-held values, perceptions, and behaviors.

Officer: In Iraq, I would never be caught without my weapon. There is no place that is totally safe. Now that I'm back (in the States), I carry a gun everywhere I go. It's just not safe.

Therapist: Did you carry a weapon with you prior to being deployed to Iraq?

Officer: No, but now I know better. The world is not a safe place, and I will not be caught with my guard down.

As one examines the neuro-physiological effects of trauma combined with the cultural adjustments of multiple lengthy deployments followed by the short re-deployments home, one becomes aware that the once tried and true ways of experiencing the meaning-giving substance of culture, the world, one's place in one's family, the experience and understanding of oneself, and the person's relationship to an ultimate concern are out of balance. There is a sense of being internally and externally scattered or separated. As the spouse of one three-time deployed soldier put it, "After twelve months, we (his family) became no more than a 'memory' to him. We are no more or less than his remembering his last vacation at the beach or the last Christmas we were together. Though we talk and e-mail and send pictures, the same is true for the children. Their daddy is not real." Families and soldiers at war live in two very different worlds with a different set of cultural values and meanings. Over time, the lines connecting the two worlds can become very thin. Their attempts to connect these worlds through e-mail are one-dimensional at best and sometimes result in a soldier fighting a war on two fronts, in two very different worlds or cultures.

THE NATURE OF SHALOM

To understand the trauma that makes for a "scarred soul" within the context of religion and spirituality, one must first have a general understanding of what makes for the healing of the soul. This author conceptualizes this by way of the concept of soul in the Hebrew Scriptures. In the Hebraic Bible a person's *soul* was not some spiritual entity that was separate from the body. S*oul* was an inclusive term. It referred to a psycho-physical organism. There was no body–soul dichotomy. A life, a living being could not be divided into parts: mental, physical, spiritual, emotional, or psychological. Soul defines a person's internal or external being. According to Naylor, Willimon, and Naylor in *The Search for Meaning,* "… the search for meaning will involve a new recognition that we are not disembodied minds or souls. We have a body. What affects us physically affects our spirit as well. Some of us are in psychological or spiritual trouble because we are in physical trouble. We are beings with feelings and ideas, but we also have hormones, muscles, aches, and pains."* To put it more colloquially, your soul is what makes you, *you* ... all of you. It includes personality, essence, desires, and life as well as limbs. In the Hebrew understanding, *soul* was an all-inclusive term for life.

Similarly, in Hebrew thought there was no such thing as spiritual health. Neither was there such a thing as physical health, or relational health, or mental health. They were all interrelated.

The model of health as holistic well-being, *the shalom of the soul*, is not a recent concept. We have come full circle in that for centuries we have compartmentalized our understanding of humanity and relationships. We separated the mind from the spirit, psychology from physiology, individual health from the broader social context. Only recently, within the past 20 years, have we resurrected the Hebraic concept of old and begun to talk and think systemically. We've finally reached the place—in this field which we call mental health—where we are beginning to ask, "How is your *shalom*?"

So what does this mean for military chaplains and mental health practitioners with respect to assisting soldiers and families in their recovery from the traumas induced by warfare? This author believes it means that mental health professionals need to keep in mind that everything one does with people in the field of mental health is very spiritual in origin. Those who are military chaplains need to remember that work with soldiers and their dependents is very secular in origin.

An example of the inseparability of the spiritual from the clinical is in the mental state of dysthymic disorder, or clinical depression (DSM-IV-TR: 300.14). When one is depressed one *feels* distant from God. Appetite changes. Social withdrawal occurs. One's self-esteem takes a nosedive. Somatic pains may surface and muscular tension may be prevalent. There is little energy for, or interest in, participating in what were once pleasurable activities. When a person is in the midst of a clinical depression, his or her soul is in pain. Clinical depression can be framed as a spiritual condition.

To take seriously the shalom or healing of the soul means that clergy or mental health professionals can no longer compartmentalize what we do. Spirituality and mental health are integrally related. They cannot and should not be separated. When we compartmentalize, we risk prolonging the healing process and possibly inflicting additional pain and trauma.

It is interesting to note that the concept of holistic health, in terms of the well-being of the soul, is not new to the U.S. Army. In fact, it was codified in 1987 under the rubric of "Spiritual Fitness" in the Army's Health Promotion Program as outlined in Department of the Army—Unclassified Pamphlet 600-63-12. This program was designed for use by commanders and department heads in military facilities for the purpose of "providing the commander with a definition of spiritual fitness and suggest alternatives to enhance the soldier's total well-being

* Ibid. Naylor, Willimon, and Naylor, *The search for meaning*, p. 202.

increasing spiritual fitness." The document provides a cookbook-like protocol for inspiring and training troops for battle by assuring their spiritual fitness. It draws its inspiration from General George C. Marshall who expressed:

> The soldier's heart, the soldier's spirit, and the soldier's soul are everything. Unless the soldier's soul sustains him, he cannot be relied on and will fail himself, his commander, and his country in the end. It is not enough to fight. It is not enough to fight. It is the spirit that wins the victory. Morale is a state of mind. It is steadfastness, courage, and hope. It is confidence, zeal, and loyalty. It is élan, esprit de corps, and determination. It is staying power, the spirit which endures in the end, and the will to win. With it all things are possible, without it everything else, planning, preparation, and production count for naught.*

The concept of spiritual fitness encompassing a holistic approach that was promoted by General Marshal in 1987 continues to the present day. A detailed analysis of holistic well-being as essential to military wellness is discussed extensively in a 2001 article in *Military Medicine*, "Soldier and Family Wellness across the Life Course: A Developmental Model of Successful Aging, Spirituality, and Health Promotion, Part II." The article highlights the conclusion of numerous studies, which show that exercise, social support, and *a strong spiritual belief system* relieve signs of stress, whether they are related to anger, anxiety, hostility, or depression. The findings of the authors show that the more religious the officer, the less likely that officer is to experience hostility, anger, and depression.†

Similar sentiments were expressed by the commanding general of the U.S. Army's 3rd Mechanized Infantry Division, Rick Lynch, in his address to troops in October of 2006. He emphasized the importance of combining physical fitness with spiritual fitness for holistic well-being and good soldiering. Says Lynch, "I've experienced combat and know the value of cardiovascular endurance and muscle strength. These are the tools you will need when you bear the weight of a wounded comrade in battle. But what strength do we need long before, during, and after the battle? Spiritual fitness is central to my commander's intent. It is part of our force well-being. It is necessary for good life balance, on and off duty, and applies to everything we do."‡

While acknowledging the importance of spiritual fitness, the Ultimate Concern to which it is directed is that of service to the U.S. Army. The Army is a culture unto itself with its own set of symbols, values, sets of meaning, and rituals. This dynamic in itself can disrupt the *shalom* of the redeployed soldier as he or she works to transition back into the family system.

---

* Department of the Army, Pamphlet 600-63-12, Spiritual Fitness, 1 September 1987. Foreword: Headquarters Department of the Army, Washington, D.C.

† Parker, LTC Michael W., MS USA (Ret.) (July 2001). Soldier and family wellness across the life course: A developmental model of successful aging, spirituality, and health promotion, part II. *Military Medicine*, 166, 561–570.

‡ Third Infantry Division, "Rock of the Marne." *CG's Message*, October 27, 2006.

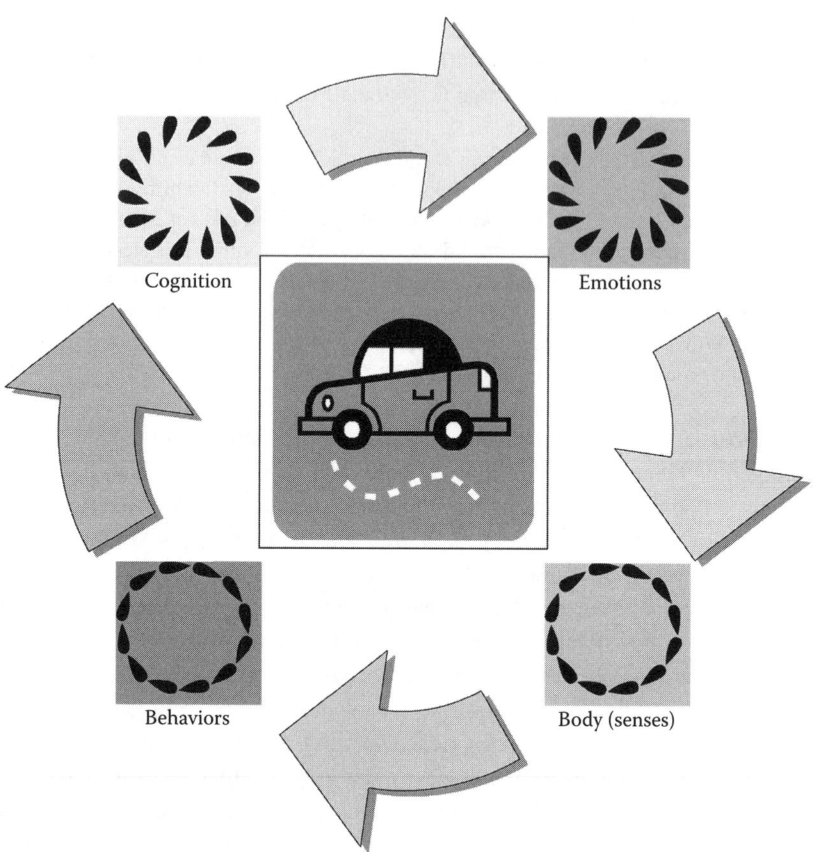

FIGURE 9.1 Normal response: holistic processing.

TRAUMA AS SPIRITUAL CRISIS

The dynamics of trauma affect a soldier's well-being in two distinct, but not unrelated, ways. The first is neuro-physiological and can be found in the official list of symptoms of post-traumatic stress disorder as presented in the DSM-IV-TR (2000). Symptoms and behaviors most often seen and expressed in the office of a therapist or military chaplain are hyper-arousal, flashbacks and nightmares, substance abuse, intrusive thoughts, domestic violence, risk-taking behaviors, marital discord, depression, suicidal ideation, generalized anger, and emotional numbing resulting in relational disconnects with spouse, children, and friends. It is beyond the scope of this chapter to detail the neuro-physiological mechanisms associated with trauma; however, the consequences of these mechanisms when one is placed in fight–flight–or freeze survival mode is that our normal way of processing events via the cerebral cortex of the brain is bypassed and our first alert system, activated by fear, kicks in within the brain's limbic system.

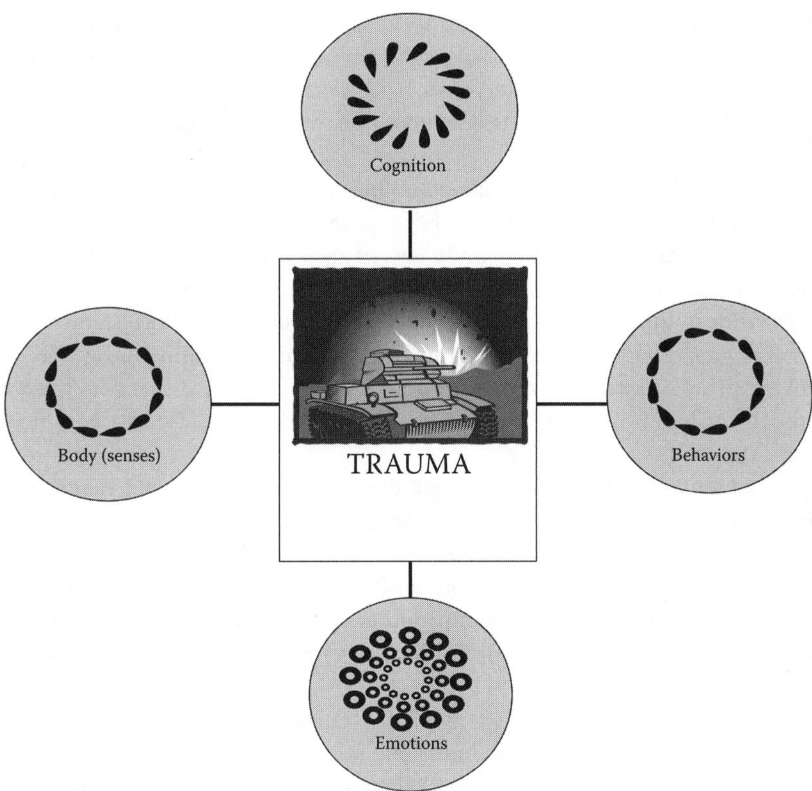

FIGURE 9.2 Combat stress response.

The end result is an immediate and hopefully short-lived segmentation or separation between our emotions, cognition, physical sensations, and behaviors. For instance, when one first learns to drive a car, the fear and level of stress involved in the simple process of coming to a halt at a stop sign may be all consuming. One may not hear the driving instructor's voice. An abrupt halt may occur due to panic and excessive pressure on the brake pedal. Coming to a four-way stop can be a harrowing experience as one concentrates on stopping and tries to remember which vehicle has the right of way. It takes concentration and singleness of focus. The rush of wind caused by a large truck passing on the interstate may initially be infused with the life-threatening fear-based reaction: "He tried to run me off the road!" Ordinarily, through time, repetition, and experience, the brain adapts and reprocesses in such a way as to make driving under normal conditions a non-threatening event (see Figure 9.1).

In contrast, the trauma of combat and constant underlying threat of harm when living in a war zone can set up neuro-physiological pathways and networks that may not be reprocessed as easily as those of a novice automobile driver. The U.S. military's training is geared toward developing muscle memory and standard operational procedures in life-threatening situations that serve to override the body's natural fight–flight–freeze response. When soldiers venture "outside of the wire" in Iraq and enter harm's way, their vigilance and training kick in. When engaged, they become a cog in a machine that has honed their reactions and function. Their adrenaline and endorphins are pumping in such a way as to heighten their senses and blunt their pain. "Mission first" and protecting themselves and their comrades become the priority (see Figure 9.2). One soldier described the excitement and chaos of an engagement saying, "It's a rush, man! There's nothing to compare it to. No drugs are that good! We were laying down fields of fire not even seeing what we were shooting at. Shit! I remember a guy that jumped up into the back of the truck as we were pulling away. He was fucking firing away on full automatic with a piece of metal sticking all the way through his leg. He said he didn't feel shit and didn't care. He just kept firing away. Man, it was awesome!"

It isn't until after the traumatic event that sights and sounds, behaviors, emotional feelings, bodily sensations, and cognitive reflection can begin to be reprocessed by the brain. The ability to do so effectively may depend upon the intensity and length of exposure, the perception of present threat versus environmental safety, the individual's history with regard to past trauma, the meaning attached to the trauma experienced, as well as other inner personal strengths and resources, one of which is spirituality.

Sgt. Joe Perez was a veteran of the first two Iraq deployments of the Army's Third Infantry Division. He was in his late 30s and had been in the U.S. Army since the age of 18. He came seeking help at the Fraser Center for PTSD due to a 3-month waiting list at the Veterans Administration hospital. He initially came in with his wife who was threatening to leave him. Symptoms presented were nightmares, non-provoked periods of anger and rage, depression, excessive use of alcohol on a daily basis, and bouts of sadness and crying. Upon entering therapy he said, "I don't understand what's happening to me. I just want to be myself again. I am always angry and don't know why. My wife can't understand this. Drinking helps me to settle down."

After an assessment, the protocol for treatment making use of EMDR* was followed and he was prepared for the process. He had been in numerous combat engagements throughout his tour of duty. The first session was to focus on a target event of pulling guard duty in the streets of Baghdad after 48 hours without sleep. Prior to the first set of visual bilateral stimulations (a technique used in EMDR), he described watching Marines race down the streets in their mechanized vehicles, one after the other, for long periods of time. There was a wreck and one of the vehicles plowed into the rear of a tow truck. Sgt. Perez was left with horrific pictures in his head of maimed, dead, and disfigured Marines. He wanted to assist the wounded but was ordered to remain at his post on guard duty. When he

* Shapiro, Francis (2001). *Eye movement desensitization and reprocessing: Basic principles, processes, and procedures.* New York, NY: Guilford Press.

initially told the story identifying the target memory, it was with great emotional affect and regret for his helplessness.

After the first set of eye movements, using the movement of my hand as the visual stimulant, his affect changed dramatically. He became hyper-aroused and intensely focused, saying, "I'm back on guard duty. When I see your hand, I see a target moving back and forth. I'm a different me. I don't know where the 'me' that felt remorse for the dead and injured Marines went. I'm back soldiering now. I don't feel anything. All I can focus on are your fingers and making sure that the situation is safe." After a similar response to the second set of bilateral movements, I made the suggestion that he imagine my hand as being vehicles in the convoy passing by, one after the next, after the next. This suggestion bridged the block and enabled the reprocessing of the incident to continue.

The traumatic stress of combat had altered the neuro-physiology of Sgt. Perez so as to allow for a triggerable dissociative process whereby this highly trained soldier-combatant remained separate from the affective, emotion-laden individual who was distressed by his inability to adjust to civilian life. His excessive use of alcohol was his way of numbing the feelings associated with the memories. His anger was generalized with no specific distinguishing cause. His sleep consisted of series after series of nightmares. The biology of trauma can in and of itself cause a separation or split between the physical, emotional, cognitive, and behavioral self, thus scarring one's soul, disrupting shalom, and making the sense of well-being brought about by spiritual connectedness all but impossible.

The second way that trauma disrupts well-being, or shalom, is existential in nature and has to do with questioning *meaning*. Traumatic events are an attack on one's meaning system, which is comprised of at least five factors:

1. What one believes about the universe
2. The nature of reality
3. One's relationship to the universe and reality
4. The search for meaning within that reality and universe
5. How one views and understands oneself in the context of reality

For chaplains in the field and for therapists following redeployment, the questions may or may not incorporate religious language. They may be laden with guilt or fraught with despair. In fact, they may not be questions at all, rather statements as couched within the following story.

In therapy, one young military physician described his routine. Day after day he triaged the wounded, removed bullets and shrapnel, and pieced together and stabilized the severely wounded and dismembered to be flown to the hospital in Laudstuhl, Germany. Daily, he was surrounded by death and disfigurement. For him, these were not the sights that traumatized. What challenged his sense of meaning, disrupted his shalom, called into question his place in the universe and reason for being was one specific incident requiring a decision. He had struck up a relationship with a wounded soldier who had been under his charge for at least

2 weeks. The physician had put a great deal of effort into the physical care and repair of this young man and connected with him on an emotional and relational level. He had recommended another day or two in recovery before allowing the soldier to return to active duty, but the soldier pleaded for an early release as his comrades were transferring to another operating base. The physician first argued, then relented and pronounced the young man fit for duty. The next day, the soldier was killed by an IED. "If only I'd kept him another day," cried the young doctor. "If I'd only kept him another twenty-four hours, he'd still be alive. It just doesn't make any sense."

Why did God allow this to happen?
If God is on our side, why did my friends die?
Why does God allow the innocent and the little children to be hurt?
Where is God when I'm ordered to blow up a hut filled with civilians?
Why is there evil in the world?

In the midst of the chaos of warfare, all of our well-formulated assumptions and presuppositions can be challenged. The problem of "theodicy" (God, good and evil), while not talked about, is present. Assumptions about the relationships and connections between the universe, the world, people, things, principles, and values are brought into question. Long-held understandings of how everyday life should be lived are relegated to a dream world called home.

There is one common comment heard by therapists who work with veterans returning from multiple lengthy deployments to Iraq, Afghanistan, and/or Bosnia. It is almost universal in nature and comes in two different forms. From spouses we hear, "I don't understand it, he is not the same person I knew before he was deployed." "She is different, changed." Similarly, from the veteran we hear, "I don't know who I am any more. I'm not the same person I was before deployment." Most often, these comments are framed within a negative context. They are usually followed by descriptive behaviors that are detrimental to familial relationships, or self-destructive or -deprecating for the soldier. These are comments that therapists do not usually hear from re-deployed veterans who have been stationed in noncombat-related zones (e.g., Korea or Germany).

Whether extensive time is spent in the constant routine of day-to-day operational boredom in a foreign land or in the momentary chaos and mayhem of combat, the questions these soldiers ask themselves are meaning filled and thus extremely religious and spiritual in nature. These questions often linger in a soldier's private thoughts and remain unverbalized until he or she returns home. These are the haunting "Why?" questions: Why am I here? Why did my buddy die or get wounded, but I was spared? What purpose do I serve in the larger picture of this war? What happens if I die? Is it okay that I took another human life? Will my spouse or girlfriend remain faithful in my absence? All of these questions are combined with a feeling of helplessness or loss of control over one's destiny. Many are fear based in that the soldiers' environment leaves them with no safe place, no familiar past life experiences from which they can internally re-frame or organize their trains of thought. Over time, their worldview is reshaped by the cultural context of living in a military complex within a foreign land. The way they view themselves and their world gradually shifts. These are the kinds of questions that, when the dynamic of hope is removed, lead to the documented increased incidents of depression and despair among this set of veterans as opposed to veterans of past military engagements. Similar thoughts and questions are birthed in combat, regardless of the war.

After describing an intense night-time fire fight with the Viet Cong in Pleiku ("Rocket City"), Viet Nam veteran Roger Lipsley writes these words:

> From that moment I knew that I was not living the life that was possible for me to live. I realized that the proximity of death was less important than the absence of real life. At that moment my search began. I was eighteen years old …*

It is very easy for a therapist to gloss over the spiritual impact of wartime deployment and focus solely on behavioral or psychological dynamics. After all, this is the stuff for chaplains, priests, rabbis, and imams. It is important, however, that therapists and chaplains alike recognize the profound spiritual effects the dynamics of lengthy separations and traumatic experiences have on the religious lives and faith-beliefs of these soldiers.

Given that values and meaning-of-life issues are central to the experience of these soldiers, the lack of religious talk within the therapy session raises its own set of questions. Various answers have been given to this phenomenon. "If we bring up the subject of religion with other soldiers in our unit, we risk being labeled a religious fanatic, or at the very least, become the butt of jokes." "No one wants to verbalize the possibility of dying or question the meaning behind the mission." From a Chaplain: "They come to us with these questions and issues, not mental health." From a soldier: "I avoid chaplains. They try to tell me 'why' my buddy died, that God 'called *him* home' but has a greater purpose for *me*." Generationally and culturally the generation of Americans in late teen or early adult years is not as oriented toward organized religion as prior generations have been. They don't typically use religious language.

Regardless of the reason, if clinicians fail to address the spiritual nature of the changes wrought by trauma and/or extended deployments, they miss opportunities for interventions that would assist the soldier and his or her family to heal from the interpersonal, relational, and cultural rifts resulting from wartime experiences.

THE FIGHT AND PLIGHT OF CHAPLAINS

Military chaplains find themselves in precarious situations with regard to their mission of being the spiritual caregivers to troops during deployments and maintaining their own shalom (mental, physical, emotional, spiritual, relational

* Lipsley, Roger & Probst, Bruce (Winter 2002). Among the Quadi, on the River Gran. Parabola (on War), pp. 48 and 50.

well-being). They find themselves between the proverbial "rock and hard place." Prior to a mission, they are there offering prayer on behalf of those who are about to "go outside of the wire" (on a mission that is outside of the security of a forward operating base). They are present upon the unit's return, offering what consolation they can provide after traumatic engagements. At times, they are caught in the middle. Unarmed, as per the Geneva Convention, it is up to their chaplain assistant to wield the weapon that provides for their defense should it be necessary.

The theological and psychological training received differs from chaplain to chaplain, yet by virtue of their mission, they are first responders to the wounded, the emotionally traumatized, the grief stricken, and the heart broken. They are expected to listen to horrific accounts of combat and respond appropriately. When psychological pain is expressed in religious language and combined with despair or anger (i.e., "Why did God let my buddy get blown to hell and I'm still here!"), chaplains are expected to be able to discern the difference and respond appropriately. In combat, distinguishing between a soldier's psychological cry of pain that is couched in religious language and an existential outburst questioning the meaning of life and faith is not an easy call to make. If a chaplain tries to answer a psychological outcry with a religious or theological answer the possibility of future rapport is often lost. As a representative of "the Divine who should have protected," the chaplain is always open to be the recipient of transferred anger directed at God.

As if the dynamics of combat are not sufficient for the toils of the day, chaplains have the additional responsibilities of providing for religious services, being inter-faith sensitive with soldiers of differing religious persuasions, mediating conflict between the troops, keeping positive troop morale, and providing individual and marital counseling for soldiers whose long-distance relationships with family and significant others are falling apart. They are required to keep personal and theological misgivings of war and conflict to themselves and focus on the needs of troops, some of whom are questioning the overall mission, which the chaplain must overtly support. For some, this conflict may remain internalized, but most are supportive of the overall purpose of the Iraq conflict and the U.S. participation in it.

Chaplains are "catch-alls" when it comes to the expectations of others upon them and their job descriptions. In other words, they have as many jobs are there are soldiers.

"IF I WANTED TO DRIVE A CHAPLAIN UP THE WALL"

- I would make the chaplain responsible for the mental health, spiritual well-being, and marriages/family relationships of all the troops and give him or her few resources with little authority and vacillating support.
- I would provide the chaplain with unclear goals not commonly agreed upon by battalion commanders, hospital administration, clinical supervisors, or chaplaincy command.

- I would ask the chaplain to fulfill expectations that are totally unreasonable—to be all things to all people in all situations (a rabbi, imam, Christian minister, Buddhist priest), to go wherever and whenever ordered into whatever situation a superior feels is most important at that time, to always be the point person in the delivering of bad news, and when called upon, to remain calm and provide spiritual guidance in life-threatening situations.
- I would expect the chaplain to be able to work 10 to 24 hours per day when deployed thousands of miles from home for 6 to 15 months at a stretch while also maintaining a peaceful and perfect marriage with well-adjusted children.
- I would place the chaplain on a tentative career advancement track that could easily be de-railed by getting on the bad side of command during one deployment (assignment) within a 20-year time frame.
- I would make the chaplain accountable to God and to the U.S. Army (not necessarily in that order!).*

The impacts of trauma and prolonged deployment exposure on combat troops have been documented; however, little study has been done with regard to the situation of these heroic caregivers called chaplains. Literature on the effects of trauma, secondary trauma, and extended deployment is, at best, sparse. One article, "Care for the Caregivers: A Program for Canadian Military Chaplains after Serving NATO and United Nations Peacekeeping Missions in the 1990s," cites a 1996 pilot program for chaplains after deployment. An adult educational model was used as the basis for the program. The article highlights the most significant aspect of the program as the opportunity for the participants (a total of 31 chaplains) to reflect on "the meaning of their ministry in the face of the apparent meaninglessness of combat-related violence." It is hypothesized that the sense of meaning may be the most critical factor in influencing vicarious traumatization. The possible shortcoming of the program was the lack of opportunity for participants to discuss the deployment stressors.†

The Fraser Counseling Center in Hinesville, Georgia, in conjunction with the Department of Psychiatry and Behavioral Science of Mercer University School of Medicine, and with the cooperation of the Chaplain Installation Command of the U.S. Army's Third Infantry Division for Ft. Stewart and Hunter Army airfield, held a 2-day workshop for chaplains in November 2003. The workshop was titled, "Trauma and Spiritual Healing: A Recovery Workshop for Chaplains." A total of 70 chaplains and their assistants were in attendance. The workshop learning model was both adult educational as well as interactive-participatory.

* Swanson, Duane (1972). If I wanted to drive a pastor up the wall. Source unknown. (Revised by author.)

† *Military Medicine*, Vol. 165, September 2000, Guarantor: Cdr. George Zimmerman, Canadian Forces; Contributors: Cdr. George Zimmerman, Canadian Forces; Wesley Weber, Ph.D., pp. 687–670.

The itinerary listed the following as subject areas to be covered: "Religious and Spiritual Dimensions of Trauma," "A Model of Stress and Coping with Trauma," "Assessing Trauma Experiences and Post-Traumatic Symptoms," "An Overview of Trauma Spectrum Disorders," and the teaching of a 12-step process that chaplains could use with troops to assist them, post-deployment, in processing combat stress and trauma.

The 2-day workshop took an unexpected turn. The participatory segments strayed from topic-focused discussions to personal and interpersonal experiences. Broken into groups of six to eight, the chaplains and their assistants (most of whom had recently returned from an Iraq deployment) began spontaneously talking about their experiences in combat. At this point in the Iraq engagement, debriefing for re-deployed chaplains had not been in the military protocol. Being away from the military installation and dressed in civilian clothes made for a setting that felt safer for personal disclosure. The Fraser Center therapists and Mercer instructors quickly became aware of the importance of modifying the agenda. Workshop staff served to facilitate the much-needed debriefing process for the war-wearied caregivers. Naming and normalizing the post-trauma symptoms in the psycho-educational presentations had provided the chaplains with a language with which to describe their own experiences. These were experiences for which most were ill prepared. "I can't get the sights and smells out of my head." "I never thought I would be walking a field picking up pieces and body parts and placing them in bags." "The heat and the sand, I can still feel the heat and taste the sand." "How do I answer a soldier when he asks me why God took his leg?"

The Third Infantry Division chaplains of Iraqi Freedom, during and following their march into Baghdad, had experienced the same combat stress as the soldiers with whom they marched. The re-experiencing of events, emotional numbing, and increased arousal were common. In seeing some of these chaplains in therapy in the months following their re-deployment, it was obvious that secondary losses as a result of post-traumatic stress disorder (PTSD) were also prevalent—the intent to leave the ministry, marital discord, and a loss or significant questioning of faith.

For many chaplains, identity and faith are inextricably tied together in a term known as a call or calling. Call is religious language for the experience of being set apart by God for an ecclesiastical vocation. Thus, his or her relationship with God is paramount in the defining and understanding of self. Therefore, when a chaplain experiences a crisis of faith following combat trauma or extended deployment, the emotional numbing and/or depression which accompany it call into question his or her self-identity as well as purpose in life. It has been the experience of this therapist that re-framing a crisis of faith as possibly due to the psycho-biological or physiological effects of primary or secondary trauma, or compassion fatigue, lowers the level of anxiety and provides hope for healing.

In another workshop in 2006 for chaplains at Ft. Gordon, an explanation of the dynamics of post-traumatic stress and its symptoms as well as its effect on spirituality served as a catalyst for a chaplain, who was a veteran of the Iraq War, to seek treatment for his PTSD. "The feelings I was having were making me question whether or not I should be in the ministry. Now I know that there is something I can do about it."

In the U.S. Army, the family life chaplains, the hospital chaplains with at least four quarters of CPE (Clinical Pastoral Education), and the CPE trained reserve and National Guard pastors called to active duty are often the only chaplains with extensive clinical as well as theological training. Weekly briefings and continuing education provided through the Chaplaincy Corps serve to fill the educational gap for most chaplains. Often the briefings are on topics such as suicide, recognizing depression, recognizing and addressing combat stress, etc. As with other branches of the military, much was learned about the nature of combat and the gaps in training from the first deployment, Iraqi Freedom (OFI1). Training for chaplains was adjusted accordingly. The gravity of combat and the complexities involved in lengthy multiple deployments called for more thorough training in psychological areas. During current deployments, referrals from chaplains to mental health specialists in the field are common.

Chaplains themselves are susceptible to primary trauma, secondary trauma from listening to the trauma stories of others, and compassion fatigue. The questions arise: Who serves as a chaplain to the chaplains? Who can a chaplain go to in order to express his or her pain or misgivings? Is there a safe person for the chaplain to confide in? The report from some chaplains is that the Chaplaincy Corps is a "pretty tight group." Unit chaplains support each other. They can always access the brigade chaplain. The brigade chaplains have ready access to the battalion chaplains who can access the division chaplain. Non-deployed chaplains in the garrison on the military post handle matters on the home front. In general, chaplains rely on chaplains for moral, emotional, and spiritual support. One wonders, however, if the military command structure and the future prospects of promotion inhibit some chaplains from approaching their colleagues. Chaplains under the stress of combat are subject to the same temptations, trauma-related stress issues, and moral misgivings as the troops whom they serve.

Perhaps there is an additional need for a cadre of clinically trained and retired military chaplains who are willing to serve as pastors to active duty chaplains and to National Guard and reserve chaplains who have recently returned to civilian life. Such a cadre may need additional clinical training and education, but the important factor is that they would be out of the military chain of command. Perhaps the Veterans Administration or local veterans organizations could secure and subsequently publicize lists of retired volunteer military chaplains who are presently serving local churches or synagogues and make these clergy available to those for whom *mission first* overrides compassion fatigue.

THE COMORBID RELATIONSHIP BETWEEN SPIRITUALITY AND TRAUMA

Spirituality, the ability to subjectively experience a connection or relationship with one's Ultimate Concern, is based on maintaining shalom, a balanced connection between mental, physical, emotional, and relational well-being. When discussing the trauma of the Iraq War, there are at lease three comorbid dynamics that affect the maintenance of this connection. In therapy settings, these dynamics have been seen singularly as well as in combination.

The neuro-physiological effects that result in post-traumatic stress disorder and/or depression often result in cognitive, emotional, and somatic impairment, resulting in internal distress (hypervigilance, avoidance, intrusive thoughts, etc.) as well as behavioral maladaptive behaviors—addictions, poor impulse control, violence, anger, marital and/or familial discord, emotional numbing. For one to feel whole, reprocessing of the trauma, making use of the accepted therapeutic modalities (EMDR, cognitive behavioral techniques [CBT], group therapy, exposure therapy) is essential. The reprocessing may need to be combined with medication management.

Specialist E-4 Janice Rogers served for 16 months in an intelligence unit of the U.S. Army's Third Infantry Division, Third Brigade.

Specialist: I've been told that I have to go to an anger management group and personal therapy.

Therapist: Were you involved in any life-threatening engagements?

Specialist: No, but every day, my wake up call was the sound of mortars going overhead. They worked us 16-plus hours per day, starting with PT at 5 am. We worked straight through the day, the same routine from day to day to day. No one slept well. I still can't sleep. I've got insomnia really bad.

Though not necessarily fitting neatly under the etiology of what makes for PTSD, the conditions under which veterans live, even while in a relatively safe FOB (forward operating base), have resulted in a disruption of soldiers' neurobiology. They endure sleep deprivation, the over-arching awareness of possible threat of physical harm, the awareness of increased incidents of sexual assault, and the experience of repetitive, monotonous daily routines over extended periods of time. Just as a computer needs to be de-fragmented in order to run smoothly and efficiently, these troops need the opportunity to reprocess their experiences in order to heal physically and emotionally from such extensive deployments.

It is not difficult to see how the impairments resulting from post-traumatic stress disorder can further complicate the experiencing of shalom when the additional challenge of a search for meaning is present. The emotional and cognitive distortions resulting from trauma often result in emotional numbing, which not only impairs relationships with families, but also affects one's ability to perceive a connection with God (or one's Ultimate Concern). If a soldier's spiritual base prior to deployment was primarily experiential—feeling God's presence—the neurobiological effects of trauma on emotions rob him or her of what was once the core of faith. If a soldier's spiritual base was primarily cognitive prior to deployment—such as with someone who has a well thought out understanding of who God is within his or her faith tradition—the neurobiological effects of trauma on cognition can disrupt the ability to grasp hold of previously faith-bolstering beliefs. This is especially true when the "why" questions that accompany the horrors of war are also challenging the meaning of life.

Sergeant Mathis is a gunner:

> The sniper in our unit was bragging about his 15 kills. We were all pumped. It was like we were shooting anything that moves ... like a game. I was ordered to take out a hut. The men and women had their hands in the air like they wanted to surrender. I can still see their eyes. You know when someone doesn't want to fight. I followed my orders. Now I see them in my dreams ... how can there be forgiveness for that?

War may be "hell," but for a soldier suffering from trauma and a lengthy deployment, home can be a purgatory within which he or she is lost. It is no wonder that soldiers and their families often have negative experiences while together during an 18-day leave in the middle of a deployment.

SPIRITUALITY, DEPLOYMENT, AND FAMILY REINTEGRATION

Multiple and extended deployments within a military culture impair the ability of soldiers to reintegrate back into the family system. Again, from Tillich, *culture is religion and religion is culture*. They are inseparable. Both are made up of systems of meaning, symbols, rites, and rituals. These serve to bring order, cohesion, and meaning to life. In lengthy wartime deployments, the culture of the military wins. The military is a highly ritualistic organization with its own set of values, which are imbedded in its symbols, slogans, and structures. Even the program of spiritual fitness, while admirable in its intent, is fitness intended to enhance the culture that birthed it. If one combines lengthy deployments filled with moments of chaos and terror overlapped by times of monotonous routines, a hostile climate/environment, and adds sleep deprivation, a new existence is created. One eats, breathes, and sleeps military, and relational bonds develop that rival the intimacy experienced within the soldier's family system. Military culture during deployment is for the most part predictable and orderly. Rituals (standard operating procedures in their own way) cover all five of Abraham Maslow's hierarchy of human needs:

1. Physiological requirements (food, water, and shelter)
2. Safety (economic security and protection from injury or disease)
3. Social acceptance (love, a sense of belonging, and membership in a group)

4. Self-esteem (prestige, power, and recognition)
5. Self-actualization (confidence, competence, and achievement)

These needs are solidified and ritualized in such a way as to provide a culture with which the family system back home can hardly compete. For many, the military as a career provides for the soldier's shalom (physical, emotional, and spiritual well-being).

Though monotonous, lengthy deployments solidify a culture that is already heavily infused with strong and vibrant symbols, meanings, rituals, and a language of its own. Once redeployed, these rituals are reinforced from military installation to military installation. For many soldiers, much of the time at home is spent in the field training. The family system becomes a sub-system of the Army and is in many ways incorporated into the military culture. When the trauma of combat enters this equation, the dynamics of extended deployments plus the effects of trauma on the soldier, the sub-system of the family may be replaced by comrades in arms. The writings of veteran Roger Lipsley illustrate these dynamics:

> In contrast, another kind of feeling can appear among soldiers: camaraderie based on mutual need, tribal in many ways—the need to trust, respect and share experiences with those one counts on for survival. It is a shared responsibility, this wish to survive, these hopes for a life outside the madness. Mutual survival is bound up with this feeling. It can be deeper than familial feeling, beyond prejudice, deeper than anything one might have felt at so young an age. It is the basis for heroic deeds, for amazing stories of courage and endurance, for a total disregard for one's own safety in order to save the life of a comrade in arms.*

RESTORING SHALOM THROUGH RITUALS

Meaning is derived from religion and culture. It is reinforced by symbols and solidified through rituals. A soldier's re-entry into civilian culture, with its once familiar yet often mundane rituals, is made more difficult by the power of some of the rituals birthed by war. Bryan Mockenhaupt illustrates this well in "I Miss Iraq. I Miss My Gun. I Miss My War." It's difficult to compete with a military culture that includes rituals reinforced by an adrenaline rush such as the one he describes:

> For those who know, this is the open secret: War is exciting. Sometimes I was in awe of this, and sometimes I felt low and mean for loving it, but I loved it still. Even in its quiet moments, war is brighter, louder, brasher, more fun, more tragic, more wasteful, More. More of everything ... Every day in Iraq, if you have a job that takes you outside the wire, you stop just before the gate and make your final preparation for war. You pull out a magazine stacked with thirty rounds of ammunition ... You slide it into the magazine well of your rifle and smack it with the heel of your hand ... You pull the rifle's charging handle, draw the bolt back, and release. The bolt slides forward with a metallic snap ... Chak-chuk. If I hear that a half century from now, I will know it in an instant. Unmistakable, and pregnant with

* Ibid. Lipsley and Probst.

> possibility. On top of a diving board, as the grad-school-science explanation goes, you are potential energy. On the way down, you are kinetic energy. So I leave the gate and step off the diving board, my energy transformed.*

The rituals in the theatre of war are extremely powerful and often reinforced by the physiology effects under extreme stress or trauma. There is no doubt that the reprocessing and healing of traumatic experiences needs to take place in order to set the stage for the restoration of shalom, and thus allow for the nurture of a soldier's spirituality, regardless of whether the soldier participates in traditional religious faith communities or not. The therapeutic tools, modalities, and techniques of reprocessing are available to the clinician who works with the military or with trauma—shalom—and can also be found in the practice of transitional rituals. These rituals provide for emotional, mental, and spiritual healing by assisting the soldier to re-enter his or her culture of origin. This culture may include the soldier's family system, church or synagogue, civic or social organizations, or any activities within the particular civilian population within which the soldier was comfortable prior to deployment. This is where clinicians and chaplains alike can play an integral role.

To utilize rituals as a strength in the therapeutic process, the therapist needs to boldly identify the faith perspective of the soldier and acknowledge its importance, or lack thereof, in the soldier's life. This may be a traditional religious denomination, or a belief system that provided meaning to the soldier's life prior to deployments. Simple but direct questions such as, "As we work together, are there important beliefs that I should know about? Has spirituality or religion been an important part of your life, and if so, have your beliefs changed? Did you ever talk with the chaplains while deployed?" may open doors, thus allowing the therapist to make use of the soldier's belief system in the healing process. They may also bring to the surface deep anger and disappointment in God, chaplains, church, or synagogue.

Chaplains need to set aside their particular denominational or personal theology and ask questions that are neutral in religious content or expectations but allow the soldier to express feelings that have been spiritual in nature to him or her. Some anecdotal reports from deployed soldiers indicate their avoidance of approaching chaplains due to fear (or negative prior experience) of the imposition of the chaplain's own belief system and theology upon their trauma-related experiences. These religious questions may take the form of, "What has sustained you? Where do you find peace? What comforts you when you are afraid or in pain? To whom or what are you most devoted? How have your experiences during deployment affected the things that bring meaning to your life?"

Once a therapist or chaplain is aware of the elements that make for a soldier's Ultimate Concern, i.e., religious or secular belief system, he or she can introduce rituals that enable a soldier to transition from the military combat-ready culture to

---

* Mockenhaupt, Brian. I Miss Iraq. I Miss My Gun. I Miss My War. http://men.men.com/chan_printarticale.aspx?cp-documentid=3042293

the culture of his or her family, home, or social group. The rituals can be as simple and mundane as the repetitive structure of off duty time such as a designated game night with children, a weekly night out with his or her spouse, or a weekly Sunday drive to explore new places, or as complex as participating in traditional religious services of worship. Therapists and chaplains should be creative and imaginative as they listen to the meaning-filled elements of a soldier's life pre-combat and deployment. Through careful listening they can assist the soldier in finding repetitive activities that fit and work for the soldier as well as for the soldier's dependents. Elements of pre-deployment life ritualized and repeated assist in re-claiming spirituality and shalom as well as making the transition from the military deployment culture of combat to the culture of home and community.

> A pediatrician placed in a mobile medical/surgical setting came in for therapy and "to figure out why I am so angry all the time." When asked about his religious beliefs he said that he was Roman Catholic during childhood but valued spirituality regardless of denominational preference. We identified possible targets for EMDR and preparation began for an internal safe place. The physician was taught and practiced self-soothing breathing exercises. Serving as his therapist, I led him through a progressive muscle relaxation exercise followed by a slow count to 10 as the soldier went to his safe place. I suggested that he incorporate something that would serve as a protective measure to keep out whatever might be disturbing or did not belong. He chose figures of Christ and angels—images from his Roman Catholic childhood faith—surrounded by radiant white light. It was obvious from the Army physician's affect that he was relaxed and calm during this trance-like state; thus, I chose to allow him to stay there for a significant period of time (ten to fifteen minutes) during the therapy session. When he mentally came back into the room he said, "That's the first time I've felt at peace in three years. The anger was gone while I was there. I've never felt so relaxed and connected to God."

This positive safe place experience was incorporated into the treatment plan and was to be practiced on a daily basis before the next therapy session. Amid the turmoil of his redeployment hospital work, the physician found sustenance and meaning in this daily safe place exercise. Along with therapy, it helped to dissipate his anger. The exercise eventually became a daily spiritual ritual and practice for the doctor. By the end of his therapy experience, he had incorporated this ritual into the context of meditation within his faith tradition.

Rituals provide us with stability, structure, social control, and meaning. They are the stuff life is made of. Robert Fulghum in his book *From Beginning to End* explains it as follows:

> Our lives are endless ritual. Patterns of repetition govern each day, week, year, and lifetime. "Personal habits" is one term we use to describe the most common of these repeated patterns. But I say these habits are sacred because they give deliberate structure to our lives. Structure gives us a sense of security. And that sense of security is the ground of meaning.
>
> Rituals flow from the life of the individual into the church. The rituals of the church are the organized, communal form of the needs and patterns of the life

> of the individual. Communal activity is one more way of supporting meaningful structure in the life of an individual.*

Consider the small rituals that one does upon waking up, the ordered steps done on a daily basis such as when one prepares to go to work: shutting off the alarm, the brushing of teeth, taking care of personal hygiene, picking out clothes and dressing, pouring a cup of coffee, eating breakfast, etc. One's daily routine is structured into small segments or blocks of rituals. If corners are cut, it leaves one feeling insecure or unsettled. Even in the process of traveling overnight, vestiges of daily rituals are packed into our suitcases. In our motel rooms, we recreate them if only in an abbreviated forms. Chances are, if corners are cut, if something is left out—no coffee, no toothpaste, no time for breakfast—it will leave a person feeling a bit unsettled, insecure, or ill at ease. Even the small rituals make for a feeling of increased well-being, security, and safety.

Since every aspect of the military culture during these lengthy deployments is reinforced by rituals, from daily maintenance rituals to ceremonial rituals, even without a traumatic experience, the transition to civilian routines of home and society comes with great difficulty and effort. For some, the transition and difficulties are such that soldiers prefer to volunteer for additional deployments rather then to work on re-establishing relationships and rituals at home. Without familiar rituals, whether military or civilian, a soldier can feel out of sorts, internally scattered, or afraid. The soldier's shalom is out of balance and the soldier experiences *soul pain.*

Traditionally defined religious rituals can serve as an additional and powerful resource in the process of restoring shalom. They can serve as containers for, and restorers of, faith at a time when the soldier's ability to perceive spiritual connections is beyond the soldier's grasp. Joseph Marshall in his book, *Walking with Grandfather: The Wisdom of Lakota Elders*, cites a religious ritual of the Lakota that allowed and promoted re-entry back into the culture of the tribe:

> … There was a cleansing and healing ceremony for fighting men. Those who had participated in battle, or battles, were placed outside the circle of the community; a dance arbor represented that circle as the people stood within it. Songs were sung to honor the fighting men, and prayers were offered for their souls so that they could be cleansed of the terrible things they had to do to defend the people. Then the men walked quietly back into the circle, back into the community, because the people allowed them to return so they could be healed. … Any community that unconditionally heals and nurtures its warriors is ensuring its own survival.†

The U.S. Army structures re-entry with numerous briefings for both soldiers and families letting them know what to expect in an attempt to assist in the transition process. At present, the re-entry ritual for the U.S. Army's Third Infantry

---

* Fulghum, Robert (1995). *From beginning to end.* New York: Random House, p. 21.

† Marshall III, Joseph M. (2005). *Walking with Grandfather: The wisdom of Lakota elders.* Louisville, CO: Sounds True, Inc. p. 74.

Division soldiers returning from Iraq consists of a patriotic celebration and welcome. The soldiers parade "through the trees." Flags and ribbons are passed out to families and members of the community, as well as a large contingent of representatives from the VFW who are on site to welcome the troops home. Army songs and patriotic songs are sung. There is a short address and welcome from garrison command. Then, there is a rush of soldiers to their families. Soldiers who are "single by location" get on buses and are returned to barracks where toiletries and gifts await them. This is followed by 2 weeks of reintegration training, including mental health surveys. Following this, they then go on block leave for approximately one month before returning to duty.

Perhaps there is something to be learned from the ritual entry of the Lakota warriors back into the community. What if the 2 days of mandatory integration training climaxed with a religious inter-faith re-entry ritual planned by the garrison chaplains? The setting could be such that the soldiers sat together on one side of the aisle and families and/or community members on the other. Through song and prayer, in addition to giving thanks to God for the soldiers' return, there could also be an acknowledgment that the scars of warfare affect everyone—families at home, Iraqi civilians, those whom we fight against, and our comrades in arms. Suffering is a part of war. This acknowledgment could be shaped into the form of a unison prayer of confession followed by an absolution (assurance of pardon and forgiveness), or verbalized in a prayer for the renewal of relationships strained, the acknowledgment of sacrifices made, the remembrance of comrades lost, and the hope for recovery and reconciliation. At this point in the service, much like the Lakota ritual for returning warriors, families and returning soldiers would cross the aisle and then sit together, not as an Army of One but as a Community of One. If not on a garrison level, the individual faith communities represented on a military installation could each devise a similar "ritual of cleansing, healing, and transition" that would be respectful of the particular traditions and beliefs of their community of faith.

SUMMARY

In discussing the effects trauma and the multiple lengthy Iraq and Afghanistan deployments, one must first expand the concept of spirituality beyond the traditional religious definitions. Traditional religion confines spirituality to a relationship with God. Spirituality needs to be reviewed in terms of relationships of connectedness within the context of both culture and religion as those relationships apply to what Paul Tillich defines as one's Ultimate Concern. Thus understood, spirituality becomes one's ability to perceive and experience relationships in the vertical, horizontal, and internal dimensions. This may include one's relationship with God, self, others, and/or society as a whole.

A broader definition of spirituality and religions as stated above is called for when trying to understand the dynamics of long deployments and combat trauma on soldiers. Often, as reported by therapists, soldiers themselves do not return from war and express their views or issues in traditional religious language.

Nevertheless, the issues that they address and wrestle with in the therapy session are extremely religious and spiritual in nature. They have everything to do with meaning, ultimate concerns, and the ability to perceive multi-dimensional relationships. The Hebraic term *shalom* as used to describe this holistic approach to restoring spirituality in therapy is a term that describes a restored wholeness of body, mind, spirit, and culture. Assisting a combat veteran in restoring his or her shalom is the goal of both the therapist and the military chaplain.

When addressing the issue of spirituality in the arena of combat, it is helpful to understand the unique and difficult positions that the chaplains, the representatives of faith and meaning, are placed in. Theirs is a 24/7 job that may be redefined at any moment depending on the special needs of the soldiers. They, too, can suffer from combat stress or trauma, both primary and secondary. They are tasked with seeing and walking the fine line between soldiers' spiritual and psychological needs. These heroic caregivers are as vulnerable as the troops they serve when it comes to the weariness of deployment, the tensions that can form over time, and the feeling of distance created within their own families. The threat of compassion fatigue is ever present. Their shalom can also be disrupted in such a way as to question life's meaning—who they are as people called by God to religious service may also be called into question. The emotional intensity of their work should not be minimized or taken for granted; rather, it is important that safe confidants are sought after (or provided) for the nurture and care of their own shalom.

The experience of trauma in combat due to its neuro-physiological effects may also result in a disruption of the multi-dimensional processing of such an event: emotional, cognitive, somatic, and behavioral. The soldier's ability to accurately perceive a world view unaffected by the trauma is impaired due to the disruptions of neuro-pathways in the brain. The result can be symptoms and behaviors categorized under the clinical definitions of either acute stress disorder or post-traumatic stress disorder. It becomes difficult for the soldier to restore his or her shalom (spirituality) without the addressing and reprocessing of the trauma in therapy.

Adding to the complexity of what it takes for a combat veteran to experience shalom and transition home from these multiple lengthy deployments is the difficulty in shifting from a military combat culture to the culture of family and community. Therapists and military chaplains alike can assist soldiers in making this transition through the creative use of rituals. Military culture, especially lengthy combat military culture, is filled with rituals, many of which fulfill Maslow's five basic human needs. Over time, these become familiar, comfortable, and safe. On the other hand, civilian (or combined civilian and military) life is filled with ambiguities. The difficulty of transitions within the cycle of re-deployment of former, non-wartime deployments cannot be compared to the present multi-deployment cycle of the Iraqi-Afghani conflict. The nature of these deployments is such that "meaning" may seem insignificant as compared to the intense experiences and relational bonding that have taken place. Traumatic experiences only complicate what may be a difficult re-entry into the family system or former social matrix of the soldier.

Rituals, both commonplace and distinctly religious, can be employed to assist in this transition between cultures. Through careful listening as the soldier describes who he or she was prior to deployments, the therapist can be creative in prescribing repetitive activities which, over time, assist the soldier in reconnecting with former meaning-filled relationships with families, religious community, and friends. Chaplains are in a position to make use of religious rituals. These rituals with their powerful symbols can serve as containers of faith and avenues or experiencing forgiveness, healing, or reconciliation. They can also serve as a meaningful recognition of sacrifices made and the welcoming transition back into a once familiar culture.

10 Secondary Traumatic Stress, Deployment Phase, and Military Families

Systemic Approaches to Treatment

Joseph R. Herzog and R. Blaine Everson

CONTENTS

> Some say a cavalry troop, others say an infantry, and others still, will swear that the swift oars of our sea fleet are the best sight on dark earth; but I say that whomever one loves is.
>
> **To an Army Wife in Sardis ~ Sappho (circa b.c. 600)**

INTRODUCTION

Military families face a great number of stresses and strains ranging from geographic relocation to deployments for extended periods of time. During wartime, deployment-related stressors become central to military families. Two of the major war-time–related stressors for military families include post-traumatic stress disorder (PTSD) experienced by some service members exposed to combat, and secondary traumatic stress that often develops within family members of those who suffer from PTSD. *The New York Times* recently reported 121 cases of crimes nationwide committed by former veterans of Iraq and Afghanistan, many of which were said to be related to exposure to combat and involved domestic violence. The focus of this chapter involves a closer look at the relationship between trauma, post-traumatic stress disorder, and the phenomenon of secondary stress transmission in spouses, as well as children, of returning veterans from Iraq and Afghanistan. We delve into other factors that may render military family members more vulnerable to the development of these problems. We also discuss effective treatment of this truly systemic problem and give case examples of families experiencing secondary traumatic stress reactions in the wake of warfare.

The traumatic nature of experiences is derived from the perception of events taking place around individuals at any given time. Human beings construct meaning based upon their experiences within a variety of contexts facilitating continued emotional suffering in the wake of life-altering events. In essence, trauma is a social construct based upon the exposure to events outside of the range of normal human experience (Herman,1997). Yet for an individual to develop secondary stress reactions, there must be an exposure to another post-traumatic stress sufferer as a prerequisite. Far from being a simple case of heightened reactivity to the stressor of an ailing family member, the secondary stress reaction may include exposure to an incendiary event like violence, abandonment, or substance use within the household. The role change required of primary group members by the return of a PTSD sufferer into the household acts as a further mechanism for inducing strain on the individual's personal emotional system, their affective ties with others, and role expectations within their relationships. Our scientific understanding of this phenomenon stems directly from research on compassion fatigue and secondary stress reactions among relief workers, members of various healthcare professions, and returning combat veterans (and their families). We are still exploring the idea that somehow the relationship involving the PTSD sufferer and his or her loved one is somehow transformed at some point by trauma into a traumatic experience itself. Whereas other non-systemic approaches tend to focus on the PTSD sufferer primarily and the loved one suffering secondary trauma as an ancillary viewed as a support in therapy (Sherman, Zanotti & Jones, 2005), or not acknowledge the secondary exposure as being traumatic at all, our approach is concerned with treating this interactional-level phenomenon. From our standpoint, the clinician must consider that the relationship with the sufferer, in and of itself, has become traumatic for the spouse, children, and/or parents of the PTSD sufferer, which alters the family structure (vis-à-vis boundaries and communication) by creating distance that further alienates the family member with PTSD and evokes an anxiety-based withdrawal response by all family members (i.e., facilitating an emotional cut-off). Perhaps, as Boss (2006) suggests, the traumatic experience stems from the ongoing ambiguity associated with the inability to reconstruct the psychological predicates necessary for family and reconnect the required emotional attachments in the aftermath of long-term absences. Regardless of one's outlook on the dynamics of traumatized families, we assert that the family experience has become traumatic in such families, primarily for spouses and for children in these families as a result of their interaction with the trauma sufferer and the secondarily impacted spouse (parent).

According to at least one recent study, up to 17 percent of combat veterans returning from the wars in Iraq and Afghanistan exhibit symptoms of post-traumatic stress disorder (PTSD) (Hoge et al., 2005). Exposure to those with PTSD can lead to secondary trauma symptoms in family members (Figley, 1998). Past research finds that trauma symptoms in veterans have had an impact on the family system of the veteran including their spouse (Dekel, Goldblatt, Keidar, Solomon & Polliack, 2005; Dirkzwager, Bramensen, Ader & van der Ploeg, 2005), and their children (Del Valle & Avelo, 1996; Rosenheck & Nathan, 1985). In fact, there are indications that family members of current combat veterans are experiencing secondary trauma symptoms (Herzog & Everson, 2007). We must add that reports on PTSD as a result of combat may be somewhat deceptive given that the focus on PTSD, to the exclusion of other causal factors for secondary traumatic stress symptoms (STSS), may distort the true picture of problems associated with returning to families after combat. What researchers have yet to study is the extent to which returning veterans suffer from other anxiety disorders, such as phobias and generalized anxiety, depressive disorders, alcohol dependence, or drug addiction. We should not assume that post-traumatic stress symptoms are exclusively responsible for all of the negative experiences within military families.

The type of secondary traumatic stress experienced by military family members varies throughout the deployment cycle, and the secondary traumatic stress process can affect different family members in a variety of ways depending upon a number of predisposing factors. Among the factors influencing this process are their position within the family system (e.g., spouse, parent, or child), age of the family member, and number of members within the family. For those exposed to PTSD sufferers, the effects vary to some degree in that a variety of emotional and behavioral symptoms may be experienced by different family members in very different ways over the course of time depending on their circumstances at any point in time. It is our goal to discuss secondary traumatic stress as an ongoing systemic process, rather than as an event, in order to provide practitioners with a family-oriented approach for assisting military family members traumatized by the effects of warfare.

SECONDARY TRAUMA LITERATURE REVIEW

Secondary trauma is a rapidly developing theory. It has variously been referred to as secondary traumatic stress reaction (Figley, 1983), secondary trauma (Rosenheck & Nathan, 1985), vicarious traumatization (Harkness, 1993), and compassion fatigue (Figley, 2002). The concept of secondary trauma can be originally found in Figley's (1983) work, where the term secondary traumatic stress reaction is described as "simply being a member of a family and caring deeply about its members [which] makes us emotionally vulnerable to the catastrophes which impact them" (p. 12). Rosenheck and Nathan's (1985) clinical experience with children of Vietnam veterans led them to coin the term "secondary traumatization," which they defined as "the relationship between the fathers' war experiences and subsequent stress disorder and their children's problems" (p. 538). According to Figley (1998), secondary trauma includes "the experience of tension and distress directly related to the demands of living with and caring for someone who displays the symptoms of post-traumatic stress disorder" as well as " the natural and consequent behaviors and emotions resulting from knowledge about a stressful event experienced by a significant other" (p. 7). Over time secondary traumatic stress can lead to emotional exhaustion and burnout. The buildup of secondary traumatic stress leads to what Figley calls secondary traumatic stress disorder (STSD) that "leads to emotional exhaustion and *emotional burnout* ..." (p. 7). This emotional burnout can lead to family burnout, which Figley states "is the breakdown of the family members' collective commitment to each other and a refusal to work together in harmony as a function of some crisis or traumatic event or series of crises or events that leave members emotionally exhausted and disillusioned" (p. 7).

FAMILY FUNCTIONING

Family functioning is often negatively impacted when a member is PTSD positive. PTSD symptoms of intrusion and avoidance appear to play a key component in families living with traumatized individuals. High levels of these symptoms have been associated with lower levels of cohesion, expressiveness, and marital satisfaction (Hendrix, 1995). Of particular concern are conflict-oriented and rigid-moral families of PTSD-positive veterans whose wives are at increased risk of psychopathology and behavioral problems (Waysman, Mikulincer, Solomon & Weisenberg, 1993). Rosenheck (1986) found that the emotional center around which family life revolved included the veteran/father's irritability, depression, aggressiveness, and periodic withdrawal. Indeed some research indicates that family dysfunction rather than secondary trauma is the primary effect of war-related trauma (Davidson, 2001).

It appears that the emotional numbing aspect of PTSD plays a critical role in combat veterans' relationships with their children (Ruscio, 2002). Combat veterans' ability to parent may be diminished through "disinterest, detachment, and emotional unavailability" (p. 355) leading to poorer relationship quality with their children. Children of traumatized and tortured parents have also been found to be at greater risk for attention deficit, depressive, behavioral, as well as PTSD symptoms (Daud, Skoglund & Rydelius, 2005). PTSD families also have more conflict and control while having less cohesion and expressiveness (Dan, 1996).

Spouse Secondary Trauma

Evidence exists of secondary trauma in spouses of those who have been traumatized. These spouses have been found to have higher rates of somatic psychiatric symptoms (Dirkzwager et al., 2005; Mikulincer, Florian & Solomon, 1995; Solomon, Waysman, Levy, Fried, Mikulincer, Benbenishty, Florian & Bleich, 1992) and emotional distress (Dekel, Solomon & Bleich, 2005). Spouses of PTSD-positive veterans are often drawn in and fused with their partner's illness (Dekel, 2005), having higher rates of negative emotions and lower rates of positive emotions (Mikulincer et al., 1995). Marital intimacy appears to be inversely related to negative emotions (Mikulincer, Florian & Solomon, 1995). These spouses have great difficulty setting boundaries and reducing ambiguity. They experience problematic marital and family adjustment with their "husband and father who is missing" spouses, who have poor parenting skills, are often violent, and fail to engage emotionally (Frederickson, Chamberlain & Long, 1996, p. 56). These spouses of PTSD-positive soldiers have been found to have poorer social support, marital relations (Dirkzwager et al., 2005), and marital adjustment (Dekel et al., 2005; Solomon et al., 1992).

Child Secondary Trauma

Secondary trauma symptoms in children are thought of as similar to but less intense than PTSD symptoms and include avoidance, intrusion, and arousal (Motta, Joseph, Rose, Suozzi & Leiderman, 1997). Figley (1998) also believes that the family member "experiences emotions that are strikingly similar to the victim's. This includes visual images (e.g., flashbacks), sleeping problems, depression, and other symptoms that are a direct result of visualizing the victim's traumatic experiences, exposure to the symptoms of the victim, or both" (p. 20).

Children of World War II veterans (Rosenheck, 1986), Vietnam veterans (Del Valle and Alvelo, 1996; Harkness, 1993; Rosenheck & Nathan, 1985) have been the subject of examination into the relationship of combat-related trauma, PTSD, and its effect on children. Rosenheck (1985) described a case study of a 10-year-old boy who exhibited symptoms including "intense involvement in the emotional life of his father; deficient development of his ego boundaries; high levels of guilt, anxiety, and aggressiveness; and conscious and unconscious preoccupation with specific events that were traumatic for his father" (p. 539). Children of parents with PTSD have more somatic complaints, social problems, attention problems, and aggression, and more intrusive thoughts of their parent's war experience than do children of substance abusers (Dan, 1996). Children are both aware of their parent's PTSD symptoms and display PTSD symptoms themselves (Del Valle, and Avelo, 1996). The symptoms the children most often display are anxiety, concentration problems, irritability, and emotional outbursts, when war is mentioned.

PRE-DEPLOYMENT-RELATED SECONDARY TRAUMATIC STRESS

The central theme of secondary traumatic stress experienced in the pre-deployment phase is anticipation of the service member being placed in harm's way. If this is a first deployment for a military family, the family is faced with the unknown. If the family is faced with a repeated deployment to a war zone, it can awaken previous traumatic stress reactions and secondary traumatic stress reactions experienced during earlier deployments.

It is not uncommon for there to be conflict within the family during the pre-deployment phase. These families may have great difficulty in saying goodbye, and conflict can serve as a means to place emotional distance between family members. Spouses may be resentful of the amount of time spent training for the upcoming deployment and grow more emotionally distant from the service member in the weeks prior to the deployment as a result.

Children experience a variety of responses during this phase of the deployment cycle. Children may engage in clingy behaviors with either (or both) parent(s) during this time, only to rebuff the departing parent as the separation draws nearer. Much of the child's response depends upon several factors, including developmental stage, parental behavior, and previous experiences with deployments. All of these reactions, of course, are evidence of the systemic nature of the events. While the inevitability of the family life cycle pushes members along a predictable trajectory, deeper strains on the affective ties that bond parents to children are associated with the phases of the deployment cycle and repeated separations caused by multiple deployments.

Domestic Violence and Household Conflict

We reported earlier that *The New York Times* (1/13/2008) had indicated over 100 homicides committed by returning combat veterans. More than a third of the victims in these killings included spouses, girlfriends, children, and other relatives of these combat veterans, and three-quarters of them were still in the military at the time of their crime. Half of these homicides involved the use of a firearm, while the rest involved beatings, strangulations, and drownings. Many reported that they had experienced post-traumatic stress symptoms, along with excessive use of alcohol and/or drugs. Furthermore, neither the Department of Defense nor the Justice Department kept records of these locally prosecuted cases at the time the story was reported. This was only one report, but in a recent data analysis of members of a National Guard unit and their spouses (by the authors of this chapter) the level of interpersonal conflict within the household was found to be the strongest mediator of the perceived development of secondary traumatic stress reaction in children under the age of 12. We certainly believe that the relationship between household conflict between family members, personal suffering by the exposed veteran, and the use of illicit substances may heighten the likelihood of secondary trauma transmission.

DEPLOYMENT-RELATED SECONDARY TRAUMATIC STRESS

Deployment-related secondary traumatic stress results from fear for the safety of the service member by the service member's spouse and child. Most directly related to the fact that the service member may be engaged in combat missions, this fear is exacerbated by intermittent communication with the service member, rumors, and media effects. Children seem to be particularly sensitive to their mother's (i.e., remaining parent's) stress reactions during the deployment. These may include reactions to rumors about attacks, wounded, or return dates.

Secondary traumatic stress manifests in different ways in the service member's family and can range from anxious to depressive symptoms. Spouses of service members may engage in hypervigilant activities in which they carry and leave their cell phones and computers on at all times, monitor news media channels with acute sensitivity to any adverse events that take place near or around where the service member may be stationed, and responding emotionally to rumors.

Children's responses to secondary traumatic stress during the deployment phase vary as well. Children can have anxious symptoms such as nightmares about the deployed parent's health and welfare, and bedwetting and episodes of panic. Children may also have depressive symptoms such as periods of tearfulness, extreme pining for their deployed parent, and depressed mood. School behavior of children may be impacted at this point in the deployment cycle. Children may take on adult-type roles within the family in order to fill the vacuum left by their deployed parent. These adult-type roles may exacerbate stress levels within the family system.

POST-DEPLOYMENT-RELATED SECONDARY TRAUMATIC STRESS

Post-deployment–related secondary traumatic stress occurs after the soldier returns from a deployment to a war zone and is related to post-traumatic stress symptoms the service member may be experiencing. What has been thought of as a joyous event of homecoming has become understood over the past half century as a period of vulnerability for families as they struggle to adjust to the re-joining of the previously absent member to the family system and alteration of the family structure that results from this addition (Hill, 1949; Figley, 1998). The development of these symptoms may also be related to the level of strain experienced by the spouses and family members during the deployment, which places them at higher risk of secondary traumatic stress development. In many ways, this phenomenon represents a significant alteration in the normative transitions that take place as part of the family developmental life cycle.

Spouses of PTSD-positive service members can take on a caretaking role in which their coping mechanisms become overwhelmed, and they become anxious or depressed themselves. As mentioned, spouses may experience PTSD symptoms themselves as a result of domestic violence at the hands of the service member and as an ancillary reaction to the increase in household conflict. It should be noted that the relationship between the spouses in military families, as in other families, seems to provide either an insulating or a detrimental effect on the overall emotional tone of family interaction, and create either wholesome (or toxic) environments for their members. It is also important to discuss the relationship between the level of a wife's marital satisfaction and her sense of personal well-being. Deployment influences both aspects of individuals' perceptions of their immediate surroundings and their worldview, in general, and must be taken into account when assessing for possible secondary stress reactions in the non-military spouse after a deployment ends.

Children may react to secondary traumatic stress in the post-deployment phase with emotional and behavioral symptoms. Herzog and Everson (2007) noted that these children may respond with behavioral acting-out both at home and in school due to a developmental inability to articulate feelings associated with the anxiety they're experiencing. Children may exhibit an increase in already diagnosed attention deficit disorder type symptoms or an increase in the prevalence of oppositional-defiant behaviors. In fact, sub-clinical levels of mental disorders may reach clinical levels, while previously existing clinical levels of mental disorders may worsen (Herzog & Everson, 2007). They may also experience anxious and depressive symptoms including isolation and withdrawal, hypersomnia, and poor school performance due to lack of concentration and increased distractibility. Children may have difficulty giving up adult-type roles, making the post-deployment transition all the more difficult.

A FAMILY SYSTEMS APPROACH TO SECONDARY TRAUMATIC STRESS

There have been a number of suggestions as to the optimal way to deal with families containing PTSD members. Some have suggested that treating the post-traumatic stress primarily and using other family as support, particularly spouses, will alleviate the symptoms and improve the system's overall functioning in the long run (Sherman et al., 2005). Others have espoused a general family systems approach (i.e., multigenerational family explorations mixed with structurally based interventions) and met with successful documented outcomes (Ford et al., 1998). Although it is entirely possible to systemically treat post-traumatic stress successfully, even Figley (1988) and others (Riggs, 2004) have cautioned that doing so depends on a wide range of factors, such as the complexity of PTSD and the disorganization of the family system as a result, and that other interventions may be needed in addition to family therapy (e.g., cognitive therapy, exposure therapy, etc.). In the present case, we are focusing not only on PTSD, but also on the treatment of the vicarious experience of trauma by family members. We propose treating the family, or couple, as a primary target, with tandem sessions for individuals or other family members. In some cases, some sessions may literally include the entire family when deemed appropriate to do so. Our approach is straightforward in the sense that we make every attempt to maintain treatment on a multi-focal basis. It is important to balance the needs of the PTSD sufferer with those of the ailing family member(s), regardless of whether they are spouses or children.

Beginning Therapy

It seems that we must discuss our approach to treatment of traumatized families in two ways, due to the nonlinear nature of a systemic approach to treating families in distress. The first issue stems from the impact of the PTSD sufferer on the family members and the creation of secondary symptomatic problems, and subsequently, the effect the family member's suffering has on the index person (i.e., with PTSD). For this approach to be effective, we use assessment measures, between session assignments, and gradual discharge with designated follow-up intervals for empirical support. These are idealized goals, since follow-up may be random due to the relocation of families during between-treatment episodes. Second, we strive to be mindful of the influence that family reactions bear on the PTSD sufferer as well. In an effort to address the varying needs of family members within the context of family treatment, our approach is multi-focused on several subsystems at once, depending on the presenting problems and those family members present in the session. This approach to treating secondary traumatic stress in military families is loosely based on the five-phase family empowerment treatment (FET) model developed by Figley in the late 1980s. While this approach was initially developed for use with families who had suffered the same traumatic experiences, in these cases of secondary traumatic stress the family experienced the separation and war in different ways and at separate times (i.e., some members experience the event *post hoc*). Our modified approach to FET as a working model has been useful given that the family environment is now perceived as traumatizing to one or more members of the family system. In the first phase of treatment, it is important to establish appropriate therapeutic goals, determine the objectives necessary to achieve the stated goals, and assess the commitment to attaining those goals. Not only is it important to assess the index person for PTSD, but it is also important to check for other symptomatology among family members. More commonly, perhaps, is the "back door" approach to post-traumatic stress treatment, where the person seeking therapy is the spouse or the child of a service member, who may (or may not) be aware of his or her problems, and the therapist may (or may not) quickly realize that the depressive symptoms observed in the civilian spouse are a reaction to an ongoing post-traumatic experience in a service member. Defining the role of the therapist is also very important at an early point in the process, and it is our belief that the therapist should seek to delineate her (or his) unique position within the family for their time in therapy. Early on in our sessions we begin to construct a genogram in order to get a more accurate picture of the extent to which problems permeate to the family environment and to tease out any intergenerational issues that may need addressing at some point in the course of family therapy. We also begin to look at the family's adaptive structuring of roles and boundaries, such as emotional cut-offs between the primary trauma sufferer and other family members, early in our clinical interviewing, as well as the presence of previous traumatic experience that may impact treatment at some point in the process. As part of our initial assessment, we also use a variety of instruments to assess marital stability, parent-child relations, interpersonal conflict, impact of traumatic events, mood and anxiety disorders, and the experiences with separation and war. Personal preference in valid and reliable tools and careful selection given the presenting issues are our only guidelines for the practitioner, as there are a multitude of clinical scales and instruments for use in these situations.

Framing Problems and Maintaining Optimal Therapeutic Environs

The next phase of the process involves framing the problem at individual, subsystem, and systemic levels, which at the outset of therapy involves the uninterrupted telling of family experiences by each member in a narrative format. Departing slightly from the FET protocol, we allow for the retelling of the emotional experiences beginning with the return from deployment, or with prospective redeployment, if such a transition is imminent. This helps focus on the family-level experiences within the system, and we allow the PTSD sufferer to discuss his or her own experiences at some point early in the course of treatment. We may include teenage and younger members of family, as appropriate by developmental stage, for the retelling of traumatic experience(s). As with all aspects of therapeutic communication, the rules of respect, mutuality, equity, and support are adhered to in these early phases, although in some cases the presenting issue may be of such importance that it requires immediate attention while other issues are dealt with as appropriate (e.g., suicidal gestures, marital separation, etc.). We also use this period of treatment as a way of allowing family members to contrast a healing narrative, which includes the processing of traumatic experiences for all members and assists with the development of empathy between family members, aiding reduction of potentially destructive structural alignments (e.g., fused relationships between parent-child subsystems or cut-offs between spouses and/or parents and children). We also use this phase of treatment to work in tandem individually with the PTSD sufferer and the family group. A referral to a colleague skilled in the use of exposure and desensitization techniques for emotional trauma may be warranted at this point depending on the severity of symptoms and the extent to which these symptoms disrupt the ongoing family treatment. The second author of this chapter has been successful with the use of Eye Movement Desensitization and Reprocessing (EMDR) and Visual-Kinesthetic Dissociation

(VK/D) with individual PTSD sufferers outside of family sessions to reduce the intensity of potentially disruptive symptoms, such as intrusive images, affective constriction, and anxious arousal (Parnell, 1997). We both have shared numerous cases where one would conduct the family sessions and the other would see one or more family members individually. This team approach to this very difficult work is very rewarding, but requires close communication among the therapists and other co-therapists working with these cases.

As this phase of treatment continues, we push families to more clearly articulate the consequence of their experiences, identify their objectives as a family in treatment (and beyond), and reduce blaming in order to alter the boundary structure and lessen emotional distance between members resulting from the trauma experience. We accomplish this in several ways, but in some cases we must allow for the presence of a certain amount of disagreement between members and a respectful discourse in differences of opinion in order to get through the lingering negativity associated with the family experiences. One of the simplest questions a practitioner can ask at this point is, "How did you get through this (experience)?" or "What have you done since …?", and very quickly the focus shifts from an orientation toward negative consequences to a conversation about resource utilization within the individuals and family. When this process begins, we seek to amplify to positive aspects of the family's attempts to overcome their problems and we also note that this point in therapy marks a transition to the next phase of treatment.

Providing Reframes, Altering Structure, and Constructing Healing Narratives

The reframe is perhaps the most powerful therapeutic tool in the therapist's arsenal. It allows for the re-learning of old information derived from past experiences in the present time. Reframing is important at both individual and interactional levels, and provides a basis for acceptance of a future where life within the family can be potentially different for members. If, as Laing (Laing & Esterton, 1964; Laing, 1967) stated, families have a negatively *mystifying* effect on family members individually and at a group level, then helping families to become "demystified" is a place where a reframe may strategically accomplish this purpose. The emotional impact of traumatic experiences may be so powerful that family members may seemingly be held in the grip of trauma and may have difficulty seeing their lives as qualitatively different at some point in the future (à la mystification). At an individual perceptual level, complicity stems from the need to avoid conflict or further upset the structural balance created by the trauma experience within the family, and therefore makes even the prospect of change unpalatable for traumatized families. At this point therapists may find themselves working very hard, as family members' anxiety levels rise and interpersonal conflict jeopardizes treatment, to help members to see their way out of the predicament(s) they find themselves in. Again, the fearfulness associated with the imbalance created by the therapy itself may create a situation where blaming and attention to negative consequence predominates the interaction inside and outside of therapy. In some cases, family members feel the need to discontinue treatment because of the strain experienced as a result of change (i.e., returning to homeostatic dysfunction or "the hell we know is preferable to what hell may await …"). It is useful in these difficult interactions for the therapist to "quieten down" the anxiety and emotional reactance within the sessions. In order to effectively accomplish this goal, therapists must pay close attention to their own anxiety and emotional reactance, and identify the reasons for their experiences of such emotions. Consultation with other therapists can be very helpful during these times. A very simple technique for quietening (dampening, de-amplifying, etc.) the interaction and regaining control of the therapeutic interaction involves bringing toys into the session and allowing family members to sit (or talk) quietly with the therapist while the children are at play, or the therapist may have members talk about a non-threatening subject. If there has been a great deal of conflict and the family can successfully discuss a non-threatening topic or make future plans together, then an exception has been created out of the interaction, which may form the basis for a therapeutic reframe at some point in the future. Unlike a cognitive restructuring exercise, we find the timely and strategic use of a reframe to be more powerful for bringing rapid change, but timing is crucial and therapists must be patient with the therapeutic process in order to ensure maximum effectiveness. A good sign of the family's readiness for a strategic reframe comes when the family trauma narrative begins to shift from a predominance of negative experiences and perhaps toward more positive references to ongoing improvements (see second case illustration for example).

There is considerable overlap in these phases of treatment. Moving toward a healing theory involves helping the family realize the significance of their insights in therapy and new interpretations of events gained as result of the therapeutic interaction. The symptoms associated with the spouse's or children's secondary reactions (e.g., anxiety, panic episodes, or depressive symptoms) should begin to diminish as a result of ongoing family therapy, or in some cases, in conjunction with copious amounts of psychotropic medications (input into the system vis-à-vis a neurochemical change in one family member). Also, the PTSD sufferer should begin to acknowledge the reduction of "reference" symptoms (i.e., those exacerbations related to negative interactions with other family members, or as one service member called it, "blowback"), which interestingly enough constitutes the presence of a double bind in the family interactional patterns where nothing changes in spite the sufferer's best efforts to do so, and in fact things often get worse, forcing the sufferer to initially seek therapy. The mutual supportiveness expressed by family members allows for a safer connection between members within the ongoing sessions. As therapy progresses, the clients begin to see the sessions as routine and begin to take ownership of the process by bringing up topics for discussion, following up on outside assignments without prompting, and simply talking more than the therapist does in the sessions, all because it feels safe to do so at this point in the process.

Closure and Follow-Up

The ending of therapy is an intricate and sometimes implicit process, and constitutes a delicately struck agreement between therapist and clients. It is best to discuss systems-based therapy with active duty families as an ongoing process, rather than viewing them as opened and closed cases. Determining successful outcomes may seem difficult given our attitude toward the expectation of ongoing contact with the same families. The difficulty associated with determining such outcomes is why we advocate the use of clinical assessments toward the end of treatment as well, in order to ascertain whether improvement has occurred. Using assessments at the beginning and the end of treatment, at a minimum, allows both the therapist and the family to observe the degree to which they have improved as far as their symptoms are concerned. However, the use of assessments is not always feasible in the hectic world of clinical practice or even necessary to determine successful outcomes. Whether the family felt they improved or not is the most basic determinant of successful therapy, and whether they know when they should return, if they need to do so. There are four essential questions built into this model that assist the therapist with helping families achieve closure, and these criteria are fairly ubiquitous to therapeutic closure. First, were the treatment goals achieved, and if so, how were they achieved? The next three questions are pretty straightforward to family systems therapies: (1) Was there a change (healing) theory and to what extent did all members buy into the new narrative(s)? (2) What new rules and skills were obtained to prevent future setbacks? (3) Did the family experience a sense of accomplishment, and how do members feel differently about their collective future as a result? Finally, were there any goals left to accomplish and can these be achieved outside of therapy?

CASE EXAMPLES

Fit for Duty

The Thomases are a U.S. Army family consisting of a 34-year-old soldier, his 32-year-old wife, and their four children. Mr. Thomas is a career soldier who has been deployed on peacekeeping missions in the Balkans, and was soon to leave for his third deployment to Iraq. This synopsis exemplifies a family dealing with post-trauma and secondary trauma symptoms.

Mrs. Thomas sought therapy for Justin, her 7-year-old son, who she believed may have attention-deficit hyperactive disorder (ADHD). Justin's symptoms include an inability to focus at home or in school, failure to complete tasks at home and at school, and impulsive acting-out behaviors at school. Justin had recently received in-school suspension for his acting-out behavior. Further testing confirmed Justin's ADHD diagnosis, and he continued in therapy both individually and with his mother to deal with the ADHD symptoms. He also saw the staff psychiatrist and was started on a course of medication. Justin's symptoms soon improved. It was at this point that Mrs. Thomas indicated she might need some counseling as well. An individual session was scheduled for Mrs. Thomas.

During the individual session Mrs. Thomas revealed that she was more anxious than usual, had disturbed sleep, was easily distracted, and had racing thoughts, increased irritability, and depression. Mr. Thomas was soon to deploy and Mrs. Thomas said the family was having great difficulty as it approached. She said that there was increased conflict between her and Mr. Thomas. She was worried about his increased use of alcohol since returning from the last deployment. In addition, the children were a worry to Mrs. Thomas. Not only was she aware of Justin's troubles, the three other children were exhibiting symptoms as well. Devonte, 12, was becoming increasingly angry, displaying hostile behavior toward her including balling his fists. He often disobeyed rules at home and had even broken some things around the house in anger. He continued to do well in school, however, and was on the honor roll. Kayla, age 10, was having difficulty with sleeping, and was withdrawing from the family and isolating herself. The symptoms Trequon, age 5, was experiencing included lying to his teachers and parents, as well as acting out in school. Mrs. Thomas agreed to have Mr. Thomas accompany her on the next session, as he was soon to leave.

Mr. Thomas arrived at the next session with Mrs. Thomas. He briefly described the same symptoms in his children that his wife had described the previous session. I then asked Mr. Thomas about his experience in Iraq. Instead, he began by telling me about an incident that happened in childhood in which he saw a schoolmate beheaded in an auto accident. He then went on to describe some of the trauma he was exposed to in the Balkans. This discussion was very intense and it came flooding out of him. His wife and I were quiet as he described the dead and injured civilians he saw in the Balkans. Mr. Thomas then began to speak of Iraq. He said an IED (improvised explosive device) hit him not only on his first patrol during his second tour, but also on his birthday and at other times as well. He described losing soldiers and intense firefights. He feared for his safety on the upcoming tour. He was having distressing thoughts and dreams about the trauma he had experienced. He also had disturbed sleep, increased irritability, isolation, and withdrawal from the family. Mr. Thomas left for Iraq the following week. His wife and children continued in therapy.

This case exemplifies the systemic impact of secondary trauma in many ways. First the father had experienced early and frequent trauma of an intense and severe nature. He was experiencing many post-trauma symptoms that appeared to be deepening. His wife had an intense emotional connection with him and at one point said that she felt everything that he felt. She became symptomatic with depression and anxiety, experiencing conflict and strife in her marriage. The children in the family experienced a worsening of (as in Justin's case) or the development of new symptoms in concert with their father's post-trauma symptoms.

"Duck and Cover, Dude ...!"

The next illustration involves excerpts from a session with a husband and wife approximately 15 months after his return from deployment in Iraq. His night terrors and nightmares were still persistent, sleep was intermittent, his level of hyperarousal was still high, and he would experience intense periods of rage, during which he would have to leave the household to calm himself. His wife suffered from depressive symptoms, including insomnia, poor appetite, apathy, feelings of hopelessness and helplessness, irritability, and indecision. She was also very anxious about their marital success given his mental condition, the status of his pending medical discharge, and the prospect of her husband being an involved father to their toddler born during his last Iraq deployment. We would classify her as suffering from secondary traumatic stress. She had not been anxious or depressed prior to his return from duty. In addition to having PTSD, he had developed a blood disorder from a skin infection for which he was treated "in theater" and upon his return (according to his medical records the diagnosis was *leishmaniasis*, caused by sand fly bites and commonly referred to in the Iraq theater as "Baghdad boil"). He had also been treated by a military staff psychiatrist and attended group therapy sessions at the military installation where they were assigned. They had sought consultation a year earlier at the behest of his senior non-commissioned officer (NCO) due to a marital separation after a violent incident a few weeks after his return from his year-long combat tour in 2005. She lived in her hometown near the military installation and he commuted for weekend visits for the first 6 months of therapy. He had moved into the house with her prior to the previous holiday season. They had been active in couple therapy for almost a year at the time of the following session excerpt.

Husband: Holy sh*t, dude! I had one of those flashback things—like we talked about—the other day when I was working around the house.

Therapist: What happened?

Husband: This guy we know has these fits or spasms, and he was over at the house the other day while I was working on a wheel on a trailer. He's talking to me and he has his kid sitting up on top of the car, right?

Wife: The guy has cerebral palsy, I think, and he lives near us … he comes over a lot. He likes Randy*. I think he's on disability or something. (Husband rolls his eyes at her.)

*(*pseudonym)*

Husband: Well, he had one of those spasms while I was working on this trailer and kind of hunches over as he's falling to the ground. In my mind, it's like "duck and cover," man. I'm on the ground with him. I'm waiting for f*cking mortars to start dropping in on us or something.

Therapist: Was that how it was in Iraq?

Husband: Hell, yeah! It happened all the time from outside of our perimeter at the FOB. For a second it was like it was happening all over again. We left his f*cking kid sitting on top of the car and everything. He was just sitting up there looking around at us laughing. I guess he thought it was a game or something, but that sh*t was for real serious.

Wife: He's 18 months old or something like that (little boy).

Husband: Then I got pissed off because the other people, her brother and kids, were laughing at us. I don't like his ass (wife's brother) anyway, but after a while I was okay, because it was probably pretty funny just looking at it. It was f*cked up though, dude.

Therapist: I can tell something about your reaction to it from the way you just explained it just then. It's still got your heart rate way up there.

Co-therapist: Yeah, I noticed that too. I was going to comment about it.

Wife: I think that's the worst one he's had though, since he's come back. Well, except for the time we got into it and I moved out the next day while he was on 24-hour duty. I mean that look he had … it was like he wasn't even there—it scared me badly, so I took the baby and left, but we've already talked about all that.

Therapist: On numerous occasions (laughing).

Husband: She even took the toilet paper when she left, man.

Wife: He always says that and I didn't take the toilet paper. I was too upset to even contemplate being malicious.

Co-therapist: I'll bet it was that brother of hers that you don't like (to husband, jokingly).

Wife: I actually think it was either my niece or aunt, but I thought we'd covered that already. Can we talk about something else (laughing)?

Therapist: Since you guys moved back in together, that's been behind us, right?

Wife: It comes up more as a joke, if anything, now than before.

Therapist: On a serious note, your irritability seems to have diminished somewhat. Is that the Zyprexa® working?

We were not pleased with the use of this medication.

Husband: Yeah, but it makes me feel really tired sometimes and I feel drugged out—you know, "draggy" and I don't want to have to take medicine for the rest of my life. I still use the Klonopin® to sleep at night.

Wife: We also did what you suggested with my mom and had her stop staying over so late at night.

Co-therapist: That's one of those things that was causing trouble that you didn't have complete control over with your cousins and their kids living in her house with her.

Husband: She was just looking for an escape more than anything, I think. I like her and we get along great, but jeez, we need some time to ourselves as well.

Wife: I see now that you had a good point, even though I was very upset with you and defensive at the time.

Lack of closure in family boundary system noted previously—follow-up by couple on clarity improved relational functioning.

Therapist: Me?

Wife: Yes. It was causing a lot of strain because we couldn't say anything about it and it was causing us to argue. Of course, when we do that I get to feeling hopeless again—like nothing's ever going to change.

Her anger comes from out of nowhere seemingly—very intense.

Therapist: You guys really need to see this as a recovery period, like we've talked about, so you can heal emotionally.

Co-therapist: He's absolutely right. This has been a time to reconnect for you two and for him to begin to recover from what happened over there.

Husband: I know she worries about me a lot. I wish she wouldn't. I'm going to be fine.

Wife: I can't help it and he p*sses me off when he says sh*t like that (tears begin to well up). I'm sorry.

Trying to re-engage husband who's "blanked out" again, in the process.

Therapist: Don't apologize—please continue.

Wife: I'm angry. (pauses) Not at him. I'm afraid. (pauses) That he won't be okay, or that he's going kill us in our sleep. I know he won't. This isn't the man I fell in love with. (looking at husband) I still love him, with all of my heart, but nothing's ever going to be the same again.

Therapist: That man's gone, isn't he?

Wife: Uh-huh.

Co-therapist: Or maybe, he's still in there somewhere (smiling at husband).

Continues to engage husband while therapist holds wife's attention.

Husband: Yeah. I'm still here.

Therapist: Some of this is the secondary stress reaction we've talked about over the past few months, which comes from being around someone experiencing post-traumatic stress and feeling obligated to care for them emotionally because of the closeness of your relationship.

Apparent depersonalization experience.

Co-therapist: You do that a lot when we talk about things that are stressful to you (husband). It's like you "zone out" on us.

Husband: I don't know what happens, but it happens a lot and happened a lot when I was over there. I still know what's going on around me when it happens.

Wife: That scares me. Sometimes I feel myself slipping back down into that "hole" we talked about a few sessions ago.

Wife's withdrawal pattern.

Therapist: It's really nothing to be afraid of, as long as you give him a few minutes. It's a common response and a way of self-protecting.

Recaps the previous reconstructing of the family healing narrative for them.

Co-therapist: It's also important to keep looking forward, as we've discussed.
Husband: I know we'll make it—it's just so hard sometimes and I wish I could go back and undo it all, but we've talked about that fantasy in here before. That's no good.
Wife: As long as he's willing to keep trying and not become isolated like he's been known to do.

This couple continued to participate in intensive therapy for the next several months. These sessions took place in tandem with the service member's involvement with off-post group sessions designed specifically for processing combat experiences and reintegrating into family settings. He eventually left military service and found employment within the state correctional system. Our focus for treatment was three phased: First, they came in seeking a reconciliation. Our primary goal was to reduce the amount of conflict between them, while improving communication skills, allowing the appropriate expression of some legitimate negative emotions. For the second phase of treatment, sustaining the couple union by maintaining positive gains in communication and building upon their affection for each other was a primary goal. Finally, we sought continued improvement in their own marriage, as well as their relationships with other family members, and a reduction in the individual symptoms experienced by the two members of the couple. The wife's secondary emotional symptoms (i.e., depression and anxiety) were almost completely ameliorated by the process of therapy. While the husband's PTSD symptoms remained, their deleterious effects were greatly reduced and he sought further medical treatment through the Veterans Administration, at our request. Although therapy was eventually discontinued, recent conversations with them (by the second author) indicate a continued adherence to the gains made in therapy, despite minor and occasional setbacks.

CLINICAL IMPLICATIONS AND INTERVENTIONS

There are two basic ways in which to approach family treatment of combination PTSD/STSR (secondary traumatic stress response) related problems. These depend on the orientation of the therapist and extent to which the problem complex has permeated the parent and child family subsystems. If the approach is couple based, we also espouse an emotionally focused approach (Greenberg & Johnson, 1988) to accomplish three basic goals: (a) elicit the expression of primary emotions surrounding traumatic events, (b) reduce negative interaction patterns associated within attachment injuries, and (c) foster the deepening of attachment bonds between spouses. Although this approach has primarily been associated with couple therapy, implications for further use with other family members as deemed appropriate are important to note as emotionally focused therapy's (EFT's) application to these treatment groups broadens and its efficacy is established in the family therapy literature. It is also important to discuss the use of older established family therapy models, such as family systems therapy (Bowenian), structural family therapy, narrative therapy, and cognitive-behavioral family therapy approaches, for the treatment of the problems associated with secondary stress reactions. A few colleagues who are adherents to emotionally focused couple therapy (EFCT) have sometimes acted as if they've discovered something previously unknown to psychotherapy in the form of human emotions, altered structures, and misaligned attachments. All of us as practitioners would do well to remember that the delving into the emotional impact of human interactions has formed the basis of the therapeutic setting since early in the 20th century whether by name or not (i.e., the cognitive behavioral techniques [CBT] practitioner is not precluded from dealing with emotional issues in counseling sessions). For example, within a structural-strategic approach, or any other systems-oriented model for that matter, part of the treatment focuses on altering structural patterns in order elicit emotional responses that are then dealt with as part of the therapeutic process (Minuchin & Fishman, 1981). As we have discussed, the family empowerment treatment model (FET) provides a combined systemic approach that espouses the inclusion of narratives around the problems experienced by the family, gives consideration to the communication patterns around the problem narrative and the structural aspects of family interactions, and allows for the strategic reframing of the impairment(s) into a more salient healing mode.

In the previous case illustration, the multiple attachment injuries were further complicated by emotional trauma from previous relational experience for both members of the couple. It also illustrated the long-term nature of these experiences and the multi-focal treatment associated with improving these symptoms. The first case presented in the chapter dealt with a variety of emotional issues within the couple and the parent-child subsystems. The therapists in both of these cases chose to contend with the presenting issues similarly, but as new problem sets emerged from the therapeutic interactions, each approach became somewhat varied based upon the therapist's specific frame of reference and the within-session cues from the clients. It is almost cliché at this point in history to suggest that the interaction becomes "layered" as more subsystems are added in the therapeutic situation.

CONCLUSION

Military family members who experience the war deployment of a loved one are at risk of secondary traumatic stress. In fact, secondary traumatic stress is the signature psychological effect for military families experiencing war deployments in Iraq and Afghanistan. Secondary traumatic stress impacts military family members throughout the deployment cycle: First, as the family begins to prepare for an upcoming deployment through a series of reorganizing behaviors and structural changes to the family system. Then, during the deployment, as they experience the physical separation, emotional ambiguity, and psychological impact of the dangers associated with the possibility of potential harm. After the service member returns from deployment, the family must re-organize and restructure, or not, with the returnee as an added actor within the system. In some cases, service members have been injured physically, psychologically, or may have experienced undiagnosed operational injuries that may impact the family system many months after their return. Applications for this model may include settings where family members and service members are pre-selected for an intensive experience, such as the U.S. Army's Warrior-in-Transition programs designed for physically and psychologically impacted service members and their families.

We feel very strongly that therapists should take a systemic approach in working with military families who have experienced war deployment. Otherwise, there is a real danger of creating an emotional imbalance as a result of overfocusing on one problem set to the detriment of others who do not initially present themselves in therapy. This approach involves carefully balancing the emotional needs of all family members involved in the course of treatment, and may take longer than a more targeted approach toward exclusively treating the primary sufferer and/or one other member. We do not, however, advocate letting severe PTSD symptoms go untreated, which is why working in a multidisciplinary team is a viable part of our approach (i.e., a parallel system to the family). Acknowledging symptoms as a product of family interaction in other members is important as well in this approach. It is not simply that a focus on PTSD symptoms in the service member or secondary trauma symptoms in a family member leads to healing in the family. Rather, it is a simultaneous focus on PTSD symptoms and secondary trauma symptoms as well as the interaction between the two in which change takes place. In taking a systemic approach in working with combat trauma survivors and their family members, practitioners can offer a new way forward with a unique and viable approach to these problems.

REFERENCES

Armstrong, K., Best, S. & Domenici, P. (2007). *Courage after fire: Coping strategies for troops returning from Iraq and Afghanistan and their families.* Berkeley, CA: Ulysses.

Boss, P. (2006). *Loss, trauma, and resilience: Therapeutic work with ambiguous loss.* New York, NY: Norton.

Coleman, P. (2006). *Flashback: Post-traumatic stress disorder, suicide, and the lessons of war.* Boston, MA: Beacon.

Daud, A., Skoglund, E. & Rydelius, P. A. (2005). Children in families of torture victims: Transgenerational transmission of parents' traumatic experiences to their children. *International Journal of Social Welfare, 14*, 23–32.

Dekel, R., Goldblatt, H., Keidar, M., Solomon, Z. & Polliack, M. (2005). Being a wife of a veteran with posttraumatic stress disorder. *Family Relations, 54*, 24–36.

Dekel, R., Solomon, Z. & Bleich, A. (2005). Emotional distress and marital adjustment of caregivers: Contribution of level of impairment and appraised burden. *Stress, Anxiety and Coping, 18*(1), 71–82.

Del Valle, L. & Avelo, J. (1996). Perceptions of posttraumatic stress disorder symptoms by children of Puerto Rican Vietnam veterans. *Puerto Rico Health Science Journal, 15*(2), 101–106.

Dirkzwager, A., Bramensen, I., Ader, H. & van der Ploeg, H. (2005). Secondary traumatization in partners and parents of Dutch peacekeeping soldiers. *Journal of Family Psychology, 19*(2), 217–226.

Figley, C. R. (1983). Catastrophes: An overview of family reaction. In C. R. Figley & H. I. McCubbin (Eds.), *Stress and the family: Coping with catastrophe, 2*. New York: Brunner/Mazel.

Figley, C. R. (1998). The transition from registered to certified traumatologist. Invited address to the Green Cross Projects Annual Conference, Tampa, Florida.

Figley, C. (1998). Introduction. In C. Figley (Ed.), *Burnout in families: The systemic costs of caring* (pp. 1–13). Boca Raton, FL: CRC Press.

Figley, C. R. (Ed.). (2002). Treating compassion fatigue. New York: Brunner-Routledge.

Ford, J. D., Chandler, P., Thacker, B., Greaves, D., Shaw, D., Sennhauser, S. & Schwartz, L. (1998). Family systems therapy after Operation Desert Storm with European Theater Veterans. *Journal of Marriage and Family Therapy, 24*, 243–250.

Frederikson, L. G., Chamberlain, K. & Long, N. (1996). Unacknowledged Casualties of the Vietnam War: Experiences of Partners of New Zealand Veterans. *Qual Health Res 6*: 49–70.

Greenberg, L. S. & Johnson, S. M. (1988). *Emotionally focused therapy for couples.* New York, NY: Guilford.

Harkness, L. L. (1993). Transgenerational transmission of war-related trauma. In J. P. Wilson & B. Raphael (Eds.), *International handbook of traumatic stress syndromes*, pp. 635–643. New York: Plenum Press.

Herman, J. (1997). *Trauma and recovery: The aftermath of violence from domestic abuse to political terror.* New York, NY: Basic Books.

Herzog, J. & Everson, R. (2007). The crisis of parental deployment on children of military parents: Implications for play therapy. In N. B. Webb (Ed.), *Play therapy with children in crisis* (3rd ed.). New York, NY: Guilford.

Hill, R. (1949). *Families under stress: Adjustment to the crisis of war separation and reunion.* Westport, CT: Greenwood.

Hoge, C., Castro, C., Messer, S., McGurk, D., Cotting, D. & Koffman, R. (2005). Combat duty in Iraq and Afghanistan, mental health problems, and barriers to care. *The New England Journal of Medicine, 351*(1), 13–22.

Johnson, S. M. & Greenberg, L. S. (1994). Emotion in intimate relationships: Theory and implications for therapy. In S. Johnson & L. Greenberg (Eds.), *The heart of the matter: Perspectives on emotion in marital therapy* (pp. 3–22). New York, NY: Brunner-Mazel.

Laing, R. D. (1967). *The politics of experience.* London: Penguin Books.

Laing, R. D. & Esterton, A. (1964). *Sanity, madness, and the family.* London: Penguin Books.

McCubbin, H. I. & Patterson, J. M. (1983). *The family stress process: A double ABCX model of adjustment and adaptation.* In H. McCubbin, M. Sussman & J. Patterson *(Eds.), Advances and developments in family stress theory and research.* New York, NY: Haworth Press.

Minuchin, S. & Fischman, H. C. (1981). *Family therapy techniques.* Cambridge, MA: Harvard.

Mikulincer, M., Florian, V. & Solomon, Z. (1995). Marital intimacy, family support, and secondary traumatization: A study of wives of veterans with combat stress reaction. *Anxiety, Stress, and Coping, 8*, 203–213.

Motta, R. W., Joseph, J. M., Rose, R. D., Suozzia, J. M. & Leiderman, L. J. (1997). Transmission of war experiences with a modified Stroop procedure. *Journal of Clinical Psychology, 53*, 895–903.

Parnell, L. (1997). *Transforming trauma: Eye movement desensitization and reprocessing.* New York, NY: Norton.

Riggs, D. S. (2004). Marital and family therapy. In E. B. Foa, T. M. Keane & M. J. Friedman (Eds.), *Effective treatments for PTSD* (pp. 280–301). New York, NY: Guilford.

Rosenheck, R. & Nathan, P. (1985). *Secondary traumatization in children of Vietnam veterans. Hospital and Community Psychiatry, 36*(5), 538–539.

Ruscio, A. M. (2002). Delimiting the boundaries of generalized anxiety disorder: Differentiating high worriers with and without GAD. *Journal of Anxiety Disorders, 16*, 377–400.

Schiraldi, G. R. (2000). *The post-traumatic stress disorder sourcebook: A guide to healing, recovery, and growth.* Los Angeles, CA: Lowell House.

Sherman, M. D., Zanotti, D. K. & Jones, D. E. (2005). Key elements in couples therapy with veterans with combat related posttraumatic stress disorder. *Professional Psychology: Research and Practice, 36*(6), 626–633.

Solomon, Z., Waysman, M., Levy, G., Fried, B., Mikulincer, M., Benbenishty, R., Florian, V. & Bleich, A. (1992). From front line to home front: A study of secondary traumatization. *Family Process, 31*, 289–302.

Section III

Systemic Solutions to the Interpersonal Challenges of Modern Military Families

11 In Support of Military Women and Families
Challenges Facing Community Therapists

Judith Mathewson

CONTENTS

A REVOLUTIONARY WAY OF DOING BUSINESS

How do women fit into the war-fighting plan in Iraq, Afghanistan, and other locations in the world today? And what psychological needs might they have when they return home? The overarching goal of this chapter is to increase counselors' awareness of gender-specific issues women face both in the combat zone and on the home front. For the civilian mental health provider, an understanding of the military culture and its impact on women is essential in order to help female military members who may be experiencing combat stress. Very few guides have been written to address the needs of women veterans, and women are finding themselves in circumstances that were unheard of 15 years ago in the military. And many misconceptions continue as women's roles expand during these turbulent yet historical times of the U.S. military.

Women are now serving as combat pilots, as turret gunners, on fire teams, and as weapons' systems operators. Since 1993, under Defense Secretary Les Aspin, all armed services opened combat aviation to women (in spite of the recommendation by the Presidential Commission on the Assignment of Women in the Armed Forces that Congress reinstate the ban). A year later, the risk rule was repealed and many units supporting ground combat operations were now open to women. As a result, 260,000 additional military positions, many of which involve combat, are now open to women. Today, about 80% of the jobs and more than 90% of the career fields in the armed forces can now be filled by the best-qualified and available person, man or woman. To quote a female veteran: "We love our country as much as any man and have made the same sacrifices as our brothers in arms" (Holmstedt, 2007).

For both men and women, war is one of the most psychologically, physically, cognitively, and emotionally stressful and demanding series of events that they can experience, even with the best of military preparation (Rizzo & Kim, 2005). There have always been inherent dangers in this career; it is the nature of the job for those who serve either at home or abroad. As the war continues in nearly 130 locations around the world, over 200,000 active duty, National Guard, and Reserves women are serving their country in many career fields; many serve on the front lines—since front lines are found everywhere in Iraq and Afghanistan—and danger lurks everywhere: in support positions, and anywhere soldiers, sailors, Marines, airmen, and Coast Guard members are needed.

Following the events of September 11, 2001, the U.S. military (all branches of the active duty, National Guard, Reserves, and Coast Guard) was activated to serve in our nation's defense. As the global war on terrorism (GWOT) continues past its 7-year mark with over one million military personnel on repeated deployments, this experience has taken psychological, physical, emotional, spiritual, and financial tolls on our servicemen and women (Figley & Nash, 2007).

The "traditional" or "M-Day" reserves military service, which was one weekend a month, two weeks annual training per year, has now become a full-time job: deployments to Iraq for 6 to 18 months, augmenting the Border Patrol in Texas, California, or Arizona, and back to a civilian way of life. Following a year at their civilian job, Reserves or National Guard soldiers, sailors, marines, or airmen may be deployed again to Afghanistan or other locations around the world. The pattern continues, depending on the career field of the service member. Unfortunately, there is no mental health support system readily available on base or in the community for these citizen soldiers or citizen airmen. Military and civilian research collaboration and a coordinated community response team can be of great assistance for veterans in need, whether in the housing, educational, vocational, medical, or mental health arenas.

WOMEN AND THEIR CONTRIBUTIONS TO THE MILITARY

To fully appreciate the contributions of women, there is historical value in acknowledging U.S. women's military service over the past 200 years. Their service includes women's roles as soldiers, nurses, and spies during the Revolutionary and Civil Wars. In World War I, women could serve in medical support positions, although they could not vote. Following the bombing of Pearl Harbor, Army and Navy nurses worked side by side tending over 2,000 wounded servicemen. The Women's Air Ferrying Service (WAFS) delivered airplanes from the United States to Europe during World War II.

But what about those who dreamed of becoming fighter pilots, military police officers (MPs), civil affairs officers, mechanics, logistical officers, and combat engineers? The Gulf War of 1991 was a turning point in history for women. More than 40,000 servicewomen went to war and one in five women in uniform was deployed in direct support of the Gulf War. In 1994, bans on women serving in combat roles were relaxed and women began to fly combat aircraft, staff missile placements, drive convoys in the desert, and participate in other roles that involved potential combat exposure (Klein, 2005). In the first Gulf War, eleven women were killed in action, and two were taken as prisoners of war.

How has this GWOT changed the roles of active and reserves military women? In today's military, women serve in many diverse career fields that were once exclusively available to males. The Department of Defense (DoD) Task Force on Mental Health (2007) stated that "female service members in combatant areas have to fight the enemy in the same manner as their male counterparts: engaging in firefights, taking prisoners, and possibly becoming casualties."

A Gulf War study of more than 3,695 deployed military personnel, including 129 women, determined that both males and females had seen air and/or ground combat and experienced at least one combat exposure (missile explosions in their vicinity, witnessing a death, or viewing dead bodies). Women were most likely to report witnessing injured or dead bodies or having a scud missile explode within one mile of their location in the war zone.

This Gulf War study defined combat experiences and exposure to include firing a weapon, being fired upon, witnessing injury or death, and going on special missions or patrols. There were no gender differences in exposure to the aftermath of battle (e.g., observing or handling human and animal remains, dealing with prisoners of war, and observing devastated communities (Vogt, Pless, King & King, 2005). Future research and separate examination of different types of combat experiences may more clearly delineate gender differences and the differential impact of various forms of exposure.

A prime example of this new asymmetric warfare is demonstrated by the heroic actions of Sgt Leigh Ann Hester, a member of the Kentucky Army National Guard. While she was part of a convoy, she and her team were overcome by insurgents and she sprang into action. Ultimately, she was awarded a Silver Star for valor in combat action in Iraq, a first for a woman since World War II. Her citation states that her actions against the enemy included the killing of at least three insurgents and saving the lives of her fellow soldiers (Holmstedt, 2007).

With the changing world, geo-political volatility, and continuous media coverage, there is a need for community mental health counselors and marriage and family therapists to have a better understanding of the challenges and stressors of the female military member and her family.

WOMEN BY THE NUMBERS IN THE DEPARTMENT OF DEFENSE

Female service members represent 20% of new military recruits, compose 17% of the National Guard and Reserves members, and are currently 15% of the active duty force. By the year 2010, 14% of all veterans will be women (U.S. Department of Health and Human Services, Center for Mental Health Services, 2008). To consider how things have changed over the last three decades and the enormity of these issues, here is a look at the numbers:

- A total of 7,500 women (mostly nurses) served in Vietnam; 41,000 women deployed during the Gulf War, as compared to 210,000 (16%) in Operation Iraqi Freedom (OIF) and Operation Enduring Freedom (OEF) in Afghanistan out of 1.4 million active duty members (DMDC, 2006).
- More than 100 female service members have died, and 570 have been wounded in Iraq and Afghanistan (Gifford, Ursano, Stuart & Engle, 2006).
- Per the DoD Report on Mental Health (2007), nearly 3,800 women diagnosed with post-traumatic stress disorder (PTSD) were treated by the Veterans Administration (VA) throughout the United States. They account for 14% of a total of 27,000 recent veterans treated for PTSD. One of the many recommendations of this report is the importance of developing treatment programs specifically geared toward the psychological health needs of female service members.
- Depression is one of the top three problems for women veterans treated by the VA (Fontana, Litz & Rosenhack, 2000).

About one out of seven female veterans (15%) who served in Afghanistan or Iraq who visited a VA Medical Center for care reported that they had been victims of sexual harassment or assault during their military duty. And more than half of these women have PTSD. Women with military-related sexual trauma had a 59% higher risk for mental health problems and other medically related problems, according to the National Center for Post-Traumatic Stress Disorder.

RECRUITING AND MILITARY BASIC TRAINING (BOOT CAMP)

For the civilian mental health provider, an understanding of the military culture and its impact on women is essential in order to be of the greatest assistance to female military members who are experiencing combat stress. Therefore, it is important to understand the foundation of basic military training. The sales pitch given by recruiters is based on determining the basic needs of the individual recruit and encouraging these volunteers to visualize how their lives can be changed for the better—for family members to be proud of their accomplishments, for their own self-esteem needs, develop a sense of belonging, becoming successful, and for a "steady" job with potential salary increases, room and board, educational and medical benefits for the recruit and for his or her family. These military members may have signed up due to their interest in getting away from home, travel, adventure, or eagerness to serve their country after the September 11, 2001, attacks on the United States. Some feel strongly about serving God and their country or following in their parent's (dad's, in particular) footsteps.

For a young adult, joining the military can promise respect, power, and a chance to test both men's and women's physical and mental limits. Boot camp or basic training consists of 6 to 9 weeks of rigorous training and instills new beliefs into the thought processes of recruits: commitment, honor, courage, integrity first, service before self, teamwork, mental toughness, and respect for the United States are part of the soldier's creed or warrior ethos and core values of the Air Force and Navy. Physically, they may develop to top condition and understand the importance of belonging to a team of well-trained professionals for the first time in their lives. They are exposed to individuals of different races, religions, values, and cultural backgrounds, and are required to meld together into a unit of leaders working together in spite of their differences.

Basic training indoctrination changes newly recruited members' civilian mind to a military mind with one purpose: to accomplish the mission. Their conditioned response becomes second nature; they become warriors and operate with a sense of duty, responsibility, loyalty to their fellow soldiers, and dedication unseen in civilian society. Being on duty 24/7 means doing their jobs thoroughly every day as military members: in comparison, there is not the same sense of dedication to the mission in the civilian world. Following basic training is technical school or advanced individual training (AIT) for specialized career training, which can last from 5 weeks to almost 2 years. Then the stress of deployment begins for both male and female soldiers; this is an unspoken responsibility in this world of military, political, and diplomatic upheaval.

THE DEPLOYMENT CYCLE AND ITS CHALLENGES

During the Cold War era of the 1980s through 2000, military field training was limited to short periods of time. Annual training was limited to 2 weeks per year and deployments were limited to a month. Since September 11, 2001, most deployments have increased from 6 months to 18 months.

However, after recently speaking to returning troops from Iraq or Afghanistan, it is obvious that when military members have completed initial training, then deploy, they are "wired as warriors." Their warrior skills of self-defense and defending their fellow soldiers become second nature. It is a matter of survival.

Unfortunately, they are not "deprogrammed" or trained down when they come home to the life they left behind prior to deployment. Coming from an adrenaline-filled 6 to 18 months of life or death situations to a very complacent and apathetic civilian world is indeed a culture shock. Survival techniques from the combat zone are still very real to the service members; they may display what appears to be erratic driving, which may have saved their lives in combat. However, back home in the United States with children in the car, driving 90 miles per hour is reckless. They may develop substance (alcohol or other drugs) use or dependency, have a tendency to isolate themselves, continue their poor sleeping habits, and demonstrate hyper-arousal reactions. These are all very common responses of returning veterans—both male and female. Symptoms of extreme fatigue, feelings of vulnerability, tendency to startle, memory lapses, and inability to concentrate are additional responses to traumatic events that veterans have identified in recent studies.

One deployed female OIF Navy clinical psychologist wrote:

> After returning home, I took three weeks of leave to be with my family. Over the next six months, before I left active duty, I struggled to reconnect with my family; jumped at every car backfire, popped balloon, and firework; lost my appetite and ten more pounds; and battled bizarre nightmares. And so I returned as a clinical psychologist in a peacetime hospital. I often found myself openly staring in disbelief at patients. I could not fathom the crises that my patients made out of their petty relationship, work, or financial stressors that brought them to tears in my office. (Kraft, 2007)

What may be the Walmart checkout counter tabloid interest of Americans who have not served in the military or possess no understanding of the combat atmosphere is of no interest to veterans. Hollywood gossip or mundane chores are irrelevant to returning veterans who may be bombarded with questions ("How many people did you kill?" "Why are we even over there?"). Veterans also state that civilians just wouldn't understand what the stress of combat is really like. They may initially be welcomed home but soon afterwards, friends and neighbors in the civilian hometown community go back to their own business, paying bills and everyday routines. With the rapidly changing U.S. economy, many veterans have lost their civilian jobs due to their extended absences, or companies have downsized and no longer need them. So the veterans feel isolated, that no one understands them, and that the welcome home is very short-lived.

Vietnam veterans, speaking of their combat service 45 years later, have identified their similar behavioral responses of impatience, frustration, insomnia, and failing physical health from stress, environmental factors such as Agent Orange, and episodes of depression. Usually, the signs and symptoms of psychological trauma will lessen with time. However, the duration and intensity of these symptoms may become health risks if the reactions interfere with the veteran's ability to carry on a "normal" life with healthy relationships. Other studies show that veterans still lack coping or resiliency skills after many years.

COMBAT'S EFFECTS ON WOMEN

The question that begs to be asked is, how does combat affect women? Both women and men experience hyper-arousal, startling easily and hyper-vigilance, spiritual stress, intrusive flashbacks and nightmares, and some physical hardships (from noise, dirt, and improvised explosive device [IED] blasts while in combat). Cognitive stress may have occurred during duty deployment: confusing or contradictory orders, lack of information, loss of a sense of identity, grief and shock of losing a battle buddy, or one's own fear of injury or death, helplessness, guilt, and shame.

From a few recent studies, women may struggle with the aftermath of combat in different ways than men. Compared with men in the military, women may be differently exposed to certain traumatic stressors that adversely affect their mental health in a gender-specific manner (Felker, Hawkins, Dorbie, Gutierrez & McFall, 2008).

Jessica Wolfe's research from the Persian Gulf War indicated that the stress of war may be associated with increases in rates of sexual harassment (defined as unwanted, unwelcome comments or physical contact of a sexual nature occurring in the workplace) and assault (defined as attempted or completed sexual attack through threat or use of physical force that took place on or off duty during the course of military service). Her study indicated that the rates of sexual assault (7%), physical sexual harassment (33%), and verbal sexual harassment (66%) were higher than those typically found in peacetime military samples.

According to a VA study, women in the military are at high risk for exposure to traumatic events, especially during times of war, as well as two and a half times more likely to experience PTSD than men. PSTD among female veterans has been associated with a variety of mental health and physical health difficulties. Overall, PTSD has been related to poor psychiatric functioning (Dobie et al., 2004; Monnier, Grubaugh, Knapp, Magruder & Frueh, 2004). Additionally, studies support a link between PTSD and substance abuse (Davis & Wood, 1999; Dobie et al., 2004; Lang et al., 2003; Ouimette, Wolfe & Chrestman, 1996). This is similar to civilian and male veteran populations, wherein 24% to 45% of individuals diagnosed with PTSD have been shown to meet criteria for substance abuse or dependence (Breslau, Davis, Andreski & Peterson, 1991; Hankin et al., 1999; Kessler, Sonnega, Bromet, Hughes & Nelson, 1995).

Combat veteran women tend to come back as stronger and more independent people, but are challenged by parenting and interpersonal relationships, according to Brandi Wilson, Minnesota Department of Veterans Affairs/Women Veterans Coordinator. She added that female vets often have a harder time finding the support they need.

How are women's experiences different from men's military experiences? When returning from deployment, men have support systems—mothers, wives, male comrades, and older male veterans from other generations—to help them cope (Vogt et al., 2005). They also have spouses or family members who urge them to seek help when their behaviors or personality has changed dramatically or they have become a danger to themselves or others. When women military members return, typically the male spouse or significant other is ready to give her back the responsibilities of motherhood, the housework, and other work responsibilities, and will often try to speed up her transition so that it becomes uncomfortable and overwhelming for the female veteran. In many cases, after returning from war, women are not the same "mommy" who left, stated Yale University Associate Professor Laurie Harkness, who runs a Veterans Affairs mental health clinic in Connecticut. Mothers in general are the emotional hub of a family, and returning home causes some conflicting emotions, Harkness added. Female veterans have identified their inability to function well with their children: they may be overly protective of their children or unable to bond with their children as they did prior to their deployment. Traumatic flashbacks of children being injured, killed, orphaned, or homeless haunt the minds of some female veterans.

Both women and men (Hoge et al., 2004) reported someone being killed or injured that they knew, saw dead bodies or remains, handled or uncovered remains, and saw ill or injured women and children. Yet only half of returning vets with symptoms of PTSD or depression actually seek help. The adage, "Suck it up and drive on"—meaning, "Deal with it and get the mission done"—is still being touted as the immediate solution to combat trauma concerns in the military. Having the time to transition, with support systems in place, to include telling their stories to other veterans who have experienced combat stressors is crucial for both men and women veterans. Seeking help should not incur a stigma of weakness; rather, it is a sign of strength.

Although the numbers of women veterans are increasing, the lack of studies and information about female veterans makes it difficult to gauge their needs. The current data obtained in this research do not point to a specific causal explanation, and the observation that women are more likely than men to seek mental health care during deployment has important implications for the design of relevant mental health services (Kessler et al., 1995). According to existing research, female veterans experience higher rates of trauma exposure in comparison to the general female population (Zinzow, Grubaugh, Monnier, Suffoletta-Maierle & Frueh, 2007). Emerging data also suggest that women who enter the military with significant trauma histories and are exposed to additional traumatic events during the course of military service are at risk for cumulative trauma exposure, significant occupational stress, and related mental and physical health problems. Thus far, it appears that women are just as likely to be involved in combat when deployed, but are less likely than men to be directly exposed to traumatic events while in combat. And perhaps most importantly, female veterans are equally or less likely than male veterans to meet the criteria for PTSD. Although their numbers have increased, women still constitute a minority of deployed soldiers. Therefore, the deployment health care system and VA may not be designed or staffed to appropriately accommodate gender-specific mental health concerns.

WOMEN AND TRAUMATIC EVENTS

Recent studies indicate that almost all female veterans (81% to 93%) experience a traumatic event at some point in their lives (Escalona, Achilles, Waitzkin & Yager, 2004), and these estimates are higher than previously reported (Suffoletta-Mairle,

Grubaugh, Magruder, Monnier & Frueh, 2003). This is likely due to a more comprehensive assessment of traumatic events. Trauma histories are highly common among female veterans, which may indicate that a substantial portion of women who join the military may be trying to escape violent environments (Sadler, Booth, Mengeling & Doebbeling, 2004). Studies suggest that more than half (52% to 54%) of female veterans experience pre-military physical or sexual abuse and that they are more likely than men to report pre-military trauma (Engel et al., 1993; Sadler et al., 2004). Studies show that prior trauma exposure is predictive of future trauma exposure, so it may not be surprising that a large portion of female soldiers experience further trauma exposure (both military and non-military). Furthermore, physical and sexual violence among wartime military samples of women has been reported at higher rates in comparison to civilian and peacetime military samples (Wolfe et al., 1998). This suggests that combat exposure represents an additional risk factor for female veterans.

SEXUAL HARASSMENT AND SEXUAL ASSAULT

Sexual harassment and sexual assault issues are prevalent in today's military toward women who bring talent, innovation, and heroic actions to all branches of the U.S. military and the U.S. Coast Guard. Female veterans are more likely than male veterans to experience sexual assault. Military law defines sexual trauma as "sexual harassment, rape, and other acts of violence." One recent study has indicated that women represent a disproportionately high percentage of those presenting for incidents of sexual assault (Felker et al., 2008). According to another recent study, prior trauma or incidences of assault at a younger age in both males and females may be a marker or precursor for a higher risk of depression and post-traumatic stress disorder (Smith, Tyler et al., 2008). In the DoD, reports on sexual assault indicate that alcohol use is a key factor in many of these incidents. Numerous studies corroborate that some women not only enter the military with significant trauma histories, but may also be exposed to additional risk factors for violence and related mental health problems during the course of military service.

The VA Military Sexual Trauma Report of 2005 indicates that National Guard and Reserves components' prevalence of military sexual trauma (MST) among females is 60% and among males is 27%. MST includes sexual harassment, sexual assault, and rape. The report also states the estimated prevalence for rape among females is 11% and among males is 1.2%. Unfortunately, numbers have increased over the past 3 years. Most studies have focused on the prevalence of sexual assault, physical assault, or combat exposure; therefore, this section will focus on these areas. Reported rates of sexual harassment in veterans and active-duty military members affect two out of three veterans, with sexual assault occurring to one out of every three female veterans (Goldzweig, Balekian, Rolon, Yano & Shekelle, 2006). National surveys suggest that one in four women veterans have experienced rape during their military service.

A Pentagon report released in 2007 indicated that the number of reported incidents of sexual assault spiked from 2,400 in 2005 to nearly 3,000 in 2006—an increase of roughly 24%. Since sexual assault is about power, someone who already has authority over a subordinate can use that power as a way to be sexually inappropriate with the subordinate. A female military member's weak personal boundaries and low self-esteem may make her vulnerable to a male soldier's compliment or inappropriate sexual attention.

From the very beginning, military personnel are trained to follow orders, and that places them at a disadvantage. Some reactions are: "It's not the enemy attacking me; it's family." It has an incest dynamic to it: "I'm supposed to trust these people; they're supposed to be part of this special organization, and now look what's happening to me" (Hunter, 2007). Demographic data is scarce, but in 2007, nearly 2,000 criminal investigations based on sexual assault reports resulted in punitive action for 1,172 people. For hundreds of other alleged offenders, the commander did not take action due to "insufficient evidence," "unfounded" allegations, or obstacles in the legal process. The DoD has responded with new procedures and requirements (restricted and unrestricted reporting) for preventing and dealing with any incident of sexual harassment and assault. This type of reporting allows the victim to keep the incident confidential or it can be pursued in court. However, little data exist to determine whether those efforts have helped.

According to a large study of former female Reservists, more than half of sexual assaults occurred at a military work site and during duty hours (National Center for Posttraumatic Stress Disorder [PTSD], 2003). Furthermore, the majority of offenders were military personnel (Sadler, Booth, Cook & Doebbeling, 2003). Some women are more acutely vulnerable if they are the primary income earners or caregivers for their children. Their careers may become jeopardized for reporting the sexual harassment or sexual assault. The stigma of reporting any sexual trauma is great, and many service members fear disclosing information to authorities (either with a restricted or unrestricted reporting procedure) due to retribution. Ultimately, they may find themselves being ostracized for reporting an incident of harassment or assault. Other job-related risk factors include isolated duty stations, independent duty (such as a recruiter), being outnumbered by males, and risky superior-inferior relationships. Some military members who experience sexual trauma feel that organizations tend to "blame the victim." What are other foundational risk factors? Victim focus, feared stigmatization for rejecting sexual advances, and exposure to patriarchal gender role norms are cited in a recent study (Messman-Moore & Long, 2003).

Rates of military sexual trauma among veteran users of VA health care appear to be 6% for women and 1% for men, even higher than in general military populations. In another recent study, 23% of female users of VA health care reported at least one sexual assault while in the military. Treatment for military sexual trauma in the VA (following discharge from the military) is mandatory; that is, the VA must provide treatment and counseling to any eligible veteran. Veterans may receive counseling at private outpatient facilities in some circumstances. However, in almost all cases, mental health professionals accept a veteran's version of traumatic events occurring on active duty.

As recently as 2007, the VA opened MST residential treatment centers due to the growing problems of sexual assault in the ranks. These intensive 60-day residential programs are designed to treat women veterans with PTSD and MST and emphasize the development of strong interpersonal skills. Many of the women who are referred to the program were sexually assaulted prior to and during their military service, and a large percentage of the women are battling addiction problems as well. The MST programs have seen a 95% success rate for women veterans from many generations.

LIFE IN A COMBAT ZONE

What are some of the combat zone conditions that increase stress levels for both men and women? In a 2006 Army Mental Health Assessment Team (MHAT) survey of 1,767 soldiers and Marines stationed in Iraq during OIF, over one-third reported the lack of privacy and personal space to be a top stressor. High caloric food in packages called Meals Ready to Eat (MREs), loss of connection with family and friends, duty 24 hours a day, sleep deprivation, small living quarters, and temperature extremes were all sources of stress. In the first month of troop deployment (August 1990) to the Persian Gulf region, the weather was extremely hot and humid, with air temperatures as high as 115°F and sand temperatures reaching 150°F. Male troops drank large quantities of water to prevent dehydration, but women drank less because of their need to urinate and safe facilities were at a premium. In some of the areas of Iraq that U.S. troops patrolled, the temperatures reach 140°F. Although the summers in the Middle East are hot and dry, temperatures in winter (December-March) are low, and wind-chill temperatures at night can drop to well below freezing. Wind and blowing sand make protection of skin and eyes imperative. Goggles and sunglasses help somewhat, but visibility is often poor, and contact lenses were prohibited in the Gulf War (Ursano & Norwood, 1997).

Some women returned home with urinary tract and bladder infections due to field conditions. These infections were due, in part, to the female soldier's fear of walking alone after dark to latrines, based on fear of attacks by male U.S. soldiers. Many women have also stated that limiting their intake of water kept them from dragging out the mission and embarrassment due to lack of bathroom facilities. Other injuries included back and knee injuries from carrying equipment and long-term running and marching injuries. Women, like men, are subjected to blast injuries from the explosion of IEDs, hearing loss, and sleep difficulties when they return home. Women have been the key military to search Iraqi women and children for IEDs and other weapons at checkpoints and in buildings in order to respect the cultural taboo against American men physically searching Iraqi women.

ADDITIONAL MENTAL HEALTH RISKS FOR WOMEN

Evidence is accumulating to support a connection between sexual trauma, health-related behavior, and physical health problems among female veterans (Dobie et al., 2004; Frayne, Skinner, Sullivan & Freund, 2003; Lang et al., 2003; Stein et al., 2004). Other conditions mentioned in the civilian literature include depression, neuro-biological alterations, and coping skill difficulties (Schnurr & Green, 2004). These potential health conditions await further study among female veterans.

Even though women and combat-exposed individuals are likely to use more health care services than men, barriers to initial or continued service use remain. For example, one study indicated that most veterans who experienced adult sexual assault and sought help reported "secondary victimization"; that is, the experience made them feel guilty, depressed, anxious, distrustful of others, and reluctant to seek further help (Campbell & Raja, 2005). Other potential barriers include decreased likelihood of receiving PTSD and substance-related diagnoses in comparison to male veterans, reluctance to disclose military-related experiences such as sexual harassment, and stigma and shame associated with the traumatic events that women are most likely to experience.

For women coming from low-income or otherwise marginalized communities, reintegration often means confronting both personal trauma and structural inequality. Without adequate support, they may have difficulty transitioning in a healthy manner. And if their combat trauma issues aren't addressed, these issues may manifest at a later time. Symptoms may appear a few weeks or months after returning from deployment in the form of self-destructive behaviors such as continued sleeping deprivation, alcohol or substance abuse, pain pill addictions, breakdowns, unemployment, medical concerns, loss of ability to properly care for their children, public assistance, homelessness, or suicide. Women may represent a particularly high-risk group for the development of mental disorders in the service, although it is equally possible that this is simply a manifestation of a commonly reported observation that women are more likely than men to seek health care in most clinical settings (Felker et al., 2008).

SEXUAL TRAUMA AND POST-TRAUMATIC STRESS DISORDER (PTSD)

With repeated deployments overseas as the norm instead of an anomaly, mental health and physical health issues are beginning to be openly discussed, such as the prevalence of sexual trauma. The VA faces radical changes in its delivery of health care now that it has become a major service provider for women sexually victimized in the military and women exposed to combat. Congress has passed laws to ensure that women's health needs would be evaluated and programs would be set into place for the female soldiers. These two acts are the Women's Health Care Act of 1992 and the Veterans Programs Enhancement Act of 1998. Unfortunately, there is a limited amount of research available about the complex aspects of traumatic exposures for women. However, more research studies have been completed on male service members' health concerns. In addition, there are barriers to care on both fronts: while the service member remains in the military and chooses to officially report gender-based violence, and following discharge or retirement from the military as she seeks post-trauma care.

In 2007, over 60,000 veterans were diagnosed with PTSD. Of these veterans, 22% of women suffered from military sexual trauma (MST), compared with 1% of men. For female veterans treated at the VA's Comprehensive Healthcare Center for Women in Los Angeles, 60% who experienced MST also had a diagnosis of PTSD.

The problem of sexual assault may be connected to PTSD from combat experiences but frequently emerges with prior sexual abuse. VA researchers in Texas have found that working with women survivors of military sexual assault were nine times more likely to suffer from PTSD than a comparison group without assault histories, yet they received fewer health care services. Many military women may not seek help because they fear embarrassment, retribution, lack of career advancement opportunities, or dishonorable discharge. Female veterans are reluctant to talk about sexual trauma or even lesser issues with someone outside the military, numerous VA MST specialists have stated. Silence and denial are also common responses for victims of sexual assault—whether in or outside the military. Women have had invalidating experiences following sexual traumas when they are ignored, not believed, or encouraged to keep silent about their experience. Sometimes, they themselves have been blamed for the experience.

These same VA MST specialists also stated that women tend to blame themselves for the sexual assault. Other barriers include the female soldier's need to show emotional strength to be perceived as tough, or may not associate trauma symptoms with military service. This can have a significant negative impact on the female soldier's post-trauma adjustment.

In 2005, a large number of female veterans with PTSD were extensively studied by the VA. As a result, Prolonged Exposure Therapy (PE) was effective in treating PTSD in active duty personnel and female veterans, achieving total remission of symptoms (Schnurr at al., 2007). Based on these results, the Department of Military Affairs created two initiatives in evidence-based practice in PTSD: Cognitive Processing Therapy (CPT) and PE therapy as an alternative means of treatment. Thirty-seven percent of female veterans of OEF/OIF have used VA or civilian community medical or psychological services (when referred by Tricare) for some type of health care at least once between 2002 and 2006. Some women seek out their own community therapist with private pay in order to keep the information out of reach of the military system. It is expected that females will increasingly seek care in any of these settings.

A female military member related this observation:

> As a woman in the military, I have observed that we definitely have unique experiences while deployed. First of all, as women, not only do we have to live in a combat zone but we also combat each other. Women here are not always supportive of other women. I tried reaching out to a couple women here, but it only backfired. I don't know what it is, or why women are so competitive with each other. We, as women, experience a different kind of loneliness too; we have no intimacy here. I don't mean physical intimacy, but emotional intimacy. Men don't seem to need that as

> badly as we do. I also see women struggle who are mothers and have to hear about their children's achievements and every day activities, and that doesn't really seem to affect the men as strongly, either. Women need to learn to support each other and not compete against each other. (What are we competing for, anyway?) Another difficult issue is mothers being away from their children. (That is why I couldn't do this if I had kids.) It's not easy.

As this enlisted member so eloquently stated, women in the military sometimes go into a more competitive stance versus a supportive one. Is it a survival instinct or do women sometimes become as competitive as men in the workplace—at home, or when deployed? The reality is, in a combat zone, it truly is a matter of life or death and serious responsibility to watch out for each other's safety. Women military members sometimes check each other out and silently ask, "Do you play the female card? Are you a "slacker"? Or are you "good to go" (meaning, squared away as a military member)?"

Gender issues may differ for females who have deployed or work in the military setting. Unprofessional behaviors from male military members may begin with sexual harassment and potentially move to sexual assault.

These data have implications for work-related stress that many military women may experience because they must continue to live and work with their perpetrators. Military-related sexual assault also affects military women's careers because a substantial portion transfer or leave the service as a result of these experiences (Sadler et al., 2003). As the following observation from a three-time deployed Air Force female stated, there are still areas of concern for women:

> We have to deal with the attitudes of the males. It's not a woman's world over here; it's a man's world still. We also have to find our way into the "boys club" and fit in. We put up with a certain amount of sexist statements and things of that nature, because if you don't, you will be an outcast. I'm not talking sexual harassment, but more like their rude behavior and jokes. Most of us have "thick skin" but when we're talking among all of us (women), we are sick of it. So there's a whole other aspect that women deal with that men really don't have to deal with. It adds another level of stress. Also, the availability for healthy food is limited, and time for exercise is not always available, either. It's not easy to cope with stress in those ways.

Unfortunately, verbal sexual harassment and sexual assault incidents continue to haunt even the most dedicated soldier, airmen, sailor, marine, or Coast Guard member. Such behavior becomes a matter of betrayal, wondering who is "watching my back" in a combat zone. Women often become "the problem" instead of being seen as victims of the system that allows them to be blamed for sexual assault.

"A woman who signs up to protect her country is more likely to be raped by a fellow soldier than killed by enemy fire," stated Rep. Jane Harman (D-CA), who introduced a bill to encourage the investigation of prosecution of sexual assault and rape cases in the military. When she recently visited a Veterans Affairs hospital in the Los Angeles area, women told her horror stories of how they were raped in the military. Doctors told her that 41 percent of the female veterans seen at the VA say they were victims of sexual assault while serving in the military. Congresswoman Harman stated that her "jaw dropped" when military doctors told her that 4 in 10 women reported being sexually assaulted while in the military. The military women told her of their terror, feelings of helplessness, and downward spirals that their lives have since taken. In addition, The DoD's 2-year-old Sexual Assault Prevention and Response Office stated there were 201 sexual assaults in 2006 within the U.S. Central Command, which includes Iraq and Afghanistan. That's up from 167 in 2005, a 20 percent increase after the Pentagon began a policy that allows victims to get medical help without launching a criminal investigation.

The DoD Task Force vision is to develop a culture of support for psychological health, where service members will receive a full continuum of excellent care, and sufficient and appropriate resources will be allocated to prevention, early intervention, and treatment. Yet there may be cultural expectations that make it difficult for society and providers to recognize women as combatants. Last of all, there is a propensity to diagnose women as having depression, anxiety, and borderline personality disorder instead of combat-related PTSD (Becker, Brady, Killeen, Saladin & Dansky, 1994).

HELP FROM COMMUNITY-BASED THERAPISTS

With this research in mind, how can family systems mental health therapists prepare to assist returning female soldiers? With the shortage of qualified mental health professionals in the military, it is essential that community and civilian therapists learn about "Military Cultures 101" (a basic course) in order to assist the military members and their families. Each branch of service has its own unique culture, and each member of the service has a pride and perception that his or her service is the finest, as compared to other services. At this time, there is no published measure specifically for sexual trauma for military women. The Sexual Experiences Survey, by Mary Koss and her colleagues, is a self-report measure that assesses unwanted sexual experiences including those associated with substance use (alcohol or drugs). Heidi Resick and her colleagues developed an interview for assessing sexual assault called the National Women's Study. It includes behaviorally specific interview questions that ask about a variety of unwanted sexual experiences. The Sexual Experience Questionnaire, by Louise Fitzgerald, is the most widely used self-report measure of sexual harassment. Most measures don't assess sexual harassment, however. Also, each family system has dynamics that influence the morale of the service member—both in a positive and negative manner. The family system may see the female service member as a victim of the military system or believe she "asked for it" when she chose to join the military. The military member's family support, an understanding faith-based community, developing a regular program of relaxation/exercise, and a trusting relationship from a non-attribution community counselor are all valuable resources on the road to recovery for the deployed military member.

Additional education regarding sensitive techniques for inquiring about and screening for sexual harassment and assault may be needed. Female (or male) military personnel won't readily provide information about their personal experiences with sexual harassment or assault. A therapist's compassion and sensitivity are essential when working with clients who are entrusting their incredible hurt to a therapist. It is important to help them to draw upon their courage to divulge such family system and military system "secrets." There are treatments available that can significantly reduce the psychological symptoms of sexual harassment and assault and can ultimately improve the quality of life of female soldiers who have experienced this specific trauma. Although there is very little empirical study on the treatment of sexually harassed or sexually traumatized military women, there are studies about civilian women that can be used to assist in educating and treating traumatized clients. Interventions for sexual trauma should address immediate health and safety concerns, as a therapist would for a civilian population client. Another family therapist strategy for female soldiers is to help normalize post-trauma reactions by providing education about psychological reactions to traumatic events, supporting existing adaptive coping strategies, and helping with the development of new coping skills. The current "gold standard" among VA therapists is utilizing cognitive behavioral therapy, exposure therapy, and virtual reality therapy with the sounds, temperatures, language, smells, and sights of their combat experience. Studies indicate that desensitizing clients will help them feel less anxious and more secure in their abilities to overcome the barriers of combat-related sexual assault. The VA also uses breath work (Dr. Andrew Weil) and yoga for stress reduction.

Community therapists can empower military women by teaching them about deep breathing and muscle relaxation techniques; recognition of their individual cognitive and affective reactions to include fear, self-blame, anger, and disillusionment; and some form of cognitive restructuring. Some forms of exposure therapy have been successful for both male and female military members who experience combat exposure, PTSD symptoms, depression, substance abuse, and sexual trauma. Family therapists can also refer to Foa and Rothbaum (1998) and Resick and Schnicke (2002) for additional information on the treatment of sexual trauma. Family therapists require accurate information on the conditions that the deployed unit members, and female soldiers, have experienced. This would include a unit climate assessment to determine perceptions of discrimination, harassment, and verbal, sexual, or physical assaults.

If discrimination, prejudice, and fear about mental health counseling are allowed to persist in the system, building a first-class system for supporting psychological health is impossible. Many sexual trauma survivors' claims are denied because VA and civilian staff lack the training to follow appropriate procedures for evaluating their complex cases. Both military and civilian leaders will need to advocate, plan, and integrate prevention, early intervention, and treatment and be supportive of the female soldier's mental health readjustment appointments upon return to her home unit.

Another key recommendation: family therapists should re-familiarize themselves with interactions between drugs such as psychotropic medications and contraceptives. Finally, when short-term intensive group treatment interventions are implemented while deployed, consideration should be given to offering a support group for female soldiers. The female military member's family of origin and their service "family" values may come into conflict. Educating families utilizing a systemic approach is not only valuable but allows the spouse, significant others, parents or children a glimpse of how a military member has been indoctrinated and accounts for some of the customs, courtesies, and behaviors of that service member. For a military member to report wrongdoing of a fellow warrior is considered "disloyal"; the culture strongly encourages military members to stick together and display a united front. Anything less is considered a betrayal of the camaraderie and esprit de corps of the unit.

A review of any deaths or serious injuries (hostile or non-hostile, suicides, or friendly-fire incidents) of personnel or encounters with insurgents would also be valuable to determine the level of traumatic exposure the unit and individual female member has experienced. Additionally, a mandatory pre- and post-mental health screening for all service members should be done at the home station at 30-, 60-, and 90-day intervals to determine specific individual and family system needs. Additional supporting agencies to assist the female veteran may include Tricare, Transition Assistance Advisors, the National Guard Bureau Psychological Health Office, and the Vet Centers in collaboration with mental health professionals found in community counseling agencies and women's centers in the local area.

As Edward Tick, psychotherapist and ordained interfaith minister has stated, "No matter how well-intentioned therapies are—stress-reduction techniques, medications, cognitive-behavioral therapy—none takes on the moral and spiritual wounds of the trauma of war." Therapies like these may help restore everyday functioning, but they do not help with spiritual healing of veterans. Tick suggested that the community help them heal and help shoulder their burden. For example, on Veterans Day, veterans should be allowed to tell their stories in a public place. In indigenous cultures, elders and medicine people used purification techniques to cleanse warriors and storytelling techniques as "expressive arts therapy."

As a therapist, I use the Native American talking stick with veterans to help each speaker gain courage to relate sadness, anger, and horrific experiences in a group setting. It can be a very healing experience for groups of female warriors. Male warriors sometimes make light of the talking stick, but once they realize the power of group interaction and the gut-level honesty of sharing the pain, holding and moving the talking stick from warrior to warrior becomes a life-changing experience. Women warriors/veterans suffer because they feel they were created to be life-givers, not life-takers. So, according to Tick, the moral trauma is more severe for them. If we understand that the warrior's role is to be protecting and preserving, not destroying and killing, we can find many women serving honorably in our military.

No one appears to have the monopoly on all the good ideas regarding issues of female combat veterans. Both 10% of men and 30% of women with a prior enlistment history of sexual or violent assault experienced an additional doubling of odds of new-onset PTSD. Options for screening and prevention need to be considered due to their additional risk factors, as well as studies of possible resiliency or vulnerability to PTSD symptoms. Further studies need to be done on specific female populations—to include issues of mothers, grandmothers, or aunts, who care for children growing up while an individual service member is deployed. Future studies are needed to better understand the effects of women's exposure to both combat trauma and sexual assault.

It is time to break down the barriers and develop a partnership of military and civilian counselors to help ease the transition of the female veteran. Ironically, the way to heal veteran's pain is by diving deeper into it. Most of the pain is caused by resistance to and denial of it. Our veterans are home in body, but they can't come home in mind, heart, or spirit. Our goal, as therapists, should be to help them with a road map (or GPS, since it is a process, over time) to lead them back into society. As a therapist, you can serve as a resource for the families and for returning female veterans; consider getting prepared to be their healthy safety net or to assist with a "tune up" for women veterans, when needed.

REFERENCES

Becker, S., Brady, K. T., Killeen, T., Saladin, M. E. & Dansky, B. (1994). Comorbid substance abuse and posttraumatic stress disorder: Characteristics of women in treatment. *American Journal on Addictions, 3*(2), 160–164.

Bray, R. M. 2003. *2002 Department of Defense survey of health related behaviors among military personnel*. Research Triangle Park, NC: RTI International.

Breslau, N. Davis, G. C., Andreski, P. & Peterson, E. (1991). *Gender, trauma, and distress. In Psychological injuries: Forensic assessment, treatment and law.* London: Oxford University Press.

Campbell, R. & Raja, S. (2005). The sexual assault and secondary victimization of female veterans: Help-seeking experiences with military and civilian social systems. *Psychology of Women Quarterly, 29*(1), 97–106.

Carney, C. P., Sampson, T. R., Voelker, M., Woolson, R., Thorne, P. & Doebbeling, B. N. (2003). Women in the Gulf War: Combat experience, exposures, and subsequent healthcare use. *Military Medicine, 168*(8), 654–661.

Davis, T. M. & Wood, P. S. (1999). Substance abuse and sexual trauma in a female veteran population. *Journal of Substance Abuse Treatment, 16,* 123–127.

Defense Manpower Data Center (DMDC) (2006). Defense Manpower Data Center (DMDC) report.

Department of Defense (2004). *Task force report on care for victims of sexual assault.* Washington, DC.

Department of Defense (2006). *Annual report on military services sexual assault* [PDF].

Department of Defense Task Force on Mental Health (2007). *An achievable vision: A report of the Department of Defense Task Force on Mental Health.* Falls Church, VA: Defense Health Board.

Department of Veterans Affairs. (2005). *Iraq War clinician guide*. Retrieved from www.va.gov

Department of Veterans Affairs (2005). *Military sexual trauma among the reserve components of the armed forces.*

Dobie, D. J., Kivlahan, D. R., Maynard, C., Bush, K. R., Davis, T. M. & Bradley, K.A. (2004). Posttraumatic stress disorder in female veterans: Association with self-reported health problems and functional impairment. *Archives of Internal Medicine, 164,* 394–400.

Doyle, M. E. & Peterson, K. A. (2005). Re-entry and reintegration: Returning home after combat. *Psychiatric Quarterly, 76*(4), 361–370.

Engel, C. C., Engel, A. L., Campbell, S. J., McFall, M. E., Russo, J. & Katon, W. (1993). Posttraumatic stress disorder symptoms and precombat sexual and physical abuse in Desert Storm veterans. *Journal of Nervous and Mental Disease, 181*, 683–688.

Escalona, R, Achilles, G. M., Waitzka, H. & Yager, J. (2004). PTSD and somatization in women treated at a VA primary care clinic. *Psychosomatics, 45,* 291–296.

Felker, B., Hawkins, E., Dorbie, D., Gutierrez, J. & McFall, M. (2008). *Military medicine: Characteristics of deployed Operation Iraqi Freedom military personnel who seek mental health care.* www.ncbi.nih.gov/pubmed/18333491.

Figley, C. & Nash, W. (2007). *Combat stress injury: Theory, research, and management.* New York, NY: Routledge, Taylor & Francis Group.

Foa, E. B. & Rothbaum, B. O. (1998). *Treating the trauma of rape: Cognitive-behavioral therapy for PTSD.* New York, NY: Guilford.

Fontana, A., Litz, B. & Rosenheck, R. (2000). Impact of combat and sexual harassment on the severity of posttraumatic stress disorder among men and women peacekeepers in Somalia. *Journal of Nervous and Mental Disease, 188*(3), 163–169.

Frayne, S. M., Skinner, K. M., Sullivan, L. M. & Freund, K. M. (2003). Sexual assault while in the military: Violence as a predictor of cardiac risk? *Violence and Victims, 18,* 219–225.

Gifford, R. K., Ursano, R. J., Stuart, J. A. & Engel, C. C. (2006). Stress and stressors of the early phases of the Persian Gulf War. *Philosophical Transactions of the Royal Society of London—Series B: Biological Sciences, 361*(1468), 585–591.

Goldzweig, C. L., Balekian, T. M., Rolon, C., Yano, E. M. & Shekelle, P. G. (2006). The state of women veterans' health research: Results of a systematic literature review. *Journal of General Internal Medicine, 21*(Suppl 3), S82–S92.

Hankin, C. S., Skinner, K. M., Sullivan, L. M., Miller, D. R., Frayne, S. & Tripp, T. J. (1999). Prevalence of depressive and alcohol abuse symptoms among women VA outpatients who report experiencing sexual assault while in the military. *Journal of Traumatic Stress, 12,* 601–612.

Hoge, C., Castro, C., Messer, S., McGurk, D., Cotting, D. & Koffman, R. (2004). Combat duty in Iraq and Afghanistan, mental health problems, and barriers to care. *New England Journal of Medicine, 351*, 13–22.

Holmstedt, K. (2007). *Band of sisters: American women at war in Iraq (p. 309).* Mechanicsburg, PA: Stackpole Books.

Hunter, M. (2007). *Honor betrayed: Sexual abuse in America's military*. Fort Lee, NJ: Hunter.

Kessler, R., Sonnega, A., Bromet, E., Hughes, M. & Nelson, C.B. (1995). Posttraumatic stress disorder in the National Comorbidity Survey. *Archives of General Psychiatry, 52*, 1048–1060.

Klein, R. E. (2005). *Women veterans: Past, present, and future.* Washington DC: U.S. Department of Veterans Affairs.

Kraft, H. S. *(2007). Rule number two, lessons I learned in a combat hospital.* New York, NY: Little, Brown and Company.

Lang A. J., Rodgers, C. S., Laffaye, C., Satz, L. E., Dresselhaus, T. R. & Stein, M. B. (2003). Sexual trauma, posttraumatic stress disorder, and health behavior. *Behavioral Medicine, 28*, 150–158.

Messman-Moore, T. & Long, P. J. (2003). The role of childhood sexual abuse sequelae in the sexual revictimization of women: An empirical review and theoretical formulation. *Clinical Psychology Review, 23*, 537–571.

Monnier, J., Grubaugh, A. L., Knapp, R. G., Magruder, K. M. & Frueh, B. C. (2004). U.S. female veterans in VA primary care: Posttraumatic stress disorder symptoms and functional status. *Primary Care Psychiatry, 9*, 145–150.

National Center for Posttraumatic Stress Disorder (2003). *Fact sheet on MST.*

NDAA 1994, HR 2401, (Sec. 543) Combat Exclusion Law.

Ouimette, P., Wolfe, J. & Chrestman, K. R. (1996). Characteristics of posttraumatic stress disorder-alcohol abuse comorbidity in women. *Journal of Substance Abuse, 8*, 335-346.

Resick, P. S. & Schnicke, M. K. (2002). *Cognitive processing therapy for rape victims: A treatment manual.* Newbury Park, CA: Sage.

Rizzo, A. A. & Kim, G. (2005). A SWOT analysis of the field of Virtual Rehabilitation and Therapy. *Presence: Teleoperators and Virtual Environments, 14*(2), 1–28.

Sadler, A. G., Booth, B. M., Cook, B. L. & Doebbeling, B. N. (2003). Women's military environmental risk factors for rape. *American Journal of Industrial Medicine, 43*, 262–273.

Sadler, A. G., Booth, B. M., Cook, B. L., Torner, J. C. & Doebbeling, B. N. (2001). The military environment: Risk factors for women's non-fatal assaults. *Journal of Occupational and Environmental Medicine, 43*(4), 325-334.

Sadler, A. G., Booth, B. M., Mengeling, M. A. & Doebbeling, B. N. (2004). Lifespan and repeated violence against women during military. *Journal of Women's Health, 13*(7), 799–811.

Sadler, A. G., Booth, B. M., Nielson, B. & Doebbeling, B. N. (2000). Health-related consequences of physical and sexual violence: Women in the military. *Obstetrics and Gynecology, 96*(3), 493–480.

Schnurr, P. P., Friedman, M. J., Engel, C. C., Foa, E. B., Shea, M. T., Chow, B. K., et al. (2007). Cognitive behavioral therapy for posttraumatic stress disorder in women: A randomized controlled trial. *Journal of the American Medical Association, 297*, 820–830.

Schnurr, P. P. & Green, B. L. (2004). *Trauma and health: physical health consequences of exposure to extreme stress*. Washington, DC: American Psychological Association.

Smith, T., Wingard, D., Ryan, M., Kritz-Silverstein, D., Slymen, D. & Sallis, J. (2008). Prior assault and posttraumatic stress disorder after combat deployment. *Epidemiology, 19*(3), 505–512.

Suffoletta-Mairle, S., Grubaugh, A. L., Magruder, K., Monnier, J. & Frueh, B. C. (2003). Trauma-related mental health needs and service utilization among female veterans. *Journal of Psychiatric Practice, 9*, 367–375.

Stein, M. B., Lang, A. J., Laffaye, C., Satz, L. E., Lenox, R. J. & Dresselhaus, T. R. (2004). Relationship of sexual assault history to somatic symptoms and health anxiety in women. *General Hospital Psychiatry, 26*, 178–83.

Tick, E. (2008). Like wandering ghosts: How the U.S. fails its returning soldiers. *The Sun.*

Ursano, R. & Norwood, A. (1997). Understanding the effects of combat stress, trauma, and extreme environments on women's health. *Military Medicine, 162*, 643–648.

Vogt, D. S., Pless, A. P., King, L. A. & King, D. W. (2005). Deployment stressors, genders, and mental health outcomes among Gulf War I veterans. *Journal of Traumatic Stress*, 271–284.

Wilson, B. CPT, MN ARNG. Women's Veterans Affairs Coordinator of the Minnesota Department of Veterans Affairs.

Wolfe, J., Sharkansky, E. J., Read, J. P., Dawson, R., Martin, J. A. & Oimette, P. C. (1998). Sexual harassment and assault as predictors of PTSD symptomatology among U.S. female Persian Gulf military personnel. *Journal of Interpersonal Violence, 13,* 40–57.

Zinzow, H., Grubaugh, A., Monnier, J., Suffoletta-Maierle, S. & Frueh, B. C. (2007). Trauma among female veterans, a critical review. *Trauma, Violence, and Abuse, 8*(4), 384–400.

12 Painting a Moving Train

Preparing Civilian Community Providers to Serve Returning Warriors and Their Families

Charles "Keith" Springle and Charlotte M. Wilmer

CONTENTS

Local community civilian providers are responsible for a very significant part of the support for returning combat veterans and families. There are a lot of reasons veterans as well as current active duty and family members seek care outside of the Department of Defense and/or the Veterans Administration (VA). Stigma and the fact that care, especially mental health care, may affect future assignments and security clearances clearly influence choice. Once a person leaves the military, whether through retirement or end of commitment, he or she may not live near military or VA treatment facilities. This is not a new issue or an issue that is necessarily the result of the current force or wars. The National Vietnam Veterans Readjustment Study found that 68% of Vietnam veterans with post-traumatic stress disorder (PTSD) who sought mental health care did so in non-military settings (Kulka et al., 1990). Military family members often feel more comfortable seeking services in the civilian community, and in some cases they may be ineligible or otherwise unable to obtain care on base.

Civilian providers clearly posses the clinical competency to provide the care, but sometimes lack the military cultural point of reference, which can be critical to successfully serving this population. To be successful, civilian providers must recognize the military communities' perception, real or imagined, that they are unique. This is especially so when the issues are related to combat experience. Thus, as with clinical practice in any culture different from the culture of the provider, one must ensure cultural competence to treat.

In early 2006, several people in the Wilmington, North Carolina, area started developing ideas for training civilian primary care and mental health providers who provide care for returning veterans. In September 2006, North Carolina Governor Michael Easley convened a summit of key leaders of the NC State Government, Veterans Administration, and Department of Defense (DoD), meeting with representatives of state and community provider and consumer groups. The summit participants were charged to develop new ideas that would help veterans succeed in getting back to their families, their jobs, and their communities after service in Afghanistan and Iraq. The Citizen-Soldier Support Program (CSSP) stepped in and began building on and cooperating with this effort. CSSP is a federally funded, national demonstration program housed at the University of North Carolina. The CSSP's mission is to mobilize and engage communities to support service members and families, particularly reservists and the National Guard and their families. The CSSP partnered with the South East Area Health Education Center (SEAHEC) in Wilmington, NC, a region in North Carolina's Area Health Education Center Program (NC-AHEC). The mission of NC-AHEC is to meet North Carolina's health workforce needs by providing educational programs in partnership with academic institutions, health care agencies, and other organizations. The AHEC system provided the delivery mechanism for training non-military and non-Veterans Administration health care providers. The CSSP and SEAHEC were joined by Dr. Harold Kudler, a psychiatrist and mental health coordinator for the Veterans Integrated Service Network (VISN) in Durham, NC, and Charlotte Wilmer, LCSW at the Community Counseling Center, Marine Corps Base, Camp Lejeune, NC.

The group ultimately produced a training program called "Painting a Moving Train." The program included a training curriculum presented in a series of 8-hour workshops designed as an attempt to fill in the gaps, and otherwise support the civilian providers who treat veterans. "Painting a Moving Train" was chosen to reflect the reality that the operations in Afghanistan and Iraq were/are ongoing and dynamic. General Robert Magnus (2007), Assistant Commandant of the U.S. Marine Corps, in his opening remarks at the 2007 Marine Corps Combat/Operational Stress Control Conference, used the term when he referred to Marine Corps efforts to provide appropriate services to our marines, sailors, and families. The consequences of service in Operation Enduring Freedom (OEF) and Operation Iraqi Freedom (OIF) continue to evolve. Likewise, the state of our knowledge about the effects of combat is evolving. We cannot wait until we have all the answers to begin to paint the train! This article provides an overview of some key components of our program, and is an invitation for providers to improve our capacity to serve the military community upon return from war.

WHO HAS BEEN AFFECTED BY THESE WARS?

We are involved in a long war. The United States has been in Afghanistan since October 2001 and in Iraq since March 2003. As of November 27, 2006, the wars surpassed the time frames of most of America's wars. The American Civil War lasted 4 years. WWI lasted about 4½ years. And lots of people have been affected by the wars in Afghanistan and Iraq. Military service, and sadly, war, are very much family affairs in 2008. As of this writing, approximately 3.5 million people serve in uniform. Over 54% of the force is married, including 70% of officers and almost 52% of enlisted personnel (Department of Defense, 2006). There are an estimated 1,865,058 family members (including spouses, children, and adult dependents) of active duty military. About 37% are married with children, 5.4% are single parents, and almost 7% are dual-career military couples. There are almost 470,000 military dependent children between the ages of 1 and 5, approximately 375,000 children between the ages of 6 and 11, and over 285,000 children between the ages of 12 and 18. In addition, there are over 8,000 adult dependents of active duty military. Almost half of the spouses of active duty members are 30 years of age or younger. Seventy-five percent of spouses of officers, who tend to be older, are 31 or older (Hall, 2008).

At any given moment over the past 7 to 8 years, approximately a quarter of a million of our active duty troops, reservists, and National Guard members are either preparing to deploy or are deployed, and three out of every five of these deployed service members have family responsibilities (i.e., spouse and/or children) (American Psychological Association, 2007). Approximately 1.6 million have served in Iraq and Afghanistan. According to the President's Commission on Care for America's Returning Wounded Warriors (2007), as of July 2007, there had been 2,200,000 deployments. According to the Rand report "Invisible Wounds," one-third of those who have deployed have served at least two tours in a combat zone, 70,000 have been deployed three times, and 20,000 have been deployed at least five times. At this writing, an estimated 700,000 children in America have at least one parent deployed (Rand Corporation, 2008).

HOW HAVE THEY BEEN AFFECTED?

War changes people's lives. No one who has been in combat returns completely unchanged. However, most combat veterans return to their families and, after a period of adjustment with some predictable challenges, successfully resume a "normal" lifestyle. The characteristics of one's experiences in these wars (i.e., ambiguous rules of engagement, multiple deployments, the intensity of the combat, and role of civilian combatants), may lead to a significant number of combat veterans and their families accessing psychological health services upon return and in the years to come.

"The war in Iraq remains very personal. Over 75 percent of OEF/OIF vets surveyed reported being in situations where they could be seriously injured or killed; 62 to 66 percent knew someone seriously injured or killed; more than one third described an event that caused them intense fear, helplessness or horror" (Office of the Surgeon General, 2006). Hoge and colleagues (2004) estimated that, using strict screening criteria, 17 percent of soldiers from brigade combat teams are at risk for developing clinically significant symptoms of post-traumatic stress disorder (PTSD), major depression, or anxiety after deployment, and that an even higher percentage (28 percent) would experience symptoms if broader screening criteria were used. The prevalence of PTSD within a year of combat deployment was estimated to range from 10 percent to 25 percent. More recent data from the Post-Deployment Health Re-Assessment (PDHRA), which is administered to service members 90 to 120 days after returning from deployment, indicates that 38 percent of soldiers and 31 percent of marines report psychological symptoms. Among members of the National Guard, the figure rises to 49 percent (Department of Defense Task Force on Mental Health, 2007).

Psychological concerns are also significantly higher among those with repeated deployments, a rapidly growing cohort. Psychological concerns among family members of deployed and returning OIF and OEF veterans, while yet to be fully quantified, are also an issue of concern. Further, hundreds of thousands of U.S. children have experienced the deployment of a parent. Clearly, the challenges are enormous and the consequences of non-performance are significant (Kulka et al., 1990).

WHERE DO THOSE AFFECTED BY WAR TURN FOR HELP?

Just where do members of the military and their families seek services? As outlined in the Department of Defense Task Force report (2007), no single mental health program exists across the DoD. There are numerous psychological health programs both inside and outside the formal military health system. Many programs are imbedded in the command element: suicide prevention, substance abuse prevention, domestic violence prevention, building resilience and capacity to withstand the combat environment challenges. While there are multiple points of access for psychological health support, there may be confusion about benefits and services, fragmented delivery of care, and gaps in service provision.

The Department of Defense's "internal" system of support for services includes the following components:

Tricare comprises the DoD's worldwide health care program for active duty and retired uniformed services members and their families. Psychological health services are provided in the purchased care system via the Tricare network.

The Military Health System (MHS) provides mental health specialty care, counseling, and preventive services. Mental health clinics are staffed by uniformed and civilian psychiatrists, psychologists, mental health nurses, social workers, and mental health technicians.

If assigned to a military installation, active duty service members are required to seek services at a **Military Health Facility (MTF)** when accessing non-emergency mental health care.

Each military Service has **substance abuse prevention and treatment programs** designed to promote readiness and wellness through the prevention and treatment of substance misuse. These programs are organized differently within each of the services and each service assigns a unique name to these agencies.

The services' **Family Support Centers' (FSCs)** mission is to support military and family members in a number of ways, including helping families cope prior to, during, and following deployment; and offering counseling for clinical disorders, including marital problems, and services to support new parents, those with financial problems, and those who need help finding a job. There are also key volunteer and family readiness support services. As with substance abuse programs, each service has a unique name for these organizations.

Each service manages and supports a **Family Advocacy Program (FAP)**, which is a broad-based program to prevent, identify, report, treat, and follow-up on cases of child and partner abuse. Psychological health assets of the FAP work closely with command and medical assets for consultation, evaluation, and treatment.

Military OneSource is a DoD-funded initiative offering a 24-hour, 7-day-a-week, confidential non-medical information and referral system that can be accessed globally through the telephone, Internet, and e-mail. Through Military OneSource, face-to-face counseling in local communities is provided to active duty and reserve component members and their families. There is no cost for up to six sessions per person per problem per year.

Chaplains are often the first point of contact for service members and family members experiencing distress. While deployed, mental health and pastoral services often work in close partnership and constitute an essential component of deployment support. In garrison or homeport, military chaplains are often sought for individual and marital counseling because stigma may be lessened and pastoral counselors can offer greater assurances of confidentiality.

Finally, upon separation from military service, many will be eligible for care within the Veterans Administration. The **Department of Veterans Affairs** provides mental health care to former service members, including those who have been medically retired, as well as specialty care for some service members who remain on active duty.

Included within this internal framework are various special programs to address special issues related to supporting the psychological health and well-being of military members and their families. Some of these programs include health promotions, sexual assault prevention and response offices, exceptional family member programs, suicide prevention programs, and combat operational stress control initiatives.

Even though there are numerous services and personnel associated with the DoD and the Department of Veterans Affairs, we can expect veterans and their families to access civilian community services.

Even if You Build It, They May Not Come ...

Many beneficiaries cannot or do not want to seek services via the direct care system and choose to get care outside of the internal system. As previously stated, this is not a new phenomenon. The National Vietnam Veterans Readjustment Study found that only 20 percent of the Vietnam veterans with PTSD at the time of the study had ever gone to the VA for mental health (MH) care. Sixty-two percent of all Vietnam veterans with PTSD had sought MH care at some point. Of those, 32 percent came to the VA and 68 percent went elsewhere (Kulka et al., 1990).

Of the 686,306 OIF and OEF veterans separated from active duty service between 2002 and December 2006 who were eligible for Department of Veterans Affairs (DVA) care, 229,015 (33 percent) accessed care at a DVA facility. Of those 229,015 veterans who accessed care since 2002, 83,889 (37 percent) received a diagnosis of or were evaluated for a mental disorder, including PTSD (39,243 or 17 percent), non-dependent abuse of drugs (33,099 or 14 percent), and depressive disorder (27,023 or 12 percent) (Veterans Health Affairs Office of Public Health and Environmental Hazards, 2006).

More and more civilian counselors are working with military members and families, both because they are going off base for assistance and because the military is now employing, through employment-assistant-type programs (EAP), civilian counselors to help with the enormity of the task (Hall, 2008). Kristin Henderson suggests in "While They're at War," that "... there's a growing gap between the civilian world and the military community ..." (Henderson, 2006). "Despite near-constant news coverage of conflict in the Middle East, young Americans have a weak knowledge of the geography of this region. Six in ten (63 percent) cannot find Iraq or Saudi Arabia on a map of the Middle East, while three-quarters (75 percent) cannot find Iran or Israel. In fact, 44 percent cannot find even one of these four countries. Nine in ten (88 percent) cannot find Afghanistan on a map of Asia" (National Geographic-Roper Public Affairs, 2006).

The "gap" in knowledge creates a significant barrier to treatment. Staff Sgt. Gladys Santos, who attempted suicide after three tours in Iraq, told investigators the following: "When I come to feeling overwhelmed … I want a one-on-one talk with a trained psychiatrist who's either been to war or understands war" (*Newsweek*, 2008). The overriding message is: *If you want to help, you must have an insight into what we've been through. You must be willing to listen.* So it's critical that those who work with military members and their families are not only trained but work to understand the worldview, mind-set and culture of the military before attempting to intervene and work with these families (Hall, 2008). You must be culturally competent.

TOWARD CULTURAL COMPETENCE: WHAT DO YOU NEED TO KNOW ABOUT YOUR MILITARY CLIENT'S WORLD?

Military Culture

"Militaries have always seen themselves somewhat apart from the larger societies that support them and that they are constituted to protect. Part of the separateness stems from the military mission and its burdens. But the American military has, during the Cold War, by its rapid rotation of people through assignments and posts and by its substantial forward presence overseas, enhanced that separateness and fostered a separate military family and society" (Zellman, Heilbrunn & Builder, 1993).

In October of 2000, one of the authors of this piece was on an assignment that placed my family in a town far away from any military bases or large concentrations of military people. I was driving with my daughter and her teammate to an out-of-town high school volleyball game. We were talking about our family history of moving and where we might next be transferred. I used the term "PCS." Her friend asked, "What's that mean?" My daughter replied, "Oh, it means permanent change of station. That's when we move from here." Her friend asked, "So when you leave here you'll move somewhere permanently?" My daughter replied, "No, that just means we are going someplace else for three years." Her friend asked, "Three years is permanent in the Navy?" My daughter chuckled and replied, "Yeah, and four years is forever."

Life is different for people who live a military life, whether at war or in times of peace. Although we probably have more in common with our civilian counterparts than differences, there are some dramatic lifestyle differences. Sometimes we are able to clearly define those differences. Other times it is difficult. We also tend to describe ourselves as different from our civilian counterparts. On another trip to another ball game my daughter and I were talking about school and life and she commented, "We are different." I must admit I was concerned to hear my teenaged daughter make this comment, so I asked her, "What do you mean?" Sensing my angst, she was quick to assure me that this was not a bad thing. She said that her experiences traveling abroad as well as being around military facilities sometimes gave her an advantage at school. "I know things other girls in the school don't know. I know a lot of things that the boys in school don't know. I think I have a broader outlook." And we continued to laugh and talk about the ways in which she thought she was different from the other kids. I can't tell you how happy I am to report that most of the things were positive. (But I understand a teenaged daughter doesn't tell her parents everything!)

If you're a clinician serving military people, you need to know that we think we are different … whether based on reality, illusion, or some combination … this is an issue for clinicians who serve military populations. To be successful, we suggest that you get to know us.

Why Do They Come and From Where?

People enter the U.S. Military from all walks of life. The reasons for committing oneself to military service vary. The educational benefits of the various versions of the GI bill post-Vietnam era and the stability of full-time employment with significant benefits have been historic enticements. Some of our people come with rich family histories of service to country; others are the first to serve. Some enlist to "see the world" or simply to "get away" … from hometowns, from abusive environments, from boredom. After the attacks of September 2001, there is no question that anger and patriotism led to an increase in enlistments.

Renowned Northwestern University military sociologist C. C. Moskos (1970, 1981), a drafted Army enlisted man who served in the late 1950s, published articles during the 1970s and 1980s warning of the danger of using monetary incentives as primary enticements for enlistment. He argued that this plan would make military service simply a job rather than patriotic duty. He was particularly concerned that the recruitment strategy would decrease one's motivation to fight during wartime. Moskos' concerns have proven to be largely unfounded in the three decades since his original thesis (Padilla, 2001). It remains to be seen what impact more than 8 years of war will have on the validity of Moskos' concerns.

After the Vietnam War and the end of conscription (the draft), many in the United States expressed concerns that the military would become dramatically different from the country it serves. Some feared that the all-volunteer force would place the burden of defending the United States primarily on the backs of the poor and African-Americans (Bachman, Blair & Segal, 1977). In fact, the face of the military community has changed. Clearly, improved access for African-Americans had an impact. Likewise, the increased access for women into operational and leadership roles increased their numbers. However, neither group is over-represented in today's military when compared to the general population (Martin & McClure, 2000). Similarly, some feared the end of the draft would lead to an enlisted community with virtually no college education (Bachman et al., 1977). College education benefits as recruitment enticements and the need for increasingly well-trained technicians have helped to prove this concern unfounded. In sum, although there is some indication that military members, as a group, are more conservative than the American population (Holsti, 1998/1999), most of the cultural diversity found in the United States is also found in the U.S. military. The military community looks very much like the local community.

We're Not in Kansas Anymore, Are We, Toto?

No matter where they come from or why, once individuals enter military service they find that there are in fact cultural differences associated with military service. Research (Kohen, 1984; Segal, 1988; Wertsch, 1991) suggests that there is a unique set of characteristics of military life. Other occupations share some of the specific characteristics discussed here, but no other replicates the combination that is uniquely military life (Martin & McClure, 2000). There are specific rules and expectations about behavior, and there are traditions and lifestyle characteristics unique to the culture of military service (Kohen, 1984). The rules and expectations change over time and are influenced by the experiences of each new member. As group membership changes the culture changes. However, change in the military culture occurs within specific cultural parameters.

The military profession, similar to medicine, the ministry, and law enforcement, is a complete lifestyle. The military family is, to some degree, immersed in the lifestyle. "The officer (or other service member) is a member of a community whose claims over his daily existence extend well beyond his official duties. The deadly mission of warfare has required that the officer be prepared at short notice to abandon his routine and personal commitments. Detailed regulation of the military style of life is expected to enhance group cohesion, professional loyalty, and maintain the martial spirit" (Janowitz, 1971, p. 175).

Some of the military cultural differences are clear, obvious, and formal. Some are sanctioned by the Uniform Code of Military Justice (UCMJ), the military system of laws. Violations can result in criminal prosecution or other punishment. Other cultural differences are not codified in formal regulation; they just "come with the territory." That is especially true for family members whose lives are profoundly affected by the culture (Stoddard, 1976; Wertsch, 1991). Spouses change jobs frequently. Children attend multiple schools and adjust to different curricula and social groups. Families live in a different house/state/country every 1 to 5 years.

DISTINGUISHING FEATURES OF THE CULTURE

The primary distinguishing features of military culture are shaped by the overall task(s) of the organization, waging war. The uniqueness of military culture is in part the result of the organization's responsibility to prepare "... to deal with ... the uncertainty of war, to impose some pattern on war, to control war's outcome, and to invest war with meaning and significance" (Snider, 1999). Military culture is an example of what D'Andrade (1984) called a constitutive rule system. People who enter the military agree to behave in specific ways. Certainly there are many other American institutions (marriage, graduate school, Elks Clubs) that require specific behavior from members. However, Snider (1999) suggests four basic features upon which military culture rests and is distinguished from the rest of American society. Each is related to preparation for war. Each impacts the military member and the military family.

Discipline

The first feature is discipline. Discipline is defined as "the orderly conduct of military personnel, whether individually or in formation, in battle or in garrison, and most often prescribed by their officers in command. The purpose of discipline … is to minimize the confusion and disintegration consequences of battle by imposing order on it with a repertoire of patterned actions …"(Snider, 1999, p. 12). Discipline further provides a way in which to ritualize the violence of war. Discipline reassures military members in combat situations and defines when and how they may violate societal norms that prohibit violence and killing (Marshall, 1988).

One of the most obvious (to those inside the military) manifestations of the discipline feature is the fraternization prohibition. The phrase "to promote good order and discipline" is typically at the center of any discussion of fraternization. The reality is that the rules prohibiting close relationships between seniors and subordinates are, in part, the result of the potential wartime requirement for a senior to order a junior into a situation that is likely to mean death. It is very difficult to do that to anyone. Close relationships can complicate the situation. This same dynamic, though rarely acknowledged, is a part of the debate about women in the military. Sexism and paternalism, fundamental characteristics of the American experience, make it difficult for a man to order a woman into danger.

Loyalty

Snider's second feature of military culture is the professional ethos, "… that set of normative self-understandings for which members define the profession's corporate identity, its code of conduct and, for the officers in particular, its social worth" (Snider, 1999, p. 13). Huntington described "… the management of violence on behalf of society as the principle determinant of the military ethos …" (Huntington, 1957, p. 80). The military ethos holds that military institutions exist only to the extent that they are needed to defend the nation and are always subordinate to civilian leadership (Snider, 1999). Thus, when the civilians say go, the military goes (no matter their private misgivings). Very rarely does a military member refuse to participate in an assignment or mission or question (in public) the appropriateness of an order or a leader. Likewise, most military families accept the mobility requirements of the culture. Much of the social worth of the military member is derived from the intense loyalty.

Ritual

Snider's third feature of military culture is ritual, often expressed in ceremony and etiquette. The military salute, uniform, rank, and formal ceremonies for weddings, funerals, promotions, changes of command, and the rituals of sending off and welcoming home ships, squadrons, and battalions are examples of the rituals that separate military culture. Burk suggests that "these ceremonies and etiquette make up an elaborate ritual and play the role that ritual typically plays in society: to control or mask our anxieties and ignorance; to affirm our solidarity with one another; and to celebrate our being, usually in conjunction with a large universe" (Burk, 1999). Constructed rituals help to guide individual conduct and provide some degree of order to the harsh reality of separation and death (Snider, 1999).

Community

Finally, Snider speaks of the cohesion and esprit de corps so often associated with military service. It is this spirit of identity and group pride that enables individuals and groups to continue to fight, even when there appears to be minimal chance for success. Behavioral studies since World War II have repeatedly shown that soldiers' capacity to continue to fight is related to (in addition to having adequate food and shelter) the group sense of cohesion and loyalty, not ideology or patriotism (Burk, 1999; Huntington, 1957; Snider, 1999).

MILITARY CULTURAL PLURALISM: WHERE ONE SITS DETERMINES WHERE ONE STANDS!

You might think that, because we all think we are different from civilians, we think we are the same, or at least similar to each other. You would be very wrong! Don't ever refer to a marine as a soldier or vice versa. We enjoy (for the most part) a rich history of inter-service rivalry and (again, for the most part) collegial feelings of superiority toward sister services. Each service has a unique personality. Over time the assigned domains of war on land, sea, and in the air led the services to develop (at times dramatically) different institutional cultures (Snider, 1999). Those differences are found in the way each service trains and fights and as well as the way families are viewed. Historically, and in very general terms, the division of labor for the military services has been as follows. The Army is responsible for large-scale land operations including combat, reconstruction, and as an occupying force. The Air Force has responsibility to maintain air superiority. The Navy is responsible for keeping the sea lanes open and projecting force from the sea. The Marine Corps is a smaller, agile force responsible for projecting force from the sea. While these have been the historic responsibilities, and remain the core responsibilities, it is very important for clinicians to understand that the requirements of OIF/OEF, perhaps more than any other war, have required the services to share resources (including personnel) and responsibilities to an unprecedented degree. This can have a significant impact on an individual's experience and dictate a specific clinical response (more on this later).

Are You Really a Warrior?

A military organization is quite complex and requires a variety of skill sets (see Figure 12.1). "U.S. Army officers may come from the infantry, armor, artillery, aviation, airborne or special forces. Navy Officers may be carrier pilots from the fighter or attack communities, anti-submarine warfare pilots, submariners, surface ship commanders or from an amphibious force" (Snider, 1999, p. 12). Like most organizations, military organizations are stratified around several issues … rank being the most obvious, but not only stratum. On most days, the warriors are at the top. One might think of a military organization as a series of concentric circles. At the center are the people who actually fight the battle. Generally, the closer one's job responsibilities are perceived to be a part of actual combat/war (in the center), the more likely one is viewed as a warrior. Military culture is subdivided in many ways including, but not limited to:

Warrior (the people who fight) versus support/staff (medical and other helpers)
Officer (leaders and decision makers) versus enlisted (technicians)
Mustang (leaders who started as enlisted) versus other officers (college boys)
Short-timers (doing a tour for the educational benefits) versus lifers (career people)
Service academy graduates (often multiple generational) versus others
Regular (full-time military) versus reserve (weekend warriors and extended service)
Active duty (currently working) versus retired (subject to recall)

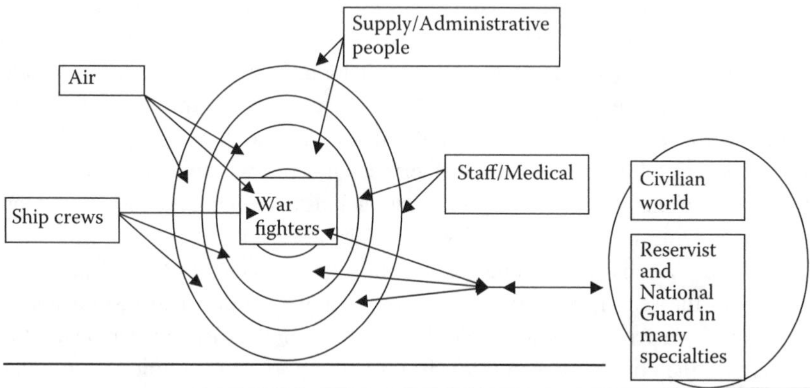

FIGURE 12.1 An example of organizational dynamics in the Navy.

Note that all of the specialties listed here might be perceived as "belonging" in multiple rings. The spot one occupies depends on many issues including job specialty and mission. For example, a fighter pilot is considered a war fighter while a cargo plane pilot who delivers supplies to the rear or an Airborne Warning and Control (AWAC) pilot might be considered in the next ring out. A pilot flying cargo within the United States or flying military passenger missions would be considered even further out. A similar dynamic applies to ship crews. Other issues such as age and rank (a few, but not too many, senior officers fly fighters or lead SEAL Teams) as well as current world situation (i.e., pre/post September 11th) influence the dynamic. The reservist and National Guard member can spend 30 years moving from the civilian world to any number of the circles, depending on individual specialty and military/world situation. *The reality in OEF/OIF is that many of these citizen soldiers spend more time deployed than in the civilian world.* Most medical people spend most of their careers on the outer ring working in the hospitals and clinics. In certain situations medical people will accompany war fighters, even into battle. However, they would never be considered war fighters and are (theoretically) protected from certain acts of war (being held as prisoners of war) by the Geneva Convention.

THE CULTURAL REALITY OF WAR: SOMETIMES THEY CHANGE THE RULES!

It is clearly beyond the scope of this chapter to discuss this topic in any significant way. One may access a plethora of resources related to the topic simply by reviewing the reading lists of any of the service academies. There are also many works specifically focused on issues relevant to mental health and community service providers. For example, Grossman's (1995) *On Killing: The Psychological Cost of Learning to Kill in War and Society*, and Grossman and Christensen's (2004) *On Combat: The Psychology and Physiology of Deadly Conflict in War and in Peace*, as well as Figley and Nash's (2007) *Combat Stress Injury: Theory, Research, and Management* provide readers with a solid foundation of the realities of war from a clinical perspective. Further, there are many first-person accounts of the realities of OEF/OIF published in print as well as on the Web. Read as much as you can! For now, we present a couple of specific issues particularly relevant for most clinical practice scenarios. …

NOT WHAT I SIGNED UP TO DO

The wars in Iraq and Afghanistan have required significant shifts in the division of labor for the services. It is very common for members of the Navy, for example, to join Army units to provide specialized service and/or to augment specific skill sets. This dynamic has existed for a long time. For many years the concept of all services cooperating in the execution of missions in war and peace (so-called joint service) has been highlighted. However, the strain on personnel from years of war leads to a far greater level of personnel sharing. For example, Naval social workers and other providers are increasingly serving with Army units both in Iraq and in places like the Landstuhl Regional Medical Center in Germany. The same happens very frequently in the line communities (warriors). Called individual augmentees, these people leave the known service environment (i.e., Navy) to work in another (i.e., Army). Most often, these individuals do not participate in the joyous, validating, welcome home activities of the units with which they serve. They simply return to duty with their own service.

Even within one's own service, when at war, one is often required to perform duties not generally part of his or her job description. For example, a Marine enlisted man trained to shoot artillery is required to serve as an infantryman in Iraq. An Army truck driver becomes an infantryman when he or she is attacked on a delivery, with little security, on what was expected to be a safe road. An Air Force mechanic may be required to serve as a construction laborer on a reconstruction project, and be able to immediately fight as an infantryman when the project is unexpectedly attacked.

Most people in these situations receive a significant amount of training prior to assuming these new roles. And in most situations, they perform well, survive, and come home feeling some level of success. However, when mistakes are made, when people die or are seriously injured while people are serving in roles other than their usual, the people involved question their own and others' actions.

Blurring of roles, multiple fronts, and nature of the fight(s) are not unique issues for these wars. However, the length of the wars, and the multiple deployments required of almost everyone who serves, is different. In recent years politicians and military leadership have begun to refer to "the long war." In essence, the term compares the current military generation's anticipated responsibilities with those of the Cold War generation at least in terms of the number of years one might expect some level of military conflict (*The Washington Post*, 2006). If accurate, this assessment surely means that the strain for military members and families will continue to grow.

WHAT DOES ALL THIS MEAN FOR THE CLINICIAN?

Where to start … exactly? In developing the curriculum for "Painting a Moving Train" we challenged our civilian colleagues first and foremost to be competent professionals trained in evidence-based interventions. But to best serve the military population, we submit, one needs to know something about our nation's military history and about our present military conflicts. You need to know something about DoD and VA health care and other benefit systems. We encourage providers to ask each and every patient/client/customer, no matter the referral source, whether or not he or she is a current or veteran service member or a family member/significant other of a service member or veteran. And it is really important to know something about military culture including knowledge of each of the service branches and some of the organizational/cultural differences. The effort will go a very long way toward preparing the civilian clinician to more successfully build rapport. Dr. Harold Kudler, a psychiatrist, long-time veteran of the VA, and a key contributor to the curriculum development and program faculty of "Painting a Moving Train," often tells the story of a lesson he learned in medical school about basic diagnosing techniques: *If you don't take the temperature, you can't find the fever!* Above all else, ask the questions and be prepared to listen to the answers. Again, you must be culturally competent.

ASSESSMENT

We suggest that you add several, very specific questions to your routine assessment tool:

1. Why did you join the Marine Corps, Army, Navy, etc.? What did you hope to accomplish?

   As discussed here, people choose to commit to military service for all kinds of reasons. The client's perception of the decision in retrospect and the degree to which one feels accomplishment of the original goals often colors self-assessment.
2. Have you served in combat? If so, how many tours, what specific location, and when were you there?

   Iraq in 2008 was still a very dangerous place, but there can be no question it is different from what it was 2005. The war in Afghanistan has at times been referred to as "The Forgotten War." Where and when one serves, while obviously dictating objective experience, can also have a tremendous influence on the subjective meaning combat veterans place on their experience, and the meaning they believe others place on the experience.
3. What is your military occupational specialty (the job you were trained to do)? What was your job in Iraq or Afghanistan?

   As previously discussed, almost everyone has experienced new job responsibilities during deployment. If successful, one might experience growth. But if things did not go well, and especially if people died or were seriously injured, the results can be disastrous for one's sense of self.
4. Were you satisfied with your training and preparation?

   There is a plethora of news and other accounts regarding lack of preparation prior to deployment to the war zones. Our task here is not to take a particular position in that discussion, and we suggest that you refrain from doing so in the clinical setting. However, be prepared to deal with the full range of emotions that come from feeling ill-prepared, especially when things do not go well in combat. Allen King (2006) provides a good example of the issue from a relatively senior prospective and Winn (2006) from the junior level.
5. Were you satisfied with your leadership and equipment?

   See question 4.

6. How do your family and friends feel about the military and your service? How do they feel about the separations?

   Deployment has always been difficult for families. When training Navy and Marine Corps members and families for routine, non-combat deployments, we have always tried to help members and family members see things from the other's perspective. There is an oft-told story (at least oft told in training sessions) of the washing machine or the car breaking down the week after he deploys. She has a romanticized vision of him sailing to exotic places while he has images of her at home where she has a warm bed, TV, and the ability to eat whatever she wants. Neither image is completely based on reality. Deployment has always been hard because life is uncertain. No matter who you are or what you do in civilian life, when you leave to go to work or school on any given morning, you don't know for certain that you will return. However, when you leave to go to war, the reality that you might not see your family again can be overwhelming. Imagine the cumulative stress of three, four, even five such deployments.

Much is written about how things have changed since the days when Vietnam veterans returned, with special emphasis on so-called support-the-troops programs and initiatives. While such efforts are clearly appreciated and helpful, be prepared for the resentment that some returning vets feel. Dominick King (2006) provides important insight: "When we got back from Iraq, me and my friend Tabor were in the car driving to Dunkin' Donuts or something in the morning, and we were at the stop sign with a car in front of us saying 'Freedom Is Not Free,' and he just looks at me. He goes, 'Can you believe this? Freedom's not free, what has he paid?'" (D. King, 2006, p. 230).

SPECIAL BARRIERS TO TREATMENT

By now it should be clear that we advocate that civilian providers view preparing to practice in a military population in much the same manner as you would prepare to practice in any other culture different from your own, whether the difference is gender, ethnicity, region, or any of the other ways in which we identify or otherwise segregate ourselves. Military populations share all of the above group identification characteristics plus our own special cultural distinctions. And we also share most of the same barriers that discourage mental-health-support-seeking behaviors: lack of knowledge, isolation, and, of course, stigma. But military populations have additional issues, for example:

Treatment beliefs not addressed: Nash (2007) described the stress of combat as "… friction to be overcome and banished from awareness." Combat vets may consider what they're doing as a normal way to respond to a frightening world. In fact, they are specifically trained to not think about that when in battle, because it can get people killed. It is very difficult to "turn off" the perspective and behaviors once you are out of the battle. And the truth is, while it's not as dangerous in Jacksonville, NC, as in Fallujah, Iraq, people get hurt here too. What most mental health providers consider trauma symptoms often feel right to the combat veteran. Veterans may appear arrogant as they often view civilians as stupid or naive when they don't see the dangers the veteran sees.

Fears of failure and fears of success: For warriors, there's usefulness in not admitting problems and avoiding fears. Despite the good faith efforts of many military leaders, the stereotype that asking for help is a sign of weakness persists. There continue to be stories of individuals being labeled as stupid, seen as damaged, and made to feel guilt and shame when seeking help. Of course, this is made worse by the reality that some people choose to use mental-health-seeking behaviors as a means to the secondary gain of release form responsibility. But there is also the very real commitment that most military members feel. Combat veterans will tell you that the last thing they want to do is have someone else take their place on a mission, and thus will do everything to avoid "being pulled." This is especially traumatic when someone is killed or seriously injured on the mission. Finally, related to labels or stereotypes, many of the current combat vets will tell you that they've all heard about and discussed the Vietnam vets. They are all homeless, crazy. Of course, this is not true but there is enough bad information in the public to influence decision making. And in reality, some of today's veterans grew up with fathers and grandfathers who suffer from combat PTSD from serving in Vietnam.

Realistic concerns: There are, at times, realistic concerns for the military member that create significant barriers to treatment. The attitude of the warrior is important. Vets will often say something like, "I'm trained to do what I did. I'm too embarrassed and I don't want people to think I'm crazy. It will hurt my career. My men won't trust me when we go back to Iraq. My security clearance will be taken away. I might lose my relationship and partner and my family will not understand." In any given situation, all of this may be accurate.

WHEN THEY DO SEEK SERVICES: A QUICK OVERVIEW OF TREATMENT MODALITIES WE FIND SUCCESSFUL

Once the service member has overcome the barriers, often because a spouse or other family member has confronted him or her, clinicians must have the specific skills to address the issues. An in-depth discussion of treatment modalities is beyond the scope of this chapter; however, attention should be paid to the evidence-based treatments as identified by the Department of Defense and the

Veterans Administration in the clinical practice guidelines, which are available at www.oqp.med.va.gov/cpg/PTSD/PTSD_Base.htm

These guidelines assist clinicians regarding available treatments, reviewing their evidence base, and making practical, patient-specific choices. They are useful from screening and initial assessment through treatment and re-assessment. The specific therapies that are most recommended by the DoD and the VA for treatment of PTSD in military and non-military populations are:

Cognitive therapy: Represents a systematic approach to challenging the negative trauma-related beliefs that many trauma survivors carry with them—feelings of guilt: "I should have prevented the trauma from happening," and so on (http://www.ncptsd.va.gov).

Exposure therapy: This is the practice that involves safe, repetitive exposure to the traumatic memory or to the traumatic stimuli that are continuing to cause distress for the survivor, thus allowing him or her to confront the avoidance behavior.

Stress inoculation therapy: Can be thought of as a set of skills for managing stress and anxiety. Skills include breathing control, deep muscle relaxation, assertiveness training, role-playing, modeling, thought stopping, positive thinking, and self talk.

Eye movement desensitization reprocessing (EMDR): Developed by Dr. Francine Shapiro, EMDR involves a number of complex procedures that require specific training. EMDR has received careful investigation and has a strong evidence base.

Patient education: Recommended element no matter what approach you select.

It has been our experience that you may use a combination of these and other therapies as assessment continues and at various stages of treatment. In addition to the DoD/VA Clinical Practice Guidelines, the American Psychiatric Association has Practice Guidelines for Patients with Acute Stress Disorder and Posttraumatic Stress Disorder and the International Society for Traumatic Stress Studies developed a comprehensive set of treatment guidelines in 2008.

Finally, although for many years the military trained personnel in the critical incident stress debrief and critical incident stress management protocols, these are being replaced by psychological first aid as a front-line defense.

CONCLUSION

In conclusion, we are fortunate to have a wealth of real-time resources to help us understand the military and wartime cultures. In our live training sessions we encourage providers to look in their favorite bookstores, and we challenge you to do the same. There are some wonderful first-hand accounts written by people who have been there (*Rule Number Two: Lessons I Learned in a Combat Hospital* by Dr. Heidi Squier Kraft, and *What Was Asked of Us: An Oral History of the*

Iraq War by the Soldiers Who Fought It by Trish Wood, for example). There are collections of communications between combat veterans and their families and friends (*Operation Homecoming: Iraq, Afghanistan and the Home Front in the Words of U.S. Troops and Their Families*, edited by Andrew Carroll). There are first-hand accounts of the key battles (Fallujah and Ramadi, Iraq, and operations in Afghanistan). PBS, Frontline, and HBO have produced remarkable accounts (*Baghdad ER*, *The Soldier's Heart*, *A Company of Soldiers*). Web sites and blogs are too numerous to mention.

If you want to work with this population, you must not only know the best interventions. You must also learn, respect and appreciate the cultures from which we come. You must be culturally competent.

ACKNOWLEDGMENTS

We have been privileged to work with some very talented people who are dedicated to serving military members and families. Our "Painting a Moving Train" program has been very well received thanks to the efforts of our fellow faculty, content developers, and coordinators. We wish to acknowledge the efforts of David Amos, Dr. Vince Arnold (Capt., USN, RET), Pheon Beal, Lt. Col. Ken Bowers, Brian Corlett, Miriam Deaver, Bob Goodale, Dennis Goodwin (Col., USA RET), Dan Hickman (Brig. General, Army National Guard, RET), Dr. Harold Kudler, SSGT. Holly Mullis, SSGT. Robbie Mullis, and Sheryl Pacelli. Thank you for your service!

REFERENCES

American Psychological Association Presidential Task Force on Military Deployment Services for Youth, Families and Service Members (2007). *The psychological needs of U.S. military service members and their families: A preliminary report.* This document was drafted by the American Psychological Association's (APA) Presidential Task Force on Military Deployment Services for Youth, Families and Service Members and adopted by the APA Council of Representatives on February 18, 2007. Although some Task Force members were serving on active duty in the U.S. military or working for either the DoD or VA, the contents of this report were neither vetted nor endorsed by any entity outside of the APA.

Bachman, J. G., Blair, J. D. & Segal, D. R. (1977). *The all-volunteer force: A study of ideology in the military.* Ann Arbor, MI: The University of Michigan Press.

Burk, J. (1999). Military culture. In L. Kurtz (Ed.), *Encyclopedia of violence, peace and conflict.* San Diego, CA: Academic Press.

D'Andrade, R. G. (1984). Cultural meaning systems. In S. R. A. & R. A. Levine (Eds.), *Culture theory: Essays on mind, self, and emotion* (pp. 88–119). Cambridge, MA: Cambridge University Press.

Department of Defense (2006). *Profile of the military community.* DoD 2006 Demographics Report.

Department of Defense Task Force on Mental Health (2007). An achievable vision: Report of the Department of Defense Task Force on Mental Health. Falls Church, VA: Defense Health Board.

Figley, Charles R., and Nash, William P. (Eds.) (2007). *Combat stress injury: Theory, research, and management*. New York, NY: Routledge, Taylor & Francis Group.

Grossman, Dave (1995). *On killing: The psychological cost of learning to kill in war and society*. New York, NY: Back Bay Books; Little, Brown and Company.

Grossman, Dave & Christensen, Loren W. (2004). *On combat: The psychology and physiology of deadly conflict in war and in peace*. USA: PPCT Research Publications.

Hall, Lynn K. (2008). *Counseling military families: What mental health professionals need to know*. New York, NY: Routledge.

Henderson, Kristin (2006). *While they're at war: The true story of American families on the homefront*. New York, NY: Houghton Muffin Company. Retrieved October 25, 2008 from www.kristinhenderson.com

Hoge, C. W., Castro, C. A., Messer, S. C., McGurk, D., Cotting, D. I. & Koffman, R. L. (2004). Combat duty in Iraq and Afghanistan, mental health problems, and barriers to care. *The New England Journal of Medicine, 351*(1), 13–22.

Holsti, O. R. (1998/1999). A widening gap between the U.S. military and civilian society: Some evidence, 1976-1996. *International Security (Winter),* 5–42.

Huntington, S. P. (1957). *The soldier and the state*. Cambridge, MA: Harvard University Press.

Janowitz, M. (1971). *The professional soldier*. New York, NY: The Free Press.

Kohen, J. A. (1984). The military career is a family affair. *Journal of Family Issues, 5*, 401–408.

King, Allen (2006), They don't have a security or reconstruction plan to implement. In Wood, Trish (Ed.), *What was asked of us: An oral history of the Iraq War by the soldiers who fought it.* New York, NY: Back Bay Books, Little, Brown and Company.

King, Dominick (2006), I am changed. In *What was asked of us: An oral history of the Iraq War by the soldiers who fought it.* New York, NY: Back Bay Books, Little, Brown and Company.

Kraft, Heidi Squier (2007). *Rule number two: Lessons I learned in a combat hospital*. New York, NY: Little, Brown and Company, Hachette Book Group.

Kulka, R. A., Schlenger, W. E., Fairbank, J. A., Hough, R. L., Jordan, B. K., Marmar, C. R., et al. (1990). *Trauma and the Vietnam War generation: Report of findings from the National Vietnam Veterans Readjustment Study.* New York, NY: Brunner/Mazel.

Magnus, Robert (2007). Opening Remarks at the 2007 Marine Corps Combat/Operational Stress Control Conference, June 18.

Marshall, S. L. A. (1988). Americans in combat. In Department of Defense (Ed.), *The armed forces officer* (p. 80). Washington, DC: Department of Defense.

Martin, J. A. & McClure, P. (2000). Today's active duty military family: The evolving challenges of military family life. In J. A. R. Martin, N. Lenora & L. R. Sparacina (Eds.), *The military family: A practice guide for human service providers* (p. 282). Westport, CT: Praeger.

Mental Health Advisory Team (MHAT) IV (2006). *Final report*, November. Office of the Surgeon General.

Moskos, C. C. (1970). *The American enlisted man: The rank and file in today's military.* New York, NY: Russell Sage Foundation.

Moskos, C. C (1981) The social psychology of military service and the influence of bureaucratic rationalism. In Charles C. Moskos & Frank R. Wood (Eds.), *Is the military more than just a job?* International Defense Publishers, Inc.

Nash, William P. (2007). In Charles R. Figley & William P. Nash (Eds.), *Combat stress injury: Theory, research, and management.* New York, NY: Routledge, Taylor & Francis Group.

National Geographic-Roper Public Affairs (2006). Geographic Literacy Study, May 2006. Retrieved October 25, 2008, from http://press.nationalgeographic.com/pressroom/pressReleaseFiles/1146580209503/1146580209520/Report_2006_Geog_Lit_survey.pdf

Newsweek (2008). February 11.

Padilla, Peter A. & Laner, Mary R. (2002). Trends in military influences on Army recruitment 1915-1990. *Journal of Political and Military Sociology, Summer*.

President's Commission on Care for America's Returning Wounded Warriors (2007). *Serve, support, simplify: Report of the President's Commission on Care for America's Returning Wounded Warriors*.

Rand Corporation (2008). *Invisible wounds of war: Psychological and cognitive injuries, their consequences, and services to assist recovery*. Terri Tanielian & Lisa H. Jaycox (Eds.). Rand Corporation Document MG-720-CCF.

Segal, M. (1988). The military and the family as greedy institutions. In Charles. C Moskos & F. R. Woods (Eds.), *The military: More than just a job*. New York, NY: Pergamon.

Snider, D. M. (1999). An uniformed debate on military culture. *Orbis, 43*(1), 11–16.

Stoddard, E. R. C., C. E. (1976). The Army officer's wife: Social stresses in a complementary role. In N. L. G. D. R. Segal (Ed.), *The social psychology of military service*. Newbury Park, CA: Sage.

The Washington Post (2006, February 3). Rumsfeld offers strategies for current war.

Veterans Health Affairs Office of Public Health and Environment Hazards (2006).

Wertsch, M. E. (1991). *Military brats: Legacies of childhood inside the fortress* (1st ed.). New York, NY: Harmony Books.

Winn, Mathew (2006). They were sending us out there in pieces of crap with no armor. In Trish Wood (Ed.), *What was asked of us: An oral history of the Iraq War by the soldiers who fought it*. New York, NY: Back Bay Books, Little, Brown and Company.

Wood, Trish (2006). *What was asked of us: An oral history of the Iraq War by the soldiers who fought it*. New York, NY: Back Bay Books, Little, Brown and Company.

Zellman, G. L., Heilbrunn, C. S. & Builder, C. (1993). *Implementing change in large organizations*. Washington, DC: Rand Corp.

13 Post Deployment
Practical Guidelines for Warriors' Loved Ones

*Judith A. Lyons and Natasha Elkovitch**

CONTENTS

Veterans' friends and families face many challenges as their relationships readjust to changes that occurred during deployment. Habits, roles, and viewpoints have usually altered in some way. Recognizing commonly observed patterns and understanding their underlying principles can help friends and family more easily navigate these changes.

This chapter[†] identifies issues that frequently emerge in re-establishing relationships after a combat deployment. (Readers interested in more detailed descriptions of some of the research studies cited in this chapter are referred to Galovski & Lyons, 2004, and Lyons, 2009.) The first section of this chapter alerts the reader to key risk factors that predict post-deployment difficulties (deployment, combat,

* Affiliations: G. V. (Sonny) Montgomery VA Medical Center: VA South Central (VISN 16) Mental Illness Research, Education and Clinical Center (MIRECC); and University of Mississippi Medical Center.

† This chapter is the result of work supported with resources and the use of facilities at the G. V. (Sonny) Montgomery VA Medical Center, Jackson, MS, with additional support from VA South Central MIRECC. The views expressed here represent those of the authors and do not necessarily represent the views of the Department of Veterans Affairs or the University of Mississippi Medical Center.

poor leadership/unit cohesion, posttraumatic stress), while emphasizing that positive adjustment is the norm. Information is then offered regarding three topics frequently encountered in post-deployment reintegration: acute fluctuations in adjustment, strained communication, and dealing with crowds. Finally, direction is provided regarding sources of additional guidance and support, as well as more formal clinical resources that would be applicable if an individual's readjustment problems become chronic or severe.

RECOGNIZING RISK FACTORS

Deployment

Military families often embody characteristics of and have access to resources that promote resilience (Jensen, Martin & Watanabe, 1996; Rentz et al., 2007). Even so, the experience of deployment and combat can leave a deep impact on those who serve. However, the details and direction of the change vary across individuals and are often mixed even within an individual. For example, Newby et al. (2005) analyzed soldiers' reports of positive and negative consequences of a peacekeeping deployment. Married soldiers were more likely to report negative consequences such as missing important family events while away. However, married soldiers were also more likely to report that deployment led to improvement in their relationship with their significant other (9.4 percent of married soldiers versus 1.2 percent of single soldiers reported such improvement). Across topics, 63 percent of all soldiers surveyed reported some positive consequence of deployment including income, self-improvement, and time to think.

Family reunification and adjustment may be particularly difficult for families who experience a long combat deployment and/or multiple tours to a war zone (Orthner & Rose, 2006). The U.S. military's Fourth Mental Health Advisory Team report (MHAT-IV; Mental Health Advisory Team, 2006) found that service personnel in Iraq longer than 6 months are 50 percent to 60 percent more likely to screen positive for mental health problems. They are more likely to have marital concerns (31 percent in longer deployments versus 19 percent in shorter deployments), report problems with infidelity (17 percent versus 10 percent), and be planning marital separation or divorce (22 percent versus 14 percent). Multiple deployments are associated with a 50 percent greater prevalence of mental health problems (9 percent among repeaters; 6 percent among first-time deployers). It cannot be overemphasized, however, that this indicates the vast majority of troops are not reporting relationship problems or mental health issues.

British (Browne et al., 2007) and American (Milliken, Auchterlonie & Hoge, 2007; Smith et al., 2008) studies have shown guard reservists are at increased risk for post-deployment mental health problems. Browne et al. (2007) found high marital satisfaction among both reservists and regulars overall, but satisfaction was lower among reservists who had deployed. The studies speculate that differences between reservists and regulars may be because many reservists did not deploy with their parent unit and lacked the cohesive support network that might have helped sustain troops in regular units; they have the extra task of transitioning back to civilian employment; and they may have less access to support and services after deployment.

Not surprisingly, deployment also affects spouses. In a study of 45 Army couples following the husband's deployment to Iraq or Afghanistan (Goff, Crow, Reisbig & Hamilton, 2007), 24 percent of wives reported their husband's deployment was the "most traumatic" event they had ever experienced. In spite of this strain, study participants were described as "overall, a highly satisfied sample of couples" (p. 352). Other studies also report only temporary or limited impact or significant negative impact only within select subgroups where other risk factors are present (Jensen et al., 1996; Ruger, Wilson & Waddoups, 2002; Schumm, Bell, Knott & Rice, 1996).

Studies on the impact of deployment and reunification on children have yielded mixed results (e.g., Jensen et al., 1996; Kelley et al., 2001). For example, Jensen et al. (1996) found some increase in symptoms associated with parental deployment, yet scores tended to remain within the normal range. Similarly, Kelley et al. (2001) found that the levels of internalizing and externalizing behavior exhibited by young children with Navy mothers fell within normal limits. Although the data are very reassuring that most children and families of service members adapt successfully and are healthy and well adjusted (Pesonen et al., 2007; Wiens & Boss 2006), periods of deployment separations can be difficult for children. Research indicates that some children struggle with internalizing (sadness, anxiety, difficulty concentrating) and/or externalizing (behavioral) problems either pre- or post-deployment (e.g., Jensen et al., 1996). These problems tend to be more likely for children when the at-home parent is struggling with his or her own mental health concerns (e.g., Jensen et al., 1996). In addition, other variables in families of warriors have been related to child problems, such as family violence (Harkness, 1991; Watkins, Taft, Hebenstreit, King & King, 2008) or the father's wartime participation in atrocities (Rosenheck & Fontana, 1998).

In sum, readers can draw encouragement from the fact that research finds that the majority of war fighters, spouses, and children adjust well to deployments.

COMBAT EXPOSURE

While warriors are trained through physical conditioning and military fundamentals (e.g., discipline, responsibility), the war zone confronts troops with a plethora of experiences rarely encountered in civilian life to the same degree. In one large-scale study, more than 90% of respondents who had been deployed to Iraq reported being shot at, and a high percentage reported handling dead bodies, knowing someone who was killed, experiencing a close call (e.g., being shielded from a bullet via body armor), or seeing injured women or children whom they were unable to help (Hoge et al., 2004). In the face of such circumstances, hypervigilance, alertness, and narrowed attention have unquestionable survival value. Innocent-looking situations can prove to be the most deadly (e.g., Alford, Mahone & Fielstein, 1988; Weiner, 2004). Tendencies for sympathy and compassion are often used as lures to entrap the unwary, e.g., the dead and wounded are often booby-trapped or used to coax additional troops into the crosshairs of a sniper. Choices may be limited to several undesirable options, forcing warriors into actions that run directly contrary to their values and beliefs. Losses are often inevitable, but rarely is there time to grieve. In order to stay alive and not jeopardize comrades, the warrior must suppress tender emotions and function in a calculated manner—a coping style that is highly effective in combat but can undermine post-war relationships.

To be ready for the unexpected attack, the warrior learns to maintain a level of combat alertness around the clock, never fully relaxing and ready to mobilize into attack mode in an instant. The chronic release of stress hormones (e.g., noradrenaline, cortisol) increases mental arousal, quickens heart rate, and boosts energy. While necessary in combat, the extreme and prolonged stress of the modern battlefield and the high levels stress hormones reach can have both psychological and physiological consequences. For example, while the hormone noradrenaline increases mental arousal, it also plays a role in enhancing the formation of memories about vivid events, helping to explain post-war re-experiencing of frightening war images (e.g., Elzinga & Bremmer, 2002). Other physical, emotional, and behavioral consequences of war-zone stress include insomnia, appetite suppression, feelings of restlessness (or feeling "keyed up"), low tolerance for frustrations, difficulty concentrating, and hypervigilance. This combat-ready level of activation can persist even after the warrier is safely home.

Even though studies from various countries show that higher levels of combat exposure are associated with increased risk of mental health problems including anxiety, depression, and acute stress/posttraumatic stress (Mental Health Advisory Team, 2006; Rona et al., 2009; Sareen et al., 2007) as well as increased rates of marital dissolution (Ruger et al., 2002), a large number of veterans demonstrate remarkable resilience even in the face of combat-related trauma (Sammons & Batten, 2008). Surviving the challenges of war can be growth promoting and associated with an increase in self-discipline, self-efficacy, appreciation for family and core values, or a greater sense of self-identity (e.g., Elder & Clipp, 1989; Waysman, Schwarzwald & Solomon, 2001).

Poor Leadership and Poor Unit Cohesion

Positive unit leadership has been demonstrated to buffer the negative effects of other risk factors such as combat exposure (Mental Health Advisory Team, 2006). It has also been found to reduce the stress reported by wives during their husbands' deployment (Schumm, Bell & Knott, 2001). Similarly, unit cohesion has been found to be an important predictor of post-deployment adjustment (Rona et al., 2009).

PTSD as a Family Risk Factor

Studies from Britain (Iverson et al., 2005), Canada (Sareen et al., 2007), and the United States (Hoge et al., 2002) report posttraumatic stress disorder (PTSD) is less common among military personnel than several other mental health problems. However, most studies continue to support the conclusion expressed by Galovski and Lyons (2004) that PTSD is one of the strongest predictors of relationship problems. Individuals with this disorder share a cluster of symptoms: (1) re-experiencing (e.g., continuing to think about combat or feeling as if one is still in combat); (2) avoidance (e.g., avoiding certain situations or avoiding talking about combat or particular events); (3) numbing (feeling detached from others, feeling closed-off emotionally); and (4) arousal (e.g., feeling jumpy, unable to sleep, getting angry quickly). One recent study estimates that one in six veterans who served combat duty in Iraq suffers with PTSD (Hoge, Terhakopian, Castro, Messer & Engel, 2007).

PTSD among male veterans has been found to predict distress in their cohabitating female partners (Beckham, Lytle & Feldman, 1996; Calhoun, Beckham & Bosworth, 2002; Dekel, 2007; Dekel & Solomon, 2006; Dirkzwager, Bramsen, Adèr & van der Ploeg, 2005; Jordan et al., 1992; Manguno-Mire et al., 2007; Sautter et al., 2006). Veterans with PTSD also report more marital distress (Cook, Riggs, Thompson, Coyne & Sheikh, 2004). Riggs, Byrne, Weathers & Litz (1998) found that 30% of couples report relationship distress if the veteran does not have PTSD. However, if the veteran has PTSD then the odds reversed and only 30% of couples did *not* report distress. In addition, the risk for domestic violence is particularly high among warriors with PTSD (e.g., Byrne & Riggs, 1996; Jordan et al., 1992; Sherman, Sautter, Jackson, Lyons & Han, 2006).

As noted regarding other risk factors, there are individual differences in how PTSD impacts partners. Dekel (2007) found that, among wives who demonstrated a secure attachment style, greater PTSD symptoms in the veteran actually predicted more positive growth in the wife. The direction of this pattern was reversed (more PTSD in husband was associated with less growth in the wife) among wives who exhibited an insecure/avoidant attachment style. Similarly, Dollar, Lyons, Kibler & Ma (2007) found that the cognitive appraisal style through which female partners view stressors predicted how distressed the women were by the veteran's PTSD; those who tended to views stressors as a challenge were less distressed.

Studies have also found children to be negatively impacted by a father's PTSD (Caselli & Motta, 1995; Davidson & Mellor, 2001; Davidson, Smith & Kudler, 1989; Rosenheck, 1986; Rosenheck & Nathan, 1985). In particular, warriors who are struggling with the avoidance and emotional numbing symptoms of PTSD may be at particular risk for impaired parenting, which in turn may be related to children's adjustment difficulties (Ruscio, Weathers, King & King, 2002).

Conversely, family distress may also contribute to PTSD symptomatology. Browne et al. (2007) found that PTSD was more closely related to problems at home during and since deployment than it was to deployment experiences such as unit cohesion or combat events. Authors of that study suggest that PTSD symptoms may have contributed to problems at home. They also speculate that domestic tension may have prevented combat distress from resolving without treatment, as occurs in most cases.

ANTICIPATING AND ADDRESSING CHALLENGES

FLUCTUATIONS IN ADJUSTMENT

In a large study of US soldiers who served in Iraq, Milliken et al. (2007) found higher reports of various problems at 4 to 10 months post-deployment than at homecoming. At homecoming, only 3 percent to 4 percent of soldiers reported conflicts with their spouse, family members, or close friends. Months later, this had increased to 14 percent of active duty soldiers and 21 percent of National Guard/Reserves troops (although some of this increase may be due to the fact that conflicts with co-workers was added to the wording of the question).

One of the intriguing findings reported by Milliken et al. (2007) is the fact that different soldiers reported symptoms at the two assessment points. Of those who met screening criteria for depression at the initial screen, 56 percent to 62 percentno longer met criteria at the second screening. Of soldiers who showed PTSD symptoms at the initial screening, 49 percent to 59 percent no longer met screening criteria for PTSD at the second assessment. This is similar to Smith et al.'s (2008) finding that more than half of military personnel who met screening criteria for PTSD prior to deployment no longer met criteria for the diagnosis after deployment. Research by Toomey et al. (2007) offers similar reassurance that problems do dissipate over time. Among veterans deployed to the 1991 Gulf War, prevalence of depression reduced from 7.1 percent during the Gulf War period to 3.2 percent a decade later, PTSD rates declined from 6.2 percent to 1.8 percent and other anxiety disorders decreased from 4.3 percent to 2.8 percent.

Fluctuations in symptoms following homecoming should not be surprising. The returning warrior may feel relief and happiness to be home and joy at reuniting with loved ones mixed with insecurities about readjustment, guilt or shame for combat decisions and actions, concern for those still in the battle zone, and/or confusion regarding their own values and character (e.g., Hendin & Pollinger-Haas, 1991; Maher, 2008). Growing interpersonal tensions after an initial "honeymoon" are understandable. Roles that shifted during separation may need to be renegotiated. Relationships may have become idealized during months of separation, or partners left behind may feel angry (or proud) that they handled matters on their own for an extended period. Under such pressures and with high expectations on both sides, the potential for unintended slights and open clashes is high (Knox & Price, 1995; Peebles-Kleiger & Kleiger, 1994). In a recent survey of married and cohabitating veterans who served in Iraq or Afghanistan, the most common familial difficulties reported include feeling like a guest in their own household (approximately 41 percent), being unsure about their family role (approximately 37 percent), and their children acting afraid or not being warm toward the returning parent (25 percent) (Sayers, Farrow, Ross & Oslin, 2009).

Reminders of combat can be expected to elicit temporary increases in anxiety or moodiness. Warriors, particularly those struggling with PTSD, tend to attend selectively to trauma-related information (McNally, 1998), so it may only take a certain smell, sight, sound, or phrase to elicit a vivid memory. Some research has found that warriors may have difficulty recalling positive personal memories (e.g., family memories prior to deployment) due to the attention that is consumed by remaining on guard for future threats or recalling trauma-related memories (McNally, Litz, Prassas, Shin & Weathers, 1994). This turn may impede their ability to envision their future in a positive, adaptive way (McNally, Lasko, Macklin & Pitman, 1995).

Common reminders of combat include anniversaries of traumatic events, weather similar to that in the combat zone, and news coverage of wars or disasters. Less obvious personal life events can also serve as cues. Promotion to a managerial position can be disquieting for the warrior who feels responsible for the failure of a military operation he commanded. For war fighters who saw children killed or discovered family photos on the corpse of an enemy combatant, their celebration of their own children's milestones may evoke as much guilt and sadness as it does joy and pride. Once the links to combat trauma are recognized so families can anticipate difficult episodes (e.g., anniversary of a battle) it becomes possible to plan in advance ways to cope with the expected anxiety or moodiness (Sherman, Zanotti & Jones, 2005).

Communication Issues

One of the most significant areas of conflict with returned warriors and their families pertains to talking about the war. Family and friends may notice certain behavior changes that can appear irrational to someone who is unaware of the warrior's combat experiences. For example, agitation if the gas gauge on the family minivan falls below half a tank is understandable once family members learn that one vehicle running out of fuel in the combat zone could place the entire convoy at risk. Veering widely around seemingly harmless debris in the road, always having an escape route planned, or insisting on always knowing the whereabouts of loved ones may also stem from lessons learned in combat.

There is almost invariably a disconnect in timing between the warrior's readiness to discuss combat experiences and others' eagerness to inquire about such experiences. Particularly outside of military environments, well-meaning friends and family may jovially ask about death and close-calls. Those who are more accustomed to military culture or simply more sensitive in their approach may find that even simple inquiries of "What was it like?" can spark an angry reply. Friends and family soon learn not to ask, or to even avoid the topic at all costs. Later, when the war fighter feels psychologically and emotionally ready to share some of those war memories, others may shy away from or no longer show interest in the topic. Months after homecoming, attempts the warrior makes to bring up the topic may elicit only well-intended advice to "put that behind you" or less sympathetic commands to "get over it."

In addition to the issue of timing, the emotional reaction of loved ones can create barriers. It is easy to feel hurt or resentment that the warrior seems unwilling to share his or her story. Many loved ones interpret the warrior's lack of disclosure as a sign of emotional distance or distrust. Many people do not realize that the high level of emotional confusion about events can take time to sort out before the stories are even in any organized fashion to tell. War fighters fear that loved ones will pity them or be repulsed or afraid if the warriors reveal what they have seen and done. Another fear many warriors report is concern that talking about their traumas will infect their loved ones with the same nightmarish images that haunt the war fighter. Such concerns reflect some real risk, as secondary traumatization is a phenomenon sometimes seen among therapists (Figley, 1995), partners (Dekel, Goldblatt, Keidar, Solomon & Polliack, 2005; Maloney, 1988), and children (Ancharoff, Munroe & Fisher, 1998; Davidson and Mellor, 2001).

The warrior may find it easier to share experiences with other veterans, even if they are strangers. Shared culture and terminology reduce fears of being misunderstood, judged, or interrupted with tangential questions. This can facilitate conversations with family and friends who are also veterans. This would seem to be an advantage, but research by Rosenheck and Fontana found it is not always enough. Studies of father–son pairs who both experienced combat trauma have reported that sons of combat veterans adjusted less well to their own combat trauma than the sons whose fathers had not experienced war trauma (Rosenheck, 1985; Rosenheck & Fontana, 1998).

Johnson, Feldman, and Lubin (1995) offer very helpful case examples of ways to facilitate positive communication once the warrior is ready to disclose personal trauma experiences. Loved ones are advised to focus on listening—resisting the desire to jump in with quick advice in an attempt to "fix" the hurt. Premature reassurances can be meant to comfort but may leave the war fighter feeling that the degree of emotion or the complexity of the moral dilemma was dismissed.

Communication challenges are not limited to war topics. Political, social, and religious views may have changed, with new ideas not yet fully integrated (so potentially contradictory) and perhaps at odds with those of loved ones. After learning to suppress emotions to function in combat, the warrior may find it difficult to risk the emotional vulnerability that intimacy requires. This may come across as uncaring and uninterested. Restless sleep may lead to separate bedrooms and further reduce intimacy. Partners are encouraged to resist taking such changes too personally, recognizing them as a common pattern among veterans. Such emotional numbing/withdrawal presents one of the biggest challenges to personal relationships (Frederikson, Chamberlain & Long, 1996; Kashdan, Elhai & Frueh, 2006; Riggs et al., 1998; Wilson & Kurtz, 1997), including those with children (Ruscio et al., 2002).

Dealing with Crowds

The noise and activity levels of parties, malls, sports events, and other such venues are very aversive to someone still in "combat mode" because monitoring potential sources of threat becomes overwhelming. Celebrations that include fireworks are particularly stressful. At the other extreme, quiet, stationary events (such as a movie or worship service) pose other challenges. Being confined to one spot can also feel risky and increase anxiety, yet such situations offer little tolerance for fidgeting or early departures. Selecting a position that offers a broad view and easy exit (e.g., back row near the door) can help keep anxiety levels manageable. Gradually re-engaging in social interactions and outings is an important step toward re-integration for the war fighter. If social isolation persists, it can erode the veteran's quality of life. Increased social withdrawal has been associated with higher levels of PTSD intensity, while increased social contact tends to decrease severity of symptoms (Solomon, Mikulincer & Avitzuer, 1998). Isolation on the part of the warrior leaves family and friends to face questions ("Why didn't s/he attend?" "Is s/he alright?") and they may also start to feel socially isolated (Sherman et al., 2005).

WHERE TO GET HELP: RESOURCES AND SERVICES

Many informational Web sites and online support groups have been developed to help families through the normal readjustment process. Courage Community's podcast *Her War* (community.couragecommunity.org) and the Walter Reed Army Institute of Research's *Battlemind* series are examples. *Spouse Battlemind Training* (www.battlemind.org) aims to prepare partners for the challenges of deployment and reunification by helping them better understand military training and the impact of this training on personal and familial functioning. The Deployment Health Clinical Center (www.pdhealth.mil) is another resource. Organizations such as Hearts Toward Home International market packaged workshops, including participant workbooks and facilitators' manuals, for returning troops who have experienced trauma and for their families (www.heartstoward-home.com). The National Center for PTSD has an excellent Web site with many pages devoted to resources for veterans and their families struggling with PTSD (http://www.ncptsd.va.gov/). This resource includes information on, among other things, combat in specific locations (e.g., Iraq and Afghanistan), treatment for PTSD and related problems, specific issues pertaining to women warriors, and links to other online resources. In particular, readers may be interested in the Web site devoted especially to returning service members of Operation Enduring Freedom/Operation Iraqi Freedom (http://www.oefoif.va.gov/).

For those who prefer a hard-copy reference, a free 102-page book titled *Veterans and Families' Guide to Recovering from PTSD* (Lanham, 2005) provides helpful information, including essays by veterans and family members and a resource directory. A number of videos about PTSD are also available. A 29-minute videotape titled *PTSD: Families Matter* (Abrams and Freeman, n.d.) depicts issues families encounter when a veteran has PTSD. It was developed by the Veterans Administration's (VA's) South Central Mental Illness Research, Education, and Clinical Center (MIRECC) and is available to licensed clinicians by contacting Michael.Kauth@med.va.gov. A video titled *Living with PTSD: Lessons for Partners, Friends, and Supporters* is accessible at the Web site www.giftsfromwithin.org. The National Center for PTSD has made available several videos that pertain to specific groups, including Asian Americans, Native Americans, Latinos, and women. This list of videos is available at http://www.ncptsd.va.gov/ncmain/veterans/videos.jsp.

As previously emphasized, most returning troops readjust well after homecoming. However, it is also true that, reportedly for the first time in history, the number of psychological/emotional injuries from combat has surpassed the number of combat-related physical injuries or deaths (Christian, Stivers & Sammons, 2008). Such injuries will generally require more than can be offered via self-help resources. Mental health services are available through the military for those who remain on active duty. The Department of Veterans Affairs also offers services at medical centers, community clinics, and Vet Centers (local services can be located via http://www2.va.gov/directory/guide/vetcenter.asp). Give an Hour (www.giveanhour.org) has recruited mental health professionals to volunteer their time to serve troops returning from Iraq or Afghanistan and their families. Family support and treatment for PTSD is also available in most communities through psychologists in private practice, community mental health centers, and private mental health clinics. Family physicians and human resources offices/employee assistance programs may assist with referrals. Finally, state psychological and psychiatric associations and local university departments of psychology may also be able to help locate therapists with expertise in treating combat-related stress and trauma.

The International Society for Traumatic Stress Studies has published a series of recommendations for the treatment of PTSD (Foa, Keane, Friedman & Cohen, 2008). These guidelines are based on an extensive review of the clinical and research literature prepared by experts in the field and are intended to assist clinicians who provide treatment for adults, adolescents, and children with PTSD. These guidelines are available online at http://www.istss.org/treatmentguidelines/. These guidelines indicate that cognitive-behavioral therapy (CBT) is the most effective treatment for adult PTSD.

The goal of CBT is to help individuals learn more adaptive ways of coping with distressing thoughts and reduce other problematic behaviors (e.g., substance use). Several types of CBT have been shown to be effective in the treatment of PTSD, including exposure therapy, stress-inoculation training, and cognitive processing therapy. The evidence for the effectiveness of exposure therapy is particularly strong. In this treatment, the following topics are typically addressed: education about common reactions to trauma, breathing or relaxation retraining, repeated imagining, talking and/or writing about the traumatic memories, and real-life exposure to non-dangerous situations that are avoided due to trauma-related fear. In other words, individuals are encouraged to confront the memory of the trauma by telling the story to the therapist over and over again. They are also encouraged to slowly confront things in life that they are not doing because they are frightening (e.g., going to concerts, driving on a rocky road).

Family and friends play a major role in recovery from PTSD. In fact, almost 20% of the variance in PTSD treatment outcome in a civilian sample was found to be explained by negative family relationships (Tarrier, Sommerfield & Pilgrim, 1999). However, two particular aspects of PTSD treatment are very easy for loved ones to misinterpret. First, it is common sense to think treatment is supposed to make someone better and that if symptoms get worse after beginning therapy, treatment should be discontinued. However, evidence-based treatments such as exposure therapy and cognitive processing therapy require focus on conflicted thoughts and feelings associated with the traumatic event. Thus, during the initial phases of treatment, increased combat-related thoughts, dreams, and anxiety are expected and can actually signify progress. A second common misinterpretation is to become jealous or resentful that the warrior will not discuss war experiences at home but is "baring his/her soul" to a perfect stranger (the therapist). Loved ones are reminded that reluctance to divulge horrible details may be motivated by a desire to protect them from gruesome images and to avoid tainting a relationship the warrior views as too important to place at risk. Being aware of these counterintuitive aspects of PTSD therapy can help loved ones resolve ambivalence they may have about the warrior seeking or continuing treatment.

Recognizing both the importance of supportive family involvement and the impact of PTSD on loved ones, there are treatments available that include family members. In a review of marital and family therapies being offered in the wake of trauma, Riggs (2000) identified two major approaches to PTSD-related family/marital treatment: systemic and support. Systemic approaches treat the relationship to reduce friction and/or strengthen bonds. Traditional marital and family therapies would be in this category. Support treatments have the goal of increasing social support for the warrior and the warrior's treatment. Supportive treatments often include teaching about PTSD symptoms and helping family members develop ways to cope with the warrior's PTSD symptoms. While these therapies are not recommended as the sole treatment for PTSD, they could be useful adjuncts to the warrior's individual treatment (e.g., Glynn et al., 1995, 1999; Monson, Guthrie & Stevens, 2003; Monson, Schnurr, Stevens & Guthrie, 2004). It is recommended that family members of an individual with PTSD find out as much as they can about the disorder and get assistance for themselves, even if their loved one does not want treatment.

CONCLUSION

The pressures of war leave a lasting imprint on the warrior. Those who survive the horrors and rigors of war may emerge with a new clarity of their own abilities and limitations, a strong sense of values and beliefs, and an ethical maturity that many others do not develop until old age—if then. An entire field of research is developing to explore the resilience and posttraumatic growth displayed by survivors of war and other traumas (Tedeschi & Calhoun, 2004). Even when the changes in the war fighter and loved ones at home are all in a positive direction, it can still create challenges as the relation shifts to adjust. Although there is no clinical magic that can undo the impact of separation and the experiences of war, clinical resources are available and can help. If one is concerned about the direction his or her relationship is headed, contact a counselor by utilizing the services through the local VA or contact a community-based therapist. Despite the challenges that sometimes present when accessing care (e.g., distance, transportation, scheduling) (Glynn et al., 1999; Lyons, 2003: Lyons & Root, 2001), the benefits of effective support and treatment can make the effort a very good investment. It is much easier to restore a relationship if problems are addressed before they multiply.

REFERENCES

Abrams, P. & Freeman, T. (n.d.). *PTSD: Families matter* (video). North Little Rock, AR: VA South Central MIRECC. Available from Michael.Kauth@med.va.gov

Alford, J. D., Mahone, C. & Fielstein, E. M. (1988). Cognitive and behavioral sequelae of combat: Conceptualization and implications for treatment. *Journal of Traumatic Stress, 1*, 489–501.

Ancharoff, M. R., Munroe, J. F. & Fisher, L. M. (1998). The legacy of combat trauma: Clinical implications of intergenerational transmission. In Y. Danieli (Ed.), *International handbook of multigenerational legacies of trauma*, (pp. 257–276). New York, NY: Plenum Press.

Beckham, J. C., Lytle, B. L. & Feldman, M. E. (1996). Caregiver burden in partners of Vietnam War veterans with posttraumatic stress. *Journal of Consulting and Clinical Psychology, 64*, 1068–1072.

Browne, T., Hull, L., Horn, O. Jones, M., Murphy, D., Fear, N. T. et al. (2007). Explanations for the increase in mental health problems in UK reserve forces who have served in Iraq. *British Journal of Psychiatry, 190*, 484–489.

Byrne, C. A. & Riggs, D. S. (1996). The cycle of trauma: Relationship aggression in male Vietnam veterans with symptoms of posttraumatic stress disorder. *Violence and Victims, 11*, 213–225.

Calhoun, P. S., Beckham, J. C. & Bosworth, H. B. (2002). Caregiver burden and psychological distress in partners of veterans with chronic posttraumatic stress disorder. *Journal of Traumatic Stress, 15*, 205–212.

Caselli, L. T. & Motta, R. W. (1995). The effect of PTSD and combat level on Vietnam veterans' perceptions of child behavior and marital adjustment. *Journal of Clinical Psychology. 51,* 4–12.

Christian, J. R., Stivers, J. R. & Sammons, M. T. (2008). Training to the warrior ethos: Implications for clinicians treating military members and their families. In S. Morgillo-Freeman, B. Moore & A. Freeman (Eds.), *In harm's way: A psychological treatment handbook for pre- and post-deployment.* New York, NY: Routledge.

Cook, J. M., Riggs, D. S., Thompson, R., Coyne, J. C. & Sheikh, J. I. (2004). Posttraumatic stress disorder and current relationship functioning among World War II ex-prisoners of war. *Journal of Family Psychology, 18*, 36–45.

Davidson, A. C. & Mellor, D. J. (2001). The adjustment of children of Australian Vietnam veterans: Is there evidence for the transgenerational transmission of the effects of war-related trauma? *Australia and New Zealand Journal of Psychiatry, 35,* 345–351.

Davidson, J., Smith, R. & Kudler, H. (1989). Familial psychiatric illness in chronic posttraumatic stress disorder. *Comprehensive Psychiatry, 30*, 339–345.

Dekel, R. (2007). Posttraumatic distress and growth among wives of prisoners of war: The contribution of husbands' posttraumatic stress disorder and wives' own attachments. *American Journal of Orthopsychiatry, 77*, 419–426.

Dekel, R., Goldblatt, H., Keidar, M. Solomon, Z. & Polliack, M. (2005). Being a wife of a veteran with posttraumatic stress disorder. *Family Relations, 54*, 24–36.

Dekel, R. & Solomon, Z. (2006). Secondary traumatization among wives of Israeli POWs: The role of POWs' distress. *Social Psychiatry and Psychiatric Epidemiology, 41*, 27–33.

Dollar, K. M., Lyons, J., Kibler, J. L. & Ma, M. (2007, March). *Feasibility and efficacy of a home study workbook for caregivers of veterans with PTSD: A pilot intervention.* Poster presented at the annual meeting of the Society of Behavioral Medicine, Washington, DC.

Dirkzwager, A. J. E., Bramsen, I., Adèr, H. & van der Ploeg, H. M. (2005). Secondary traumatization in partners and parents of Dutch peacekeeping soldiers. *Journal of Family Psychology, 19*, 217–226.

Elder, G. H. & Clipp, E. C. (1989). Combat experience and emotional health: Impairment and resilience in later life. *Journal of Personality, 57*, 311–341.

Elzinga, B. M. & Bremmer, J. D. (2002). Are the neural substrates of memory the final common pathway in posttraumatic stress disorder (PTSD)? *Journal of Affective Disorders, 70,* 1–17.

Figley, C.R. (1995). *Compassion fatigue: Coping with secondary traumatic stress disorder in those who treat the traumatized.* New York, NY: Brunner/Mazel.

Foa, E. B., Keane, T. M., Friedman, M. J. & Cohen, J. A. (2008). *Effective treatments for PTSD: Practice guidelines from the International Society for Traumatic Stress Studies* (2nd ed.). New York, NY: Guilford Press.

Frederikson, L. G., Chamberlain, K. & Long, N. (1996). Unacknowledged casualties of the Vietnam War: Experiences of the partners of New Zealand veterans. *Qualitative Health Research, 6,* 49–70.

Galovski, T. & Lyons, J.A. (2004). Psychological sequelae of combat violence: A review of the impact of PTSD on the veteran's family and possible interventions. *Aggression and Violent Behavior, 9*, 477–501.

Glynn, S. M., Eth, S., Randolph, E. T., Foy, D. W., Leong, G. B., Paz, G. G. et al. (1995). Behavioral family therapy for Vietnam veterans with posttraumatic stress disorder. *Journal of Psychotherapy Practice, 4*, 214–223.

Glynn, S. M., Eth, S., Randolph, E., Foy, D. W., Urbaitis, M. et al. (1999). A test of behavioral family therapy to augment exposure for combat-related posttraumatic stress disorder. *Journal of Consulting and Clinical Psychology, 67*, 243–251.

Goff, B. S., Crow, J. R., Reisbig, A. M. & Hamilton, S. (2007). The impact of individual trauma symptoms of deployed soldiers on relationship satisfaction. *Journal of Family Psychology, 21*, 344–353.

Harkness, L. L. (1991). The effect of combat-related PTSD on children. *National Center for PTSD Clinical Newsletter, 2*, 12–13.

Hendin, H. & Pollinger-Haas, A. (1991). Suicide and guilt as manifestations of PTSD in Vietnam combat veterans. *American Journal of Psychiatry, 148,* 586–591.

Hoge, C. W., Castro, C. A., Messer, S. M., McGurk, D., Cotting, D. I. & Koffman, R. L. (2004). Combat duty in Iraq and Afghanistan, mental health problems, and barriers to care. *The New England Journal of Medicine, 351*, 13–22.

Hoge, C. W., Lesikar, S. E., Guevara, R., Lange, J., Brundage, J. F. et al. (2002). Mental disorders among U.S. military personnel in the 1990s: Association with high levels of health care utilization and early military attrition. *American Journal of Psychiatry, 159*, 1576–1583.

Hoge, C. W., Terhakopian, A., Castro, C. A., Messer, S. C. & Engel, C. C. (2007). Association of posttraumatic stress disorder with somatic symptoms, health care visits, and absenteeism among Iraq war veterans. *American Journal of Psychiatry, 164,* 150–153.

Iversen, A., Dyson, C., Smith, N., Greenberg, N., Walwyn, R., Unwin, C. et al. (2005). 'Goodbye and good luck': The mental health needs and treatment experiences of British ex-service personnel. *British Journal of Psychiatry, 186*, 480–486.

Jensen, P. S., Martin, D. & Watanabe, H. (1996). Children's response to parental separation during Operation Desert Storm. *Journal of the American Academy of Child and Adolescent Psychiatry, 35*, 433–441.

Johnson, D. R., Feldman, S. & Lubin, H. (1995). Critical interaction therapy: Couples therapy in combat-related posttraumatic stress disorder. *Family Process, 34*, 401–412.

Jordan, B. K., Marmar, C. R., Fairbank, J. A., Schlenger, W. E., Kulka, R. A., Hough, R. L. & Weiss, D. S. (1992). Problems in families of male Vietnam veterans with posttraumatic stress disorder. *Journal of Consulting and Clinical Psychology, 60,* 916–926.

Kashdan, T. B., Elhai, J. D. & Frueh, B. C. (2006). Anhedonia and emotional numbing in combat veterans with PTSD. *Behaviour Research and Therapy, 44,* 457–467.

Kelley, M. L., Hock, E., Smith, K. M., Jarvis, M. S., Bonney, J. F. & Gaffney, M. A. (2001). Internalizing and externalizing behavior of children with enlisted Navy mothers experiencing military-induced separation. *Journal of American Academy of Child Adolescent Psychiatry, 40*, 464–471.

Knox, J. & Price, D. H. (1995). The changing American military family: Opportunities for social work. *Social Service Review, 69*, 479–497.

Lanham, S. L. (2005). *Veterans and families' guide to recovering from PTSD (3rd ed.).* Annandale, VA: Purple Heart Service Foundation. (While supplies last, a free copy should be available through your local Vet Center, http://www.va.gov/rcs/VetCenterDirectory.htm).

Lyons, J. A. (2003). Veterans Health Administration: Reducing barriers to access. In B. H. Stamm (Ed.), *Rural behavioral health care: An interdisciplinary guide* (pp. 217–229). Washington, DC: American Psychological Association.

Lyons, J. A. (2009). Intimate relationships in the military. In S. M. Freeman, B.A. Moore & A. Freeman (Eds.), *Living and surviving in harm's way: A psychological treatment handbook for pre- and post-deployment of military personnel* (pp. 371–393). New York, NY: Routledge/Taylor and Francis Group.

Lyons, J. A. & Root, L. P. (2001). Family members of the PTSD veteran: Treatment needs and barriers. *National Center for Posttraumatic Stress Disorder Clinical Quarterly, 10*, 48–52.

Maher, C. (2008). Grief and guilt in the military. In R. G. Stevenson & G. R. Cox (Eds.), *Perspectives on violence and violent death* (pp. 127–132). Amityville, NY: Baywood Publishing.

Maloney, L. J. (1988). Posttraumatic stresses on women partners of Vietnam veterans. *Smith College Studies in Social Work, 58,* 122–143.

Manguno-Mire, G., Sautter, F., Lyons, J., Myers, L., Perry, D., Sherman, M. et al. (2007). Psychological distress and burden among female partners of combat veterans with PTSD. *Journal of Nervous and Mental Disease, 195,* 144–151.

McNally, R. J. (1998). Experimental approaches to cognitive abnormality in posttraumatic stress disorder. *Clinical Psychology Review, 18*, 971–982.

McNally, R. J., Lasko, N. B., Macklin, M. L. & Pitman, R. K. (1995). Autobiographical memory disturbance in combat-related posttraumatic stress disorder. *Behaviour Research and Therapy, 33*, 619–630.

McNally, R. J., Litz, B. T., Prassas, A., Shin, L. M. & Weathers, F. W. (1994). Emotional priming of autobiographical memory in post-traumatic stress disorder. *Cognition and Emotion, 8,* 351–367.

Mental Health Advisory Team (2006). *Mental Health Advisory Team (MHAT) IV Operation Iraqi Freedom 05-07: Final Report.* Office of the Surgeon Multinational Force-Iraq and Office of the Surgeon General United States Army Medical Command. Retrieved July 9, 2007 from http://www.scribd.com/doc/134591/mhat-iv-report (alternative source: www.armymedicine.army.mil/news/mhat/mhat_iv/MHAT_IV_Report_17NOV06.pdf).

Milliken, C. S., Auchterlonie, J. L. & Hoge, C. W. (2007). Longitudinal assessment of mental health problems among active and reserve component soldiers returning from the Iraq war. *JAMA, 298*, 2141–2148.

Monson, C. M., Guthrie, K. A. & Stevens, S. P. (2003). Cognitive-behavioral couple's treatment for posttraumatic stress disorder. *Behavior Therapist, 26*, 393–402.

Monson, C. M., Schnurr, P. P., Stevens, S. P. & Guthrie, K. A. (2004). Cognitive-behavioral couple's treatment for posttraumatic stress disorder: Initial findings. *Journal of Traumatic Stress, 17*, 341–344.

Newby, J. H., McCarroll, J. E., Ursano, R. J., Fan, Z., Shigemura, J. & Tucker-Harris, Y. (2005). Positive and negative consequences of a military deployment. *Military Medicine, 170*, 815–819.

Orthner, D. K. & Rose, R. (2006). Deployment and separation adjustment among Army civilian spouses. Washington, DC: Army Research Institute for the Behavioral and Social Sciences.

Peebles-Kleiger, M. J. & Kleiger, J. H. (1994). Re-integration stress for Desert Storm families: Wartime deployments and family trauma. *Journal of Traumatic Stress, 7*, 173–194.

Pesonen, A. K., Räikkönen, K., Heinonen, K., Kajantie, E., Forsén, T. & Eriksson, J. G. (2007). Depressive symptoms in adults separated from their parents as children: A natural experiment during World War II. *American Journal of Epidemiology, 166*, 1126–1133.

Rentz, E. D., Marshall, S. W., Loomis, D., Casteel, C., Martin, S. L. & Gibbs, D. A. (2007). Effect of deployment on the occurrence of child maltreatment in military and non-military families. *American Journal of Epidemiology, 165*, 1199–1206.

Riggs, D. (2000). Marital and family therapy. In E. B. Foa, T. M. Keane & M. J. Friedman (Eds.), *Effective treatments for PTSD: Practice guidelines from the International Society for Traumatic Stress Studies* (pp. 280–301). New York, NY: Guilford.

Riggs, D. S., Byrne, C. A., Weathers, F. W. & Litz, B. T. (1998). The quality of the intimate relationships of male Vietnam veterans: Problems associated with posttraumatic stress disorder. *Journal of Traumatic Stress, 11,* 87–101.

Rona, R. J., Hooper, R., Jones, M., Iverson, A.C., Hull, L., Murphy, D. et al. (2009). The contribution of prior psychological symptoms and combat exposure to post Iraq deployment mental health in the UK military. *Journal of Traumatic Stress, 22,* 11–19.

Rosenheck, R. (1985). Father-son relationships in malignant Post-Vietnam stress syndrome. *American Journal of Social Psychiatry, 5*, 19–23.

Rosenheck, R. (1986). Impact of posttraumatic stress disorder of World War II on the next generation. *Journal of Nervous and Mental Disease, 174*, 319–327.

Rosenheck, R. & Fontana, A. (1998). Transgenerational effects of abusive violence on the children of Vietnam combat veterans. *Journal of Traumatic Stress, 11*, 731–741.

Rosenheck, R. & Nathan, P. (1985). Secondary traumatization in children of Vietnam veterans. *Hospital and Community Psychiatry, 36,* 538–539.

Ruger, W., Wilson, S. E. & Waddoups, S. L. (2002). Warfare and welfare: Military service, combat, and marital dissolution. *Armed Forces and Society, 29*, 85–107.

Ruscio, A. M., Weathers, F. W., King, L. A. & King, D. W. (2002). Male war-zone veterans' perceived relationships with their children: The importance of emotional numbing. *Journal of Traumatic Stress, 15,* 351–357.

Sammons, M. T. & Batten, S. V. (2008). Psychological services for returning veterans and their families: Evolving conceptualizations of the sequelae of war-zone experiences. *Journal of Clinical Psychology, 64*, 921–927.

Sareen, J., Cox, B. J., Afifi, T. O., Stein, M. B., Belik, S. L., Meadows, G. & Asmundson, G. J. (2007). Combat and peacekeeping operations in relation to prevalence of mental disorders and perceived need for mental health care: Findings from a large representative sample of military personnel. *Archives of General Psychiatry, 64*, 843–852.

Sautter, F., Lyons, J., Manguno-Mire, G., Perry, D., Han, X., Sherman, M. et al. (2006). Predictors of partner engagement in PTSD treatment. *Journal of Psychopathology and Behavioral Assessment, 28*(2).

Sayers, S. L., Farrow, V. A., Ross, J. & Oslin, D. W. (2009). Family problems among recently returned military veterans referred for a mental health evaluation. *Journal of Clinical Psychiatry, 70,* 163–170.

Schumm, W. R., Bell, D. B. & Knott, B. (2001). Predicting the extent and stressfulness of problem rumors at home among Army wives of soldiers deployed overseas on a humanitarian mission. *Psychological Reports, 89*, 123–134.

Schumm, W. R., Bell, D. B., Knott, B. & Rice, R. E. (1996). The perceived effect of stressors on marital satisfaction among civilian wives of enlisted soldiers deployed to Somalia for Operation Restore Hope. *Military Medicine, 161*, 601–606.

Sherman, M. D., Sautter, F., Jackson, H., Lyons, J. & Han, X. (2006). Domestic violence in veterans with posttraumatic stress disorder who seek couples therapy. *Journal of Marital and Family Therapy, 32,* 479–490.

Sherman, M. D., Sautter, F., Lyons, J., Manguno-Mire, G., Han, X., Perry, D. & Sullivan, G. (2005). Mental health treatment needs of cohabiting partners of veterans with combat-related PTSD. *Psychiatric Services, 56*, 1150–1152.

Sherman, M. D., Zanotti, D. K. & Jones, D. E. (2005). Key elements in couples therapy with veterans with combat-related PTSD. *Professional Psychology: Research and Practice, 36*, 626–633.

Smith, T. C., Ryan, M. A. K., Wingard, D. L., Slyment, D. J., Sallis, J. F. & Kritz-Silverstein, D., for the Millenium Cohort Study Team (2008). New onset and persistent symptoms of post-traumatic stress disorder self reported after deployment and combat exposures: Prospective population based US military cohort study. *BMJ online*. Retrieved January 16, 2008 from http://www.bmj.com/cgi/content/full/bmj.39430.638241.AEv1

Solomon, Z., Mikulincer, M. & Avitzuer, E. (1998). Coping, locus of control, social support, and combat-related posttraumatic stress disorder: A prospective study. *Journal of Personality and Social Psychology, 55,* 270–285.

Tarrier, N., Sommerfield, C. & Pilgrim, H. (1999). Relatives' expressed emotion (EE) and PTSD treatment outcome. *Psychological Medicine, 29*, 801–811.

Tedeschi, R. G. & Calhoun, L. (2004). Posttraumatic growth: A new perspective on psychotraumatology. *Psychiatric Times, 21* (4). Retrieved October 7, 2005 from http://www.psychiatrictimes.com/p040458.html

Toomey, R., Kang., H. K., Karlinsky, J., Baker, D.G., Vasterling, J. J., Alpern, R. et al. (2007). Mental health of US Gulf War veterans 10 years after the war. *British Journal of Psychiatry, 190*, 385–393.

Watkins, L. E., Taft, C. T., Hebenstreit, C. L., King, L. A. & King, D. W. (2008). Predictors of child behavior problems among children of female Vietnam veterans. *Journal of Family Violence, 23*, 135–140.

Waysman, M., Schwarzwald, J. & Solomon, Z. (2001). Hardiness: An examination of its relationship with positive and negative long term changes following trauma. *Journal of Traumatic Stress, 14,* 531–548.

Weiner, T. (2004). *Voices of war.* Washington, DC: National Geographic Society.

Wiens, T. & Boss, P. (2006). Maintaining family resilience before, during and after military separation. In C. Castro, A. Adler & T. Britt (Eds.), *Military life: The psychology of serving in peace and combat (vol. 3): The military family* (pp. 13–38). Westport, CT: Praeger Security International.

Wilson, J. P. & Kurtz, R. R. (1997). Assessing posttraumatic stress disorder in couples and families. In J. P. Wilson & T. M. Keane (Eds.), *Assessing psychological trauma and PTSD*. (pp. 349–372). New York, NY: Guilford Press.

14 The Long Way Home
The Aftermath of War for Service Members and Their Families

R. Blaine Everson and Charles R. Figley

CONTENTS

In a country's memory, her brave are immortal

—Memorial to the Confederate Dead, Broad Street, Athens, Georgia

This final chapter focuses on the readjustment to life after warfare, not only adaptation required by veterans and their families, but for our society as well. We hope to offer an overview of the various issues associated with the aftermath of war experiences for the systemic practitioner, and suggest ways in which the systemic intervention comprises a crucial part of the ongoing care plan for veterans of military service and their families. Men and women who serve in our armed forces may head these households, and should be thought of synonymously in terms of their experiences with military service and warfare. As the conflict in Afghanistan lingers toward a full decade and the occupation of Iraq continues for the foreseeable future, providing comprehensive services for returning veterans will be of utmost importance (Armstrong, Best & Domenic, 2007). During the past century, as military campaigns ended, the aftermath of warfare was often inaccurately depicted as a time of celebration and rejoicing, but for many service members and their families these celebrations were often short-lived. Even our collective memories have become distorted across the span time and by revisionist history citing the "greatest generation" returning from the big war. Childers

(2009) provides frightening accounts of returning WWII veterans' difficult experiences with "readjustment" to post-war life, and how these real problems were glossed over (with the nostalgia that has become familiar to many of us) as the country became swept up in the euphoria of victory for the remainder of the decade of the 1940s. As it turns out, many of those veterans experienced significant difficulties, but with few available treatments for psychiatric disorders available, many were fearful of being institutionalized. Family scholars are reminded of Hill's (1949) seminal work with readjustment in families of returning veterans from this period to understand that troubled times lay ahead for many. Our struggle, as a society, will involve focusing on the reality of the aftermath of conflict for many in order to provide proper care for those service members and families truly in need. Historians are now turning their attention toward reconstructing the lives of men, women, and children on the home front during past wars in American history with the idea that we better understand our current situation by constructing a more realistic view of our past (Yellin, 2004). With these ideas in mind, we now turn our attention toward the closing chapter of this volume and some final thoughts regarding some of our current concerns and recent trends in the care of returning service members.

MYTHS AND LEGENDS

Our current military families are different from families who experienced previous conflicts and from those in the population at-large, in many ways, as noted throughout this book, especially in their enduring the number of, duration of, and down time between deployments. Yet throughout history warriors have left their families to wage war in distant lands and have often returned home to find the difficulties they face equally challenging. From the age of antiquity survive tales of mythological heroes who take up the challenge of conflict. Many of these tales have implications for current experiences in the wake of warfare and resonate strongly within our collective consciousness as individuals, families, and societies. We are all familiar with the heroic exploits of Achilles, Hector, and Odysseus on the plains of Troy, as well as the treachery of Agamemnon and cowardly Paris, whose well-placed arrow led to Achilles' untimely demise (Green, 1958/1994). Some would hasten to add that Achilles' death spared him the innumerable travails later encountered by the Greeks who sailed for home after the fall of Troy and the immeasurable suffering experienced after they returned to the relative safety of their homes (Shay, 1995). In essence, their lives were never to be the same given their experiences.

Regardless of the account, there appear to be four basic components to each warrior myth: the exuberance experienced as the heroes take up the task (of war), the perils that are overcome as they engage in the tasks before them, the misfortunes often associated with the arduous voyage home, and the difficulties that await the returning warriors once they are finally home (Buxton, 2004). There are countless renditions of these tales throughout art, literature, and science, including Shay's (2002) excellent parallel experience of Vietnam veterans and the travails of Odysseus after the Trojan War. Myths have long found a home within the modern psychotherapy literature since Freud's famous use of Oedipus' patricide and Electra's motherly disdain as metaphors for unconscious sexual conflicts in young children. Even our most prevalent Axis II malady (DSM-IV-TR, 2000) is named for the youth who could not tear his gaze away from his reflection in the water and died of thirst rather than disturb his image by drinking from the pool.

As for women in modern warfare, the mythic Amazonians may serve as a model for the sacrifices made by women in the line of duty, where they may not only experience the travails associated with combat, but cope with a variety of risks posed by males serving within their own ranks (Wise & Baron, 2006). After all it was Hippolyta, the queen of the Amazons and daughter of the god of war, whom Heracles brought to Athens to be wed to Theseus, after obtaining her girdle. The Greek historian Herodotus wrote of a tribe of women warriors, known as the Sauromatians, who were not to allowed to mate and bear children until they had taken the lives of three male enemies. It is interesting to note that a much older tribe of women warriors were thought to sever their right breast and were known as the Caucasians (or Circassians) living in the region of the Black Sea and from whom the term "amazon" (Greek trans. "no breast") is thought to have originated (Hobbes, 2003). Contrary to our mythologized notions, in reality these ancient women were also expected to raise their children, tend to their domestic duties, and form relationships with their male counterparts. The symbolism associated with these ancient female combatants, as it relates to modern female service members, is uncanny. The image of young women in modern combat roles and the uniqueness of their experiences are pertinent at this point in history of warfare, but their importance may unfortunately be overlooked due the multiple roles they play within their families and the military, and the institutionalized nature of gender disparity in modern American society (Holmsetdt, 2008). In a very real sense, female soldiers, sailors, airwomen, and Marines may find the experience of adaptation particularly difficult as the needs of their loved ones take precedence over their own. Some myths may have very real modern applications.

Jason and the Argonauts

One myth related to this phenomenon that hasn't been discussed recently in reference to the individual warrior's experience is the tale of *Jason and the Argonauts*. The tale of Jason (Æson) is one known by many around the world (Martin, 1991). Jason and the Argonauts were sent on a quest for the Golden Fleece by King Pelias, his wicked uncle. Jason and the Argonauts sailed around the known world and into many adventures. Among his crew were other yet-to-be-famous heroes of antiquity including Heracles (Hercules), Perseus, Orpheus, and Atlanta, who disguised herself as a male in order to become a member of the crew of the *Argo* (Buxton, 2004). She found life somewhat mundane after her mythic voyage, the epic foot race for her hand (in marriage), and the legendary Caledonian boar hunt (Martin, 1991). Along the way, the crew received divine guidance and tools to aid them in their journey.

At the heart of this tale, Jason was a young man of misfortune, given a "fool's errand" in order to earn his rightful place in his father's kingdom (Martin, 1991). Many of the perils the Argonauts faced were ameliorated by the sorcery of Medea, who upon their return became Jason's wife and, of course, the mother of their ill-fated children (Green, 1958/1994). Life after great adventure rarely produces the much sought after excitement for both young men and women. Many of today's young warriors, of both sexes, may encounter a similar fate, because an interesting paradox has developed in American society since the advent of an all-volunteer military in the late 1970s. While voluntary military service has been encouraged throughout history for the sake of morale, conscription was at times a necessity in the face of international crises, sudden attacks from malefactors, and/or troop shortages after long military campaigns. In recent history, military planners have seen the benefits of a well-trained voluntary fighting force that is constantly "at the ready," or as our Army clients would say, "locked, cocked, and ready to rock." It has become commonly accepted that our nation's young people can gain valuable life experience or social advancement by volunteering for military service, but serving in the military seems to have become as much about gaining the intrinsic rewards associated with a uniquely achieved status for individuals inhabiting the military system as it is about carrying out the actual warfare. We are not suggesting, of course, that completing military service is simply an outgrowth of the survival mentality, but it is now seen as a stepping stone to bigger and better things in American life. On the other hand, there are seductive aspects to military service, such as the physical and psychological risks associated with combat—many of which are rarely ever talked about openly until after the fact.

MYTHS VERSUS REALITIES OF WAR

Our thinking has become synonymous with the commonly held cultural notions of the ancient Greeks whose myths reflected what was best and worst about their society and the "hero" myth (i.e., the need to be something more than one is currently or accomplish something noteworthy) remains a driving force in many young people's lives today. Yet this notion of heroism is juxtaposed against the harsh reality of warfare for some. This is illustrated by what one young soldier related from his first battle experience in 2003:

> The chaplains came around and prayed with us, that was nothing. When I got really scared was when the medics came around and told us where to put our dog tags before we rolled out … that's when I first realized that I may not see any of that college money the recruiter promised me!

A young woman who attended a Warrior-In-Transition workshop recently, after she'd served as a Marine combat medic in Iraq, expressed to the first author the ongoing impact of her war experience on her life as follows:

> I still think about "*my guys*" a lot, you know? I'm not there with them anymore, but knowing what that's like and having my husband back over there is the worst torture you could imagine. I feel like people just don't understand, although they try—they just don't get it.

How does one return to an ordinary civilian life after such an experience? There is, however, much wisdom to be derived from these statements. Military service in the modern American armed forces may have become more about personal attainment than about being part of something bigger than oneself. This parallel process is easily understood from a systemic frame of reference when considering the disparity between an idealized future and a life-long reality disfigured by the horrific experiences imposed by war on service members (and subsequently, their loved ones). Many young service members return with their families to a civilian world devoid of the familiar structure to which they've become accustomed in any recognizable form.

To a lesser extent perhaps, hero myths still permeate the fabric of modern societies. Modern war experiences provide young men and women with a sense of purpose, belonging, and accomplishment at a relatively young age. In essence, it is a head start on a life story that others are still attempting to write by middle age in some cases. Some would argue that the necessity of a personal narrative is merely an outgrowth of a narcissistic, post-modern society that rewards the duplicity associated with finding characters on reality television more interesting than those whose lives are scripted as part of a contemporary sitcom, but these are the circumstances in which this generation of service members have been socialized (Douglas, 2003). Whether we agree with such a harsh assessment or not, our awareness of personal narratives is a part of our existence in the 21st century.

Many of those currently serving in the armed forces were born after 1980 and consequently were raised in the fast-paced culture of an information society knowing very little about constancy and adapting to change as we turned every corner of history during the past quarter of a century. For them, the military provides something akin to stability, sincerity, and security. What are they to do when they return to a humdrum world of assembly lines, office cubicles, elementary school classrooms, corporate boardrooms, and educational institutions where they can be easily outflanked and outmaneuvered because they cannot be assured of who "has their back" anymore in those settings? "Leave no man behind" becomes an anachronism; a vestige from a time in their lives where there was order even among the chaos of combat. They are no longer "ten feet tall and bulletproof," because the rules governing camaraderie simply may not apply anymore. Thus, having survived their war experience unscathed in many cases, these individuals may face escalating feelings of isolation, loneliness, mistrust, and alienation. These factors may produce or exacerbate symptoms commonly associated with depression, anxiety, or bipolar disorders that may not be service related, but certainly can stem from pre-existing expectations and ideals of a successful transition to civilian life.

Finding the Way Back

There are varying opinions as to why some families experience less stress associated with life cycle transitions than others. Adaptation is the key to successful transition from military life into the civilian world whether at the end of short term of service or retirement from a long military career for service members and their families. How does one adapt successfully to such transitions? As we have asserted throughout this book, a systemic viewpoint may help us to better conceptualize this transition process for former service members and their families. The flexibility, communication, and cohesion dimensions of Olson's circumplex model may be applied in order to explain why transitions are more easily made by some families than others. Families who tend toward marginality or extreme in these dimensions tend to disintegrate (i.e., *dis-integrate* or become less integrated in form or function) more easily or fall apart altogether. The impact of ongoing and added stressors on coping, perception, and adaptation, which form the centerpiece of Family Stress and Resiliency theory (see Hill, 1958; Boss, 2003), help explain this phenomenon as a process. In fact, family dimensional types are a key aspect of how members perceive and cope with stressors individually and collectively.

The debate surrounding successful transitions may be merely a matter of perception. This perception of success may be skewed by some families being unwilling to seek help or being ignorant of the fact that assistance may be required. In some cases, the necessary assistance may be unavailable to them or necessitate a lengthy drive to a larger community.

What Lies Ahead

As the conflict in Iraq begins to wind down, today's service members return to a social climate where our economic system is wracked by economic woes. As evidence of the potential struggle faced by service members, *USA Today* recently reported that the unemployment rate for returning veterans was nearly 3 percent higher than for those similarly aged members of the general population (March 20, 2009), which has prompted many to remain in the armed services for extended periods of time. Along with these re-enlistments, of course, comes the imminent possibility of further tours of duty in Iraq as part of an ongoing occupational force, or further combat in Afghanistan, for those service members who re-enlist and remain on active duty. Add to this the burden of caring for disabled veterans suffering from combat (or non-combat) related injuries, along with the loss of wages from these otherwise healthy workers across a lifespan, and the true cost of injuries (both physical and emotional) for the over 750,000 discharged veterans from Iraq and Afghanistan, as of December 2007, is conservatively estimated at $372 billion (Stiglitz & Bilmes, 2008). These figures fail to take into account the true cost of long-term mental health disabilities, quality of life impairment, and the strain on veterans' family members, of course. Were they to do so, the costs would certainly be much higher than those projected by economists, according to Stiglitz and Bilmes (2008), and would add a further $367 billion to the aforementioned figure.

At this time, the civilian community in America has become increasingly aware of the post-service needs of service members and their families. There are news reports almost weekly of new programs being initiated by the Department of Defense, the Veterans Administration (VA), and numerous other contracted providers, which prompts us to be hopeful that the needs of veterans and their families will not be overlooked within the next decade. Yet we make this statement with some degree of trepidation that these efforts to foster post-war re-adjustment will fall by the wayside as funding priorities shift or as the perceived need for long-term services changes. For example, as we conduct workshops for military family care around the country, many private providers are initially excited by the prospect of working with military families. That is, until they realize how difficult this therapeutic work can be, or until they realize that many post-service families are no longer covered under military benefits and they lack the equivalent private insurance coverage to make their treatment economically viable for the therapist. One of our fears is that many mental health professionals will sign up as panel providers without realizing the difficult nature of this work and will subsequently burn out, thereby reducing the number of service hours they provide and leaving many families who truly need their assistance in-the-lurch. Providing some insight into various aspects of working with military families has been the partial aim of this volume.

An entire generation of therapists will be affected by the experience of the Iraq and Afghan conflicts. Many young people now entering the helping professions have their own military backgrounds to enhance their understanding of the unique aspects of the transition from a military life after service. A large number of therapists who are now nearing retirement age experienced the aftermath of Vietnam, where large numbers of veterans returned to a healthcare system inept at dealing with the long-term consequences of guerilla warfare, and suffered due to a society ill prepared for the impact of these problems on veterans and families for the next 30 years (Coleman, 2006). Some of these veterans are still being treated for emotional issues, relational problems, and long-term mental disorders today. Hopefully, we are better prepared for the rising tide of family problems that will result from the military conflicts of the last decade. There are those who fear that we are not as prepared as we need to be. Galbraith (2008) questions the government's commitment to returning veterans and their families due to an over-extension of monetary resources to the war effort in Iraq (and Afghanistan) and an under-allocation those resources toward dealing with the aftermath of these protracted military engagements, except where continued political stabilization is needed in those countries. Should these trends continue, we run a substantial risk of a failed Vietnam-era approach to the problems of service members and their families. There are positive signs that we, as a society, understand the impacts of warfare on veterans and family members. Today, veteran centers are extending their outreach services into smaller communities and receiving funding at unprecedented levels, yet for all the increase in funding, the emphasis remains primarily on veterans to the exclusion of family. As an example, while they have been admitted to practice within the Department of Defense at many military installations, licensed marriage and family therapists (MFTs) are still struggling to gain the necessary recognition to practice within VA settings.* MFTs have been (first and foremost) systemic practitioners and this focus encompasses our entire approach to clients, regardless of the families' backgrounds. Until the time comes that MFTs are allowed full access to jobs within this sector, many will remain in an ancillary role with treatment centers providing services for vets, and these individuals utilizing systemic interventions with vets and families from their private practices. It is impossible to meet every need of active duty service members, veterans, and family members, but somehow care providers must make every attempt to understand, appropriately treat, and advocate for their military family clients in order to narrow the potential cracks through which many may fall. To some extent, this lack of concern for the needs of members of the armed forces post-military service has been pervasive after previous conflicts and those lessons were hard learned by American society for the future benefit of these individuals and families.

We have been heartened by recent efforts on the part of public advocacy groups to work with families of returning service members within local communities, the collaborations between the Defense Department and healthcare consortiums to provide services for wounded service members and their families, and by Web-based nonprofit entities seeking to provide information, as well as referral sources, for military families in need. These grassroots organizations have begun in many states around our country, and in essence help bridge the gap created when service members leave the military and when they begin civilian life (now it is more difficult to separate these two aspects of life anymore). In many ways these efforts represent new thinking in terms of how we view services members, the jobs they perform, their families, and the lives they lead. Whereas military service was often a premarital part of life during the mid-20th century, today's service members are likely to be spouses and parents in addition to their military service. These public/private partnerships certainly represent a unique approach to 21st century problems associated with post-military life for many who have proudly served.

CONCLUSIONS

With the proposed withdrawal of a sizable portion of U.S. troops engaged in the hostilities in Iraq, many members of the armed services and their families will begin a new phase in their lives. For some, this means ending their terms of service and returning to civilian life. For those who remain in the military, the future will involve promotions, different assignments to other combat zones, and

* See the testimony before the House Committee on Veterans' Affairs by Charles R. Figley, June 18, 2008. Available at http://veterans.house.gov/hearings/Testimony.aspx?TID=33480&Newsid=186&Name=%20Charles%20%20Figley,%20Ph.D.,%20LMFT (accessed June 16 2009).

preparations for future conflicts in yet-to-be-determined parts of the world. For American service members, their families, and our society as a whole, the future will be full of challenges as we seek to reintegrate these individuals back into our communities. In some cases this task will be made more difficult by the physical and emotional injuries suffered by service members as a result of combat exposure, the long-term separations imposed on their families by deployments, and the lack of ongoing support from social institutions designed to assist service members after their service has ended. Already we have seen a number of problems synonymous with the aftermath of previous conflicts develop, such as improper screening for combat-related post-trauma symptoms, inadequate treatment for physical injuries suffered during engagement with the enemy, an escalation in the divorce rate among military couples, increasing incidences of domestic violence involving service members, and the overall lack of monetary funding in the federal budget for ongoing economic support for veterans (Stiglitz & Bilmes, 2008). The lack of appropriate funding may continue as a byproduct of what Filkins (2008) sees as our ongoing war without borders that began sometime around 1998 with the U.S. embassy bombings in Nairobi and Dar-es-Salaam, and continues in Afghanistan and Iraq at this time. It is a war that has yet to end and will almost certainly require the involvement of several hundred thousand more U.S. service members into the near future. While wars are very expensive, caring for those who have fought them is as well. We hope that the significance of their service will not be soon forgotten.

When this project was first conceived, our armed forces were heavily engaged in a protracted occupation of Iraq and an ongoing incursion against terrorist forces (and their supporters) in the mountains of eastern Afghanistan. These were hostile environments that posed new challenges to all branches of our military and, as a result, to the men and women who fill their ranks. We understood that families of service members were coping with the strain of lengthy and dangerous deployments that would impact each member, both positively and negatively, for many years to come. We felt that it was important to provide a set of clinical tools that allowed new clinicians, those unfamiliar with family systems approaches and those systemic practitioners new to military family practice, a frame of reference for their work with these families. To this end, we have attempted to collect a wide variety of perspectives in our effort to create a work that is both educational and experiential as related to the practice of systems-based therapy with military families. We hope that the readers found what they were looking for as a resource when they received this volume. There are certainly omissions from this text, but the inclusion of the chapters and topic areas were carefully considered given our time constraints. We welcome any feedback from our readers and the opportunity to collaborate on future volumes in this topic area. What is unique about this volume is the fact that we have collected an extensive set of systemic clinical accounts from a wide variety of civilian and military practitioners. During the past 2 years of writing and editing this book, many of our authors have experienced the effects of warfare in a very personal way, whether through their practice with military families, the deployment of friends or loved ones, or due to their own deployment to a theater of operations. Some have paid a hefty price in providing services to members of our armed forces and their families, whether through extra hours in their practices, time away from their families due to deployment-related separations, or in some cases the loss of their own lives. We sadly lament that one of our own contributors died in the line of duty while serving in Iraq (see dedication) in the spring of 2009. Needless to say, his loss will impact both his own family and the families of those service members that he would have potentially assisted in their transitions through military service and into civilian life.

REFERENCES

Armstrong, K., Best, S. & Domenici, P. (2007). *Courage after fire: Coping strategies for troops returning from Iraq and Afghanistan and their families.* Berkeley, CA: Ulysses.

Boss, P. (2003). *Family Stress: Classical Contemporary Readings*. Thousand Oaks: Sage.

Buxton, R. (2004). *The complete world of Greek mythology.* London: Thames & Hudson.

Childers, T. (2009). *Soldier from the war returning: The greatest generation's troubled homecoming from World War II.* New York, NY: Houghton Mifflin Harcourt.

Coleman, P. (2006). *Flashback: Post-traumatic stress disorder, suicide, and the lessons of war.* Boston, MA: Beacon.

Douglas, W. (2003). *Television families.* New York, NY: Lawrence Erlbaum Associates.

Filkins, D. (2008). *The forever war.* New York, NY: Alfred A. Knopf.

Galbraith, P. W. (2008). *Unintended consequences: How war in Iraq strengthened America's enemies.* New York, NY: Simon & Schuster.

Green, R. L. (1958/1994). *Tales of the Greek heroes.* London: Penguin.

Hill, R. (1948). Generic Features of Families Under Stress, *Social Casework, 49*, 139–150.

Hobbes, N. (2003). *Essential militaria.* London: Atlantic Books.

Holmstedt, K. (2008). *Band of sisters: American women at war in Iraq.* Mechanicsburg, PA: Stackpole.

Martin R. P. (1991). In T. Bulfinch (Ed.), *Bulfinch's mythology.* New York, NY: HarperCollins.

Shay. J. (1995). *Achilles in Vietnam: Combat trauma and the undoing of character.* New York, NY: Simon & Schuster.

Shay, J. (2002). *Odysseus in America: Combat trauma and the trials of homecoming.* New York: Scribners.

Stiglitz, J. E. & Bilmes, L. J. (2008). *The three trillion dollar war: The true cost of the Iraq conflict.* New York, NY: W. W. Norton.

Wise, Jr., J. E. & Baron, S. (2006). *Women at war: Iraq, Afghanistan, and other conflicts.* Annapolis, MD: U.S. Naval Institute.

Yellin, E. (2004). *Our mother's war: American women at home and at the front during World War II.* New York, NY: Free Press.

Appendix: Developmental Overview and Brief History of Systemic Family Therapy

R. Blaine Everson and Thomas G. Camp

CONTENTS

A BRIEF HISTORY OF FAMILY THERAPY DEVELOPMENT AND PRACTICE

BACKGROUND

There is a difference between the family systems approach as a paradigm for understanding the dynamic nature of the relationships among family members and the application of the methods derived from family systems as theory. Part of this difference stems from the way in which the concepts have been applied in family therapy and related professions. There are generally two acknowledged views of systems with the world: one interpretation is more organic and describes living systems, while the other is more tailored for explaining complex machines and structural mechanisms. Both sets of ideas have found their way into the language of family systems at various times over the past half-century.

Maturana coined the term "autopoiesis" as he discussed the self-regulation of complex organic systems within the natural sciences, and the mathematician Weiner in 1948 used the term "cybernetics" to elaborate on the concept of feedback as a corrective action in mechanical systems using ballistics as an example during the early 20th century (Guttman, 1991). The biologist von Bertalanffy in the 1960s introduced the concept of human systems as utilizing feedback, information, and communication into the social sciences, in the form of general system theory (Colapinto, 1991). If cybernetics is the study of effective organization, then its application to family can be defined as the study of (at times) ineffectual organization. Although systemic thinking has been part of the natural sciences, sociological theory, and the understanding of mechanical structures since before the second world war, systems theory as applied to the current practice of family therapy can be traced to the work of Bateson and his colleagues with communication patterns among families of schizophrenics in Palo Alto, California, in the 1950s (Guttman, 1991). Many of those who shaped the thinking of future systems-based practitioners were members of this project over the course of its first 20 years as this project evolved into the Mental Research Institute (e.g., Don Jackson and John Weakland). Among the members of this group, the further application of systemic concepts as strategic family therapy by Jay Haley stands out as seminal for the establishment of family therapy as a method of practice for reducing dysfunctional relationship patterns in families (Nichols & Schwartz, 1997).

One primary concept sets the work of the Palo Alto group apart from that of others during the same time period: the "double bind," which is a structural- and communication-based maladaptation creating anxiety within members of families across multiple generations. Largely disregarded as a primary explanation of the development of schizophrenia, the double-bind concept remains applicable to the development and maintenance of anxiety-provoking patterns of dysfunctional interaction within families and is often viewed by practitioners as the third point of a triangulated relationship. The double bind, as a process, is a contributor to and a manifestation of problems within family relational systems (see Guttman, 1991, p. 47). Many systemic practitioners still feel it is a primary factor in the presenting problems of those counseling for emotional maladies, such as depressive disorders or anxiety (e.g., an adolescent prone to panic attacks may control them well until the onset of problems within the parent dyad). Moreover, within the field of traumatic stress, the development of secondary traumatic stress symptoms may be viewed as a double-bind situation for the person in closest emotional proximity to the post-traumatic stress disorder (PTSD) sufferer and responsible for the emotional well-being of other members (accordingly, "burn-out" may also be viewed as a product of the double bind).

Major Models and Schools of Thought

Many early family systems practitioners began work on the problem of family interactions as a basis for the development, and the perpetuation, of schizophrenia. Murray Bowen introduced the concept of emotional triangulation based upon lack of differentiation into the theory of schizophrenic families (Roberto, 1992). Carl Whitaker (perhaps incorrectly) challenged the notion that schizophrenia was biogenetically predisposed. His approach to individual schizophrenics was based on the idea that psychotic symptoms were symbolic attempts at adaptation, and these symptoms themselves were a byproduct of the anxiety experienced within certain families. The innovation of involving multiple family members in sessions, much to the dismay of other psychotherapy practitioners at the time

(Roberto, 1992), and Whitaker's addition of a co-therapist rapidly set the budding practice of family therapy apart from other person-centered approaches in the mid-20th century.

During the 1960s and 1970s, the practice of family therapy was seemingly dominated by a few prolific private and institute-based practitioners whose ideas were entering more mainstream realms of psychotherapy, including Bowen, Whitaker, Salvador Minuchin, Jay Haley, Peggy Papp, Monica McGoldrick, and Virginia Satir. Haley originally brought the work of Milton Erickson to the field of family therapy (see *Uncommon Therapy: The Psychiatric Techniques of Milton Erickson, M..D.*) and helped develop a model for dynamic family change that became known as strategic therapy. Many see this approach as an outgrowth of his earlier work with Bateson, Jackson, and others at the Mental Research Institute. Within this approach, therapists are interested in the maintenance of symptoms by the family structure (feedback loops, power struggles, etc.) and the alteration of the interactional patterns as a way of reducing symptoms functioning and fostering systemic change (Madanes, 1981). Minuchin's work with family structure was similar, in some ways, but focused on the development and maintenance of roles, rules, coalitions, boundaries, and subsystems as the sources of problematic dynamics within family systems (Colapinto, 1991). Many of the ideas and concepts basic to the practice of systemic family therapy stem from what some consider the formative period of family therapy from the late 1950s through the 1970s, and will be discussed more in depth later in this chapter.

More Recent Developments

In the 1980s, as more graduate programs began to develop, family therapy sought to establish a research-based approach to family problems (i.e., a craft to be taught to others versus an art form to be cultivated by a few). Although a variety of approaches have developed out of systems thinking in the past 25 years, most family therapy practitioners today work from models or paradigms that unify systems thinking into multiple levels of interaction and encompass the notion that changes within the system may be disruptive and chaotic. A good example of current systems application is Olsen's circumplex model for family functioning, which accounts for three dimensions of systemic phenomena: adaptability to change, relationship structure, and communication patterns (Olson, 2003). The Beavers Family Systems (Beavers, 1985; Beavers & Hampson, 2003) model seeks to incorporate family-level change across the span of time and the parent–child personality dynamics into a conceptualization of the problems experienced between members of couples and in subsequent family outcomes. Within family systems theory, Remer (2005) has also been influential in the inclusion of the chaos model within systems thinking for understanding flux and the underlying dynamical nature of change within family systems.

Yes, But Is It Family Therapy?

As we began the final decade of the 20th century, several new models emerged that deviated from the more traditional expressions of systems thinking. Collectively these approaches have become known as "postmodern" in the sense that they do not start with many of the basic premises so familiar to family therapy practice. However, many systems-oriented therapists have integrated many concepts into their ongoing practices. The narrative approach to family therapy espoused by White and Epston (1990) is based on the basic notion that meanings are socially constructed by individuals and families out of their interpretations of their experiences, and these meanings are subject to change as a result of therapeutic interventions. Seeing problems as external, rather than internal, allows for the redefinition of issues stemming from problems first through a deconstruction of the problem narrative and (then) the reconstruction of a more satisfactory one. The ultimate goal is symptom relief by altering erroneous conclusions stemming from incorrect stories about events. The applicability of the narrative approach to systemic work relies on the realization that everyone has a story about almost everything and that our stories often emerge out of family interactions. Minuchin's own work in structural family therapy acknowledged a basic narrative process, or family story, that was evidence of, and reinforced, family roles, rules, and beliefs (Minuchin & Fischman, 1981). The solution-focused and problem-oriented approaches to family therapy sought to focus solely upon problem definition and the resolution of presenting issues as a means of ultimately creating positive systemic change that could be built upon for future familial forays into the therapist's office. The idea that that therapy can be brief, of course, is not new to systems-based therapy practice.

What's Next?

With the sequencing of the human genome, increased understanding of behavioral genetics, and advances in neuroscientific principles, such as the interactive processes between the nervous, endocrine, and immunological systems, many systemic therapists see a need for the biogenetic factors as an influence on the organ systems, the person as an individual system, and families as a repository for all of these systems. Indeed, these ideas have gained popularity in area of stress studies in particular in recent years (Boss, 2002). These developments represent a general trend among mental health practitioners toward integration of multiple systems at numerous levels into an over-arching unified framework of care.

The bio-behavioral family model (Wood, 1993; Wood, Klebba & Miller, 2002) has also been utilized with families suffering from the emotional effects of a member's long-term illness, and is another example of a more *unified* approach to systems thinking, as well as the family stress and resiliency theory (an extension of the original ABC-X model) for understanding familial responses to the impact of stressors and strains (McCubbin, Thompson & McCubbin, 2001). Each approach considers the meaning of interactions (i.e., symbolic nature of behaviors) between participants, that these interactions are regulated by internal affective states within the participants (i.e., the perceptions of the interaction), and the accompanying (sometimes) uncontrolled physiological changes within the body that impact the aforementioned levels and (by reference) the other members of the interactional process. As an example, both Gottman (1999) and Johnson (Johnson & Denton, 2002) have provided widely applicable approaches considering this multi-level interactional system to couple and family therapy.

Gottman's approach relies on the understanding that physiologically based emotional reactions spark detrimental conflict in relationships, while the emotionally focused approach of Greenberg and Johnson adheres to the notion that insecure, or mismatched, attachment styles form the basis of problematic interactions in close relationships. These two therapy models dominated the field of family and couple therapy during the 1990s and into the early portion of the 21st century, due mostly to the empirical support found in long-term outcomes research into couple dynamics by Gottman (Gottman, Driver & Tabares, 2002) and the emphasis on clinical effectiveness of the emotionally focused approach (Johnson & Denton, 2002). Given that students of most graduate therapy training programs have been exposed *en masse* to these two approaches over the past 20 years, they will continue to be influential to family and couple therapy for the foreseeable future.

Currently, Schwartz's (2007) internal family systems provide family therapy practitioners with a unique set of concepts that extend previous notions of the internalization of family interactional patterns, the reintegration of various aspects of self, and their impact upon ongoing relationships between family members. This model describes the process by which external family patterns become internalized as aspects of self, such as intrapsychic system "managers," which act as protectors and allow us to continue with our lives, and "exiles" that represent portions of ourselves that have been split-off through negative interpersonal experience and must be protected by other actors within the internal family system. By refocusing attention on the intrapsychic processes in addition to family interaction patterns, this approach (Schwartz, 1997) offers a unique way of helping individuals attain better integration between "self" by reclaiming its (self) disparate parts and others through the facilitation of more emotionally genuine interactions, and has led us "full circle" back to our "roots," in a sense, through the integration of internal emotional forces within the larger context of external interactions with those around us.

REFERENCES

Beavers, W. R. (1985). *Successful marriage: A family systems approach to couples therapy.* New York, NY: Norton.

Beavers, W. R. & Hampson, R. B. (2003). Measuring family competence: The Beavers systems model. In F. Walsh (Ed.), *Normal family processes* (3rd ed.) (pp. 549–580). New York, NY: Guilford.

Colapinto, J. (1991). Structural family therapy. In A. S. Gurman & D. P. Kniskern (Eds.), *Handbook of family therapy: Volume II* (pp. 417–443). New York, NY: Brunner Mazel.

Gottman, J. M. (1999). *The marriage clinic.* New York, NY: Norton.

Gottman, J. M., Driver, J. & Tabares, A. (2002). Building the sound marital house: An empirically derived couple therapy. In A. Gurman & N. Jacobson (Eds.), *Clinical handbook of couple therapy* (3rd ed.). New York, NY: Guilford.

Guttman, H. A. (1991). Systems theory, cybernetics, and epistemology. In A. S. Gurman & D. P. Kniskern (Eds.), *Handbook of family therapy: Volume II* (pp. 41–62). New York, NY: Brunner-Mazel.

Johnson, S. M. & Denton, W. (2002). Emotionally focused couple therapy: Creating secure connections. In A. Gurman & N. Jacobson (Eds.), *Clinical handbook of couple therapy* (3rd ed.). New York, NY: Guilford.

Madanes, C. (1981). *Strategic family therapy.* San Francisco, CA: Jossey-Bass.

McCubbin, H. I., Thompson, A. I. & McCubbin, M. A. (2001). *Family measures: Stress, coping, and resiliency: Inventories for research and practice.* Honolulu, HI: Kamehameha.

Minuchin, S. & Fischman, H. C. (1981). *Family therapy techniques.* Cambridge, MA: Harvard University Press.

Nichols, M. P. & Schwartz, R. C. (1997). *Family therapy: Concepts & methods.* New York, NY: Allyn & Bacon.

Olson, D. H. (2002). The circumplex model of marital and family functioning. In F. Walsh (Ed.), *Normal family processes* (3rd ed.) (pp. 514–548). New York, NY: Guilford.

Remer, R. (2005). Family disruption—Chaos vs. havoc: A chaos theory (dynamical systems) view of family structure and change. In V. L. Bengston, A. C. Acock, K. R. Allen, P. Dilworth-Anderson & D. M. Klein (Eds.), *Sourcebook of family theory & research.*

Roberto, L. G. (1998). *Transgenerational family therapies.* New York, NY: Guilford.

Schwartz, R. C. (1997). *Internal family systems therapy.* New York, NY: Guilford.

White, M. & Epston, D. (1990). *Narrative means to therapeutic ends.* New York, NY: Norton.

Wood, B. L. (1993). Beyond the psychosomatic family: A biobehavioral family model of pediatric illness. *Family Process, 32,* 261–278.

Wood, B. L., Klebba, K. B. & Miller, B. D. (2002). Evolving the biobehavioral family model: The fit of attachment. In Boss, P. (Ed.), *Family stress management: A contextual approach* (2nd ed.). Thousand Oaks, CA: Sage.

Index

D

E

R

S